Adaptation for Animation

Adaptation for Animation

Transforming Literature Frame by Frame

Hannes Rall

CRC Press
Taylor & Francis Group
Boca Raton London New York

CRC Press is an imprint of the
Taylor & Francis Group, an **informa** business
A FOCAL PRESS BOOK

CRC Press
Taylor & Francis Group
6000 Broken Sound Parkway NW, Suite 300
Boca Raton, FL 33487-2742

Printed on acid-free paper

International Standard Book Number-13: 978-1-138-88647-6 (Hardback)
International Standard Book Number-13: 978-1-138-88648-3 (Paperback)

Visit the Taylor & Francis Web site at
http://www.taylorandfrancis.com

and the CRC Press Web site at
http://www.crcpress.com

Preface

As a child, I enjoyed reading books a lot. And all of the characters started to come alive in my mind's eye: Robin Hood, Doyle's Sherlock Holmes, Stoker's Dracula, Poe's Raven, and figures from countless fairy tales and legends. Soon, the desire grew to share these visions with others, and so I started to draw my own versions: illustration and comics first, followed by animation. I (hopefully) grew more adept at this over the years, but this youthful infatuation remained to this day.

In 1999, I adapted Edgar Allan Poe's *The Raven* as an animated short film, and there was no looking back since then. Johann Wolfgang von Goethe's famous poem *Erl-King* was next in 2003, followed by adaptations of the German fairy tale *The Cold Heart* (2013); the Southeast Asian folk tales *Si Lunchai* (2014), and *The Beach Boy* (2015); and the popular Shakespeare monologue *All the World's a Stage* (2016). In the past three years, I have engaged even more with the fascinating universe of the Bard from Avon. Currently, I am working on completing an animated documentary about "Shakespeare in Singapore" titled *Shaking a Singapore Spear*, an animated adaptation of *As You Like It* and a virtual reality (VR) "mashup" of *Macbeth, The Tempest*, and *A Midsummer Night's Dream*, scheduled for release throughout 2019 and 2020.

Simultaneously, I engaged in scholarly writing that looked at animated adaptations from a theoretical angle that remained firmly rooted in the investigation of artistic practice.

With many other essays to follow, the book chapter *"Adapting Gothic Literature for Animation"* (co-authored by Daniel Keith Jernigan) in the book *New Directions in 21st-Century Gothic: The Gothic Compass* (edited by Piatti-Farnell and Brien, Routledge 2015) was a first major step in that direction.

I later had the honor to guest-edit the 2016 *Animation Journal* Special Issue on Adaptation, edited by Maureen Furniss.

The first idea for this book was to share my insights from this artistic and scholarly journey with a wider public. While this would have already allowed for a thematically diverse insight into practice-based and theoretical concepts for adaptation, I soon realized that I had to cast a much wider net. The voice of the creator(s) still remains at the center of this book; yet, it now includes a widely diverse collection of international artists and scholars who have engaged with adaptation in practice and theory.

Adaptation for Animation begins with in-depth interviews with two of the most important animation historians of our time: Giannalberto Bendazzi and John Canemaker. They provide an overview and an evaluation of adaptation approaches throughout the history of the medium. By no means is this meant to be a "complete history" of animated adaptations—a task far beyond the means of this book. Instead, they point out important aspects to define a research framework for the following investigations. Being an Academy Award–winning filmmaker himself, Prof. Canemaker also provides an elegant bridge to the subsequent exploration of creative practice for adaptation.

Organized by adaptation topics and genres, the middle section of this book examines the "making of" a multitude of animated adaptations. This includes many exclusive interviews with the directors and adds a lot of previously-unpublished development art. I firmly believe in the importance of talking to the creators when investigating artistic practice. This is indispensable to avoid misinterpretations and to obtain factually correct information on the production process. Further evidence is provided by the wealth of visual material that directly corresponds with the text. Animation is an audio-visual art form: What is discussed must be seen and analyzed in detail.

Owing to the availability of interview partners and exclusive production materials, the focus lies on independent animated short films. Another reason for this preference must be seen in the fact that non-commercially motivated production often results in artistically outstanding films, which, of course, doesn't mean that such excellence cannot be found there as well. When looking closely, the reader will soon discover that examples of adaptation development for feature film and TV series are also discussed and embedded in this book.

Adding external perspective are important curators and experts: Thomas Zandegiacomo del Bel, director of the world's most important poetry film festival ZEBRA, looks at the field as a whole before exemplary case studies follow. Prof. Michael Dobson, director of the Shakespeare Institute in Stratford-upon-Avon, discusses Shakespeare adaptation in general and in context with his participation in some of the author's projects.

Throughout adaptation, scholarship is cross-referenced to integrate the examination of practice with recent and current theory. Among many others, the excellent essay of Paul Wells *Thou Art Translated* must be named (in *Adaptations: From Text to Screen, Screen to Text*, edited by Cartmell and Whelehan, Routledge 1999, 199–213). It was one of the first thorough scholarly contributions to this particular field. The groundbreaking article remains an excellent foundation for any further investigations of animated adaptations and is cited repeatedly here.

Another aspect that merits mention is the globally-diverse selection of examples for the book.

Thanks to brilliant work of Giannalberto Bendazzi (and others), animation has been recognized as a world history, meaning the whole world. This is hopefully reflected in this book as well, as much as possible. Quite deliberately, young Asian filmmakers are represented to a good extent here, representing the growing importance of the region in the world.

Since I have been teaching and researching for 14 years in Singapore, I can contribute my own experiences in the chapter on transcultural adaptation. The same chapter features the work of an ingenious animation director who somewhat impersonates a transcultural approach to animation: Ishu Patel.

The third and final section of this monograph focuses entirely on visual development for animated adaptations. Together with the young (and brilliant) Singaporean concept artist Jasper Liu, I explore different strategies for production design through various case studies. The aim is to unearth the intrinsically linked connections between the requirements of the adaptation narrative and the visualization method.

I believe that the volume at hand will have something to offer to animation practitioners, beginners, seasoned professionals, academics, and students. This book is certainly only a start, a beginning in many ways. But what I hope for most is to inspire new, exciting animated adaptations that will reward further academic investigation.

And, as a "positive side effect," some of the mentioned source texts might motivate further reading of classic and contemporary literature—exciting discoveries await!

I wish every reader equally fascinating journeys through this book as I enjoyed when writing it.

Hannes Rall
Singapore

Author

Hannes Rall (aka Hans-Martin Rall) is a tenured associate professor at the School of Art, Design and Media at Nanyang Technological University Singapore and the coordinator of the Digital Animation area. In August 2018, he won the Nanyang Education Award (School) for his outstanding teaching. He is also a successful director of independent animated short films. His films, primarily animated adaptations of classic literature, have been shown in over 650 film festivals worldwide and won 69 international awards.

Hannes has recently completed a script for an animated feature film adapted from the German national epic *Die Nibelungen*, funded by MFG Film Funding Baden Wuerttemberg. In December 2019, he was awarded a development contract for the animated feature film project *Westboy* by renowned German Studio 100 (with co-author Jörg von den Steinen).

His conference presentations include FMX, ACM SIGGRAPH, ARS ELECTRONICA, and the Annual Conferences of the Society for Animation Studies. In 2016, he was the chair of the 28th Annual Conference of the Society for Animation Studies, The Cosmos of Animation, in Singapore.

He is a member of the scientific committee of the CONFIA conference in Portugal and preselection jury member for the Stuttgart Festival of Animated Film (ITFS). Hannes is also a member of the advisory board of the book series *Animation: Key Films/Filmmakers* and the editorial board of the book series *Palgrave Animation*. He has published books and book chapters with Routledge, UVK Verlag, Julius Springer, and J.B. Metzler Verlag. His book *Animation: From Concept to Production* (CRC Press/Focal Press) was published in December 2017.

Currently, he has already started work on his new book for CRC Press: *Beyond the Screen—Expanding Animation for VR, AR and Immersive Environments.*

Contents

An Interview with Giannalberto Bendazzi

"It is the World, Which is within the Head of the Artist": A Closer Look at the History of Animated Adaptations

Figure 1.1: Giannalberto Bendazzi (2016).

Giannalberto Bendazzi is an internationally renowned film critic and historian and has been studying animation since his late teens. In 1980, Bendazzi was one of the founding members of the Society for Animation Studies, the leading association for scholarly investigations into the field. As a result of his decades-long journey, Bendazzi must be seen as possibly the most important animation scholar of the past three decades: In 1994, he published *Cartoons: 100 Years of Cinema Animation*, a history of the medium that has been translated into several languages. Bendazzi relied on personal interviews and meticulously conducted research to create a comprehensive world map of animation for the very first time. This challenged prevailing notions that saw animation almost exclusively as a medium that flourished and emerged in North America. He was looking deeply into previously under-researched regions and countries such as China, Russia, Africa, and Latin America and uncovering many unknown artists and their work.

His book also widened the angle of research substantially beyond an investigation of commercial (American) mainstream animation by focusing equally on independent animation worldwide and its masters. T. Lindvall stated about the book (1995): "Its scholarly breadth, richness, and attention to detail, along with its amazingly readable and engaging narrative, make this the most indispensable text on world animation history. Enthusiastically recommended as both a fascinating story and an incredible reference resource for both scholars and aficionados of the art of film."

Since then, Bendazzi had continued his tireless investigative journey into the ever-expanding universe of world animation. He published more articles and books, for example, an edited tome about the Russian master Alexeieff (2001). But, in 2016, what must be seen as his crowning career achievement finally emerged: *Animation: A World History, Vols. 1–3*, a vastly expanded and revised continuation of his revolutionary 1994 book that brings the story up to date.

We are looking at no less than the most comprehensive chronicle of world animation ever published, unrivaled in its depth, accuracy, and sheer volume. It is also an indispensable resource to track the myriad changes that have come with the digital revolution that occurred almost precisely during the last 30 years.

What always made Giannalberto Bendazzi's research stand out to the author is his keen interest in the artistic creation process and his ability to understand it and write about it in the most engaging way possible. Instead of relying on implausible speculation, he always went to the source—be it the artists themselves, co-workers, or production materials—to substantiate his findings with hard facts. Who else then would be a better qualified person to start this book with a deeper look into the concept of animated adaptations?

The following interview was conducted at Prof. Bendazzi's office at Nanyang Technological University on November 18, 2014.

Hannes Rall (interviewer)
Giannalberto Bendazzi (interviewed)

Dear Giannalberto, we have come together to talk a little bit about adaptation for animation.

Adaptation, literary adaptation.

Yes, adapting literature for animation and what the specific requirements, if any, would be. Starting with my first question: Basically, I believe the history of animation is also very much a history of adaptation, because, from the earliest days on, fairy tales, myths, and legends have been adapted for animation, for example, by Disney. And these are often modified for the adaptation. Can you elaborate about that, about the historical developments? What I am particularly interested in is how the European fairy tales are changed for American adaptation.

The history of cinema in itself is a history of adaptations. So, it is not strange that animation followed. The first European animated feature film was made in Germany in 1926, and it was *The Adventures of Prince Achmed* by Lotte Reiniger; it was an adaptation from the *1001 Arabian Nights* (Anonymous 2002).

Figure 1.2: Film still from *The Adventures of Prince Achmed.* © Christel Strobel, Agency for Primrose Film Productions, Munich.

Of course, in 1937, Walt Disney made *Snow White and the Seven Dwarfs* (dir. Hand), which was an adaptation from the old fable; the most famous version had been the one by the Grimm brothers. But the adaptation, as such, is the normal approach. You take an idea, you remake it for the tastes of the audience, be it European or Northern American, or both, and you create a new thing. I make a difference between adaptation and illustration, because in many cases, you have short films that are made as adaptations from literary text, short novels, or poems. Of course, the adaptation involves a lot of creativity from the part of the adapter. And it is not strange that the Disney style overcomes the original story, because the main difference between the Grimm brothers' *Snow White* and the Disney film is that each of the seven dwarfs in the film has a special character, and in a way, they carry on the film; they are the most interesting characters. While in the original story, they are a bunch of people without a special name. There is no point discussing the "authenticity" of this fairy tale, because there are at least 50 different versions that have been handed down through generations; it is a very often told and changed story. The adaptation is important, because for the market, the well-known title is a guarantee of success. And this is the main reason why the adaptations are so favored in Hollywood. Also, they are the guarantee for the public that they will not hear or see the same old story. They will be surprised. So, there is this double guarantee of success.

Figure 1.3: European illustrations from the late nineteenth century by the German illustrator Alexander Spitz (date unknown) and Swedish artist Jenny Nystrøm (ca. 1890). They are examples of a stylistic tradition, which also becomes evident in Disney's *Snow White and the Seven Dwarfs*.

With *Snow White and the Seven Dwarfs*, you mentioned the importance to create seven very individual characters for the dwarfs, as a crucial ingredient for the success of the animated adaptation. A recent filmic adaptation comes to mind: *The Hobbit* film series by Peter Jackson (2012–2014). There was the challenge to individualize Bilbo's (Martin Freeman) 13 different travel companions, which turned out to be a huge problem. Ishaan Tharoor categorizes them as "a baker's dozen of dwarfs, who amble along in Tolkien's narrative with little individual distinction" (2012). In comparison, the individual characters of seven dwarfs were a huge success and worked out very well in the Disney adaptation of *Snow White*. I don't know how familiar you are with *The Hobbit* films, but it would be interesting to examine this problem further: Why did Jackson (arguably) fail, while Disney succeeded? Is it because of the sheer number of dwarfs you have to deal with? Or is the reason inherent to the adapted source material? In the original J.R.R. Tolkien book, the dwarfs are more treated as an almost anonymous group, with the notable exception of their leader Thorin Oakenshield. Disney applied a similar change compared to the source fairy tale, but he seemingly fared better.

In my opinion, the problem in this case is caused by the audience. The market has an audience, or the audience has a market. Peter Jackson is addressing his film to people who love the original book and to people who protect the original book, through constantly ongoing (online) communication. It has become a myth in our society, in our current society. So, the less Jacksonian the film is, the better it serves to save his box office results. While Disney had no comparison to make, he was free, because the story was nobody's story. It was a legend more than a fairy tale. So, he could do whatever he wanted and whatever he did to the story was a (welcome) addition; it was something more; it was a gift for the viewers.

Peter Jackson, in some instances, seems to be actually more artistically successful in his *The Hobbit* series, when he moves away from the original Tolkien text. On the other hand, some of the decisions he made, like trying to individualize 13 different (dwarf) characters, were, in my opinion, just not working out narratively.

The Hobbit was much more difficult to make than *The Lord of the Rings*, because *The Lord of the Rings* is so vast that you can do without a lot of the things. *The Hobbit* is shorter, and you are like in a cage.

Yes, that makes it more difficult. An interesting aspect of adaptation is also that almost every adaptation (or many adaptations) would already qualify as a parody in some ways. But then there is, of course, the deliberate parody in itself as a spoof of the original. One of the most interesting examples to consider in that respect would be *What's Opera, Doc?* (Jones 1957), because it is obviously a parody, a spoof, and then, it is simultaneously a *very* abridged version of the second part of Richard Wagner's *Ring der Nibelungen* cycle, *Die Walküre* (1870). But I find that parts of it obviously also are really a lovingly created homage to the original source material. So, it would be good to have your thoughts about it, about that specific film, and about the relation to the topic of Wagner, of all things.

I hope you will be forgiving me, but in my opinion, cinema is a bourgeois means of...

Please feel free to say whatever you think about it...

It is for the middle class. Even *Battleship Potemkin* (Eisenstein 1925) is not a truly epic film. So, in my opinion, every film adaptation or animation that has been trying to transform an epic story into an epic film was a failure or, even worse, an unwanted parody. I think of, for instance, of Fritz Lang's version of the *Nibelungen* (1924a and 1924b). It is ridiculous, because the *Nibelungen* are a fairy tale, are a legend; the *Nibelungen* are not human. The *Nibelungen* are ghosts, are semi-gods. Siegfried cannot look like a young blond man; Siegfried is the idea of the young blond man. I could say the same of Murnau's *Faust*. I know that I am on the edge of blasphemy here...

Figure 1.4: Fritz Lang. *Siegfried's death*. Publicity still for *Die Nibelungen I* (1924). Circa 1924. German postcard by Ross Verlag, Berlin, Germany.

No, these opinions are very welcome because they add to the discussion; that is important.

I don't love Fritz Lang's *Nibelungen*, but I love Murnau's *Faust* (1926) a lot by the way. So, my answer is that it is impossible to make something else other than a parody out of an epic story, in our age and in our medium. You cannot even imagine a smaller and non-Hollywood production to do something like that.

But what I was trying to get to was that *What's Opera, Doc?* goes beyond a conventional spoof or parody: It actually not only evokes laughter and amusement in the audience, but through the very powerful combination of layout, staging, and colors in the film, it also creates real drama.

This is the point. What makes *What's Opera, Doc?* a masterpiece is not the *Nibelungen* subject, it is the expressionist style. The highest achievement that I ever witnessed in terms of a parody or style, the background, the singing, or the staging: This is what matters for Chuck Jones; this is what his subject is. I mean, it is the "petit bourgeois" viewing of the epic, the "petit bourgeois" staging, the "petit bourgeois" opinion; I am talking about the middle class: We, you and me, everybody on this planet, when we go to the opera house and see Wagner, we think, through the suspension of disbelief, this must be the Walküre. But it is not. This really is just the small heart of a clerk, which lets his fantasy go and imagines the Walküre as suggested by Wagner. Therefore, in this small heart of a clerk lies the irony of *What's Opera, Doc*? And also, the final line is very interesting: Because of course, Bugs Bunny is not dead, but with the suspension of disbelief, he is supposed to be perceived as dead. And then, he looks up into the camera and says, what do you expect from an opera, a happy ending?

I believe the comedy within the film only works because the drama is taken seriously. The opening shot from the film comes to mind: We see a huge shadow cast upon a mighty rock. There really is beautiful, expressionist staging—drama of the highest order. But then, the camera pans downs and reveals a very small figure there, casting this huge shadow. If the initial drama would not have been staged convincingly, the whole gag would fall flat, of course. So, that is important.

Returning to our initial discussion: A central point in academic and fan-based debate about "serious" adaptations is the aspect of fidelity to the original source material (e.g., Starr 2012, Collin 2014, and McCabe 2011). Your point of view is very interesting: You rightfully mentioned that the Grimms' tales were collected folk tales, which underwent many transmutations or changes because they were delivered by oral tradition versus a written form. So, maybe, it is in some ways kind of redundant or even actually not appropriate to speak of authenticity in a stricter sense, right?

Absolutely, yes, it is impossible to speak about authenticity. But in the case of authenticity, let us take *Pinocchio*; there is a real and a final text written by Carlo Lorenzini, also known as Collodi (1883), and Disney changed it completely (1940). They not only changed the story, keeping some of the events and leaving most of them out, but also the setting is completely different. In fact, the Disney Pinocchio is a German, while the Lorenzini Collodi Pinocchio is Tuscan. And the two cultures are different.

Figure 1.5: Early original illustrations for Carlo Collodi's *Le avventure di Pinocchio, Storia di un Burattino*, immediately reveal the significant differences compared to the later Disney version (dir. Luske 1940). (Chiostri and Bongini 1902 and by the first illustrator Enrico Manzantini 1883).

What also comes to mind in that connection is the case of *The Hunchback of Notre Dame*. Obviously, there is the original text, the novel, by Victor Hugo (1831), and what became of it in the Disney version is drastically changed: There is a happy ending instead of a tragic ending. And to me, although it is probably very hard to make a general case, that was not artistically successful. So, how do you look at that? Would you agree?

The original material that you adapt is like the clay that you adapt to the shape that you want to give to your sculpture. So, the filmmaker or the rewriter is free to utilize anything in the way he wants. In a way, every adaptation is a parody, or a re-stylization, like in painting, every painting is a stylization or a caricature.

But how would you then define the success of an adaptation? Is the most relevant criterion, if the adaptation succeeds as a self-contained piece of art, independent from the source material?

This is what I mean. If you look for faithfulness to the original text, you have to think of illustrations, which are sometimes successful as works of art by themselves. But also, mainly, they are related to the original text. Let us talk about a very clear example for illustration: *The Nose* (1963) by Alexandre Alexeieff. The original literary source is a very sarcastic story (*editor's remark: by Nikolai Gogol [1980] between 1835 and 1836*), a very scorching story about the flaws of the Russian characters. In the Alexeieff case, you have the same story told by an emigrate, who recalls this nostalgia, those beautiful old times, so you don't have anything polemic. You have an idealized world, a Russian world, and you have all the elements that will belong to surrealism, like to dream the impossibility, the absolutely, and so on, that continue, and then, the rest is left out. So, this is an illustration, a very successful illustration in my viewpoint, but it is not an adaptation, because the material is there; Alexeieff stays faithful to the text and only takes out things that are not interesting for him.

Paul Wells speaks about the distinct (artistic) vocabulary, which distinguishes animation, despite all the communalities, from film (1999, pp. 199 and 212). So, there are specific terms of expression, of a stylistic tool set, which allow animation to add other levels of artistic expression. There, for example, is metamorphosis as one such tool. Do you believe that animation, as Paul Wells proposes, lends itself even more than film to adaptation—because it can really express what is implied in literature in very meaningful and interesting ways?

In my opinion, animation is an ace up your sleeve, because animation can invent things that you don't have to look for in the reality, in the real world. So, the language of animation is physically based on the possibility to invent, to paint, to mold, to create the things that you are filming. Therefore, the style of the painter or the draftsman is fundamental for telling a story. I will take another example, which in my opinion is very important, two maybe. *The Hangman*, by Les Goldman and Paul Julian (1964), is a vision of a bad, or not particularly good, poem by Maurice Ogden (1954), which has a very down-to-earth message. You have to defend yourself, basically. And you have to be close to your friends and fight along with them. Don't be selfish. The whole story is visualized in the paintings of Paul Julian and through the camera movements of Les Goldman—the tragedy of a small town in the Midwest in the nineteenth century, with all the charm of this town.

Figure 1.6: Painting by Paul Julian from *The Hangman* (1964). © Melrose Productions.

Yet, it is very different from the famous Edgar Allan Poe adaptation *The Tell-Tale Heart* (dir. Parmelee 1953) that featured paintings by Paul Julian as well. So, the style and the language of animation in this sense are very important, because that transports you to a special world—that is not any available world; it is the world that is within the head of the artist. And in this case, the means (*editor's remark: the actual animation both for The Hangman* and for *The Tell-Tale Heart*) are very limited, and there is all this exception. Another example like that is, in my opinion, *The Man with the Beautiful Eyes* (dir. Jonathan Hodgson 2000), which is based on a short story by Charles Bukowski. And the quality of the artwork is so high that you lose the touch of the story and you get into the imagination of the visual artist.

Figure 1.7: Production still from *The Man with the Beautiful Eyes* (2000) by Jonathan Hodgson. © Jonathan Hodgson.

Animation is word building from scratch, and it also very often presents a highly personal world view: The majority of independent animated short films offer a very subjectified vision, which might also help to add images or to express feelings and faults visually, which might be described in internal monologues in literature.

Yes. And to go back to Paul's opinions about the "animated vocabulary," you use a tool that is the most flexible and the most wide that you can utilize in the creative world.

Right, because basically, and even more so now in the digital age, only your own imagination holds you back. You can do almost everything, if time and budget allow for it.

Probably, yes.

It is great that you already mentioned *The Tell-Tale Heart*, a film to which I will return to later in this book. Let's compare once again with *The Hangman*, the other brilliant animation piece with paintings by Paul Julian. I rewatched it recently: If you compare the original poem and the film, the film really adds so much. Because it provides concrete images with multiple layers of meaning. It also offers more ambiguity within itself than the original poem. In the poem, you are free to imagine how the hangman would look like, and in the film, it is all there right in front of your eyes, and the vision of Paul Julian is very strong. What I find interesting is that the film has very limited animation, as you mentioned, and still, it works beautifully. Maybe you can offer a few thoughts on why this is the case, what is the specific strength?

I have my own answer. My own answer is based on the concept of mask. I always maintain that masks exist not to conceal, not to hide, but to reveal. A mask, in my opinion, reveals because it takes away all that is superfluous. So, let us make a comparison between *The Tell-Tale Heart* and *The Hangman*. They are painted by the same person, and the animation is relatively limited in both cases. What is the limitation of *The Tell-Tale Heart*? It is the fact that you see the face of the old man, of the victim. You never see the face of the killer, which is good. But you see the face of the victim, which is not good, because in this case, you have an individual; you recognize those features. So, this special person is the victim, and you don't care very much about him because he is not you. If you wouldn't see his face, you would care for him, because it could be you. In the case of *The Hangman*, the hangman has a face too, but it is not a face. It is a mask. It is the mask of death. So, it is an ugly face, a terrible face, a menacing face, a hopeless face. I think that it doesn't give you hope. So, it is the mask by itself, and in this case, it works, because you are always terrified by the mask of death, even in Halloween or even in carnival.

Right. That is a very strong moment toward the end of a film, where this becomes increasingly evident, and this is one of the moments where the animation or metamorphosis is actually used to a stronger effect. But that is, maybe, because it is just used in the important moments, in a way that makes it all the more efficient or effective in that sense, I guess.

Exactly, I agree completely with you, at that time where you realize that the destiny of man, not the mediocre poem of Maurice Ogden, is involved.

And precisely that elevates the film to a different level. Obviously, there is a connection between the style of the animator and the choice of a source material chosen for adaptation. Most animators have some kind of style. They are actually more inclined to a style that largely defines their artistic personality. Obviously, with Paul Julian, there is a great match between the choice of topic and the artistic style. So, in your long history of investigating animation and talking to animators, do any other examples come to mind? Or, did you hear statements from animators about this? When they work on an adaptation, what initially drew them to the material and why they chose a particular literary source, like a specific story or poem?

Well, in my opinion, the most capable animator of adapting written literature that exists is Caroline Leaf (1977). She made three masterpieces, and they are all based on books. *The Metamorphosis of Mr. Samsa* (1977) is based on Kafka and is very powerful. I dare to say as powerful as the original text, although it is different—it is an adaptation; it is her work, not Kafka's work. A completely different approach, but at least as successful is *The Street* (1976), with a different style, painting on glass, and adapted from Mordecai Richler, based a lot on dialogue also. It is an exquisite way of telling a story of an old woman dying and her room becoming free for the next generation. The third masterpiece is *Two Sisters* (1990), and for that, she wrote the original text herself.

Figure 1.8: Production stills from *The Street* (1976) and *Two Sisters* (1990) by Caroline Leaf. (From *The Street* ©1976 and *Two Sisters* ©1990 National Film Board of Canada. All rights reserved.)

And in this case, the story itself is a piece about a writer and about her recent imprisonment made by her sister. So, again, we are right in the middle of literature and writing and so on. And it is a pity that she stopped making films from then on. In my opinion, literature is basic, and it is fundamental in Caroline's work. But again, it is not literature per se; it is not the scholar's literature. It is the literature as a creative exercise. In a way, she creates literary films because she writes with images, with movements and time. But in my opinion, she never was a woman of images. She always was a woman of feelings, and her feelings were easier for her to tell through images than with words.

So, in her case, you believe that the strength of her narrative is absolutely necessary to reach her artistic maximum quality.

Yes, in my opinion, her best films succeed because of the strength of her narratives.

We already mentioned *The Tell-Tale Heart* as one of the most famous adaptations at United Productions of America (UPA). It is also interesting to maybe talk a little bit about another UPA adaptation, *The Unicorn in the Garden*, based on a short story written by James Thurber. Once again, I'm interested in how the original text source and the final film relate. You explained this already so well with *The Hangman*. How do the artistic means relate to the adapted narrative?

Well, again, we go back to our original definitions. In this case, in my opinion, it is an illustration of the book, of the text, first of all, because Bill Hurtz utilized the original drawings by James Thurber himself, just adding colors to the original drawings. And then, he utilizes the typical animation device to tell the illustrated story. But he is very faithful to the feelings, to the meaning, to the rhythm, to the timing of the original story. You don't feel a special kind of stealing from the side of Bill Hurtz; he realizes that he is telling you what Thurber is thinking. You don't perceive an underlying theme of misogyny from Bill Hurtz's animated version. If there was any misogyny in the original story by Thurber, then it is smoothed out by Bill Hurtz's film, because it has to be accepted by a female audience as well. In his film, it is the general victory of good against evil, and in this case, evil happens to be a woman. While in the case of Thurber, it was an actual misogyny. I will also give you an example of the utilization of animation in the film: The narrative use of the animation tools. When the protagonist has to close the curtains, he doesn't move his butt, he only elongates his arms. This you can do with drawings only; you cannot imagine an actor with an arm that becomes 3 meters long. So, to keep the faithfulness to the original, he uses a very typical animation tool.

Figure 1.9: Production still from *The Unicorn in the Garden* (dir. Hurtz 1953). (From *Unicorn in the Garden* ©1953 renewed 1981 Columbia Pictures Industries. All rights reserved.)

Yes, that is a very good example, because it really clearly illustrates what animation can add there as a very specific tool, which is not available elsewhere.

And very simple, very easy to make. Most people don't even realize that it happens. They are not surprised. So, it is simple, clear, and functional.

It just struck me that, obviously, there is a whole subcategory in terms of adaptation: If a director adapts a children's book, it would be a picture book actually, which already offers a certain style of visualization. This is very different from an adaptation from a purely written text without illustration. In that sense, it is a whole different ballgame, because if the director decides to adapt literally the style of illustrations, one artistic decision is already being made in that sense. But by adding all the additional elements of cinematography, editing, and sound, plus animated movement itself, it still can become its very own artistic piece, right?

Figure 1.10: Self-portrait by John Tenniel (1889) and one of his famous original illustrations (№25. 1865) for Lewis Carroll's *Alice in Wonderland*. These iconic images formed a strong visual tradition that Disney had to address for his animated adaptation: He, therefore, even purchased the rights to the Tenniel illustrations in 1931 (*Through the Keyhole* 2011).

I could give you an example for enforcing this idea of the different media that illustrate a literary text. Let us take the *Divine Comedy* (ca. 1308–1320) by Dante. I don't know whether you have seen Botticelli's illustrations. The pieces that he made, they are not many, but they are very powerful. Botticelli is a painter, and he thinks in colors. So, the inferno for him is difficult to illustrate, because it doesn't have shadows, it doesn't have that in his repertoire. Therefore, in his brush, there is not the tragedy of the darkness; the tragedy of the tragedy doesn't become evident. Botticelli is not able to convey the feeling of despair.

Figure 1.11: Sandro Botticelli, detail from *The Map of Hell* from the *Divine Comedy*, illustrated by Botticelli illustrating canto XVIII in the eighth circle of Hell. C. 1485.

Let us take Gustave Doré. He is so elegant, and he uses etchings, and his etchings, as such, being black and white, are very dark, because the images are very clear, very light, and the frame, the background, is very dark. This gives you the feeling of despair; it doesn't give you the feeling of sorrow, of punishment, because it is so elegant; there is beauty there, and beauty doesn't have anything to do with despair.

Figure 1.12: Gustave Doré's illustrations for *Dante's Inferno*. Plate II: Canto I and Plate LXV: Canto XXXI. 1857.

Let us take a very little-known example of the 26th canto of the *Inferno*, made by the Italian Manfredo Manfredi (1997). This is made in animation, and it is short, and it picks up various suggestions from the imaginary of the twentieth century. So, there is even an influence from the nineteenth century; there is an image that very clearly recalls Eadweard Muybridge's sequential photographs. And you don't feel that these images are clashing with the classic story or the classic text. You hear the voice-over, and you see the imagination, and you see that all those eclectic elements loop together very well, to the point that Virgil doesn't even have a face, because Virgil is the pod, and the pod reflects everything that is around him. While Dante is a man, he is the protagonist, the witness of what he sees. And in a way, he looks like Ulysses, who is going to have the last adventure of his life. So, in my opinion, as strange as this might seem, in the twentieth century, the most faithful adaptation or illustration. In this case, it is difficult to clarify. This arrived after 700 years from a normal, uncelebrated filmmaker with an almost uncelebrated film, just because this person was finally able to combine various suggestions to convey a general feeling of despair, punishment, hope, pride, courage, and eventually hubris, which were the basis of the story that Dante was telling in this canto.

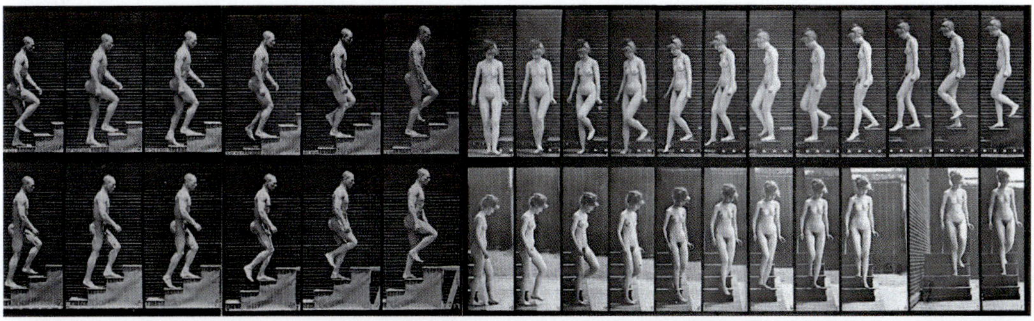

Figure 1.13: Two examples of Eadweard Muybridge's groundbreaking photographic sequences of human and animal locomotion: *Man Ascending Stairs* (1884–1885) and *Female Nude Motion Study* (1887).

I want to raise another example to further examine the relationship between adapted source material and artistic style chosen for the animated adaptation: *The Old Man and the Sea* (1999), the Hemingway adaptation by Aleksandr Petrov. This film won not only the Academy Award for animated short film in 2000 but also the Annecy Grand Prix in the same year; it also was nominated for a BAFTA Award. There obviously is a lot of critical acclaim for the film. The art style being employed is almost naturalistic, but then also, the used technique (oil painting on glass) adds a more artificial element. Can you share your opinion about the film?

Well, I have to ask you for pardon, and the people who will read these words, for pardon, but I am one of the few people in the world who don't like Aleksandr Petrov's work. I like *The Cow* (1989, adapted from Platonov), but I find the other things that he made very "kitschig," and the most "kitschig" one is the *The Old Man and the Sea*, because I find that very cheap, although very laborious. I know that he spent a lot of time and energy and that the technique is magnificent, but it is like making a copy of the Notre Dame cathedral with toothpicks. In my opinion, he has a bad palate; his painting is too realistic, his style is too cheap—cheap in the sense of the quality of the style. I know it is expensive in terms of money and time, but the result is cheap. And there is a kind of exhibition of bravura look what I am able to do.

Exactly, you could look at it like just playing to the gallery, trying to demonstrate the special abilities of the artist or technique over the substance, in a way, instead of really considering how to do the source material justice. Although I find it easy to succumb to the sheer technical mastery on display.

And I don't think that even the Hemingway text itself is a real masterpiece. I think it is a very made-up story. It is much more eloquent than poetic.

I think it is a general discussion of a more literal approach versus a poetic re-interpretation of the world. This links back to the former point in our discussion: About the big advantage of animation that animation can actually provide a highly individual and very subjective point of view of an artist of the world and the interpretation of a literary text. One certainly could argue that Petrov sticks to a highly polished, almost naturalistic approach, without really adding a very strong personal vision there.

Yes, this is correct. He is not appropriating the text or the meaning or changing the meaning; he is illustrating. But it is a children's book illustration; it is not a high-level illustration, in my opinion. And he is so detailed, so fussy in the details, that he even shows the interiors around the lamp of the tavern where the people are arm-wrestling. I mean, with all these details, these perfections, you can fill an Imax screen, you can impress a festival jury, but in the end, what do you have in your hands? You have a lot of bad paintings, and you don't have a story. Because you don't care about the older fisherman, you don't care about his fight against the sharks. You don't care about his difficult life. And you don't care even of the lines he dreams. So, it is, again, an exercise, to look at what I can do.

And also, one might argue as well that to get to the essence of the story, you might rather take away than add on and on.

Yes, certainly.

Because at the very heart, it is still very much a story about the struggle for life, but then also, the inevitable, in the end, it is a deeply desperate story, and that desperation does not really come through.

You feel that you have a foreigner trying to tell an American story. You should have some Russian subject within the story to have some truth. Otherwise, it is only some masquerade.

Speaking of a Russian story, that is the last film I want to talk about: Piotr Dumala's *Crime and Punishment* (2000, adapted from Dostoevsky). Here, we have a Polish animator adapting a Russian story. An interesting constellation in many ways. And in my opinion, an excellent adaptation with a wonderful choice of style to fully realize or even go beyond the potential of the source material for animation. I am not sure if you agree, but this shows a very different way of approaching visual adaptation. Certainly, also with high skill, but it is much more successful, because there is still a very individualized artistic vision at work here.

There is something very comic to what you are saying. It is that you are saying that Dumala's film was arguably even more successful than Dostoevsky's original story. We could say the same of Dumala's adaptation of another Dostoevsky story, *Gentle Spirit* (*Lagodna*) (1985)—the story of a lady who committed suicide. The comic thing is that a few months ago, I was sitting in Krakow in a café with Dumala, and I told him, you know that your adaptations were better than Dostoevsky's original novel(s). And he started saying horrible things about Dostoevsky.

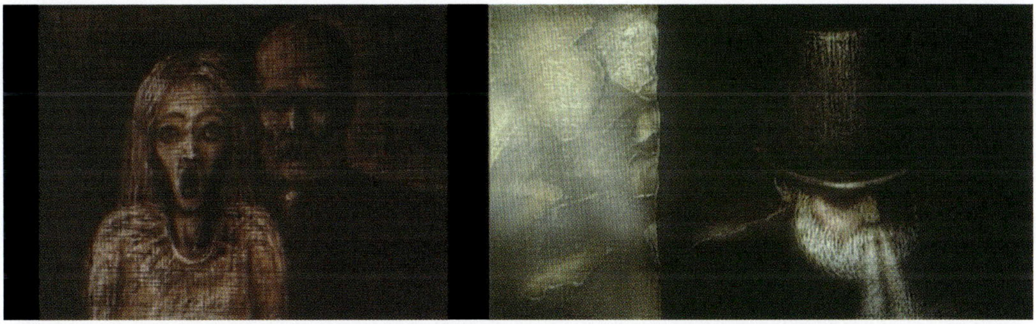

Figure 1.14: Production stills from *Gentle Spirit (Lagodna)* and *Crime and Punishment.* © Piotr Dumala.

That is very comic, you know, in that connection, because the usual cliché of adaptation is somebody sitting there, basically paralyzed by a masterpiece, and then almost not daring to touch it, and that turns the whole thing on its head.

In this case, my humble, very extremely totally humble opinion is that Dostoevsky's work grew old. It is outdated. He was a genius of the nineteenth century, but he is full of flaws of the nineteenth century that now are clear. While reading those two texts, especially *Gentle Spirit* (*Lagodna,* Oxford University Press, 1999), you realize how many exaggerations he put in there for rhetoric reasons. Dostoevsky is full of rhetoric. It is just full of rhetoric. And nowadays, rhetoric doesn't work. And the films that Dumala has made, he took away the rhetoric, and this makes them worth watching today. Maybe in 100 years, they will be outdated too, or there will be a reverse opinion, but nowadays, in the year 2014, I still subscribe to the same; I put my signature under the same words that I told him in June: Your films were better than Dostoevsky's originals.

Speaking of staying current, adapting artistic languages to changing times, you already mentioned Lotte Reiniger as a major representative of adapting fairy tales for animation. If you look at her work, where would you find potential for development, for contemporary artists to add something to it?

If you watched *The Mysterious Geographic Explorations of Jasper Morello* (Lucas 2005), this film is the "son" of *The Adventures of Prince Achmed*, so the answer is yes. The basic strengths of Lotte Reiniger's films are three. One is the music. The second one is the color. And the color, the way she was forced to use it. And the third is the filigree of the imagery. Even if you can take them all away, what still remains is the idea of the shadow puppet and the silhouette. Then, from this point on, you can add anything. I mean, the technique and the style and the approach that she made famous are there for everybody to build from. Provided that, everybody doesn't try to imitate her but to just start from the basics of her concept: Let me take your brush, and I will be painting another masterpiece.

When you look at her own work throughout the various stages of her life, a certain variety is already there. As you mentioned, some films create the impression of stained glass window colored backgrounds, like

The Star of Bethlehem (1956), her film about the nativity story. And then, there were these almost "psychedelic" backgrounds in *The Adventures of Prince Achmed*.

Well, it was a common style of the silent film, a common feature of the silent film, to paint segments of the films itself. When it was night, blue was used. If it was in a lit interior, you have orange; when you are outdoors, it is yellow. When there is a fire, it is red. So, it was a kind of visual use of music. It sets the mood, and this is a trick that you can't use nowadays.

Right, because it was very much tied to its time.

It would be an archaeological approach, which is useless.

But, what all the more seems to make for a really good argument is that redefining a style for changing times is possible, if not even required. You cannot apply exactly the same aesthetic.

That is a very good suggestion. You can quote it. But you cannot use it extensively.

Exactly. Or, you would just look into a specific artistic concept, for example, the contrast, between the silhouette, the black, and the color. And you can redefine it, in a very different way for today, because, I think, this underlying concept is always strong.

Black and blue instead of black and white. Black and red instead of black and white.

Right, so there are just like a lot of options there. And of course, although impressive in her time, the level of sophistication of the animation could be addressed differently nowadays.

Absolutely. The *Prince Achmed* animation should not be seen as an example to follow for anybody. There are (some) good animations, but it is mainly not very well animated.

Which also has a certain logic to it, because given the limitations of the technique at that time, really being required to animate straight ahead only, it certainly was not easy—although there are examples of brilliant animation in her films.

It was even too well animated for the conditions in which they were working. They were animating kneeling on the floor. So, it was very difficult to keep figures in their position.

In my opinion, what made the films really stand out, as you said, is the use of music and the color but, certainly, also the design—the design probably over the quality of the animation, because the design has the intricacy of beautiful printed illustrations.

Yes, absolutely, this is the main feature of the film. This is absolutely stunning; it is a wonderful achievement. And it is, by the way, not merely illustrated. It is just a work of art in itself.

When you look at *The Adventures of Prince Achmed*, it is also an interesting example of adaptation in the sense that it only quotes, makes its own eclectic choices from the *Tales of 1001 Nights*, which in return has the same history of being also an oral tradition and existing in many permutations. When you compare this to music, it would be a very modern approach: Basically, sampling from the source material and reassembling in a new context, just taking elements and putting them all together in their very own way and creating another framing story. So, in that sense, it is also interesting to analyze in terms of adaptation strategies.

Many films of the twentieth century owe a lot to the Italian opera of the nineteenth century. So, I would say that *The Adventures of Prince Achmed* owes a lot to Puccini's *Turandot* (1926), the opera that he did not finish, because it is a re-appropriation of a story that does not belong to your tradition and you make it your own story. So, the music for the *Prince Achmed* has nothing to do with either China or Arabia, or anything else, but it has a lot to do with the European tradition. But it is a very strong quality point for the success of the film. I will never forget the love theme; it is so sweet, so successful, and so Wagnerian in some ways.

I am currently working on another film that would use a similar approach for adaptation: *The History of the Spectre Ship* (1855), a classic fairy tale by the German author, Wilhelm Hauff, who also wrote the original novel *The Cold Heart/Das kalte Herz* (1827), which I previously adapted as an animated short film. This new film is actually a horror story. It is a gothic fairy tale, which is basically a kind of Middle Eastern re-interpretation of *The Flying Dutchman* legend. It takes place in an Arabic setting, and the original story is also heavily influenced by *1001 Nights*. So, we are basically kind of paying homage to *Prince Achmed* in some ways, but we are also looking for a new style. Now, my question is, when you think about the genre of horror, like straight on horror, really making people afraid, do you know of any examples that come to mind in animation? Can you think of any animated film that would have made people seriously afraid at all?

The Mask of the Red Death (1971) by Manfredo Manfredi, Pavao Stalter and Branko Ranitovic from the Zagreb school. *The Mask of the Red Death* is really shaking, in my opinion.

Figure 1.15: Production still from *The Mask of the Red Death* (dir. Manfredi et al. 1971). (Adapted from Edgar Allan Poe by Manfredo Manfredi, Pavao Stalter and Branko Ranitovic © Zagreb Film.)

And why is that the case? What does that film do in terms of design, in terms of cinematography, in terms of sound, to make it work?

Well, it works because the paintings in the film are made by Pavao Stalter, a great painter, who is even better than Paul Julian. But, basically, because it tells a story without any hole, so this is what gives you the feeling that you are shocked. It is definitely shocking, because there is no way out. And I always witnessed people reacting very badly to the message; they admire the film, but they are disturbed.

Of course, because an audience longs for the happy ending and for deliverance instead of the curse. But at the end of the story, we are looking to adapt—there is going to be deliverance for the crew of the ghost ship. But still, we are intending to instill moments, if possible, of real horror. And that is the challenge right now, which we are trying to address. What we have not mentioned in our investigation so far is the important role of sound, when you analyze horror film in general. What do you think of that in terms of supporting the shocking moment, like the quiet against the sudden noise or the use of sound and music in general?

In my opinion, a horror film should be very sparse, very basic in terms of music. In a horror film, they should have, most of the time, sound effects and voices, and distorted voices. Music is too cheap a tool to provoke emotions. So, if you have a true horror film, you have to find something that is different from suggestions, you have to find something that is stating horror. And what states horror is not death, because death is eventually static. It happens, and that is it. What makes me feel horrified is the impossibility of breathing, for instance, or all the phobias that you can have, or the loss of identity or the loss of parameters; these are the things that provoke horror. And you can get these things only with narration.

You think narration is important in that sense? That is a very good point to know, because we are also looking at that option actually. And, ultimately, it is more about, as the name says, fear is the fear about potentially losing, that is the interesting part, because if it is already happening…

Fear is about something that hasn't happened yet; fear is an expectation.

Exactly, it is an expectation, because the fear is actually happening before the actual event. Obviously, when death really occurs, the fear is actually over.

I have a strange story to tell you that just comes to my mind: Once upon a time in Sri Lanka, in Selon, there was a king who was so afraid of his brother to take his kingdom away that he built a fortress on a strange mountain that exists actually in this island. I don't remember the name of the fortress. And he took a lot of the soldiers, because they were unconquerable. And eventually, the brother moved over to him; after decades of him fortificating himself in the fortress, the war actually happened. And what did the king do? He descended from the fortress and had an open battle with his brother.

So, all the precautions and premonitions were not enough. It is actually quite telling, drawing an interesting parallel with *The Mask of the Red Death*. Taking all these precautionary measures, trying to protect yourself, actually proved moot, because in the end, the red death gets all of them anyway, as an intruder to that party, and that is a very powerful thought. Particularly considering the implications for adapting the horror genre for animation, how do you create fear? I think we have covered a lot of ground now in terms of looking at a wide variety of animated adaptations in different genres: We were discussing different artistic strategies to succeed or fail in this field. Thank you for your comprehensive insights into the many aspects of animated adaptations through history. I am sure our readers will find a lot of inspiration for their own creative exploits or scholarly studies.

Following on from this introductory conversation, the next chapter will present an interview with another legendary animation historian, who can also offer the angle of practitioner and studio teacher.

References

Alexeieff, Alexandre, dir. 1963. *The Nose.* Animated short film.

Alighieri, Dante. 1472. *Divine Comedy.* Ca. 1308–1320. First published version: Foligno, Italy: Johann Numeister and Evangelista Angelini da Trevi.

Anonymous. 2002. *The Thousand and One Nights.* Trans. Husain Haddawy. *The Norton Anthology of World Literature*, edited by Sarah Lawall. New York: W.W. Norton & Company.

Bendazzi, Giannalberto. 2016. *Animation: A World History. Vol. I: Foundations—The Golden Age.* Boca Raton, FL: CRC Press.

Bendazzi, Giannalberto. 2016. *Animation: A World History. Vol. II: The Birth of a Style.* Boca Raton, FL: CRC Press.

Bendazzi, Giannalberto. 2016. *Animation: A World History. Vol. III: Contemporary Times.* Boca Raton, FL: CRC Press.

Bendazzi, Giannalberto. 2001. *Alexeieff, Itinéraire D'un Maitre.* 2001. Annecy, France: Centre International Du Cinéma d'Animation.

Bendazzi, Gianalberto. 1994. *Cartoons: One Hundred Years of Cinema Animation.* London, UK: John Libbey.

Carroll, Lewis. 1865. *The Adventures of Alice in Wonderland* (aka *Alice in Wonderland*). London, UK: Macmillan.

Collin, Robin. 2014. How Peter Jackson ruined The Hobbit. *Telegraph* (UK), December 12, 2014. Accessed May 22, 2018. https://www.telegraph.co.uk/culture/film/11285677/From-warm-and-witty-to-carnage-adapting-The -Hobbit.html.

Collodi, Carlo. 1883. *Le avventure di Pinocchio, Storia di un Burattino.* Florence, Italy: Libreria Editrice Felice Paggi.

Dostoevsky, Fyodor. 1866. *Crime and Punishment.* In: *The Russian Messenger.* Moscow.

Dostoevsky, Fyodor. 1999. A gentle creature. In: *Gentle Creature, and Other Stories*, edited by Fëdor Dostoevskij, Alan Myers, and William Leatherbarrow. Oxford, UK: Oxford University Press.

Dumala, Piotr, dir. 1985. *Gentle Spirit* (*Lagodna*). Animated short film. Warsaw, Poland: Studio Minitur Filmowych (production).

Dumala, Piotr, dir. 2000. *Crime and Punishment.* Animated short film. Warsaw, Poland: Bow and Axe (production).

Eisenstein, Sergeij, dir. *Battleship Potemkin.* Silent feature film. Moscow: Mosfilm (production)/Goskino (distribution), 1925.

Gogol, Nikolai. 1980. The nose. In: *Nikolai Gogol: A Selection*, edited by Sergi Mashinsky. Moscow: Progress Publishers.

Goldman, Les, and Paul Julian, dirs. 1964. *The Hangman.* Animated short film. Melrose Productions (production).

Hand, David, dir. 1937. *Snow White and the Seven Dwarfs.* Animated feature film. Los Angeles, CA: Walt Disney Productions/RKO Radio Pictures.

Hauff, Wilhelm. 1827. *The Cold Heart/Das kalte Herz*, published in two parts in the novel Das Wirtshaus im Spessart in Märchen-Almanach auf das Jahr 1828 für Söhne und Töchter gebildeter Stände. Stuttgart, Germany: G.Schwab.

Hauff, Wilhelm. 1855. *The History of the Spectre Ship.* Translated from German by George Payn Quakenbos. New York: D. Appleton and Company. Accessed September 3, 2016. http://www.gutenberg.org/files/24593/24593-h/24593-h.htm.

Hemingway Ernest. 1952. *The Old Man and the Sea.* New York: Charles Scribners Sons.

Hodgson, Jonathan, dir. 2000. *The Man with the Beautiful Eyes.* Animated short film. London, UK: Sherbet (production)/Artificial Eye (distribution).

Hugo, Victor. 1831. *The Hunchback of Notre-Dame.* Paris, France: Charles Gosselin.

Hurtz, William T., dir. 1953. *The Unicorn in the Garden.* Animated short film. Los Angeles, CA: United Productions of America (UPA) (production)/ Coumbia Pictures (distribution).

Jackson, Peter, dir. 2012. *The Hobbit: An Unexpected Journey.* Live action feature film (with animated elements). Wellington, New Zealand: WingNut Films; Los Angeles, CA: New Line Cinema; Beverly Hills, CA: Metro-Goldwyn-Mayer (production). Los Angeles, CA: Warner Bros. Pictures (distribution).

Jackson, Peter, dir. 2013. *The Hobbit: The Desolation of Smaug.* Live action feature film (with animated elements). Wellington, New Zealand: WingNut Films; Los Angeles, CA: New Line Cinema; Beverly Hills, CA: Metro-Goldwyn-Mayer (production). Los Angeles, CA: Warner Bros. Pictures (distribution).

Jackson, Peter, dir. 2014. *The Hobbit: The Battle of the Five Armies.* Live action feature film (with animated elements). Wellington, New Zealand: WingNut Films; Los Angeles, CA: New Line Cinema; Beverly Hills, CA: Metro-Goldwyn-Mayer (production). Los Angeles, CA: Warner Bros. Pictures (distribution).

Jones, Chuck, dir. 1957. *What's Opera, Doc?* Animated short film. Los Angeles, CA: Warner Bros. Cartoons (production). Los Angeles, CA: Warner Bros. (distribution).

Lang, Fritz, dir. 1924a. *Die Nibelungen Pt. 1: Siegfried.* Silent feature film. Potsdam-Babelsberg, Germany: Universum Film AG (UFA) (production).

Lang, Fritz, dir. 1924b. *Die Nibelungen Pt. 2: Kriemhilds Rache.* Silent feature film. Potsdam-Babelsberg, Germany: Universum Film AG (UFA) (production).

Leaf, Caroline, dir. 1976. *The Street.* Animated short film. Montreal, Canada: National Film Board of Canada (production and distribution).

Leaf, Caroline, dir. 1977. *The Metamorphosis of Mr. Samsa.* Animated short film. Montreal, Canada: National Film Board of Canada (production and distribution).

Leaf, Caroline, dir. 1990. *Two Sisters.* Animated short film. Montreal, Canada: National Film Board of Canada (production and distribution).

Lindvall, Terry. n.d. Choice review for *Cartoons: 100 Years of Cinema Animation.* Accessed March 4 2019. https://bepl.ent.sirsi.net/client/en_US/default/search/detailnonmodal/ent:$002f$002fSD_ILS$002f0$002fSD_ILS:847829/ada.

Lucas, Anthony, dir. 2005. *The Mysterious Geographic Explorations of Jasper Morello.* Animated short film. Australia: 3D Films (production). Dublin: Monster Distributes (distribution).

Luske, Hamilton, and Ben Sharpsteen, dirs. 1940. *Pinocchio.* Animated feature film. Burbank, CA: Walt Disney Productions/RKO Radio Pictures.

Manfredi, Manfredo, Branko Ranitovic, and Pavao Stalter, dirs. 1971. *The Masque of the Red Death/La Maschera della Morte Rossa.* Animated short film. Italy: Corona Cinematografica (production).

Manfredi, Manfredo, dir. 1997. *Canto XXVI° dell'Inferno di Dante.* Animated short film.

McCabe, Colin, Kathleen Murray, and Rick Warner, eds. 2011. *True to the Spirit: Film Adaptation and the Question of Fidelity.* Oxford, UK: Oxford University.

Murnau, Friedrich Wilhelm, dir. 1926. *Faust - Eine deutsche Volkssage.* Silent feature film. Potsdam-Babelsberg, Germany: Universum Film AG (UFA) (production).

Ogden, Maurice. *The Hangman.* 1954. Masses and Mainstream, 7(1).

Parmelee, Ted, dir. 1953. *The Tell-Tale Heart.* Animated short film. Los Angeles, CA: United Productions of America (UPA) (production). Los Angeles, CA: Columbia Pictures (distribution).

Petrov, Aleksandr, dir. 1989. *The Cow.* Animated short film. Moscow: Pilot Moscow Animation Studio (production).

Petrov, Aleksandr, dir. 1999. *The Old Man and the Sea.* Animated short film. Tokyo, Japan: Dentsu Tec (production). Plattsburgh: Direct Source (distribution).

Platonov, Andrei Platonovich, ed. 1999. The cow. In: *The Return and Other Stories.* London, UK: Harvill.

Puccini, Giacomo. 1926. *Turandot.* Opera in three acts. Milan, Italy: Teatro alla Scala (premiered April 25).

Reiniger, Lotte, dir. 1926. *The Adventures of Prince Achmed.* Animated feature film. Berlin, Germany: Comenius-Film Berlin/Louis Hagen (production).

Reiniger, Lotte, dir. 1956. *The Star of Bethlehem.* Animated short film. London, UK: Primrose Productions (production).

Starr, Charlie W. 2012. Adaptation versus Transformation-Peter Jackson's Hobbit Experiment. Accessed May 22, 2018. http://www.cslewis.com/adaptation -vs-transformation-peter-jacksons-hobbit-experiment/.

Tharoor, Ishaan. 2012. Bilbo's Band of Bearded-Folk. Accessed May 22, 2018. http://entertainment.time.com/2012/12/13/times-guide-to-the-hobbits-13-dwarves/.

Through the Keyhole A Companion's Guide to Alice in Wonderland. *Alice in Wonderland: 60th Anniversary Edition*. 2011 Blu-Ray. Burbank, CA: Walt Disney Home Entertainment.

Wagner, Richard. 1870. *Die Walküre.* Opera in three acts. Munich, Germany: Königliches Hof-und Nationaltheater (premiered June 26).

Wells, Paul. 1999. Thou art translated: Analysing animated adaptations. In *Adaptations: From Text to Screen, Screen to Text*, edited by Deborah Cartmell and Imelda Whelehan. London, UK: Routledge.

An Interview with John Canemaker

"Animation Can Aspire to Poetic Imagery and Feeling"

Figure 2.1: John Canemaker at work in his studio (2017). © John Canemaker.

When it comes to further discussing the topic of animated adaptations, one can hardly imagine a more suitable conversation partner than famed animation historian and animation teacher John Canemaker. A full professor at New York University's (NYU) Tisch School of the Arts and head of its animation department, John has excelled in all of his capacities: As an independent animation director, he won an Oscar for his short film, *The Moon and the Son: An Imagined Conversation* (2005), as well as an Emmy. As a historian, he must be considered among the world's foremost authorities on American animation in general and Disney animation in particular. This is demonstrated by his many book publications that stand unrivaled in depth of analysis and meticulously researched detail: *The Animated Raggedy Ann and Andy* (1977), *Treasures of Disney Animation Art* (1982); *Winsor McCay: His Life and Art* (1987), *Felix: The Twisted Tale of the World's Most Famous Cat* (1991), *Tex Avery: The MGM Years* (1996), *Before the Animation Begins: The Art and Lives of Disney Inspirational Sketch Artists* (1996), *Paper Dreams: The Art and Artists of Disney Storyboards* (1999), *Walt Disney's Nine Old Men and the Art of Animation* (2001), *The Art and Flair of Mary Blair* (2003), *Two Guys Named Joe: Master Animation Storytellers Joe Grant and Joe Ranft* (2010), *The Lost Notebook: Herman Schultheis and the Secrets of Walt Disney's Movie Magic* (2014), and a revised and updated edition of *Winsor McCay: His Life and Art* (2018).

Figure 2.2: The jacket of the revised edition of *Winsor McCay—His Life and Art* (CRC Press, 2018). © John Canemaker/ CRC Press.

Giannalberto Bendazzi has pointed out in his preceding interview that the history of Disney animation is often synonymous with a history of animated adaptation. But John's immersion extends far beyond that. In his work as an award-winning animation director, he has frequently revisited animated adaptation(s) over the years. His 1982 film *Bottom's Dream* is a highly original adaptation of Shakespeare's *A Midsummer Night's Dream*. The renowned animation scholar Paul Wells (1999, 211) has high praise for this interpretation: "He essentially abstracts Shakespeare's narrative into a visual poem, highly empathetic with the transmutation of perceptual and emotional states that is the play's chief theme. Canemaker energizes the 'Romanticism' of Shakespeare's plot, however, by emphasizing the 'animality' of passion and desire. The primal instincts aroused through Bottom's transformation are represented in the intuitive and looser formations of Canemaker's 'styles'. His free use of the plasmatic potential within the open vocabulary of animation captures and develops the 'experience' in the text and the spirit of the word."

Figure 2.3: J.C. lecturing on Winsor McCay and Gertie the Dinosaur. Nemo Academy of Digital Arts, Firenze, 2018. (Courtesy of Ruth Miriam Carmeli.)

The following interview provides detailed insights into the creation process of *Bottom's Dream* and other animated adaptations, including John Canemaker's most current project. But it all begins with an innovative piece of animation that initially drew the author of this book to John's art more than 30 years ago.

The following interview was conducted by Hannes Rall with John Canemaker in his office at NYU Tisch School of the Arts on February 27, 2017:

Hannes Rall (Interviewer)
John Canemaker (Interviewed)

The very first I ever saw of your animated work was the beautiful sequence you created for the live action feature *The World According to Garp* (dir. Hill 1982). This was an adaptation of the famous book by John Irving. And we can see examples of conceptual work for the film right here. I understand that you storyboarded and designed two sequences, of which only one was finally used as an animated segment in the live action feature film.

Figure 2.4: Concept art for the animated sequence that was completed and used in the finished film. © John Canemaker.

Yes. What I sent you was actually some of the conceptual and animation drawings for both sequences. And all of the children's drawings were mine in the film, so there was an enormous amount. There was also the tale of the whale that was in the novel, but which was cut out, but they had me actually develop the whole whale story, which I have no copies of.

Okay, that is a pity, but what is there is already very impressive in its daring aesthetic approach. You also sent me some excerpts from the script that the initial idea to realize certain sequences as animation already came from the scriptwriter, is that right?

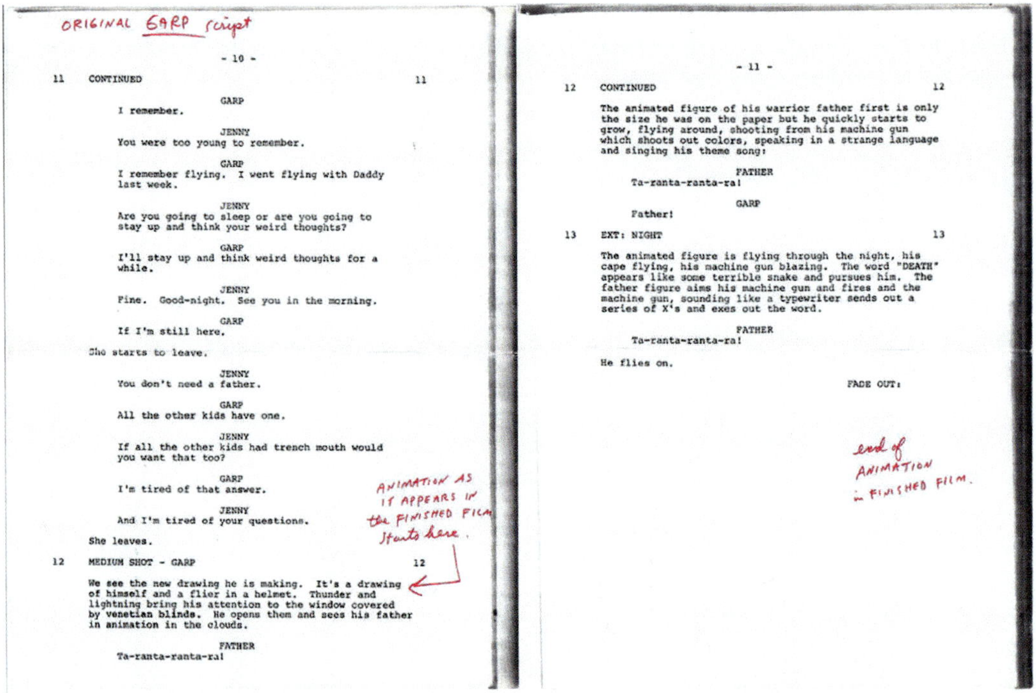

ORIGINAL GARP script

\- 10 -

11 CONTINUED 11

GARP
I remember.

JENNY
You were too young to remember.

GARP
I remember flying. I went flying with Daddy last week.

JENNY
Are you going to sleep or are you going to stay up and think your weird thoughts?

GARP
I'll stay up and think weird thoughts for a while.

JENNY
Fine. Good-night. See you in the morning.

GARP
If I'm still here.

She starts to leave.

JENNY
You don't need a father.

GARP
All the other kids have one.

JENNY
If all the other kids had trench mouth would you want that too?

GARP
I'm tired of that answer.

JENNY
And I'm tired of your questions.

She leaves.

ANIMATION AS IT APPEARS IN the FINISHED FILM starts here.

12 MEDIUM SHOT - GARP 12

We see the new drawing he is making. It's a drawing of himself and a flier in a helmet. Thunder and lightning bring his attention to the window covered by venetian blinds. He opens them and sees his father in animation in the clouds.

FATHER
Ta-ranta-ranta-ra!

\- 11 -

12 CONTINUED 12

The animated figure of his warrior father first is only the size he was on the paper but he quickly starts to grow, flying around, shooting from his machine gun which shoots out colors, speaking in a strange language and singing his theme song:

FATHER
Ta-ranta-ranta-ra!

GARP
Father!

13 EXT: NIGHT 13

The animated figure is flying through the night, his cape flying, his machine gun blazing. The word "DEATH" appears like some terrible snake and pursues him. The father figure aims his machine gun and fires and the machine gun, sounding like a typewriter sends out a series of X's and exes out the word.

FATHER
Ta-ranta-ranta-ra!

He flies on.

FADE OUT:

end of ANIMATION in FINISHED FILM.

Figure 2.5: Corresponding excerpt from the original script of *The World According to Garp*, which already suggested the use of animation. © John Canemaker.

As far as I know. Because it also, of course, had to be approved by George Roy Hill, the director. Now, it may have originated in conferences with George Roy Hill and the writer, I don't know, but what it ended up with was the script that he showed me. George, when we had our first meeting said, "Do you think you can do this?" It was just these two paragraphs, and I said, "Oh, of course I can do this." I wanted the job, so I took the stuff away, and within 2 weeks, I had done all of these storyboards, which by the way are available at the Museum of Modern Art Film Study Center (see references).

They are the actual boards that were sent to California and back and many sequences that were considered, including the one that's in pencil test.

This was the planned sequence of Jenny's (Garp's mother) story about conceiving her child. The animation was considered too funny. George had a habit of asking everybody in the crew what they thought. So, I'd be sitting there, and they'd look at the pencil test, and he'd ask the editor, and then, he'd ask the assistant editor, and they said, "Well, it's too funny. It will just break the mood of this mother-son relationship." So, he said, "Well, cut it out." I saved the pencil test, and it's now on YouTube.

Speaking about the topic of fidelity to the source material, when I read the original novel, it was already clear to me that there would be a need for significant alterations from the source material to transfer it to the screen.

But I also think that there was not really any implication of using animation in the novel itself.

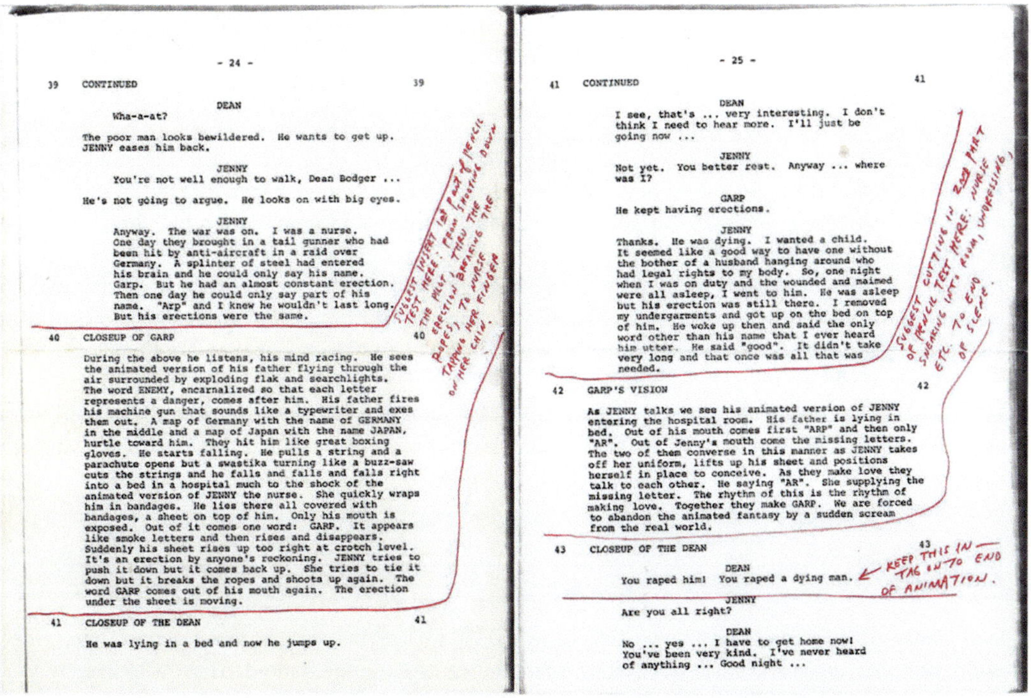

\- 24 -

39 CONTINUED 39

DEAN
Wha-a-at?

The poor man looks bewildered. He wants to get up. JENNY eases him back.

JENNY
You're not well enough to walk, Dean Bodger ...

He's not going to argue. He looks on with big eyes.

JENNY
Anyway. The war was on. I was a nurse. One day they brought in a tail gunner who had been hit by anti-aircraft in a raid over Germany. A splinter of steel had entered his brain and he could only say his name. Garp. But he had an almost constant erection. Then one day he could only say part of his name. "Arp" and I knew he wouldn't last long. But his erections were the same.

40 CLOSEUP OF GARP 40

During the above he listens, his mind racing. He sees the animated version of his father flying through the air surrounded by exploding flak and searchlights. The word ENEMY, encarnalized so that each letter represents a danger, comes after him. His father fires his machine gun that sounds like a typewriter and exes them out. A map of Germany with the name of GERMANY in the middle and a map of Japan with the name JAPAN, hurtle toward him. They hit him like great boxing gloves. He starts falling. He pulls a string and a parachute opens but a swastika turning like a buzz-saw cuts the strings and he falls and falls and falls right into a bed in a hospital much to the shock of the animated version of JENNY the nurse. She quickly wraps him in bandages. He lies there all covered with bandages, a sheet on top of him. Only his mouth is exposed. Out of it comes one word: GARP. It appears like smoke letters and then rises and disappears. Suddenly his sheet rises up too right at crotch level. It's an erection by anyone's reckoning. JENNY tries to push it down but it comes back up. She tries to tie it down but it breaks the ropes and shoots up again. The word GARP comes out of his mouth again. The erection under the sheet is moving.

41 CLOSEUP OF THE DEAN 41

He was lying in a bed and now he jumps up.

SUGGEST INSERT 1st part of PENCIL TEST HERE: FROM SHOOTING DOWN THE PILOT, THRU THE ERECTION BREAKING THE ROPES), TO NURSE TAPPING HER FINGER ON HER CHIN.

\- 25 -

41 CONTINUED 41

DEAN
I see, that's ... very interesting. I don't think I need to hear more. I'll just be going now ...

JENNY
Not yet. You better rest. Anyway ... where was I?

GARP
He kept having erections.

JENNY
Thanks. He was dying. I wanted a child. It seemed like a good way to have one without the bother of a husband hanging around who had legal rights to my body. So, one night when I was on duty and the wounded and maimed were all asleep, I went to him. He was asleep but his erection was still there. I removed my undergarments and got up on the bed on top of him. He woke up then and said the only word other than his name that I ever heard him utter. He said "good". It didn't take very long and that once was all that was needed.

42 GARP'S VISION 42

As JENNY talks we see his animated version of JENNY entering the hospital room. His father is lying in bed. Out of his mouth comes first "ARP" and then only "AR". Out of Jenny's mouth come the missing letters. The two of them converse in this manner as JENNY takes off her uniform, lifts up his sheet and positions herself in place to conceive. As they make love they talk to each other. He saying "AR". She supplying the missing letter. The rhythm of this is the rhythm of making love. Together they make GARP. We are forced to abandon the animated fantasy by a sudden scream from the real world.

43 CLOSEUP OF THE DEAN 43

DEAN
You raped him! You raped a dying man.

JENNY
Are you all right?

DEAN
No ... yes ... I have to get home now! You've been very kind. I've never heard of anything ... Good night ...

SUGGEST CUTTING IN 2nd PART OF PENCIL TEST HERE: NURSE SNEAKING INT. ROOM, UNDRESSING, ETC. TO END OF SCENE.

KEEP THIS IN — TAG ON TO END OF ANIMATION.

Figure 2.6: The corresponding directorial comments by John Canemaker for the scene of Garp's conception in the script. © John Canemaker.

No, in fact, the book's author, John Irving, did not like the idea of using animation. The director told me that Irving wasn't happy to see us drawing those scenes. I never got to meet him, but he wasn't happy about the idea of animation—that it was in there at all. But George, the director, thought, what a good way to get into this through children's drawings, the child Garp's drawings, and so, it was done.

And I thought, when I was watching the movie and comparing it to the novel, that the changes were well chosen and well conceived. One of the theories I am proposing in this book is that the transition to the moving image requires to really change things—it is an entirely different medium after all.

It is, and the producer and director were very good to me. I mean, I was taken care of. They brought me out to the Long Island studio to watch them shoot Glenn Close's first scene, and she was talking to the child, who was also there, and I watched the whole scene right next to the camera. The producer said, "You're going to stay here by the camera." And the crew were not terribly happy that I was standing so close to the camera, but I did, and I saw the whole thing. I remember Glenn Close speaking very quietly on camera, and I thought, oh, this woman; this is her first film, and it will probably be her last because she's so quiet.

It turned out quite differently.

Indeed. On the screen, she was just wonderful. I learned a lesson about the difference between film and stage acting.

So, I would be interested to learn a little bit more about the production process, whether there were approvals of the pre-production sketches by the director, and then, how did it go on through the different stages?

Well, the first thing was getting the job. Someone at Warner Bros. saw my *Confessions of a Stardreamer*, an earlier animated short (1978). So, they sent that to George, and he liked it. Then, he brought me in, and showed me the two script pages and said, "Do you think you can come up with something for this?" And I said, "Sure, I can do storyboards based on that."

At the Museum of Modern Art (MOMA), you can see the different boards and how they changed. They were much more extensive in terms of the transformation of the little cartoon boy character into one thing or another; he became a bird at one point, to fly, to catch up with its father, that sort of thing.

It's always the motivation of trying to please his father or to find his father. He never knew who his father was. He (Garp) was conceived, as you saw, in the book, and then, his father dies soon after ejaculation. So, you know, it's touching in a strange way. But I did numerous conceptual sketches and storyboards that were quite large, and they sent them off to California. When they came back, I found coffee stains and smudges on the boards, so they were well examined in LA.

I understand there were some edits in the boards coming back from these story conferences and some suggestions.

Sure. I mean, the boards were cut down. George would say, we'll do this, we'll do that, not this. Then, I would re-do the boards again and finally got exactly what they wanted. George wanted to have a finish on the first sequence, in which we pull back from the animation, and the kid's asleep on the last drawing. Well, that had to be done by R/Greenberg, a special effects company here in New York, who matched my drawing using an optical printer—this was before digital; the optical printer pulled back from the animation field into the live-action set.

So, it was an interesting process. An older executive producer looked at the pencil test and said, "Well, is there going to be any color?" And I said, yes, eventually. He said, "What's that flickering?" I said, well, it's the paper, the underlit paper levels are changing. "Oh." And then, I thought, oh, I've lost the job now. But George and a younger producer, Robert Crawford Jr., came through for me. They understood what the animation process was. In fact, Crawford's mother-in-law, Tatiana Riabouchinska, was the great Russian dancer, and she was a model for one of the hippos in *Fantasia* (dirs. Algar et al. 1940).

Figure 2.7: Typical for the workflow in animation, scenes will first be animated in black and white, tested if the animation works properly, and only subsequently colored. Concept art and color models for the "flying sequence" from *Garp*, which is in the film. © John Canemaker.

That's an interesting side story.

She's also in a Disney film titled *Two Silhouettes*, from *Make Mine Music* (dir. Cormack et al. 1946).

Then there was the second sequence about the conception, nurse Jenny's sexual encounter with the dying man named Garp. It was screened in the Midwest in pencil test form within the live-action rough cut. People laughed; they thought it was hilarious, but that killed it. The director decided, no, no, it has to be more serious. So, they just deleted that animation. So, at least the flying sequence survived.

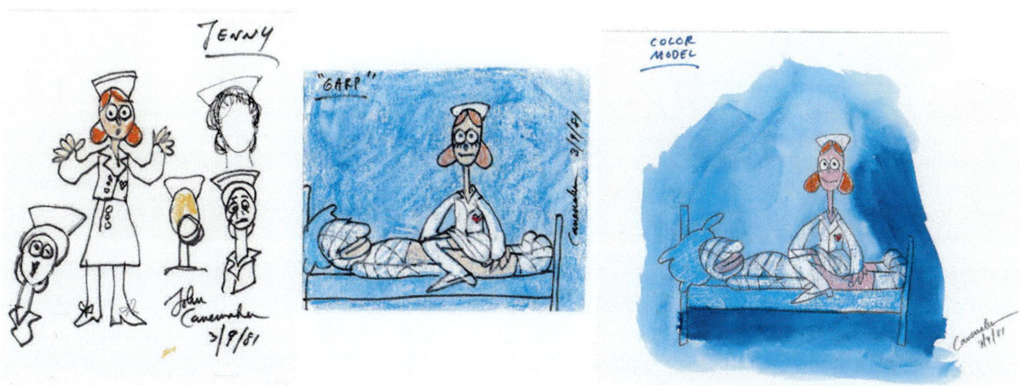

Figure 2.8: Concept art in different stages for the ultimately cut animated sequence depicting the conception of Garp. It is a wonderfully staged little scene with highly imaginative use of timing and framing. And funny as hell. While it unfortunately did not end up in the finished film, it is available to watch on YouTube as a pencil test. © John Canemaker.

Which is, actually, a pity, when you think about it... I mean, from a personal point of view, because I think it would have been a great addition, actually.

Well, it's on YouTube.

That is great! So everybody can still enjoy the wit of the sequence. So, you said that all of the drawings are yours. Does it also mean that you animated the whole thing completely by yourself?

Yes.

So, without assistants even...

I had one person coloring with crayons. But I did all the animation, and I mean, it was only 90 seconds, and I enjoyed it very much.

What I really always loved about the animation is the use of this children's drawing style that is very fitting. Maybe in a way, at that time, Irving didn't see that, but I find it highly appropriate in the specific context of the two scenes. And, in a bigger context, it is entirely in line with the tone of the movie as a whole, which itself is kind of "weird" in a way, in a good way. So, I think that something unconventional in the way of bringing the sequence(s) to the screen really enhanced the artistic quality.

Figure 2.9: Concept art from the animated segment used in *The World According to Garp*. © John Canemaker.

I also felt comfortable working in that style, and I've used it in a number of films. They're also on YouTube, including a film I called *Break the Silence: Kids Against Child Abuse* (dir. Peltier 1994)—there is a very child-like look in that—and also, *You Don't Have to Die* (dir. Clarke, Guttentag 1988), an HBO Special that won an Academy Award for the producers; it was about children with cancer. This childlike stylistic approach can be very powerful.

And, of course, it gives you a chance to kind of "getting" into the mind...

Of the child.

Animation gives you the chance to express internal mindsets.

Well, the great thing about animation is that it can personify thoughts. It can become an emotion. Pixar's *Inside Out* (dir. Docter 2015) did that. Disney did it earlier with the World War II short, *Reason and Emotion* (dir. Robert 1943).

And that's something I used, for example, when the child in *You Don't Have to Die* is getting chemotherapy. So, I misspelled the word on purpose, as a child might with the lettering, and then drew this very simple bottle containing a green liquid as the chemo. When the tube goes into the child's arm, he fills up with the green liquid as if he's an empty bottle. The child's voice-over says, "It made my hair fall out." The liquid comes up to the top of his head, and poof, his hair falls out. He tries to put it back, fails, and runs off. They're very simple drawings, but they click; they resonate with people.

Figure 2.10: Drawing from *You Don't Have to Die* (1988). © John Canemaker.

It makes the experience felt, somehow. There is a relatable emotion to it, and it also shows this other property of animation: Exaggeration comes to help here, and you can use that to really draw people in emotionally.

Animation is such a potent art form in terms of making strong statements with symbolic imagery. It can condense time; it can use metamorphosis, if you want to. Most of the Disney films want to convince you of the reality of the work. They don't want you to think that it's a drawing. For Walt Disney, that was a "no-no." It's also what Winsor McCay tried to do with his films. He wanted to convince you that his *Gertie the Dinosaur*, a 1914 film starring a cartoon dinosaur, was real and had an individualistic personality, and it worked. Disney was the ultimate propagator of that concept.

Suspension of disbelief, right?

That's right, to convince you that a cartoon is real. Interestingly, when they used metamorphosis in the early days, *Felix the Cat*, *Mickey Mouse*, and *Oswald the Lucky Rabbit* were all over the place—all stretchy and looked like they were made out of rubber, the rubber hose and circle cartoony style, and could morph into different characters and objects. And you know, it's totally impossible, but you think, what a funny cartoon character! But then, Disney wanted to convince you that if a punch made the character extend, it would also hurt. So, how to solve that problem? Also, whenever metamorphosis is used in the Disney features, for example, in *Snow White* (dir. Hand 1937), the Queen takes drugs, before she changes into a crone. There is a rational reason for her morphing.

Right, right, because, otherwise, it would break the concept of the believable narrative framework.

Think of the surreal "Elephants on Parade" sequence in *Dumbo* (dir. Sharpsteen 1941): Dumbo must get drunk before he can see those wild nightmare visions.

It is introduced as a dream, a hallucination, in fact.

Which brings me to another interesting question, which is actually referring to your adaptation of a part, a segment from Shakespeare's *A Midsummer Night's Dream*, your film *Bottom's Dream* (1983): Discussing suspension of disbelief, in this film, you deliberately reveal the artificial character of the drawings as drawings.

Figure 2.11: These excerpts from the storyboards of *Bottom's Dream* demonstrate the stylistic diversity and the deliberate reveal of the creation process. ©John Canemaker.

The process.

I would be very interested to learn about what led you to that decision and, on the other hand, also of what potentially refers to a dreamlike quality of the source material.

Figure 2.12: A beautiful background and cel setup for a horizontal pan from *Bottom's Dream*. © John Canemaker.

I've always felt that the pencil tests are one of the most interesting, beautiful parts of the animated film process. To see an inert pencil line come to life has always fascinated me. I love the Hubleys' works (*editor's remark: John and Faith Hubley*), because they actually took the rough pencil character drawings, including their construction lines, painted black around them, and cross-dissolved them onto watercolor backgrounds. Gorgeous, gorgeous. That way, they matched and merged the character's look with the backgrounds. I love that.

Another influence for me in terms of process is George Dunning's short film *Damon the Mower* (1972); do you know this film?

No, it's quite new to me. Of course, I know *Yellow Submarine* (1968, directed by George Dunning).

Very experimental, but Dunning's *Damon the Mower*, which is on YouTube, is adapted quite freely from a poem by Andrew Marvell (1621–1678). Dunning came up with the concept of animating little flip-book pages: You see the tape marks around the individual numbered pages, and the desk that they rest upon, so the camera field is high up, looking down on this little flip-book. And the imagery presents a continuous motion of nature and how death is coming into a pastoral setting teeming with life levels everything with a scythe.

The imagery includes cycles of sheep jumping and a grasshopper springing off a grass blade, and it's all on these pencil drawings, and you're seeing the process of animation, bringing the inert to life. Each drawing's numbers are seen going by on the flip-book pages—sound effects, no music. It's magical, and I was fascinated by the film.

One time in London, I went to see John Coates, Dunning's producer, and I asked to see the drawings. Dunning died in 1979. To my surprise, it wasn't just a flip-book placed on a desk. Dunning attached each drawing to separate cels. So, there was registration and control. He was very purposeful in doing that.

I can definitely recognize the influence on *Bottom's Dream*. In the film, you used so many different techniques: pencil, crayon, then some painting techniques, and the line tests themselves. So, was it any intention from your side to use this kind of collage of techniques to evoke some atmosphere of dreaming?

When I start a project, I make a lot of concept drawings and experimentation first. I like so many of the concepts, I think that, well, maybe this would work here or maybe this would work there. So, it becomes a collage, really, in a way. My film *The Moon and the Son: An Imagined Conversation* (2005) is very much a collage, including live action, documentary footage, home movies, and my drawings in different mediums and techniques. Sometimes, it goes from a photograph into a cel of an abstraction of my parents, me, and my brother, and then, it goes into something else. I'm a Gemini, so I think it's an aspect of my restless short attention span.

But it might also resonate very well with adapting Shakespeare, because when I conducted interviews over years with a director of the Shakespeare Institute, Professor Dobson, he is amazingly open in his assessment of how Shakespeare can be adapted.

He posits that Shakespeare himself is so playful in his pieces and in his plays that it can be deemed appropriate to be equally playful and experimental in an animated adaptation.

And poetic. Shakespeare's the great poet, and animation can aspire to poetic imagery and feeling. He's been adapted in so many different ways. Dunning was working on *The Tempest*, when he died. Just beautiful, magical stuff. Wished he'd finished that film. What's on YouTube is only a small part.

Figure 2.13: Film still from George Dunning's uncompleted version of *The Tempest*. © George Dunning estate.

It's an absolutely fascinating excerpt, but was there a plan for this as a feature film? One would assume that he really considered this as a long-form project.

But, ultimately, he doesn't really specify that in the interview you did with him in 1978 at the Ottawa International Animation Festival.

I think it was to be a feature. But he was doing it all himself pretty much. A labor of love. Again, I looked at the original drawings when I was with Coates, and they are just amazing. Dunning stated that the reason why he used the little flip-books was "I have a place in the country and I was dragging my animation disc and light box, and all this paraphernalia back and forth from the city to the country." So, he decided that he'll just make these flip-book sketches into a film. And that was it: born out of necessity.

I know the feeling, because I have a place in Long Island, and every other weekend, I'm carting out there all of these drawings and art materials.

I think this is a well-known circumstance for animators: I have also an apartment at the university campus and one in downtown Singapore. So, despite the digital, there always have to be these considerations, what do I bring from here over there, and backwards? And I still animate a lot, also, traditionally, so it's always about transporting things, bringing them from one place to another. So, I can understand that.

Yeah. I think it's common with many animation people: We're pack rats and trying to figure out how and where to work.

When I read the interview (Canemaker n.d.) that you conducted with George Dunning, I found it very interesting that he was extremely concerned about changing anything from the original Shakespeare text. Particularly given that I recently went to talk to some of the leading Shakespeare scholars in the world, and they rather encouraged me to depart from a too literal interpretation. Maybe, I don't know, the attitude has changed compared to 30 years ago? Or is there still a discrepancy in the perception of how sacred the texts are supposed to be?

I think you always need to be concerned about that—about whether or not you're desecrating the text with the freedom that's available in animation. But animation does beg for a different approach, and I agree with Dunning, who said, "I'm not trying to do a play. I'm not trying to do a live-action movie." Animation is a special art form, and it should have a special way of doing it. It's funny that he was so concerned about Shakespeare, because when he did *Damon the Mower*, based on a classical poem, he first had a voice-over reading the poetry. "Hark how the Mower Damon sung, with love of Juliana stung!" and so on. Then, he thought, "What about doing away with all of it?" So, he does away with the text; it's all sound effects of crickets, of wind, whoosh, and the scythe going, and then, sometimes, an explosion. It's life and death.

Figure 2.14: Film still from George Dunning's uncompleted version of *The Tempest*. © George Dunning estate.

You also decided to use text or voice only very sparsely in your own *Bottom's Dream*, right? It's just a few quotes.

Yes, a couple lines from Shakespeare for Titania.

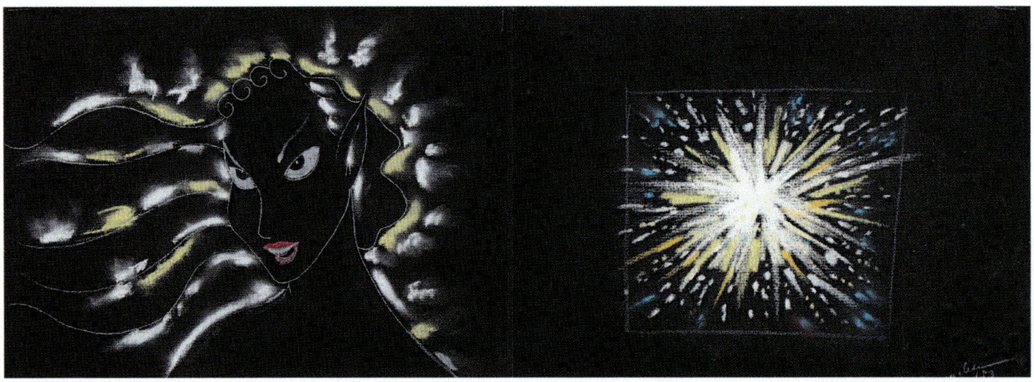

Figure 2.15: Two more examples for the variety of design styles used to give *Bottom's Dream* its enchanting and dreamlike quality. Here, crayon on black paper is used—a technique that reminisces traditional fine art techniques. © John Canemaker.

All these berries and fruits come out of her mouth, and she is very close to the camera at one point and sort of glows. I sent a print of it to Frank Thomas and Ollie Johnston, my long-distance mentors. I never worked at a big studio in California, but they sympathized with my working as an independent. They very kindly, over the years, would look at my films and give me tough love critiques. Frank, I remember saying, "Oh, boy, how do you think of all these things?" You know, *Bottom's Dream*, and he said, "How do you come up with all those concepts?" He also said, "I wish you'd kept some of those images on there for more than one scene." Which was good advice. I was very fortunate to have such great mentors in my life.

I think that very often, in my experience, there is a different mindset, in the sense that feature animation character animators are really seeing themselves as actors, primarily. Then only, to a lesser extent, they consider the design aspect as a tool of communication as well. I see that very much. I admire these animators tremendously as professionals. Yet, if I look at Hans Bacher (famous production designer) and Andreas Deja (legendary character animator), there is a very different approach: Hans is first and foremost a designer, and a great one at that, whereas Andreas is a wonderful animator, an absolutely genius character animator, and I think, it happens not so often that this is all rolled into one person. When it is, it's more in the arc of independent animation, but it is definitely rare.

Well, I'm certainly not a great animator. I'm someone who does what I can do with my own limitations and such. So, I try to make the most of them that way, but I could never approach what Andreas does, or Glen Keane, or Frank Thomas, or Ollie Johnston. They're just beyond me, but Frank and Ollie were generous mentors and friends to me—they looked at my films through the years and advised me. What a privilege! I learned from them and try in my own way to adapt what they taught me. I'm finding working again in animation, after so many years, is very labor intensive; it's just tiring.

It is, but your specific approach is also something Paul Wells enthuses about when he talks about *Bottom's Dream*, and I completely agree with him. It's very rewarding that you bring together the classic animation techniques and a certain level of craft in animation with these more challenging design concepts. For me, that was never a contradiction but a beautiful complementary process and approach.

Figure 2.16: Two-cel background setups. They demonstrate how the film's art direction also expertly quotes Disney craft traditions as on display in *Fantasia* (dir. Armstrong et al. 1940). Particularly, the *Nutcracker-Suite* sequence from the film comes to mind. © John Canemaker.

Thank you.

Looking back, of course, there was UPA; there were great animators also working with quite interesting design concepts and, even within Disney itself, for example, what Ward Kimball did, just to name one of the exponents of that approach. I think, it is something that can really bring a distinct and refreshing approach to the art form. And I think, at the time you did it (1983), was it perceived as something new you created there? I would think so, probably, in terms of combining classic Disney with strong influences of the modern.

Figure 2.17: This further example shows how the film the embraces the appeal of the artistic process, moving away from pre-modernist notions that beautiful art needs to look "complete" or "finished." One could rather argue that the spontaneity and intuitive grace of the sketch can rarely be captured in the cleaned-up form in animation. © John Canemaker.

In this context, I must again mention the Hubleys, John and Faith. When they worked on their films, going back to *Adventures of an* * (1957), *Moonbird* (1959), and even in the commercials that John Hubley did before that, there was always a wonderful modernist design sense. John Hubley wasn't an animator; he was basically a designer who hired great animators.

Moonbird was animated by Bob Cannon, and there were a couple of other great animators who found a way to bring personality animation to these very, almost-expressionistic creations—Tissa David, for example, who was another of my mentors. She was sole animator on John and Faith Hubley's *Eggs* (1971) and *Cockaboody* (1974). She had a direct, economical yet highly emotional way of animating. So, that was always a great inspiration for me.

I didn't invent really anything; I just try to express myself and gain courage and inspiration by observing certain animation filmmakers I admire.

But looking back at my art school days in the late 1980s and early 1990s, there was still this funny perception that all things Disney were "bad" and "commercial" as opposed to the "original" and "experimental" art one was supposed to create in the academic environment. You were somewhat expected to move away from any "traditional" skill level, because it was assumed to hinder your artistic expression. I think, *Bottom's Dream* is a very convincing example that this is really not the case. It definitely demonstrates that you can do very interesting, innovative things without necessarily giving up on the tradition; you can embrace it.

Have you seen *Bridgehampton*? It is one of my earlier films (1998).

It's available online through the MOMA. It's on their "Destination Art" website, a tour of MOMA for children.

It starts with a train ride, so you see shadows going by, and then, you get out to the country, and the titles come on, and it's a jazz score by Fred Hersch, who's a terrific jazz pianist. And the imagery, based on my watercolor paintings, sometimes goes from abstract to representational back to abstract again. It's all different techniques.

Figure 2.18: Image from *Bridgehampton* (1988). © John Canemaker.

I really love the strong visual flow here, based on these lines; it's basically what I call pure animation. You got all of this kind of line of action and the transitions from convex to concave, all of these things going on, and the dynamics are just beautiful.

Coming back to *Bottom's Dream*, Jena Burgess says about it, "The film is a tour de force, a summary of the license of Disney, and the post-Disney age with constant changing of styles and colors." Which, actually, sums it up quite nicely.

She's a wonderful historian.

Before we move on to other topics, I have one final question on *Bottom's Dream*:

What I found interesting is the choice of music for the film (*A Midsummer Night's Dream Scherzo* by Felix Mendelsohn), obviously, a piece that was already inspired by the play itself. So, was there any other consideration at the time for an alternative approach to the music, or did, possibly, the music come to you first?

That's what attracted me first. I love the music. So, I thought, gee, I'd love to do something freeform with that, you know, as free as the music. My friend Ross Care, who's an animation historian himself, is also a musician, and so, he arranged, transcribed, and supervised the music for the film. He created the track, and I worked to the track. *Bridgehampton* is a film about my garden on Long Island, and I showed jazz pianist Fred Hersch my storyboards, and he composed and recorded the soundtrack, and I worked to his track, the same with *Bottom's Dream*; it usually works that way.

Would you also do a frame-by-frame sound breakdown?

Oh, yes.

Ironically, nowadays, using digital tools, you still do it, basically with the old method: dragging the soundtrack back and forth and really listening to where the sounds are. That way, you still get the most accurate results.

So, now, of course, I'm also curious about the current project you're working on.

It's also an adaptation, right?

Well, it's an adaptation of a short story from Sherwood Anderson's book *Winesburg, Ohio* (1919). *Hands* is the one I've adapted. This project goes back to my 2009 grant from the Rockefeller Foundation, for a residency in Bellagio, Italy. I started by reading the story, the original story.

Figure 2.19: Image from John Canemaker's new short film project *Hands*. © John Canemaker.

So, how does your filmic version compare to the book?

It was a question of being respectful of the writing, because the book from 1919 was extremely important for Hemingway, Faulkner, and Thomas Wolfe, who were all influenced by it.

So, I wanted to be respectful of the writing. And it's a very strange story; it's about this grotesque person, whose restless hands are described as "like the beatings of an imprisoned bird."

You have created a lot of wonderful short animated pieces. Referring back to George Dunning's amazing version of *The Tempest*, do you believe that he could possibly have extended it to an animated feature film? And achieved artistic success?

It would probably have been very difficult. And in a way his *Tempest* is as perfect as it can get in terms of just being an intriguing short piece. I think, in general, that animation works best in the short form. I'm not a big fan of feature length, although I love many and totally admire people who can direct an entire feature. But, unless you have a studio behind you, it's daunting, even when you have a big crew. The whole production pipeline for a short is quite challenging.

I've been very lucky in that I've made my avocation my vocation. My career is split up into making animated films when and how I want to and writing about animation history and also teaching animation at NYU.

I feel like it's really a gift, if you're in that fortunate situation where you can combine your interest in the history with creating and then also teaching, and again, one thing that is very visible in your work is how one thing beautifully informs the other in a way.

Well thank you, I hope it does... I came into animation in the early 1970s, and I was fortunate enough to meet several of the surviving pioneers of the art form: Otto Messmer (*editor's remark: creator of Felix the Cat*), for example, and I met Winsor McCay's assistant, John Fitzsimmons, and produced and directed a documentary film about each of them in 1976 and 1977, respectively. I met John Bray, the so-called Henry Ford of animation studio production methods. I met eight of Disney's famed nine old men: four of them became my friends, two of them very close mentors to me, the aforementioned Frank and Ollie. I feel so fortunate, even to be able to converse with and interview someone like George Dunning, Faith Hubley, Tissa David, or Chuck Jones, or Richard Williams, who has been a close friend for over 40 years. Through my books and teaching, I hope to pass on what I have learned from and about these amazing filmmakers.

That is something that I find very fascinating, and it's immensely rewarding when you have a chance to talk to these heroes in person... and also it inspires you for your own work.

Well, look—you're passing it on here. It's the same thing. Maybe we're twins. Separated at birth *(laughter)*.

What you showed me now, about your new film project *Hands*, this is really something very much to look forward to. So, is there a general motivation why frequently over the course of your career you've been drawn to adaptations?

Well, I think it gives you a grounding. It gives you a real solidity, if the characters and basic plot have already been worked out, and then, you can take off from there. When I teach storyboarding, I give the students a choice of three literary properties to create a storyboard from—it could be a fairytale, a folk tale, or a short story, all public domain material. I don't allow them to do their own scripts. I want them to take off from something solid, a story that has a beginning, middle, and an end, and characters that have dimension to them. And then, how do you visualize that in story sketches and animation, how do you adapt it? That's the big challenge.

The students ask, "how to begin?" I asked the same thing when I interviewed story artist Vance Gerry at Disney. He said, "Well, I dream into the title." I thought that was a great answer. He said, "Sleeping Beauty. Well, there you've got two words. You have Beauty, and she's asleep. Show that in some pictures. Let one picture lead to the next."

And that's what I encourage students to do. Icarus, who disobeyed his father and flew too close to the sun. What do you see in your imagination? How do you see him flying? Does his father instruct him? How do you see Icarus when he goes too close to the sun? How might he have fun when he's flying? Does he play with birds and fishes as he flies? How do you visualize him showing fear when he's flying? That'll give you several pictures right there. Draw them. Pin them up, and let's talk about them. So, the process is very much having a grounding in a real story, with elements of suspense, comedy, characterization, or joy, or whatever it is, and then, letting the story artist take off from there.

I use a similar approach in my graphic storytelling class, which is about comics, but the students also really need to work out the visual storytelling language. I always give them a classic fairytale to reinterpret, for the same reason: Because it's already something that has a grounding, and then, literally, they can take off. And I think that's a really good metaphor also, taking off, taking flight with a fantasy and imagination.

I have many students who have never really drawn; they're afraid to draw, so I do a lot of convincing. I say, "Don't worry about it, it's going be *your* drawing style, and we'll work with it." And we do. And we do silhouetting exercises—drawing occupations, activities, or emotional states as silhouettes to strengthen visual communication skills. I also have them draw scenes in a sequence from, say, *Black Narcissus* (dir. Powell/Pressburger 1947). In the finale, there are 15 scenes that we freeze-frame and ask, "Why is the camera here? Draw it. Talk about it. What do you think the director was thinking? Why did the editor cut here? How many frames in this brief scene?"

Students' lives have been changed by the animation courses they take in school. Some, who never thought of storyboarding as a career, go into it. We have several at Disney, DreamWorks, Blue Sky, and Pixar, and one woman, Erin Chapman, who 20 years ago was my student in storyboarding, is now New Media Content Manager at the American Museum of Natural History (AMNH); she produces, storyboards, shoots, and animates AMNH videos for online informational series. She and many other former animation students return to inspire and encourage my current students.

That's wonderful, always the most rewarding experiences. It just started with our students who started graduating from 2009, so that now we're almost 10 years later that some of them have followed their career paths, and it will continue over years, which is always very nice.

We already talked a little bit about the fact that we both share the opinion that change is necessary for adaptation for animation.

Yes.

Maybe just a few more thoughts from your side about this, particularly when it comes to an original text, let's say a short story, and then, you take it animation, to an animated short. Why is it necessary to change?

Because it is a different form. I go back to the fact that to take the story as it is, there are descriptions there that need to be visualized, and depending on what you are trying to say as the filmmaker, you may want to start out with an interesting image, a strong visual statement. Where do you find it? Jean-Luc Godard said, "stories should have a beginning, a middle and an end, but not necessarily in that order." So that's a good philosophy for thinking about adaptation. At the beginning of the *Hands* film, I have the hands forming the letters, and that's intriguing to start with. But where does it go from there with imagery? I'm still considering what to leave in and what to cut. I'm having an interesting time; it's a struggle, but that's the creative process, and I'm indulging myself.

Also, it refers back to what you said when you showed me the original story and how you start in your adaptation is that certain things really piqued your interest, like that. And I think, that is something I heard of before, that often, in other interviews with filmmakers, it's important to find a strong way to get into the story in terms of imagery, because animation is a visual medium, right?

Look at any of the great stories; they intrigue you visually. *Pinocchio* (dir. Luske, Sharpsteen 1940) opens with an insect on a book, singing. It's great. He starts to tell the story, turning pages of the book. And then, you go into the village and on to Geppetto's toyshop, and so on.

I also talked with Giannalberto Bendazzi about adaptation in general and Disney adaptations in particular, and he was very strong in his opinion that there is of course a necessity to change. Beginning with *Snow White and the Seven Dwarfs* (dir. Hand 1937), Disney had to go beyond what the original fairy tale has on offer, and it's a very daunting task—to actually create an animated story that works for a feature film.

The story is personality-based, and that's what Disney's forte always was: make you believe in the characters and relate to them in some way. You know that famous memo that he sent, the 8-page 1935 memo (see references): all of it's there, all of his ideas about what animation could be, this *personality* animation that makes the characters and their emotions real to audiences. When Snow White runs through the forest, trying to escape from the huntsman, she falls, and one of the story people says, "Oh dear, she could hurt herself." And then, at the end of the film, the seven dwarfs are weeping about the death of another cartoon character, and audiences weep, too. They forget they are watching cartoons. They are swept up by the believable personalities of the characters.

With *Pinocchio*, there was a design problem. How do you make this angular, wooden, rude creature, as he is depicted in the original book, appealing? He was very much a cruel puppet when they first drew the concepts at Disney. Animator Milt Kahl suggested that they change Pinocchio into a charming, round little boy who had wooden joints on his limbs. This affected the storytelling. The design softened the personality of Pinocchio, making him rather passive. Jiminy Cricket, more active and assertive, became the film's de facto star.

When thinking about visualizing animated adaptations for Disney, another fabulous artist comes to mind: Mary Blair and her outstanding color designs, whose influence could be felt in *Saludos Amigos* (dirs. Ferguson et al. 1942), *The Three Caballeros* (dirs. Ferguson et al. 1944), *Cinderella* (dirs. Geronimi, Jackson, Luske 1950), *Alice in Wonderland* (dirs. Geronimi, Jackson, Luske 1951), and *Peter Pan* (dirs. Geronimi, Jackson, Luske 1953).

You certainly did earn some merit to make a broader public aware of the work through your books.

In 2014, I also curated a large exhibit of original Mary Blair art at the Walt Disney Family Museum in San Francisco, almost 200 pieces of her art.

Figure 2.20: John Canemaker authored *The Art and Flair of Mary Blair*, published in 2014 by Disney Editions. (With kind permission of Disney Editions. © Disney Enterprises Inc.)

Whereas there were only a few instances where her work really reached the screen in an unaltered form, would you consider that a lost opportunity?

Yes. I personally would have loved to see a stronger influence of her flat modernist style, but then, it wouldn't be Disney. It would be UPA *(editor's remark: United Productions of America=highly influential modernist US studio post WWII).* Oddly, she claimed not to understand UPA. Blair had her own style, and it drove the animators crazy, because Walt wanted so-called "illusion of life" rounded characters, you know? But he also said, "I want Mary Blair there, too." How do you square that? It was an impossible thing, and the closest they came, which doesn't really look like a Disney film, is *Once Upon a Wintertime* (sequence in *Melody Time*, dir. Geronimi, Jackson, Kinney, Luske 1948). Very close. She thought that the only time it happened was the little pink train with a square wheel in *The Three Caballeros* (dir. Ferguson et al. 1944), because it is her drawing; she painted the backgrounds as well as did the character design and colors. But otherwise, in Disney's films, there were elements of Mary Blair in the décor, the furniture, and mostly the vibrant colors.

The colors, of course. It's also something—if, arguably, I mean not even arguably, but for sure, something like Peter Pan, that she did a lot of concepts for—if that style would be the final movie, it would be an entirely different movie, speaking of adaptation.

Oh yes. It would be not what it is.

The question would be, how would you then transport something like the menace of Captain Hook in a compelling way. You would have to reinvent the idea of how to do that entirely.

Figure 2.21: Left: A historic photograph (1906) of *Peter Pan* author James Matthew Barrie (as Captain Hook) playing with child actor Michael Llewelyn Davies (as Peter Pan). The illustrations (on the right) by Francis Donkin Bedford (from the 1911 Charles Scribner's Sons edition) display a more realistic and menacing style than the one ultimately used for the 1953 Disney film.

The concept work of David Hall shows another approach. It's very close to live action, and it's an illustrators approach. But Mary Blair goes off into this not quite abstract but almost expressionist universe. That's what appealed to Disney; he saw the childlike quality of her work and liked it. The Mary Blair color styling really puts Disney on the map in a different dynamic way, when she starts to get going in the South American films.

Let's change to another topic that addresses Disney's approach to adaptation. I mean, there's this recent Disney live action feature *Saving Mr. Banks* (dir. Hancock 2013) that retells the adaptation of *Mary Poppins* (dir. Stevenson 1964). So, do you know more about the backstory there? There are original notes, letters, between Disney and P. L. Travers, the author of the book.

There is a documentary online that the BBC did, Channel 4 in London. It's very revealing about what she was like as a person, and then, it goes into some of the Disney stuff as well. But I don't know that much personally about it. I think Walt Disney was used to dealing with the estate rights of dead authors, so there was a problem with a living author arguing with him about "It's not my interpretation." But his children loved *Mary Poppins* as a story, and he'd always wanted to do the film. So, he worked with her, and things changed. The relationship changed. If you think about it, all of those features that he did, *Snow White, Pinocchio, Peter Pan*, and all of them, the authors were gone. They were just open and ripe for his interpretation.

And it was public domain in the end, right?

Some of it was. I think with *Peter Pan*, he had to pay something to the orphanage.

But, obviously, with the fairy tales, it was always public domain. Another aspect is that fairy tales have very often been handed down through generations. There was never one final or "definitive" version really, and they often transformed.

And the Disney version of *Snow White* was adapted from a play, not really from the Grimm brothers' version. The play was adapted from the Grimm version.

It's sometimes difficult to lay a claim to what the correct source material of a certain adaptation really is. More often than not, many, many different versions of a fairy tale exist, and there's a certain variety and leeway to adapt.

Sometimes, you pick and choose.

Another work, which was inspired by fairy tales or mythology is, of course, Lotte Reiniger's pioneering film *The Adventures of Prince Achmed* (1926), the first surviving animated feature film. It combines story elements from the famous collection of Oriental fairy tales, *One Thousand and One Nights* (Anon. 2002). This anthology itself exists in many different versions, particularly when it was translated and transformed for Western readers. If you would make a comparison, where would you see the main differences in the adaptation approach between Lotte Reiniger and Disney's method with *Snow White*? I know that this is a very complex question to answer, but I am sure you can offer some interesting insights?

You have to go back to the philosophy that the filmmakers had about what animation should be. Reiniger is much more open to metamorphosis, happening magically, changes that occur in a fantastic world. They are part of that world. We already mentioned that Disney was trying to find a rational reason for such "unrealistic" or magical events in his feature films. Alice has a dream and gets to surreal Wonderland that way. In *Snow White*, the wicked Queen takes her potion and shape-shifts into a crone. There you go.

Figure 2.22: Film still from *The Adventures of Prince Achmed*, showing the complex use of silhouetted characters. © Christel Strobel, Agency for Primrose Film Productions, Munich.

And also, the technique of animation is so different *(editor's remark: cardboard cutouts animated in stop motion technique [Reiniger] vs. hand drawn cel animation [Disney])*. Yet, there are also similarities. Disney always asked for strong silhouetted poses, storytelling poses. And Reiniger animates silhouetted profiles for the most part, so there's a certain flatness to it, although she did use her version of a multi-plane camera to photograph backgrounds and characters on different levels of glass to give the films a dimensional quality. This was more than a decade before Disney's use of a multi-plane camera in 1937. So, she was quite a film pioneer—a female producer and brilliant animator of great wit and subtlety and the creator of one of the earliest animated feature films.

Another difference was that she was basically an independent producer. She had a small crew of about six, I think, at the most. So, there are similarities, but many differences—the budget, her and his sensibilities about filmmaking—all of those things factor into why her film is what it is and Disney's is what it is.

I think a very important point you mention is the suspension of disbelief, which is by far not as important to her as it is to Disney. Because I think there is a certain element of theatricality to her work, because she's coming also from a performance background, as a shadow puppet player herself.

A similarity between the two of them is their belief in the importance of clarity in communicating with an audience. I mean, it was essential for them both. You have to understand what the characters are doing. And the Disney and Reiniger characters express themselves basically through body language. And so, the clarity of the poses and the timing of the characters' gestures are wonderful. They are both great entertainers.

That's right, and also within her specific style, she still had an interest in some character animation. There's still really something there. So, this is not just about graphic experiments. There really is character animation at work there.

Absolutely. She had the design and the look of the characters found in the ancient Asian shadow-puppet tradition. The "actors" moved as they should—elderly characters, female characters, heroic characters, and villains. All their expressive emotions are motivated by clear, readable actions.

And for whatever the limitations were by the cutout technique she was using, she was using them quite impressively. I was watching her films as a child; it still felt to a certain extent real to me.

In a way, it makes you wonder, regarding the supposed necessity to apply more naturalism to the Disney *oeuvre*. I mean, people believe in Bugs Bunny; they believe what he's doing, though he's obviously a cartoon. So, I think people become engaged with the characters up to a certain extent. I think, the audience's imagination comes halfway and meets that of the animator. One may not need to go overboard with realism.

And, of course, also by using silhouettes, you offer some open canvas for the imagination of the audience.

That's right. A Disney film is a very passive experience for an audience, because everything is worked out for you. But Lotte Reiniger's style is more challenging, because it's something you need to get used to a little bit more than you do with the Disney films. And she was working basically in pantomime. But she was very witty. Did you ever see *Galathea* (dir. Reinger 1935)? That's one of her funniest films. Galathea walks through town nude, the reaction of the townsfolk, how they follow her, chastise her, lust after her... it's great.

Figure 2.23: Film still from *Galathea*. The film is a variation of the Greek *Pygmalion* legend. © Christel Strobel, Agency for Primrose Film Productions, Munich, Germany.

The other filmmaker who we immediately touched on in our correspondence on animated adaptation is Jiří Trnka.

He was just amazing. So beautiful his elegant, stylized designs. And again, unrealistic yet so subtle in terms of the movement. The face never changes on these puppets. It's all in the body expression and the lighting effects. So, again, you needn't be too realistic to get ideas across.

That is one amazing thing that you can actually emotionally engage an audience without being overly realistic. So, Trnka—I think you mentioned him as a master of adaptation in general but particularly for his Shakespeare-related work?

Yes, definitely.

I think one of the important aspects about him is that the design is incredibly beautiful.

As it is in his children's books.

There is also a parallel with Lotte Reiniger, of having this strong style as an illustrator and then bringing that to animation.

I saw her in person, demonstrating her work years ago at the first Ottawa Animation Festival in 1976. There she was, demonstrating moving figures around a light table. She was elderly, a large woman, but with dexterous fingers working with scissors, and I was privileged to be in her presence. It was a great festival. Norman McLaren was there, and he talked and demonstrated. Grant Munro made us move like he did in the film *Neighbors*. He showed us how to fly in pixilation; you know, jump, and tuck your legs underneath and take a single-frame picture.

Coming back to Disney adaptations: There is an ongoing discussion, mainly among fans, but also some academics, about how much *The Lion King* (dir. Allers, Minkoff 1994) would actually be a thinly disguised version of *Hamlet*?

Well, maybe.

Even if it would be, what would be the problem?

I don't think it is a problem.

If that's what they were thinking of in the conception of it... it certainly worked out.

I think this discussion has been circulating on and off for basically decades now.

Well, what does Hans (Bacher) say? He worked on it.

I think he was not really interested in this as a theory at all. Actually, it really is quite pointless, because even if it would be the case, what would actually speak against it? If it would have been an adaptation, then why not? It would have been this well-done adaptation in certain respects. On the other hand, there is this completely different ending, because there is this happy ending with *The Lion King*, which would speak against an adaptation. I think it is crucial that it does not claim to be an actual adaptation.

There's also the death of his parent, which is a continuing theme with Disney.

The absent father. Frank Thomas animated the lamentation scene in *Snow White*, which was a big breakthrough in terms of animation. How to so convince the audience that this was real to moviegoers—and worth their tears. People also cry when Bambi's mother is shot. They cry when Dumbo's mother is incarcerated.

The Lion King tried to go even further for a modern audience—the little lion cub touches the dead father, doesn't he? It may have been unnecessary. There were attempts to get Walt to show the body of the dead mother deer in *Bambi*, but he didn't do it.

It became all the more powerful for it.

Off-screen violence always effectively puts the viewer in charge, in terms of imagining the horrid details.

And there you go: This is one of the cases where Disney has some projections, some space for the audience to fill in the blanks, in a way, and probably that is more terrifying than presenting the events onscreen.

You don't see what happens to the witch when she falls in *Snow White*. So, you imagine her corpse.

And, by the way, *Bambi* (1942) is also a good example for another adaptation, which very much went its own way; it had to go way beyond the book (Salten 1928). Because they had to figure out how to make the audience feel for these animals that are drawings and enable it to empathize.

That's the fascinating thing with Disney. There are so many ways of interpreting, explaining, and critiquing the work.

And you certainly offered some wonderful insights. Not only on Disney films, but also on your own artistic involvement with adapting literature for animation. I look forward to seeing your new film. Thank you for this interview.

John Canemaker's films are distributed by **Milestone Films** https://milestonefilms.com/search?q=canemaker

References

Algar, James, Samuel Armstrong, Ford Beebe Jr., Norman Ferguson, David Hand, Jim Handley, Wilfred Jackson, Hamilton Luske, Bill Roberts, Paul Satterfield, Ben Sharpsteen, and T. Hee, dirs. 1940. *Fantasia*. Animated feature film. Burbank, CA: Walt Disney Productions (production). New York: RKO Radio Pictures (distribution).

Allers, Roger, and Rob Minkoff, dirs. 1994. *The Lion King*. Animated feature film. Burbank, CA: Walt Disney Pictures (production). Burbank, CA: Buena Vista Pictures (distribution).

Anderson, Sherwood. 1919. *Winesburg, Ohio*. New York: Benjamin W. Huebsch.

Anonymous. 2002. *The Thousand and One Nights*. Trans. Husain Haddawy. *The Norton Anthology of World Literature*, edited by Sarah Lawall. New York: W.W. Norton & Company.

Canemaker, John. 2018. *Winsor McCay: His Life and Art* (revised and updated edition). Boca Raton, FL: CRC Press.

Canemaker, John. 2014. *The Lost Notebook: Herman Schultheis and the Secrets of Walt Disney's Movie Magic*. San Francisco, CA: Weldon Owen.

Canemaker, John. 2010. *Two Guys Named Joe: Master Animation Storytellers Joe Grant and Joe Ranft*. Glendale, CA: Disney Editions.

Canemaker, John. 2003. *The Art and Flair of Mary Blair*. Glendale, CA: Disney Editions.

Canemaker, John. 2001. *Walt Disney's Nine Old Men and the Art of Animation*. New York: Hyperion.

Canemaker, John. 1999. *Paper Dreams: The Art and Artists of Disney Storyboards*. New York: Hyperion.

Canemaker, John. 1996. *Before the Animation Begins: The Art and Lives of Disney Inspirational Sketch Artists*. New York: Hyperion.

Canemaker, John. 1996. *Tex Avery: The MGM Years*. Nashville, TN: Turner Publishing.

Canemaker, John. 1991. *Felix: The Twisted Tale of the World's Most Famous Cat*. New York: Pantheon.

Canemaker, John. 1987. *Winsor McCay: His Life and Art*. New York: Abbeville Press.

Canemaker, John. 1982. *Treasures of Disney Animation Art*. New York: Abbeville Press.

Canemaker, John. 1977. *The Animated Raggedy Ann and Andy*. Indianapolis, IN: Bobbs-Merill.

Canemaker, John, dir. 2005. *The Moon and the Son: An Imagined Conversation.* Animated short film. New York: John Canemaker Productions (production).

Canemaker, John, dir. 1998. *Bridgehampton.* Animated short film. New York: John Canemaker Productions (production).

Canemaker, John, dir. 1983. *Bottom's Dream.* Animated short film. New York: John Canemaker Productions (production).

Canemaker, John, dir. 1978. *Confessions of a Star Dreamer.* Animated short film. New York: John Canemaker Productions (production).

Canemaker, John. 2010. Canemaker meets Dunning-1978. Michaelspornanimation.com. Accessed May 17, 2018. http://www.michaelspornanimation.com/splog/?p=2090. (Originally published under the title *One has to live* in the Jan-Mar 1980 issue of *Animafilm* magazine).

Comack, Robert, Clyde Geronimi, Jack Kinney, Hamilton Luske, and Joshua Meador, dirs. 1946. *Make Mine Music.* Animated feature film. Burbank, CA: Walt Disney Productions (production). New York: RKO Radio Pictures (distribution).

Clarke, Malcolm, and Bill Guttentag, dirs. 1988. *You Don't Have to Die.* Live action documentary with animated inserts. Los Angeles, CA: Filmworks (production).

Disney, Walt. 2010. How to train an animator. Accessed August 12, 2018. http://www.lettersofnote.com/2010/06/how-to-train-animator-by-walt-disney.html.

Docter, Pete, dir. 2015. *Inside Out.* Animated feature film. Emeryville: Pixar Animation Studios (production). Burbank, CA: Walt Disney Studios Motion Pictures (distribution).

Dunning, George, dir. 1968. *Yellow Submarine.* Animated feature film. London, UK: Apple Corps (production). Beverly Hills, CA: United Artists (distribution).

Dunning, George, dir. 1972. *Damon the Mower.* Animated short film. London, UK: TV Cartoons (production).

Ferguson, Norman, Clyde Geronimi, Jack Kinney, Bill Roberts, and Harold Young, dirs. 1944. *The Three Caballeros.* Animated feature film. Burbank, CA: Walt Disney Productions (production). New York: RKO Radio Pictures (distribution).

Ferguson, Norman, Wilfred Jackson, Hamilton Luske, Jack Kinney, Bill Roberts, dirs. 1942. *Saludos Amigos.* Animated feature film. Burbank, CA: Walt Disney Productions (production). New York: RKO Radio Pictures (distribution).

Geronimi, Clyde, Wilfred Jackson, and Hamilton Luske, dirs. 1953. *Peter Pan.* Animated feature film. Burbank, CA: Walt Disney Productions (production). New York: RKO Radio Pictures (distribution).

Geronimi, Clyde, Wilfred Jackson, and Hamilton Luske, dirs. 1951. *Alice in Wonderland.* Animated feature film. Burbank, CA: Walt Disney Productions (production). New York: RKO Radio Pictures (distribution).

Geronimi, Clyde, Wilfred Jackson, and Hamilton Luske, dirs. 1950. *Cinderella.* Animated feature film. Burbank, CA: Walt Disney Productions (production). New York: RKO Radio Pictures (distribution).

Geronimi, Clyde, Wilfred Jackson, Hamilton Luske, and Jack Kinney, dirs. 1948. *Melody Time.* Animated feature film. Burbank, CA Walt Disney Productions (production). New York: RKO Radio Pictures (distribution).

Hancock, John Lee, dir. 2013. *Saving Mr. Banks.* Live action feature film. Burbank, CA: Walt Disney Pictures (production). Burbank, CA: Walt Disney Studios Motion Pictures (distribution).

Hand, David, dir. 1942. *Bambi.* Animated feature film. Burbank, CA: Walt Disney Productions (production). New York: RKO Radio Pictures (distribution).

Hand, David, dir. 1937. *Snow White and the Seven Dwarfs.* Animated feature film. Burbank, CA: Walt Disney Productions (production). New York: RKO Radio Pictures (distribution).

Hill, George Roy, dir. 1982. *The World According to Garp.* Live action feature film. Pan Arts (production). Burbank, CA: Warner Bros. (distribution).

Hubley, John, dir. 1974. *Cockaboody.* Animated short film. New York: Hubley Studios (production). Santa Monica, CA: Pyramid Media (distribution).

Hubley, John, dir. 1971. *Eggs.* Animated short film. New York: Hubley Studios (production). Santa Monica, CA: Pyramid Media (distribution).

Hubley, John, dir. 1959. *Moonbird.* Animated short film. New York: Hubley Studios aka Storyboard Studios (production). Brooklyn, NY: EastWest Entertainment (distribution).

Hubley, John, dir. 1957. *The Adventures of an *.* Animated short film. New York: Hubley Studios aka Storybord Studios (production).

John Canemaker's films are distributed by Milestone Films: https://milestonefilms.com/search?q=canemaker.

Luske, Hamilton, and Ben Sharpsteen, dirs. 1940. *Pinocchio.* Animated feature film. Burbank, CA: Walt Disney Productions (production). New York: RKO Radio Pictures (distribution).

McCay, Winsor, dir. 1914. *Gertie the Dinsosaur.* Animated short film. New York: Winsor McCay (production). Fort Lee, NJ: Box Office Attractions Company (distribution).

Museum of Modern Art Film Study Center. n.d. Accessed August 12, 2018. https://www.moma.org/research-and-learning/study-centers/film-study-center.

Peltier, Melissa Joe, dir. 1994. *Break the Silence: Kids Against Child Abuse.* Live action documentary with animated inserts. Los Angeles, CA: Arnold Shapiro Productions (production).

Powell, Michael/Pressburger, Emeric, dirs. 1947. *Black Narcissus.* Live action feature film. London, UK: The Archers (production). Universal City, CA: Universal Pictures (distribution).

Reiniger, Lotte, dir. 1935. *Galathea: Das lebende Marmorbild.* Animated short film.

Reiniger, Lotte, dir. 1926. *The Adventures of Prince Achmed.* Animated feature film. Berlin, Germany: Comenius-Film Berlin/Louis Hagen (production).

Robert, Bill, dir. 1943. *Reason and Emotion.* Animated short film. Burbank, CA: Walt Disney Productions (production). New York: RKO Radio Pictures (distribution).

Salten, Felix, Whittaker Chambers, John Galsworthy, and Kurt Wiese, dirs. 1928. *Bambi: A Life in the Woods.* London, UK: Jonathan Cape.

Shakespeare, William. Ca. 1595–1596. *A Midsummer Night's Dream.*

Shakespeare, William. 1611. *The Tempest.*

Sharpsteen, Ben, dir. 1941. *Dumbo.* Animated feature film. Burbank, CA: Walt Disney Productions (production). New York City: RKO Radio Pictures (distribution).

Stevenson, Robert, dir. 1964. *Mary Poppins.* Live action feature film with animated segments. Burbank, CA: Walt Disney Productions (production). Burbank, CA: Buena Vista Distribution (distribution).

Wells, P. 1999. Thou art translated: Analyzing Animated Adaptations. In: *Adaptations From Text to Screen, Screen to Text,* edited by Deborah Cartmell, Imelda Whelehan, 199–213. London, UK: Routledge.

Animated Ever After
The Fairy Tale Adaptation

We already learned this: The history of animated adaptations begins with the adaptation of fairy tales. Therefore, it is self-evident to begin the deeper investigation into the strategies of animated adaptations with a chapter about animated fairy tales. The topic would very easily merit its very own book and could be examined from many different perspectives. This makes it necessary to decide for one specific angle: The author decided to choose a thread of case studies that can be supported by detailed insights into the production process. They are also connected through their aesthetic approach and the historical perspective provided.

In the first chapter, Giannalberto Bendazzi has already pointed out Lotte Reiniger's fairy-tale adaptation *The Adventures of Prince Achmed* (1926) as the first animated European feature film.

The German animation artist Lotte Reiniger (* 2. Juni 1899 in Charlottenburg; † 19. Juni 1981 in Dettenhausen near Tübingen) is known as one of the most important pioneers of the art form. Moreover, her style of animation using silhouettes has proved to have a huge influence on subsequent generations of animators and continues to do so to this day.

The artistic style of *Achmed* was strongly influenced by Chinese shadow puppet play, as the website lotte-reiniger-film.com notes in the article "Der Einfluss der chinesischen Schattenspielkunst auf Lotte Reinigers Frühwerk," about Asian influences on Reiniger's early work. What makes her work so groundbreaking is the fact that she transformed this art form into something entirely new by redefining it for the new medium of animation. Scott Nye (2013) offers a wonderful explanation about the magic at work here: "But that's nothing compared to how she gets them moving. Each character is imbued with a life at once all their own—a convincing sensuality in the women, sensitive stoicism in the male heroes, quick, sneaky movements in the villains—yet fitting within the aesthetic Reiniger reflexively establishes. The tactile nature of her medium hardly prevents her from using some of animations more outlandish tropes, allowing characters to morph and transform, exaggerating physicality for emotional effect."

Adaptation is present in her work here under two different aspects: For one, she adapts the traditional theatrical art of shadow puppet play for animation by adding new tools of expression from the unique vocabulary of animation (such as metamorphoses, exaggeration, weight, and physicality).

Second, she has also pioneered the art of animated adaptation (particularly of fairy tales) in a longer format, by creating the first surviving animated feature film. The blog *The Cinematic Frontier* confirms in its article "The Adventures of Prince Achmed" and "One Thousand and One Nights" that the film is indeed "based on *One Thousand and One Nights* (specifically elements from *The Story of Prince Ahmed and the Fairy Paribanou*)." Nye (ibid) also cites *1001 Arabian Nights* (Anon.) as Reiniger's source for *Achmed*. He summarizes the plot of the film as the "story of Achmed, a passionate adventurer continually in conflict with a wicked African sorcerer, who first sends him far into the sky on a flying horse before, as always, stealing from him the woman he loves. As often as we've seen these types of stories onscreen (and, more familiarly for the animation crowd, the Aladdin tale that eventually factors in)..."

It becomes quickly evident from this description that Reiniger did not faithfully adapt one particular story from *1001 Nights* but chose plot elements from different stories to create her own feature-length narrative. This narrative truly carries the film and weaves a continuously enthralling thread that keeps the audience fully engaged.

It is all the more amazing that she achieved such dramaturgic mastery for animation at a time when the medium was still in its infancy. At this time (1926), Disney was yet well on his way to expand the boundaries of the art form beyond the anecdotal storytelling that dominated animation narratives.

Fairy tales were absolutely central in the work of Lotte Reiniger. She once famously said: "I believe more in fairy tales than in newspapers" (Kayser 1979). Preceding *Achmed*, Reiniger had already completed adaptations of single fairy tales, for example, in 1922, *Aschenputtel (Cinderella)*, based on the famous fairy tale by the Brothers Grimm. In later years, Lotte Reiniger repeatedly (re)turned to adapting some of their most famous and lesser known fairy tales in the short film format: 1934 *Der gestiefelte Kater* (*Puss in Boots*) or 1944 *Die goldene Gans* (*The Goose That Lays the Golden Eggs*). Between 1953 and 1954, Lotte Reiniger created a series of 13 fairy tales with her team, among which were the Grimm fairy tales *Der Froschkönig* (*The Frog Prince*, 1954/1961), *Snow White and Rose Red* (1954), the extremely popular *Hansel and Gretel* (1955), and the Wilhelm Hauff adaptation *Kaliph Stork* (1954). For her adaptation of the Brothers Grimm fairy tale *The Brave Little Tailor*, she received the prize "Silver Dolfin" for the best short film at the 1955 Venice Biennale.

Figure 3.1: Still frames from Lotte Reiniger's fairy-tale adaptations: *Die goldene Gans (The Goose That Lays The Golden Eggs)*, top left; *Hansel and Gretel*, bottom left; and *Kaliph Stork*, top and bottom right. © Christel Strobel, Agency for Primrose Film Productions, Munich, Germany.

The author assumes that the decision to return to single story subjects was largely owing to budgetary requirements. After Reiniger's second animated feature film, *Dr. Doolittle and His Animals* (1928), had also failed to become a commercial success, she was not able to secure funding for further animated feature films. Therefore, the congruence between the length of the source material and the production format (short film) might have been the decisive factor here.

Reiniger also had an opinion to offer about the constantly debated question of fidelity to the original source: The essay *Lotte Reiniger und die Gebrüder Grimm* quotes her remark that "once you have decided (to adapt) a good writer, one should try to work as faithfully (close to the original) as possible."

Continued and Lasting Influence on Animation Art

Beyond her importance as an animation pioneer, the continuous and continuing influence of Reiniger on her artistic successors cannot be overestimated. A whole artistic tradition in animation can be identified through the work of artists who followed in her footsteps to varying degrees of success. In the best cases, the later animators managed to not only quote or replicate her artistic techniques but also expand on them by introducing new elements. This kept silhouette animation alive and vibrant to this day, as it allows for a constant evolution and renewal of the art form.

In the former German Democratic Republic, the state-owned production company Deutsche Film-Aktiengesellschaft (DEFA) produced over 70 silhouette-style animations between 1954 and 1990 (Benner n.d.). Among those were fairy-tale adaptations such as *Die Bremer Stadtmusikanten* (1954), *König Drosselbart* (1956), *Prinzessin Springwasser* (1956), and *Die Prinzessin und der Ziegenhirt* (1973) by Bruno J. Böttge. Of note is also *Hans mein Igel* (1984) by Horst Tappert. Böttge created almost 50 films in this technique (Happ 1982, S. 47).

An important contemporary filmmaker to be mentioned in that context is the acclaimed French director Michel Ocelot. In his films *Princes et Princesses* (2000) and *Les Contes de la Nuit* (2011), he clearly demonstrated the influence by Reiniger by using black silhouetted figures against colored backgrounds throughout. In an interview, Ocelot explicitly named the films of Lotte Reiniger as an important influence for his own work (Benner n.d., Triebold 2011). Even more important in our context, Ocelot collects a series of fairy-tale adaptations in these compilation features.

The work of the author Hannes Rall has often been seen as a continuation as well as an evolution of the work of Lotte Reiniger.

"Rall describes his drawing-style as a mixture between German expressionism, contemporary influences, such as comics and graffiti, and stylistic elements of Reiniger's work. Even if Hannes Rall does not work with physical paper cutouts, the parallels to Reiniger can hardly be overlooked. His drawings are often black and white and frequently resemble woodcuts." (Junge 2012).

Further evidence for Hannes Rall's role as a successor and innovator of Lotte Reiniger's artistic tradition is provided by the selection of his film *The Erl-King* (2003) for the eminent exhibition *Animation und Avantgarde: Lotte Reiniger und der absolute Film* (2016–2017). This exhibition was shown in the two important museums in Germany that archive the artistic heritage of Lotte Reiniger: The Stadtmuseum Tübingen and the Filmmuseum Düsseldorf. Hannes Rall was also invited to show a retrospective of his whole body of work at both venues in 2016.

Figure 3.2: Still images from *Si Lunchai* (2014), directed by Hannes Rall. Character designs and background paintings by Cheng Yu Chao.

The influence of Lotte Reiniger on Hannes Rall's work is possibly most evident in his 2014 film *Si Lunchai*, adapted from a Southeast Asian folk tale. Here, Rall is deliberately referencing the local shadow puppet play Wayang Kulit. Asian shadow puppet play had already inspired Reiniger's work in the 1920s. Now, this specific type of silhouette animation came full circle by realizing it in the very cultural environment by which it was initially inspired. While not fundamentally changing the aesthetics, the digital production process enables more subtleties in animation and lighting of the (virtual) environment.

Previously, a new academic collaboration with the Eberhard Karl's University at his hometown Tübingen had further instigated Rall's interest to explore Reiniger's work through the means of academic research as well: Prof. Susanne Marschall contacted the author in her role as the co-director of the film *Lotte Reiniger: Dance of the Shadows* (Bieberstein, Marschall, Schneider 2012). This is the first fully comprehensive documentary about Reiniger's life and work. The film was shown in many festivals worldwide, including the *Berlinale*.

It features an interview with the author, where he talks about the ongoing importance of the animation pioneer for contemporary animation. Rall also exclusively created a short animated segment in silhouette style for the film, with color design by Hans Bacher.

Figure 3.3: Film still sequence for an animated segment that Hannes Rall created in silhouette style for the film *Lotte Reiniger: Dance of the Shadows* (2012).

Rall also directed a short animated homage to Reiniger, created by an international group of animators: *Reiniger Reinvented* (2012). It was included as a bonus feature on the DVD-release of *Lotte Reiniger: Dance of the Shadows* (Absolut Medien 2013).

Rall and Jernigan (2015) suggest that, for Hannes Rall's 2013 film *The Cold Heart*, Lotte Reiniger, the legendary pioneer animation artist and inventor of the silhouette film *The Adventures of Prince Achmed* (1926), also deserves to be mentioned here as an important influence. The frequent use of silhouettes, influenced by Reiniger's work, but in a drawn version, is also central to the design for *The Cold Heart*.

This deep connection between traditional and current practice leads to a closer investigation of two more recent productions in this chapter: *The Cold Heart* (2013) and *The History of the Spectre Ship* (in pre-production), both adapted freely from fairy tales by Wilhelm Hauff and directed by Hannes Rall.

An obvious reason for these choices is the very recent production dates that will allow contemporary practitioners to relate them to their own projects.

In terms of specific adaptation challenges, the longer narrative form of *The Cold Heart* (29 minutes) can be directly compared with the classic short format of *The History of the Spectre Ship* (8 minutes). The films are based on a novella and a short story, respectively.

Involved with the creation of both films were the renowned animation production designer Hans Bacher and animation director and writer Kathrin Albers (for the second film).

Another reason for choosing the two films is the option to deeply engage with the creative process of two current productions, with uninhibited access to visual material.

The author can also provide a firsthand account of the decision-making process, the pre-production, and production of this duo of Wilhelm Hauff fairy-tale adaptations.

The high number of very recent filmic adaptations of *The Cold Heart* also allows to compare several entirely different adaptation approaches during roughly the same time frame. This elevates the investigation beyond an isolated case study.

The Cold Heart - a classic romantic fairy tale (*Das kalte Herz*)

The Cold Heart (*Das kalte Herz*) must be counted among the best known fairy tales (Neuhaus 2002) by Wilhelm Hauff (1802–1827), one of the greatest authors of German romanticism. It was adapted by Hannes Rall as a medium-length (29-minute) animated short film (2013).

The *Cold Heart* story that takes place in the Black Forest of the nineteenth century remains a central work, not lastly because it deals with a timeless, current issue: The core element of the story is about the destructive power of greed and how it can change a person.

It is therefore a ghost story set in the Black Forest, a classic work of fantasy, which, however, owing to its themes, possesses an almost uncanny currency.

The plot has been summarized as follows:

> "Peter Munk is a poor charcoal burner whose only burning desire is to have money and standing in the community. When, one day, he meets a forest ghost who grants him 3 wishes, Peter believes heaven exists. Though his greed and lack of wits lead to him doing the wrong things; so Peter resorts one day to bartering with the evil Dutchman, Michael, who offers him all the riches in the world. Though, he wants Peter's heart in exchange."
>
> (Deutsche Film-und Medienbewertung [FBW] press release, 2012a)

For his adaptation, Rall chose to translate the title as *The Cold Heart* instead of the occasionally used *Heart of Stone* (McDonnell 1903). The author believed this translation to be more apt to illuminate the original message that Hauff wanted to communicate: A cold heart is the opposite of a warm heart. It means nothing else than the complete inability to engage with human emotions such as love and compassion. Instead, these are replaced with greed, cruelty, and ruthlessness. For clarity purposes, the author will further refer to the English title of *Das kalte Herz* as *The Cold Heart.*

Wilhelm Hauff is largely acknowledged to be one of the major authors of German romanticism (Martini 1971). Eppelsheimer (1960, 460) does attest to his enormous popularity as well. Kleeberg (2010, n.d.) offers a thematic categorization of Hauff's works as "narratives, gothic novels in the tradition of Walter Scott, fairy tales, poetry."

The big difference between Hauff and the Brothers Grimm lies in the fact that Hauff wrote his own fairy tales, while the Brothers Grimm were primarily collectors of traditional tales, which they recorded in writing.

David Blamires has intensively examined the lasting impact and the popularity of Wilhelm Hauff in his excellent book chapter *The Fairytales of Wilhelm Hauff* (2009). He claims that "of those writers who composed their own tales Wilhelm Hauff heads the list. His Märchen, whether published as a book or separately, have kept a firm place in German children's reading from the time of their first appearance right to the present day."

Further evidence for this claim is provided by the ongoing string of filmic adaptations in the 2010s, particularly of *The Cold Heart/Das kalte Herz.* Hannes Rall's animated half-hour version (2013) preceded two live-action adaptations: The feature-length adaptation for German TV broadcaster Zweites Deutsches Fernsehen (ZDF) by Marc-Andreas Bochert (2014) and the cinematic adaptation directed by Johannes Naber for Schmidtz Katze Film Kollektiv (2016).

In the context of adaptation studies, it is particularly interesting to examine how faithful these adaptations were and to understand the reasoning for any deviations from the source material.

As Bendazzi has pointed out in his introductory overview of animated adaptations, faithfulness does not automatically equal an artistically successful outcome.

Sometimes, quite the opposite can be the case, as the material demands to be substantially transformed to work in a very different, filmic medium.

How, then, did these two most recent live-action adaptations fare?

There are generally two ways to evaluate this: For one, the filmmakers themselves can explain their approach, and an insight into the logic of their production decisions might provide convincing artistic arguments. The critical researcher can examine those on their conclusiveness and investigate the results on the narrative and artistic criteria:

Is the essence of the source material preserved in the screenplay of the adaptation?
Is the story engaging and the plot built logically?
Have the characters been cast well for their roles, particularly when it comes to iconic characters?
Does the visual design reflect the atmosphere of the fairy tale adequately?
Is the production design artistically cohesive?
Are technical and artistic categories, for example, cinematography, editing, and sound design, carried out well and in full support of the audiovisual storytelling?

On the other hand, editorial reviews, as soon as available, can deliver an independent (yet not necessarily neutral) point of view on the artistic merit of the adaptation. Controversy is often high though, particularly when it comes to the adaptation of well-known material. Not only must the film succeed on its own terms, but the presented visualization might also collide with the individual vision of any spectator who is familiar with the source material. And that (naturally) includes film critics too.

Having said that, a closer look reveals some interesting comments and facts for both adaptations: Tilmann P. Gangloff (2014), a renowned German TV critic, categorizes Bochert's 2014 feature-length TV adaptation for the ZDF (Germany's biggest public broadcaster) as "old-fashioned and (too) literally adapted from the novel."

The story remains largely faithful to the source material, only entirely omitting the religious undertones of the fairy tale. The casting is referred to as largely adequate, yet the adaptation is overall seen as too conventional, with only the cinematography acknowledged as partially outstanding. Yet, one has to keep in mind that this film was created with a TV budget and with the expectations of a family audience in mind. Overall, the film is not seen as a failure by this reviewer, but as an eventually too safe retelling of the familiar tale, competent but not thrilling.

Figure 3.4: Film stills from the ZDF production "Das kalte Herz": Peter Munk (Rafael Gareisen, l.) cannot feel anything anymore after the trade with the Dutch Michael. The Glass Manikin (Tilo Prückner, right) can't help him. (Courtesy of ZDF/Sandra Bergemann.)

The commissioning editor for the 2014 ZDF version, Jörg von den Steinen, adds a different perspective here and convincingly justifies the adaptation method: "This is a great adventure with many, many stations. Partly almost already pre-conceptualized for adaptation by Wilhelm Hauff. In this respect, of course, one could simply adopt some of this proposed structure. However, for dramatic or dramaturgical reasons we focused on something that Wilhelm Hauff neglects for a very long time, or doesn't need for his story. That was the person Lisbeth. We have brought the love story with her to the fore as a central point. That means that we very quickly have encounters with Lisbeth. And it is very clear that she is the engine for what our hero Peter Munk does. Wilhelm Hauff tells it differently. He first lets him lose his warm heart. And with a cold heart again, he wants to have a beautiful wife and the prettiest woman from the Black Forest as a trophy, so to speak" (Rall 2017).

This explanation demonstrates two general strategies for adaptation: For one to find a specific and unique angle on the source material—here, it is the focus on the love story—and second, to match the narrative focus with the budget available to tell the story.

Von den Steinen (ibid) further explains: "We could not work with many visual effects. And because of that we shifted our focus more in the direction of a realistic film adaptation, i.e. more towards the social drama. We still included these magical elements. But it's still more like the here and now, that is to say the here and now of that time, which clearly is a fairytale world (…) We have surely made ourselves do with smaller tricks, backdrops which we added, as we needed them. Johannes Naber (*editor's remark:* in his 2016 theatrical adaptation) added some individual farms as digital matte paintings. They looked great. That's a money factor and an expense factor that has an impact. I sometimes have the choice and must decide: will I be able to tell this story for the money I have?"

Figure 3.5: Film stills from the ZDF production "Das kalte Herz": Lisbeth (Laura Louisa Garde) comforts her husband Peter (Rafael Gareisen), who meanwhile accuses himself of his mean and unfeeling behaviour towards her. (Courtesy of ZDF/Sandra Bergemann.)

The German film-rating board FBW (2016) comments on the most recent theatrical live-action version by Johannes Naber. It attests to the quality of the film by awarding its highest distinction—the seal of approval "highly recommended."

The jury states that the film is taking creative chances by adapting Hauff's fairy tale very freely and ultimately artistically succeeds by doing so. The reviewers agree that, by expanding some narrative elements while neglecting others, the filmmakers create a modern parable.

This verdict lends further support to the theory that well-considered deviations from the original can lead to an artistically superior result.

The Cold Heart had already been filmed multiple times before: There was the excellent theatrical version from East German studio DEFA (dir. Paul Verhoeven 1950)—now considered a classic. It employed highly impressive visual and special effects for its time that still hold up extremely well today. Its suggestive color design, impressive sets, and brilliant cinematography render it a filmic masterpiece. Its daring integration of horror elements is also remarkable and might be considered challenging for a youthful audience in today's socio-cultural climate. There were also several adaptations as a TV series (version for ZDF, Reinhold 1978, and an abridged serialized version for ARD series *Lemmi und die Schmoeker* 1978). All of these, however, were live-action adaptations; an animated adaptation did not exist before the 2000s.

The emergence of *The Cold Heart* (2013 animated adaptation)

Therefore, the option of a fully animated version presented itself as a pioneering effort, when author Hannes Rall first considered it in 2003–2004. In the early 2000s, an animated version of the movie offered the possibility of giving the work a new form of expression that was able to emphasize the central message of the story by using exaggeration, stylization, and metamorphoses.

A lifelong fascination with the work had preceded this idea, ever since the author read the classic fairy tale as a child. The two magical characters of the Glass Manikin and the Dutch Michael in the darkly alluring environment of a haunted Black Forest came alive before his eyes. The idea to create a visual adaptation was further inspired by the existing body of contemporary and classic illustrations, for example, by French nineteenth century illustrator Bertall or the German artist Ruth Koser-Michaels.

Figure 3.6: Comparison between a nineteenth-century illustration for *The Cold Heart* by French illustrator Bertall (1869) and the same scene from Hannes Rall's 2013 animated adaptation.

Figure 3.7: Early concepts for *The Cold Heart*. Hannes Rall, pencil, ca. 2006.

Economic Realities and Narrative Requirements

An animated short film of almost 30 minutes needs a substantial budget; an author can hardly create it all by himself.

Many European and some Asian countries offer opportunities for public funding.

The applicant needs to give the funding institution an idea, if the project is worthwhile supporting. How can this be accomplished when applying for funding?

Figure 3.8: The character design for the evil ghost Dutch Michael and Peter Munk, the tragic hero. Hannes Rall, 2004, ink on paper and digital.

Figure 3.9: Early production painting of a key scene from *The Cold Heart*: The Dutch Michael presents his collection of human hearts to the terrified Charcoal Peter. Hannes Rall, ink on paper/digital, 2004.

First, the central challenge consisted of converting the original work into a 30-minute-long version, which required abridging the content and deciding for a specific narrative focus. Central to the work on the screenplay (Rall 2005–2007) was to decide which aspects of the story should take center stage. In collaboration with the script advisor, Martina Döcker, it became clear very quickly that it should focus on the spiritual journey of the protagonist, Peter Munk.

Figure 3.10: An iconic scene from the original story that was eventually deleted from the screenplay: The evil Dutch Michael throws his huge walking stick (actually a tree trunk) after Peter Munk. It transforms into a gigantic snake that attacks Peter.

His change from a simple-minded but warm-hearted young man into a ruthless and emotionless monster formed the leitmotif for developing the screenplay.

Figure 3.11: Early character designs for the character of Glass Manikin. Hannes Rall, ink on paper/digital, 2004.

All the story lines and figures from the original novel were therefore checked for redundancy in this respect and abridged, if necessary.

So, the timeless currency of the fundamental issues should also stay in focus, while especially homely and folkloric elements were reduced as far as possible or, in any case, integrated as subtly as possible.

Exactly, this approach is also mirrored in the design of the movie:

Form follows function: The expressiveness and abstraction in the design of characters and backgrounds are designed to avoid Black Forest clichés. In its stead, German expressionism and exaggeration serve as inspiration through the power of the silhouette.

Here, genuine German sources of inspiration were used to create—German in the best sense of referencing great artists who were ostracized in the Third Reich. Hans Bacher, the movie's color designer, wrote about this in his blog (2012):

> "Hannes (Rall) chose a stylistic mix of ingredients from German expressionism, things that remind one of painters and xylographers (woodcut-artists) like Ernst Ludwig Kirchner, Karl Schmidt-Rottluff, Emil Nolde, Ernst Barlach, Max Beckmann, Otto Dix, Erich Heckel, Kaethe Kollwitz and Max Pechstein, As well as movies like *The Cabinet of Dr. Caligari*, *The Golem* and *Nosferatu*."

Last but not least, the influence of Lotte Reiniger should obviously also be mentioned again.

The use of silhouettes—though in an animated version—equally creates a central element in the design of *The Cold Heart*.

Once the screenplay, storyboards, and character designs were completed, the next step was to record the dialogue: For animation, this step always occurs before the actual production is done, as the voice recordings are required to be able to animate the characters' lips accurately frame by frame.

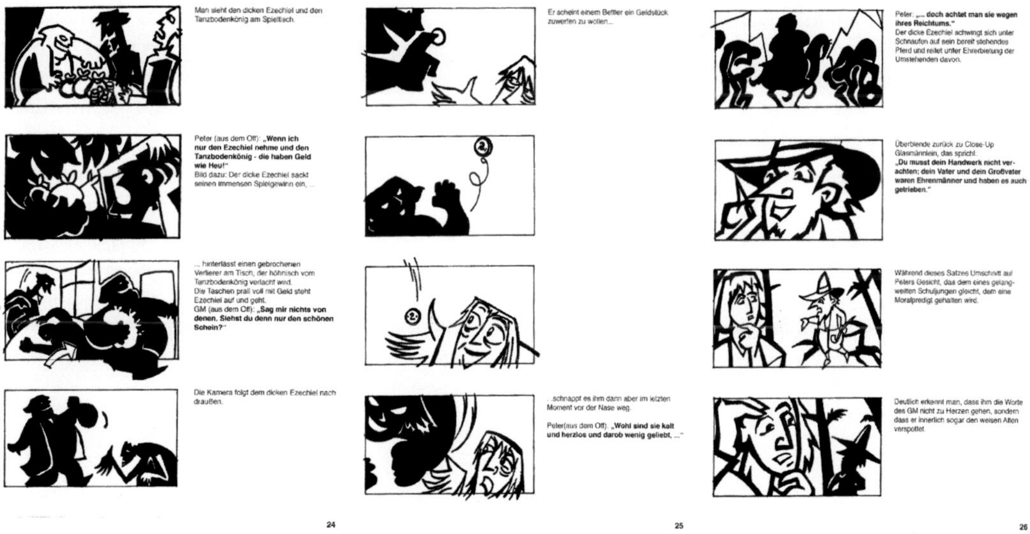

Figure 3.12: *The Cold Heart* storyboards: Storyboards break down the written screenplay into camera settings (for instance, full shots and medium shots). For animation, these often also define edits and animation-specific scene transitions (for instance, morphs), which always have a big role to play in Rall's movies. Hannes Rall, ink on paper, ca. 2007.

Casting the right voices is always one of the most important decisions for an animated film that has dialog. To underline the duality of the characters, Rall deliberately chose to cast the roles of the good and evil forest spirits, the Glass Manikin and the Dutchman Michael, with the same speaker: Karl-Michael Vogler. In the role of the Karl May hero (see also the chapter on visual development) in "Kara Ben Nemsi" (dir. Guenter Gräwert, 1973/75, ZDF), Vogler had won immense popularity in Germany (and with the author) in the 1970s and was one of the leading character actors of the German cinema scene. He was also employed in Hollywood (*Those Magnificent Men in Their Flying Machines*, 1965; *Patton*, 1970).

Because of his height and distinguished appearance, if nothing else, he was frequently typecast as the classic Prussian officer and gentleman, which sometimes hid his enormous versatility as a character actor. Naturally, he was able to let this range flow excellently into the so fundamentally different roles of the diminutive Glass Manikin and the heavily built, brutal Dutch Michael, and he delivered a truly remarkable performance. Unfortunately, Karl-Michael Vogler was not able to experience the completion of this film, as he died, completely unexpectedly, in June 2009. The movie is dedicated to his memory.

For the no-less-important role of the young "hero," Charcoal Peter, Phillipp Moog, an established voice actor, was signed up. He had, among other things, provided the German voices for Ewan McGregor and Orlando Bloom. This role was no less demanding, as it required a performance that adequately reflected the fundamental transformation of Peter. Finally, the smaller role of his wife, Lisbeth, was taken by the young actress Sabrina Litzinger, and the sound recording of the German version was completed in the summer of 2007 at the Floridan Studio in Stuttgart.

After a further refinement of the storyboard to the layout of the individual scenes, the animation work could finally begin in 2008. Hannes Rall took over large parts of the animation and prepared all scenes in detail, in order to implement important concepts of editing, movement, and design throughout the movie. In addition, the director had to coordinate a team of animators that was, in part, international. It is not realistic to transform a full-length novel into an animated film of just under 30 minutes unless one accommodates (minor) compromises in quality or has unlimited time.

The Cold Heart was created as a traditionally animated film. All the production steps before the colorization were done in the traditional way on paper, including the final artwork. That is why, in contrast to three-dimensional (3D) computer animations, there is no uniformly used virtual model with which all the animators work. Then, there's the final artwork created on the basis of the pencil-drawn animations. This makes it necessary to have exact control of the designs at all times—different animators tend to draw differently.

Figure 3.13: Style guide for the Dutch Michael, the evil spirit of the forest. Hannes Rall, pencil, ca. 2011.

In order to be able to guarantee the extremely important stylistic uniformity of the movie, the director had to create detailed style guides for all the important characters. The style guide described the characters in different poses through character-model sheets and gave instructions as to how to turn these principles into reality. That is enormously important, because, especially with a somewhat-abstract impression, there's a risk that the animators involved would deviate from these principles, because they wanted to draw something "right" (that is, make it look "real" in the sense of a more representational art style).

Continuous communication about all interim results, therefore, became an indispensable part of the production.

Figure 3.14: Style guide for Peter Munk, the hero. Hannes Rall, pencil, ca. 2011.

By its very nature, actually animating the movie took the lion's share of the production time, from 2008 to 2010/2011: Ralf Bohde (Studio Filmbilder), Michael Meier, and Jochen Rall from Germany worked alongside the director, while animators Davide Benvenuti, Lorna Sun, and Norman Baculi collaborated on an international level.

The final artwork proved to be very time-consuming. From the simple pencil line drawings ("rough animation"), final artwork had to be made by using a brush pencil in artfully varied line widths, which gave the impression of woodcuts. This led to the longest part of the production process that overlapped with the animation from 2010 to 2011.

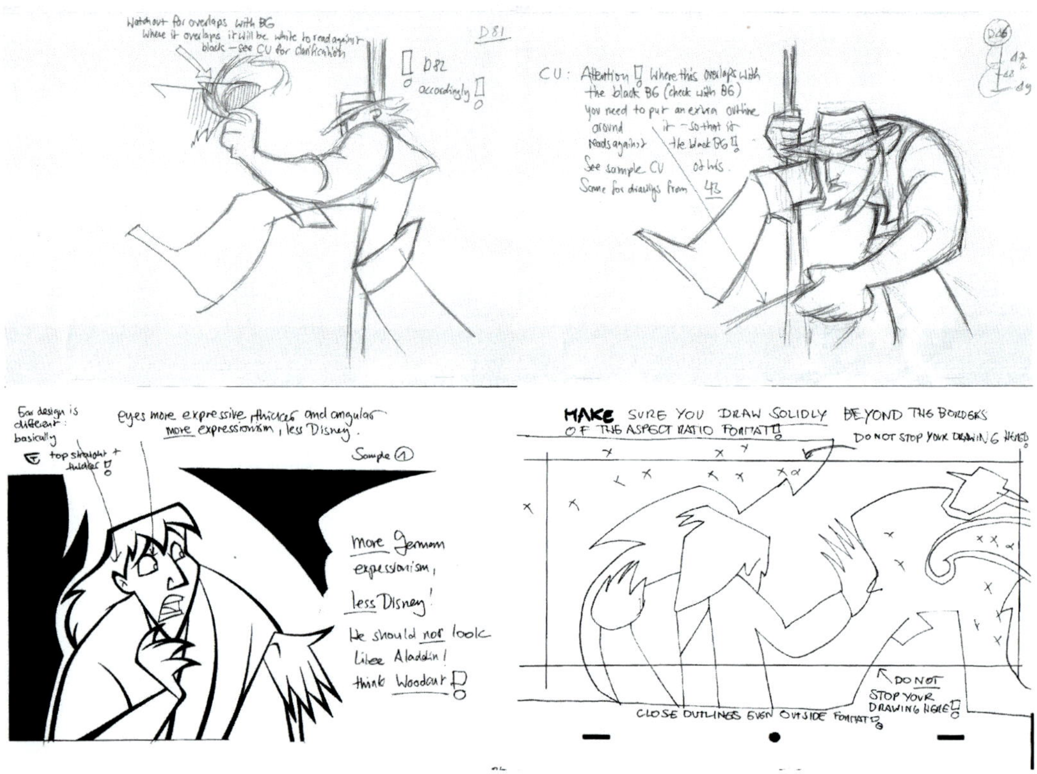

Figure 3.15: Cleaning up the rough animation drawings proved extremely labor-intensive. As demonstrated here, it required very precise instructions and corrections by the director to keep the overall look consistent, despite the clean ups being drawn by an international team of artists. Drawings by Davide Benvenuti and Tan Wei Keong (top) and Hannes Rall (bottom), 2011.

Naturally, before the computerized colorization of the scanned final artwork, it was first necessary to set the color scheme for the movie. Toward this end, a so-called "color script" was created, which, motivated by the dramatic structure, defined the color palette throughout the movie. This method guaranteed a link between the film's message and the color design in a consistent and logical way.

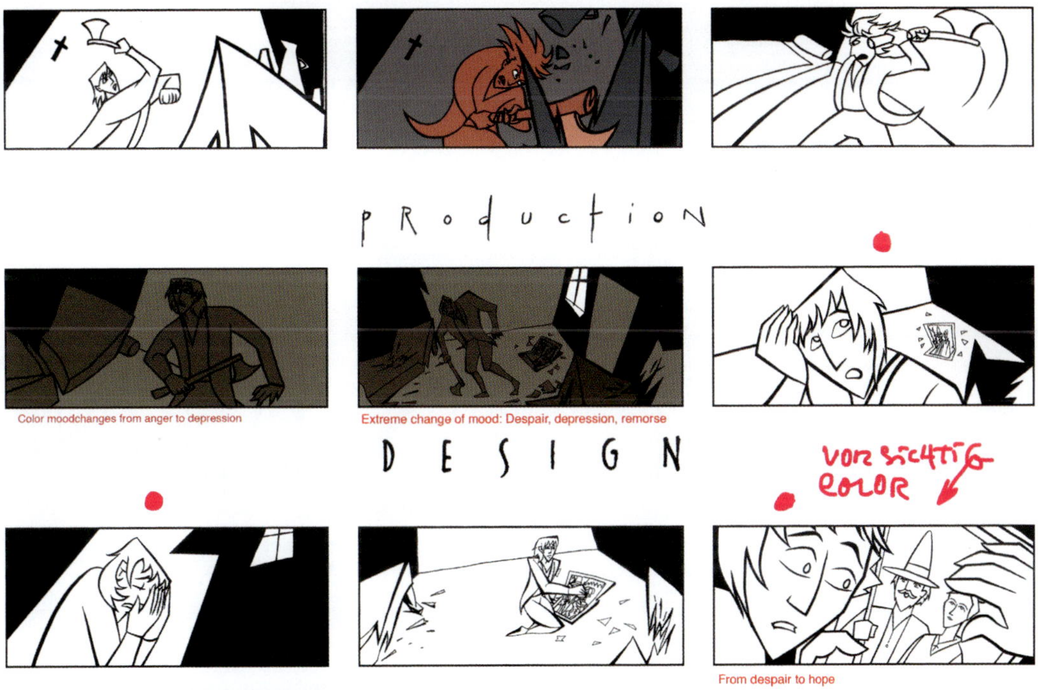

Figure 3.16: Example from the color script for *The Cold Heart* by Hans Bacher. The director's comments on the sheet indicate where a color accent is needed for dramatic purposes. Hans Bacher (color)/Hannes Rall (drawings), digital, 2012.

The author/director enjoyed the great good fortune of being able to employ Hans Bacher, one of the most well-known color designers for animated film anywhere in the world.

He is the author of the reference work *Dreamworlds: Production Design for Animation* (Focal Press, 2007), and he worked for many years at Walt Disney Feature Animation as a visual development artist and color designer.

Among other projects, he contributed significantly to *Beauty and the Beast* (Trousdale, Wise, 1991), *Aladdin* (Menken/Clements, 1992), and *The Lion King* (Allers, Minkoff, 1994). He was mainly responsible for the production design of *Mulan* (Bancroft, Cook, 1998).

For his color script, Hans analyzed the color palettes of expressionist paintings as well as the colors of traditional Black Forest clothing. In close consultation with the director, dramatic climaxes in the film were defined and their corresponding colors set. Particular attention was paid to subtle color cross-fades in characters and backgrounds that sensibly emphasized emotional turning points.

Figure 3.17: Another example for the definition of color transitions from the color script by Hans Bacher (with director's comments). It showcases the meticulous planning to optimally support the narrative through the color choices. Digital, 2012.

Coloring of the scanned drawings on computer was carried out between January and April 2012 by Scrawl-Studios in Singapore by using the color script created by Hans Bacher. At the same time, the final versions of the title sequence and the credits were outlined with additional animations added by Jochen Rall, using Adobe After Effects; these were added in the compositing phase. Robert Mack, from Spot Service in Stuttgart, then undertook the mastering for the various video formats, namely, Digital Cinema Package (DCP), 35mm film, and Blu-ray disc. Creating a successful 35mm version of the purely digitally created colors proved to be a special challenge. Though, the problem was solved successfully, thanks to the meticulous collaboration of Robert Mack with the light grading specialist at the film lab. The final version of the film was completed in late 2012.

Figure 3.18: Still frames from the completed film.

It's not for nothing that there's a basic principle that states that up to 50% of a movie's effect can be achieved through sound and music alone. As director of *The Cold Heart*, Rall always had the vision of a dark romantic and fully symphonic movie soundtrack that would be optimally balanced with the dialog. It was also important to him to have the individual characters supported by corresponding musical themes.

Eckart Gadow, a graduate of the movie soundtrack degree program at the Baden-Wuerttemberg Film Academy, has been Rall's partner in scoring his movies for several years now. He has gained lots of experience by working both for the big screen (among other projects, *Elefantenherz*, Aladag, 2002) and for numerous TV commissioned productions (among other projects, *Polizeiruf 110-Einer trage des anderen Last*, von Castelberg, 2012).

Director and composer deliberately made the joint decision to refrain from using classical sound effects and to support the action in the movie by using onomatopoeic musical accents only where it made sense in the context. By using the highest-quality orchestral samples, the soundtrack was created completely digitally, which is dotted through with an abundance of instrumental tones and the varying themes.

So, for instance, musical glasses were used for the Glass Manikin, while the entry of the Dutch Michael was signaled by the use of the full orchestra, with extra emphasis on the brass section.

Figure 3.19: Key scenes from the movie: First encounters of the hero Peter Munk with the forest spirits Glass Manikin and Dutch Michael. Production paintings (ink/digital) by Hannes Rall ca. 2004.

A subtly balanced Dolby Surround-Mix, which balanced the narrator's voices with the music, completed the scoring work.

After the German version of the movie was completed at the end of November 2012, recording for the international, English dubbed version was begun in December.

Again, the director decided in favor of a somewhat unusual artistic solution: Michael Mendl, one of the most well-known German character actors, took over the dual role of the Glass Manikin/Dutch Michael, while Peter was voiced by Timothy Peach, a prolific actor and native speaker.

Figure 3.20: Audio recordings with Timothy Peach and Michael Mendl.

All of this creates a delightful contrast between the English spoken by the Dutch Michael and the Glass Manikin's voice, which has light German undertones, and the diction of Peter.

This adequately mirrors both the plot's setting and the gothic, dark atmosphere in the movie. The results confirmed the decision: Michael Mendl performed excellently in the role of the Dutchman, Michael, voice-acting dramatically with striking volume, and he elegantly established the character of the Glass Manikin by using finer modulations.

By 2013, the film was on its way to film festivals. Since then, it has traveled the festival circuit with great success, being selected for a total of 93 international film festivals and winning 14 awards. This included acceptances for official competition in several top-tier festivals such as the 2013 Chicago International Children's Film Festival, Melbourne International Animation Festival, New Hampshire Film Festival, DC Shorts, and the Festival of Animated Film Stuttgart.

The first award had been the seal of approval "Highly Recommended" [besonders wertvoll] by the highly reputable German film-rating board FBW in Wiesbaden (2012b). The jury laudatio commented as follows:

> "Wilhelm Hauff's fairy tale is animated here using an expressionist style of drawing. The archetypal figures are outlined in an expressive way. In the traditional style, being hand-drawn and animated, the images are constantly moving. With these constantly flowing impressions he gives an expression to the emotions as told in the story, rather than painting them decoratively or even realistically. So the Dutch Michael, looms threateningly over Peter Munk who, as a poor sinner, threatens to sink further within himself and whose mouth is consumed with shock. With the danger, the warning color of red increases more and more. The angular, 2-dimensional drawings remind one of silhouettes, and the constant movement, that is also irritating at times, only makes the action appear much more intensively. Karl-Michael Vogler and Philipp Moog tell the tale using accents that are old-fashioned and perfectly matched to the story, and their lines are dotted with antiquated terms and sayings. These are likely to have been taken directly from the original text by Hannes Rall. Even the atmospheric, dark, romantic music strengthens the fairy-tale atmosphere. So this story, just like all other universal works, is as valid and current today just as it was when it was first created."

In his 2017 conversation with the author, ZDF editor and producer Jörg von den Steinen sums up in comparison: "What I find impressive about your version, is its huge expressivity—achieved through the visualization. This is shown through these flowing, morphing large shapes. The power of the Dutchman Michael is immense, the force he embodies. And he really comes across as divine, the way he pours his powers over Peter Munk, the tiny creature. And you really do use all the possibilities of animation to communicate big emotions to the viewer. As I said, if I were to rank (the adaptations) solely by that criterion, I would say that yours achieves the greatest emotional and expressive impact, so to speak. Then comes Paul Verhoeven's adaptation. The one who just does that through the exaggerations of his fairy-tale world. And ours is still moving below. As I said, we intentionally didn't make it so expressive now. But deliberately decided for a more quiet approach (..) So that means more subtle. You can make it bigger and more extreme. And you can make it more subtle. You also have to consider your target audience. "Our" *Cold Heart* targeted a family audience: we decided that we cannot tell this story so harmlessly that it is recommended even for preschool. We will not succeed in that. So we said that it has to be recommended for audiences from the age of six and up." (ibid).

These illustrations are shown over the end-credits of the film: They continue Peter's and Lisbeth's story after the happy ending: Returning to his mansion, Peter finds it destroyed. But much to their delight they find a new house instead. After the birth of their first child, the glass manikin presents them with another gift and they live happily ever after.

Figure 3.21: End-credits illustrations by Hannes Rall. Ink on paper/digital. 2012.

The examination of several adaptations of *The Cold Heart* has demonstrated that there are multiple factors that can lead to very different strategies for the transposition from written text to screen. These can be solely driven by the artistic intent of the adapter but also be determined by budgetary restrictions or considerations on the target audience. To really be able to assess the "quality" of an adaptation, these are well worth considering. Certain decisions might also be driven by the format and the need to play to its various strengths: A live-action TV adaptation will naturally rely more on the quieter aspects of the source material, while on the other end of the spectrum, an animated version can fully exploit the dramatic potential of the super-natural.

The following case study will provide further evidence to the theory that animation is a medium particularly well suited to visualize the magical elements of a story (Wells 1999, 211).

The History of the Spectre Ship

The History of the Spectre Ship is another well-known story by Wilhelm Hauff. It does not rank quite as high in popularity as *The Cold Heart*, but it still stands out from the many fairy tales that Hauff created in his short (yet very prolific) life span. One reason is that it could be described as a very dark fairy tale or might even be categorized as a gothic horror story in an Oriental setting. In short, the legend of the *Flying Dutchman* transported to the world of *1001 Nights*. Different from *The Cold Heart*, it is written in a classic short-story format, with a suitable length to be adapted for a circa 10-minute animated short film.

Hannes Rall started to develop this adaptation in 2014, together with his colleagues Asst./Prof. Kathrin Albers as a co-author and Assoc. Prof. Hans Bacher as a collaborator for visual development. This adaptation has progressed through the stages of script and storyboard, visual development, and finally an animatic. At the stage of writing, the development is still ongoing, in terms of both the narrative and the final art styles.

But particularly for that reason, the multiple iterations of narrative and artistic development can demonstrate the various solutions and remaining challenges really well.

Hauff Again?

Multiple reasons led to the idea of developing an adaptation of this mesmerizing tale for animation. These were equally artistically motivated as well as connected to an ongoing research project of the author: *Reiniger Reinvented—Re-Creation of Classic Animation in a New Digital Environment*. This research project set itself the goal to explore how the pioneering artistic efforts of Lotte Reiniger can be contextualized and redefined for digital animation. Many artists (e.g., Michel Ocelot) had already artistically explored new means of expression for silhouette animation with digital tools, yet a dedicated academic study was still missing. It is also of particular interest that Reiniger herself had adapted one of Hauff's Oriental fairy tales with *Kaliph Stork* (1954). This provided a point of reference from which the authors needed to depart, to create their own original Hauff adaptation in the context of *1001 Nights*.

In that sense, adapting *The History of the Spectre Ship* offered an opportunity to create an animated adaptation that was also helpful to answer to the research questions.

This specific adaptation study also serves extremely well to demonstrate the integration of theory (research) and practice (artistic creation). In other words, how can academic research and artistic creation be mutually beneficial?

Connection to Research

One major reason to choose this specific story for adaptation was that it takes place in the same Oriental environment in which Reiniger had set her most famous film *The Adventures of Prince Achmed*: The world of *The Thousand and One Nights*, offering ample opportunity for comparison (see also the aforementioned Reiniger adaptation of *Kaliph Stork*).

Reiniger had been looking at the world of Oriental mythology with the eyes of a Western artist, just like Hauff had been setting a Western tale in a fictional Middle-Eastern world.

The origins of *The Thousand and One Nights* are highly complex and cannot be clearly associated with one culture or country in the Middle East. Different versions are plenty, but all are clearly non-European in terms of their original inception.

From the eighteenth century onward, though, European translations (Irwin 2003, 14) that often altered and expanded on the original tales emerged, albeit largely drawing from various Middle-Eastern sources.

In that sense, both Hauff and Reiniger continued an already firmly established tradition. How can an animated adaptation create visual equivalents for Hauff's Western look at Oriental fairy tales? And how can Reiniger's earlier interpretation of Arabic art styles be developed in a digital setting?

Figure 3.22: Visual development by Andre Quek (top right) and Hannes Rall from *The History of the Spectre Ship* (2014). Ink on paper/digital.

Artistic Appeal and Creative Challenges

First and foremost, this is a story with high potential for visual dramatization, and this quickly becomes evident from many previous illustrations. Particularly, the iconic image of the pirate ship's captain, nailed to the mast, stands out. It has been depicted by many artists since its original inception.

Figure 3.23: Original illustration by Theodor Hosenmann (1869) for *The History of the Spectre Ship.*

Figure 3.24: Original illustration by Bertall (1869) for *The History of the Spectre Ship*.

The serious undertones, adult themes, and mature topics also resonated well with the artistic sensibilities of the team developing the film. As mentioned earlier, a congruence between the narrative content and the artistic abilities of an animation director should be a key factor to determine the choice of adaptation material. In other words, if the director's artistic style matches darker material, it can prove an ideal combination.

Figure 3.25: Visual development (digital, 2014) by Hans Bacher for the film's opening sequence: The merchant's small ship in the storm. © Hans Bacher.

Therefore, the authors were attracted by the prospect to create an animated horror film. Horror is still a vastly underrepresented genre in the medium. Although there are a few animated classics of the genre, the majority of topics, even in contemporary independent animation, lies elsewhere. Although R-rated horror is of course also only a niche genre in live-action films, still the percentage of horror movies compared with animation is significantly higher. One reason for that seems to be very obvious:

It remains a real challenge to create animated images that prove truly frightening to audiences, even more so when one is combining stylized drawn animation with stop motion, as the authors planned to do.

A key factor for sufficiently scaring the spectator is to allow him to identify (or at least strongly empathize) with the characters on screen. This will become increasingly difficult once there are no "real persons" represented but drawn or sculpted avatars of human beings instead.

Figure 3.26: Visual development by Hannes Rall (2014): Mutiny on board/split screen. Ink/digital.

Last but not least, his previous Hauff adaptation *The Cold Heart* had allowed Hannes Rall to deeply engage with Wilhelm Hauff's body of work. He had already explored the specific opportunities and challenges for animated adaptation. His previously successful animated interpretation provided a solid indication that he was up to the task. This would also serve well to enhance confidence levels for the project at film-funding institutions and potential private investors.

Such supporting evidence becomes important, if not crucial, once an independent animated short film moves ahead from the initial development and pre-production stage and funds are needed for the actual production. Any investor, private or public, will always favor a tried-and-tested concept over a completely unknown conceptual entity. This might be rightfully lamented from a purely artistic point of view but remains a reality that needs to be considered to successfully secure funding.

Comparison Between Original Story and Adaptation Screenplay

The short story of *The History of the Spectre Ship* superficially posed less of a challenge for adapting its narrative for an animated short than the novel-length *The Cold Heart.*

Yet, there are difficulties of a different kind that needed to be addressed when transforming the original story for animation.

Hauff's tale describes the encounter of two castaways with a mysterious ghost ship.

After being shipwrecked, they find it to be their only rescue, and they climb on board, only to encounter a horrible situation: The whole deck is full of corpses, and the captain is stuck to the mast, with a nail through his head. But things get even worse, as they are faced with the ultimate horror by night: All the dead pirates come alive. Each night, the disastrous act of mutiny gets re-enacted, which leads to the demise of all.

Hauff's heroes find out about the crew and captain's tragic backstory that left them cursed to their horrible fate. With the support of the Koran and a wise sage's advice, they finally succeed in breaking the curse and deliver the former pirates from their tragic destiny.

Finding A Style: Transcultural Explorations

If we agree that adaptation for animation means transformation, how can this be carried out successfully? One approach can be to define visual equivalents of the author's literary approach.

A defining characteristic of Hauff's narrative is its underlying transcultural concept.

It was the goal of the adaptation to emulate a point of view that would resonate with the author's original vision. And Hauff's story is decidedly "non-authentic," clearly not an attempt to create a journalistic essay on Arabic culture but a poetic (European) interpretation of an Oriental fairy tale.

Vice versa, the investigators decided to forego the idea of being "authentic" or "realistic." Instead, the authors deliberated to focus on creating a visual language that would echo the idea of a rather romanticized representation of Middle-Eastern mythology.

This decision helped to define the approach for the visual development.

Production and Color Design: Defining General Concepts

Intensive artistic research is usually the starting point for any visual development process. The designer(s) would look into previous visual adaptations and collect potential artistic influences. What has been done before? Where can design ideas come from?

What are the different historical, cultural, and contemporary artistic approaches to illustrate: Oriental fairy tales or authentic cultural studies? The goal of this development stage is to explore a multitude of options and to keep an open mind for diverse sources of inspiration.

Hans Bacher (2015, 138) describes this process:

> "The research takes a very, very long time: Two to three months for sure during which you are intensively looking for the best reference: In photos, in illustrations of other artists who have worked in a similar direction, or art

in general exploring the artistic variety the last couple of centuries."

The aforementioned "art in general" can be further broken down into concrete fields, including architecture, film, fine arts, and animation from different cultures and time periods.

The result of this widely open artistic research will result in the creation of mood boards.

These are collections of many artistic samples that might (or might not) contribute to the definition of the project's aesthetics.

Suffice to say that these will obviously already be informed by the designers' own artistic preferences.

From that point on, a stricter selection process will help to narrow down the possible artistic choices. Could it fit into our own artistic concept? Can we develop a new style by merging, integrating, or newly interpreting these influences? What to integrate, what to exclude?

In a way, this is a process of visual adaptation of artistic tradition and various design styles that mirrors the way choices are being made when adapting a narrative.

That selection will happen simultaneously with drawing many sketches that will merge external artistic influences with the designer's own artistic "handwriting."

Very often, this integrative process will result in the evolution of visually innovative styles.

The old combines with the new and Western culture with Eastern art tradition, a fusion that can yield inspired results, if executed with taste and sound artistic judgment.

Figure 3.27: Visual development studies inspired by Arabic calligraphy (Hans Bacher, ink on paper, 2014). © Hans Bacher.

In the case of the *Spectre Ship*, the artistic research would follow two main strands:

- On the one hand, the designers were looking at Western interpretations of Middle-Eastern culture and mythology, because these reflected the approach taken by Hauff and Reiniger, respectively. The visual development should look into the connection between the author of the source material and the way contemporary artists were reflecting this in their imagery.
- On the other hand, the team was going back to the original sources to draw inspiration from. As Hans Bacher further notes (ibid): "If a story takes place in a certain cultural environment, I should use this as a reference."

Figure 3.28: Visual development of waves inspired by Arabic calligraphy. (From Hans Bacher, digital, 2014).
© Hans Bacher.

Hans Bacher's own version of (fictional) Arabic calligraphy led to the development of the wave designs that were used to develop the style of the waves for the adaptation. This is a good example of how an inspiration from traditional artistic reference can literally merge with a designer's handwriting to inspire an innovative artistic approach.

Figure 3.29: Production painting (digital, 2014) by Hans Bacher for the dramatic opening sequence of the film. © Hans Bacher.

Figure 3.29 shows a small vessel in high seas during a ravaging thunderstorm. The basic design of the waves developed can now be seen in a piece that emulates the design and color of the final film.

Figure 3.30: Another exploratory study for the opening sequence. (By Hans Bacher, digital, 2014.) © Hans Bacher.

The art in Figure 3.30 also impressively pictures the drama of a ship lost in the battle of the elements, albeit in an entirely different design. The artistic style is inspired by traditional nineteenth-century painting. As common in visual development, the piece explores an alternative approach to test it for the adaptation. Despite its most impressive evocation of the atmosphere and the highly competent artistic execution, this approach was ultimately rejected. This was due to its lack of any Middle-Eastern design motifs, which would have put the scene at odds with the general design concept. For visual development, it is not crucial if a piece succeeds on its own but is crucial if it will fit the overall design context of the film. Inconsistency in the production design would fail the creation of a visually cohesive universe—a believable world.

Figure 3.31: Another early try-out for the opening sequence. (Courtesy of Hannes Rall 2014. Ink on paper, digital.)

Figure 3.31 shows a highly stylized approach for the same scene that heightens the drama through the use of expressionistic imagery and heavy blacks. The tiny white vessel of the hero (barely visible on the right) encounters the gigantic ghost ship during the storm. The use of a small positive space (vessel) against a huge negative background (wave) supports the composition. What appears to be too subtle in a static image will become more obvious in movement.

Similar to the previous image, this demonstrates the initial openness of the design approach that embraces a plethora of artistic styles.

Further down the line in the pre-production process, a final choice will be made regarding the design style that fits the adaptation the best. In this case, it turned out to be a stylized character design approach combined with backgrounds and environments that strongly display influence from Arabic calligraphy and ornaments. At the same time, the designers opted to also integrate influences of modernist European artists. This eclecticism resonates with the source text that displays the Western vision of a romanticized Oriental world.

Figure 3.32: Further visual development by Hans Bacher—here for architecture and ships (ink on paper, 2014). The elegance of Arabic calligraphy remains an influence here. © Hans Bacher.

Figure 3.33: A color and environment study by Bacher (digital 2014), exploring the visual tone and possible prop-background combinations. © Hans Bacher.

Figures 3.32 and 3.33 demonstrate how such seemingly idiosyncratic elements can be combined to create a visually cohesive world, a world that also demands an approach to character design that creates figures that "fit in."

Character Design

The lead principles for the design were identified as purity, elegance, and simplicity. These are the qualities that can be found in both the curvy shapes of Arabic calligraphy and the beautiful stylization of a painter like Henri Matisse. Figures 3.34 through 3.36 demonstrate that such influences can be combined successfully: They shape a concept for character design that sits well with the overall design approach.

Sheherazade is a figure in the film that is used in similar ways as in the original stories of *1001 Nights*: She will be the narrator of the story, therefore setting her apart from the main character cast. This also allows for more flexibility in the character design.

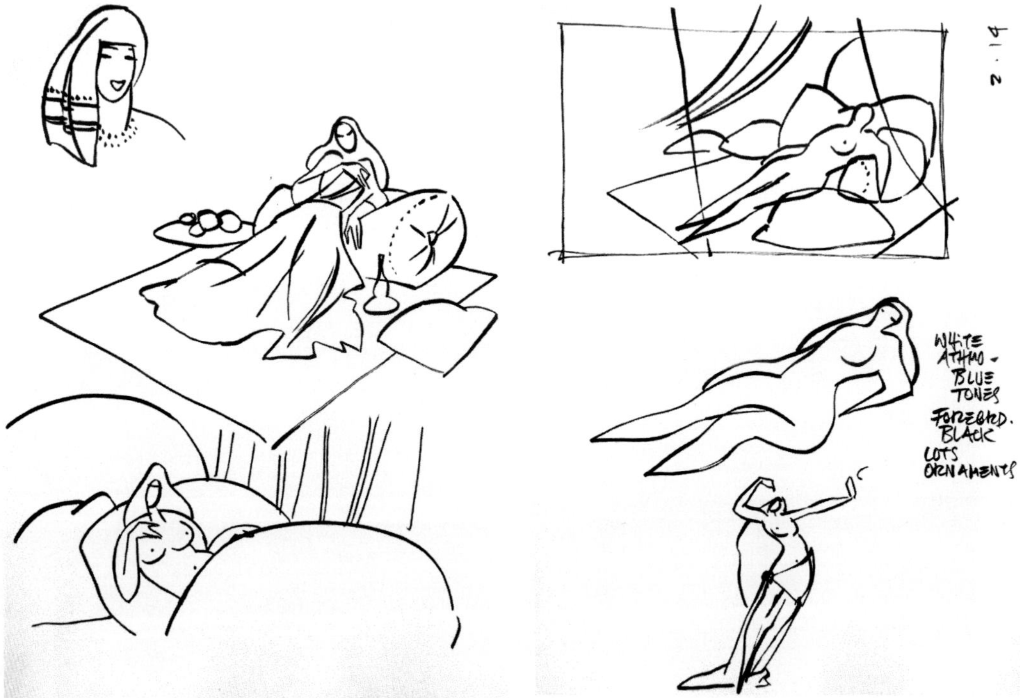

Figure 3.34: Character development of Sheherazade by Hans Bacher. Ink on paper, 2014 © Hans Bacher.

Figure 3.35: Character development of Sheherazade by Hans Bacher. Ink on paper and digital, 2014 © Hans Bacher.

Figure 3.36: Character development of Sheherazade by Hans Bacher. Digital, 2014 © Hans Bacher.

Figure 3.37 shows another important element of character design: In silhouette, all characters must be easily distinguishable from each other and provide interesting contrast in shape.

The same applies for each character design: Each figure is built from strongly contrasting basic geometrical shapes. This creates tension within the character design and adds to the appeal of the character.

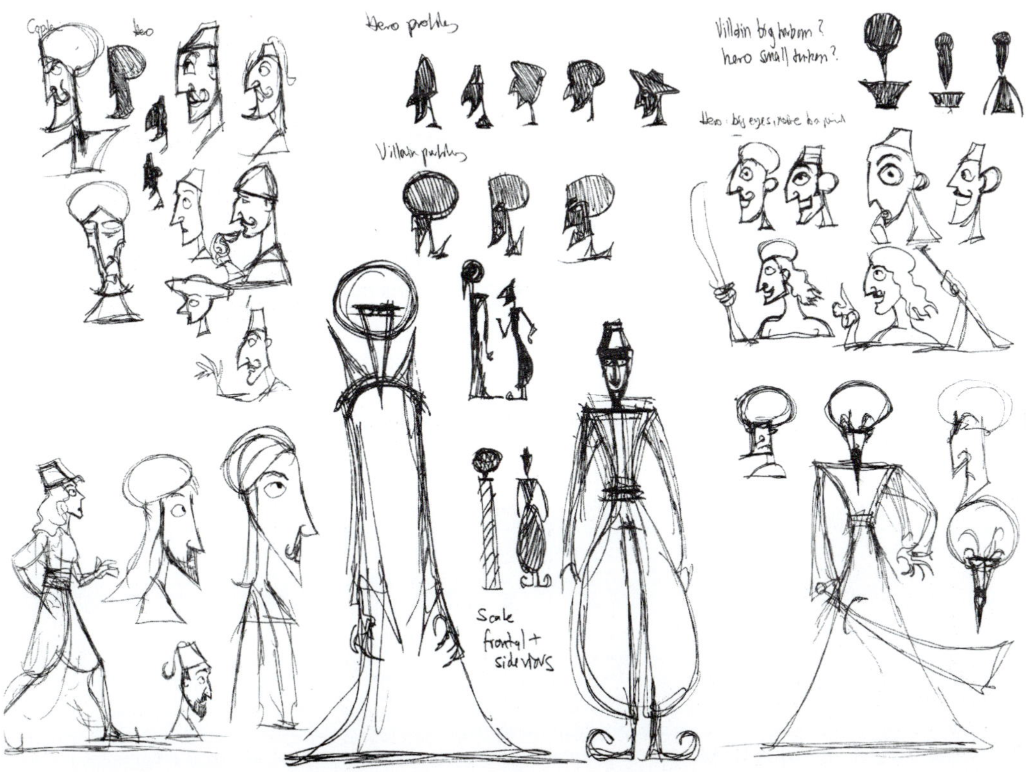

Figure 3.37: Character development for the main cast by Hannes Rall. Ink on paper, 2014.

Coming Full Circle: Marrying Story and Visuals

The original fairy tale features two main protagonists: The hero, who tells the story in the first person, and his faithful servant. The curse of the pirate ship is lifted after the protagonists visit some wise sage on land. He gives advice on how to achieve deliverance for the cursed:

They are to be brought on land, which will relieve them from eternal damnation.

The screenwriting team of Hannes Rall and Kathrin Albers made some significant changes for the animated adaptation. Instead of using the original framing story by Hauff, the story is told by Sheherazade—a decision to contextualize the story in the tradition of *1001 Nights*, which also cross-references Reiniger's earlier *Prince Achmed*.

Second, the authors decided to use only one main hero. The reason was to allow a clearer focus for filmic adaptation and to also reduce the amount of animation needed.

The whole plot was relocated to entirely take place onboard the ship. This confined spatial arrangement heightens the tension and adds suspense.

Figure 3.38: Modified character designs for the new story approach. Characters in their 2D versions for daytime (left) and a silhouetted stop-motion pirate by night. Andre Quek, digital, 2015.

The narrative change with the most crucial implications for the graphic development was a visual storytelling decision: The duality of daytime, during which the pirates are dead, and nighttime, when they come alive, is illustrated through the use of two different animation techniques: traditional two-dimensional (2D) animation during the day and stop motion by night.

Figure 3.39: Excerpt from the storyboard by Hannes Rall (top) and final look exploration of the same scene by Andre Quek. Ink on paper and digital, 2015.

The stop-motion style is reminiscent of Lotte Reiniger's earlier works, albeit reconsidered for digital animation.

Only the hero that intrudes their world stays in his drawn incarnation at all times. In this form, he cannot be seen by the ghostly pirates. The scene pictured in Figure 3.39 plays with that tension: He is hiding from the pirates, then fears himself discovered, only to ultimately realize that the pirate who found him can't see him.

The scene plays with the expectations of the audience that would fear for the hero and share his relief later on. Timing and pacing the scene the right way will be crucial for its success on screen: The menace of potential discovery needs to be smartly drawn out, before the sharp relief sets in with a fast pace.

The screenplay generates further suspense from the effect that the hero gradually turns into a stop-motion character himself, the longer he stays on the ship. This would eventually lead to him being discovered by the pirates when they come alive at night. Therefore, he desperately seeks a resolution from the curse during the daytime, when the pirates remain dead.

This new constellation adds a more urgent motivation for the main character. The strong connection between the narrative and the visuals plays to the strengths of the animation medium. This is a very different approach compared with Lotte Reiniger's introductory remark that states that "one should try to work as faithfully (close to the original) as possible." Reiniger's fairy-tale adaptations do, however, demonstrate that she competently deviated from this rule at times. Not least of all, her masterful re-contextualization of story elements from *1001 Nights* in *Prince Achmed* evidences the supremacy of creative re-imagination over (too) literal adaptation. Moreover, the oral traditions of fairy-tale storytelling even suggest embracing change as part of a continued tradition.

This chapter already examined two darkly romantic fairy tales with integrated horror elements. The next will be fully dedicated to the investigation of the Gothic in animated adaptations.

References

Anonymous. 2002. *The Thousand and One Nights*. Trans. Husain Haddawy. *The Norton Anthology of World Literature*, edited by Sarah Lawall. New York: W.W. Norton & Company.

Bacher, Hans. 2015. Interview with Hans Bacher. In: edited by Hannes Rall, *Animationsfilm. Konzept und Produktion*, 138. Konstanz, Germany: UVK Verlag.

Bacher, Hans. 2012. *Heart of Stone*. Accessed November 2, 2013. http://one1more2time3.wordpress.com/2012/08/05/das-kalte-herz/.

Bendazzi, Giannalberto. 2014. Interview with Hannes Rall. November 8. Nanyang Technological University, Singapore.

Benner, Julia. n.d. Reiniger, Lotte. Accessed September 3, 2016. http://www.kinderundjugendmedien.de/index.php/autoren/1479-reiniger-lotte.

Bertall. 1869a. *Der Köhler Peter in der Hand des Holländer-Michels*. Illustration. In: edited by Wilhelm Hauff, *Mährchen für Söhne und Töchter gebildeter Stände*, 379. Stuttgart, Germany: Rieger'sche Verlagsbuchhandlung.

Bertall. 1869b. *Piratenspuk*. Illustration. In: edited by Wilhelm Hauff, *Mährchen für Söhne und Töchter gebildeter Stände*, 36. Stuttgart, Germany: Rieger'sche Verlagsbuchhandlung.

Bieberstein, Rada, Susanne Marschall, and Kurt Schneider, dirs. 2012. *Lotte Reiniger: Dance of the Shadows*.

Documentary feature film. Stuttgart, Germany: Eikon-Südwest (production). DVD release: Berlin, Germany: Absolut Medien, 2013.

Blamires, David. 2009. The fairytales of Wilhelm Hauff. In: *Telling Tales: The Impact of Germany on English Children's Books 1780–1918*, David Blamires, 181–203. Cambridge, UK: Open Book Publishers.

Bochert, Marc-Andreas, dir. 2014. *Das kalte Herz*. Live action feature film (TV). Mainz, Germany: ZDF (production/broadcaster/distribution).

Böttge, Bruno J., dir. 1954. *Die Bremer Stadtmusikanten*. Animated short film. Dresden, Germany: DEFA (production).

Böttge, Bruno J., dir. 1956. *König Drosselbart*. Animated short film. Dresden, Germany: DEFA (production).

Böttge, Bruno J., dir. 1956. *Prinzessin Springwasser*. Animated short film. Dresden, Germany: DEFA (production).

Böttge, Bruno J., dir. 1973. *Die Prinzessin und der Ziegenhirt*. Animated short film. Dresden, Germany: DEFA (production).

Der Einfluss der chinesischen Schattenspielkunst auf Lotte Reinigers Frühwerk. lotte-reiniger-film.com. Accessed September 26, 2016. http://www.lotte-reiniger-film.com/china.html.

Eppelsheimer, Hans W. 1960. *Handbuch der Weltliteratur*. Dritte Auflage. Frankfurt am Main, Germany.

FBW. 2012a. *Das kalte Herz*. Press release for awarding the Seal of Approval: Highly Recommended. Accessed September 18, 2016. http://www.fbw-filmbewertung.com/film/das_kalte_herz.

FBW. 2012b. *Das kalte Herz*. Jury's laudatio for awarding the Seal of Approval: Highly Recommended. Accessed February, 11, 2013. http://www.fbw-filmbewertung.com/film/das_kalte_herz.

FBW. 2016. *Das kalte Herz*. Jury's laudatio for awarding the Seal of Approval: Highly Recommended. Accessed September 27, 2016. http://www.fbw-filmbewertung.com/film/das_kalte_herz_1.

Gangloff, Timann P. 2014. *Fernsehfilm "Das kalte Herz"* (review), tittelbach.tv. Last updated 29 November 2014. Accessed September 27, 2016, http://www.tittelbach.tv/programm/fernsehfilm/artikel-3464.html.

Happ, Alfred. 1982. Scherenschnitt und Schattentheater im 20. Jahrhundert. In: Licht und Schatten. Scherenschnitt und Schattentheater im 20. Jahrhundert, 8–84. Ausst.-Kat. Puppentheatermuseu m im Münchner Stadtmuseum. München, Germany.

Hauff, Wilhelm. 1827. *Das kalte* Herz, published in two parts in the novel *Das Wirtshaus im Spessart* in *Märchen-Almanach auf das Jahr 1828 für Söhne und Töchter gebildeter Stände*. Stuttgart, Germany: G.Schwab.

Hauff, Wilhelm. 1855. *The History of the Spectre Ship*. Translated from German by G.P. Quakenbos. New York: D. Appleton & Company. Accessed September 3, 2016. http://www.gutenberg.org/files/24593/24593-h/24593-h.htm.

Hosenmann, Theodor, artist. 1869. *Die Geschichte von dem Gespensterschiff: Achmet und sein Diener entdecken die Leichen der Seeleute*. (English translation: *The Story of the Spectre Ship. Achmet and his servant discover the corpses of the sailors. Gespensterschiff: Achmet und sein Diener entdecken die Leichen der Seeleute* Illustration.

Irwin, Robert. 2003. *The Arabian Nights: A Companion*. London, UK: Tauris Parke Palang-Faacks.

Junge, Janine. 2012. *Lotte Reinigers Einfluss auf gegenwärtige Künstler – Der Animationsfilmer Hannes Rall*. Accessed September 3, 2016. http://www.lotte-reiniger-film.com/rall.html.

Kayser, Beate. 1979. *"Ich glaube mehr an Märchen als Zeitungen."* Gespräch mit der Trickfilmerin Lotte Reiniger. Munich, Germany: TZ.

Kleeberg, Michael. 2010. "Wilhelm Hauff-Das kalte Herz." Accessed March 23, 2014. http://michaelkleeberg.de/seite/wp-content/uploads/2010/04/Wilhelm-Hauff.pdf.

Lotte Reiniger und die Gebrüder Grimm, lotte-reiniger-film.com. Accessed September 26, 2016. http://www.lotte-reiniger-film.com/grimm.html.

Martini, Fritz. 1971. "Wilhelm Hauff." In *Deutsche Dichter der Romantik: Ihr Leben und Werk*, edited by Benno von Wiese, 532–562. Berlin, Germany: Erich Schmidt Verlag.

McDonnell, Cicely, translator/adaptor. 1903. *Hauff's Fairy Tales*. London, UK: Dean & Son.

Naber, Johannes, dir. 2016. *Das kalte Herz*. Live action feature film. Berlin, Germany: Schmidts Katze (production).

Neuhaus, Stefan. 2002. *Das Spiel mit dem Leser: Wilhelm Hauff: Werk und Wirkung*. Goettingen, Germany: Vandenhoeck & Ruprecht.

Nye, Scott. 2013. *Scott Reviews Lotte Reiniger's The Adventures of Prince Achmed*. Blu-ray review. criterioncast.com. Accessed September 26, 2016. http://criterioncast.com/reviews/blu-ray-reviews/scott-reviews-lotte-reinigers-the-adventures-of-prince-achmed-blu-ray-review.

Ocelot, Michel, dir. 2000. *Princes et Princesses*. Animated feature film. La Fabrique Les Armateurs, Salud Productions, Studio O (production).

Ocelot, Michel, dir. 2011. *Les Contes de la Nuit*. Animated feature film. Paris, France: Studio Canal, Nord-Ouest Films, Studio O (production).

Rall, Hannes, and Daniel Keith. 2015. *Adapting Gothic Literature for Animation*. In: *New Directions in 21st-Century Gothic: The Gothic Compass*, edited by Lorna Piatti-Farnell, Donna Lee Brien. London, UK: Routledge.

Rall, Hannes, dir. 1999. *The Raven*. Animated short film.

Rall, Hannes., dir. 2003. *The Erl-King*. Animated short film.

Rall, Hannes., dir. 2012. *Reiniger Reinvented*. Animated short film.

Rall, Hannes., dir. 2013. *The Cold Heart*. Animated short film.

Rall, Hannes, dir. 2014. *Si Lunchai*. Animated short film.

Rall, Hannes, dir. 2016. *All The World's a Stage*. Animated short film.

Rall, Hannes. 2017. Interview with Jörg von Steinen. Unpublished. Recorded December 1, 2017. Stuttgart, Germany.

Reiniger, Lotte, dir. 1926. *Aschenputtel*. Animated short film.

Reiniger, Lotte, dir. 1926. *The Adventures of Prince Achmed*. Animated feature film.

Reiniger, Lotte, dir. 1928. *Dr. Doolittle and His Animals*. Animated feature film.

Reiniger, Lotte, dir. 1936. *Der gestiefelte Kater* (*Puss in Boots*). Animated short film.

Reiniger, Lotte, dir. 1944. *Die goldene Gans* (*The Goose That Lays The Golden Eggs*). Animated short film.

Reiniger, Lotte, dir. 1954. *Der Froschkönig* (*The Frog Prince*). Animated short film.

Reiniger, Lotte, dir. 1954. *Kaliph Stork*. Animated short film.

Reiniger, Lotte, dir. 1954. *Snow White and Rose Red*. Animated short film.

Reiniger, Lotte, dir. 1955. *Hansel and Gretel*. Animated short film.

Tappert, Horst, dir. 1984. *Hans mein Igel*. Animated short film. Dresden, Germany: DEFA (production).

'The Adventures of Prince Achmed' & 'One Thousand and One Nights.' The Cinematic Frontier. Posted on November 22, 2013. Accessed September 26, 2016. https://cinematicfrontier.wordpress.com/2013/11/22/the-adventures-of-prince-achmed-one-thousand-and-one-nights/.

Triebold, Wilhelm. 2011. *Die wunderbare Welt des Zeichen trickfilmers und Märchenerzählers Michel Ocelot*. In: tagblatt.de. Accessed September 3, 2016. http://www.tagblatt.de/Home/kino/filmregion_artikel,-Die-wunderbare-Welt-des-Zeichentrickfilmers-und-Maerchenerzaehlers-Michel-Ocelot-_arid,152681.html.

Wells, Paul. 1999. Thou Art Translated: Analysing animated adaptations. In *Adaptations: From Text to Screen, Screen to Text*, edited by Deborah Cartmell and Imelda Whelehan, 211. London, UK: Routledge.

Things That Go Bump on the Screen

Adapting Gothic Literature for Animation

Introduction: Gothic Literature and Animation

Studies on Gothic adaptation—particularly for animation that focuses on the connection between narrative content and its means of visual expression (i.e., the narratology of these works) —are an under-researched area (Rall, Jernigan 2015). The reason is that the field of research is still comparatively young in terms of academic investigation.

The other aspect that comes into play here is the fact that filmic adaptations have often been, if at all, examined only from the angle of literature and media studies.

This naturally led to a very different angle of investigation, as these studies lack the insight of the researcher who is also a practitioner in the field—the point of view of the artist.

I argue that this aspect should and ultimately cannot be neglected, at least not in the field of animation studies. This is because the deeper understanding of the artistic creation process will enable entirely new and, most importantly, factually correct insights into the rationale of any artistic adaptation for animation. Therefore, the topic is approached here through case studies of animated adaptations and through interviews with the filmmakers.

The author also shares the creation process of some of his own films, which negotiate Gothic adaptation. In these cases, he presents only verifiable facts, together with peer review--based assessments to balance artistic subjectivity with objective evaluation.

To start this investigation, it is still necessary to understand the adapted literature genre better. This will make it possible to evaluate later on, if the animated adaptations are succeeding in transposing the source material to the screen.

What is Gothic Literature?

The academic discussion about a precise definition of the term "Gothic literature" is still and continuously ongoing in literature studies. But the focus of this investigation is not to add to and engage with this discussion. It would prove impossible for me to discuss all of the various definitions, theories, and hypotheses about the Gothic novel here, and it is not what I am aiming for. The goal of this chapter is to primarily engage with the special challenges posed by adapting literature that includes elements of the supernatural, weird, and darker aspects of the human soul. Often sub-summarized by the terms "horror" and "dark fantasy," yet going beyond that, this genre has many facets, and the range of the genre keeps expanding.

Therefore, the scope of examples and aspects negotiated here will not be limited to a rigid definition of the genre, as it might be appropriate for literature studies.

Instead, a wider kaleidoscope of literature with Gothic elements is embraced for examining their adapted animation counterparts.

Having said that, a look at what is commonly is perceived as Gothic literature is necessary to create a foundation for the following discussions on the adapted animation counterparts.

Melani (2012) offers the following definition: "The English Gothic novel began with Horace Walpole's *The Castle of Otranto* (1765), which was enormously popular and quickly imitated by other novelists and soon became a recognizable genre."

This point of view is often supported in literature scholarship, for example, by Cornwell (2012, 64) and Murray (n.d.). *The Castle of Otranto* proved to be the starting point for the development of the whole genre.

More famous works soon followed, which inspired a continuation of the genre until today:

> "During the mid-nineteenth century in America, Nathaniel Hawthorne and Edgar Allen Poe were writing Gothic tales. At the end of the nineteenth century, Bram Stoker's *Dracula* (1897) and Oscar Wilde's *The Picture of Dorian Gray* continued the Gothic tradition. Today, the Gothic remains popular in the novels of Steven King and Anne Rice as well as in films like Tim Burton's *Corpse Bride*." (Murray n.d.)

The narrative content of these still-widely-known novels (not the least through a never-ending stream of filmic adaptations) already suggests the thematic framework that defines Gothic literature, not only in a less academically rigorous public perception but also in academic discussion. Lilia Melani (2002) has assembled a list of narrative elements and plot devices that can be seen as indicators to identify a work as Gothic:

- "A castle, ruined or intact, haunted or not,
- Ruined buildings which are sinister or which arouse a pleasing melancholy,
- Dungeons, underground passages, crypts, and catacombs which, in modern houses, become spooky basements or attics,
- Labyrinths, dark corridors, and winding stairs,
- Shadows, a beam of moonlight in the blackness, a flickering candle, or the only source of light failing (a candle blown out or an electric failure),
- Extreme landscapes, like rugged mountains, thick forests, or icy wastes, and extreme weather,
- Omens and ancestral curses,
- Magic, supernatural manifestations, or the suggestion of the supernatural,
- A passion-driven, willful villain-hero or villain,
- A curious heroine with a tendency to faint and a need to be rescued–frequently,
- A hero whose true identity is revealed by the end of the novel,
- Horrifying (or terrifying) events or the threat of such happenings."

In my opinion, I found this comprehensive yet non-limiting assembly of topics highly convincing.

It embraces the prospect of a wider definition of the genre and goes a long way toward explaining the diversity within the field. Based on this list, a darkly romantic period novel taking place in an old castle and a modern ghost story could equally qualify as Gothic literature in a wider sense.

Melani concludes her essay with a fitting summary that addresses the underlying universal concepts of the human condition and the wider appeal of Gothic literature:

> "The Gothic creates feelings of gloom, mystery, and suspense and tends to the dramatic and the sensational, like incest,

> diabolism, and nameless terrors. Most of us immediately recognize the Gothic (even if we don't know the name) when we encounter it in novels, poetry, plays, movies, and TV series. For some of us—and I include myself, the prospect of safely experiencing dread or horror is thrilling and enjoyable."

This eloquently explains the lasting fascination and continuing evolution of the genre, particularly in its various adapted incarnations. In other words, we are immersed in the Gothic in its diverse forms, because it resonates strongly with human nature. Who doesn't like to be afraid? Melani's list allows for a wider categorization of the genre. This opens up the options for analyzing a wider range of literary source material and the respective animated adaptations.

Possibly, the most important is the notion that a plethora of classic and contemporary literary works might defy a categorization as Gothic literature in the strictest sense yet contain clearly Gothic elements in significant amounts. Two examples will further explain what I mean here:

The dark magic in the *Harry Potter* book series (Rowling 1997–2007) is certainly a very Gothic element, as are the haunted castle of Hogwarts and many other elements in the books. Arguably, *Harry Potter* would therefore even fully qualify as a piece of Gothic literature, although it might venture outside the classical tropes of the canon at times.

This point of view is shared by Elizabeth Murray (n.d.) in her thorough examination of this specific topic: "The *Harry Potter* series possesses many commonalities (atmosphere and setting, emphasis on the past, use of the supernatural, heroes, heroines, and villains, and mystery) with classic Gothic texts like *The Mysteries of Udolpho, The Castle of Otranto*, and *Frankenstein*."

Pre-empting the soon-to-follow discussion about adapting Gothic literature for animation, it is worth mentioning that the filmic adaptations of the series had only one option to go to visualize the Gothic, that is, supernatural elements of the source novels: digital animation and visual effects.

The other case where a full classification as a Gothic piece of work might not apply, yet Gothic elements are very present, is another mightily popular book series turned into a global adaptation franchise: *The Lord of the Rings* (*TLOTR*) (Tolkien 1954–1974).

Beyond any reasonable doubt, *TLOTR* must be seen as the prime example and definitely the defining work of the genre and the concept of high fantasy. Yet, closer inspection quickly reveals that there are a multitude of Gothic elements present in the books: first and foremost, the dark powers of the one ring, and then, also the sorcery, dark magic, supernatural events and creatures, an army of the dead, and so on.

This is only logical because in creating *TLOTR* Tolkien had drawn from multiple sources, including ancient and medieval mythologies—sources Gothic literature has been inspired by as well.

Without a doubt, Tolkien was fully aware of the Gothic tradition, and one might even suspect a resonance of Mary Shelley's *Frakenstein* in the ungodly creature Gollum and the creation of the superpowered Uruk-Hai in the laboratories of the dark sorcerer Saruman.

Fact is the crucial role that digital animation and motion capture play to bring Gollum to life in the film adaptations by Peter Jackson (2001–2003). One might very convincingly argue that only the application of these techniques enabled a believable integration of this fantastic creature (altered by the dark powers of the ring) into a live-action environment.

The equivalent of Gollum in *TLOTR* is Dobby, the house-elf, in the *Harry Potter* films, (dirs. Columbus, Cuaron, Newell, Yates 2001-2011) a fantastic creature brought to life by the magic of animation (a good case for animators as our modern sorcerers). Both series, *Harry Potter* and *TLOTR*, are therefore also examples for the increasingly blurred boundaries between live-action and animated films (Oxoby 2003).

Is a pattern already emerging here? Why is animation seemingly more suitable or even indispensable when bringing Gothic novels and dark fantasy alive on screen?
Which specific visual storytelling techniques in animation answer to the requirements of Gothic adaptation in superior ways?

The following sections will deeply investigate this question. But to understand the bigger context, I will begin with a more general examination of the cinematic history of Gothic screen adaptations.

The Connection between Gothic Literature and Animated Adaptation

> "Gothic, as a genre born in darkness, has a natural affinity with the cinema."
>
> Heidi Kaye (2012, 239)

Moreover, in our modern media landscape, the attention of the modern audience has often shifted from the literary source to the adapted version. Therefore, the enduring quality of the literary source can increasingly be deducted from its lasting popularity for adaptation.

Gothic literature has been used as a major source for cinematic adaptation in live-action movies from the earliest days of the moving image (see, e.g., *Nosferatu* [Murnau 1922], which is, according to Kaye [2012, 242], "an uncredited retelling of Dracula").

Kaye explains further: "The Gothic texts that have been most influential in cinema are the nineteenth century works, Mary Shelley's *Frankenstein*, Robert Louis Stevenson's *Dr. Jekyll and Mr. Hyde*, and Bram Stoker's *Dracula*."
Kamilla Elliott (2008, 24–25) concurs that "most scholars of gothic film identify James Whale's *Frankenstein* (1931), Tod Browning's *Dracula* (1931), and Rouben Mamoulian's *Dr. Jekyll and Mr. Hyde* (1931) as a foundational triptych, from which they in turn look back to earlier Gothic films and forward to later ones."

Their shared hypothesis is further supported by the fact that the recent TV series *Penny Dreadful* (Logan 2014–present) successfully combines characters and plot elements precisely from these three novels. The series has been extremely well reviewed and has been extraordinarily successful, proving how much these classic Gothic narratives still resonate with a modern audience.

Heidi Kaye, in her insightful essay "Gothic Film" (2012, 239), also provides insight into the early link between animation and the visualization of the fantastic:

> "Stage magician Georges Méliès experimented with effects such as disappearances, stop-motion animation, double exposure, running film in reverse, and optical illusion rooms with angled walls and floors which made an actor seem to grow from dwarf to giant. Not surprisingly, Gothic films created spectacles and excited audiences' emotional responses, just as Gothic novels had always done."

Georges Méliès (1861–1938) was one of the most important film pioneers of early cinema to create landmark films such as *A Trip to the Moon* (1902) and *The Impossible Voyage* (1904).

His work is also to be seen in line with the presentation of animation as performance, delivered by a stage magician and the incorporation of animation as almost a "magical trick" within such framework.

Second, it is also animation in a role that supports live-action filmmaking—more in the role of early special or visual effects.

The history and development of special and visual effects continued throughout the following decades of film history and led to new artistic heights, including the aforementioned examples.

While the role of experimental animation and character animation is integral within these developments, I want to disregard live-action/animation hybrids in further course.

For clarity purposes, I want to focus on investigating the relationship between animation in its "pure" form and Gothic literature.

Animation as a standalone medium developed to full bloom throughout the 1920s and early 1930s, in such diverse techniques as traditional hand-drawn animation and stop motion in its various incarnations: puppet animation and "flat" cutout animation.

The majority of productions throughout that time period were animated short films, until the first widely recognized and commercially successful animated feature film emerged: Disney's *Snow White and the Seven Dwarfs* (Hand 1937).

While it is impossible to fully represent the list of achievements and milestone films during that era, a few other landmark films should be named.

The oldest surviving animated feature film *The Adventures of Prince Achmed* by Lotte Reiniger (1926) and *The Skeleton Dance* (Disney 1929), the first entry in Disney's *Silly Symphonies* short-film series. Quite obviously, I choose these three examples, because they feature strong Gothic elements.

Reverting back to the list of Melani, we will find magic, the supernatural (the witch and her sorcery in *Snow White*, sorcerers and magical creatures in *Prince Achmed*, and the undead in *Skeleton Dance*), haunted forests, and dark and creepy environments. But either these are not really adaptations (in the case of *Skeleton Dance*), or the source material is not widely accepted as "Gothic" in nature (in the case of *Snow White* and *Prince Achmed*, which would primarily be recognized as fairy tales).

Equally important is the fact that the prime target audience for these films were families, meaning children. That held animated adaptations back for a long time to push the scary, downright frightening elements of Gothic literature to its very extremes and therefore come up with an animated adaptation that "pulls no punches." Having said that, some of these scenes, for example, the scenes with the witch of the haunted forest in *Snow White* are certain to get (very young) children scared, testing limits.

The macabre aspects of *The Skeleton Dance* are also amazingly daring, dating from an age when today's prevalent political correctness was largely unknown.

But still, these aspects are not held up throughout the entirety of the movie; in *Snow White*, the extremely Gothic moments are outnumbered by the literally lighter scenes in tone and setting.

Similarly, the character and production design of *The Skeleton Dance* do not truly push the Gothic aspects of the material, as it largely adapts a "cartoony" rounded approach for the characters.

Rall and Jernigan (2015), therefore, claim that it took considerably long before adaptations began to surface in animation that could be considered Gothic in any strict sense. They identified the 1953 animated short film *The Tell-Tale Heart* (Parmelee) as a notable early example that is widely recognized as one of the first animated horror films. It is based on the short story of the same name by Edgar Allan Poe, whose work is seen as one of the defining examples of Gothic literature and has been acknowledged as highly influential in transforming and expanding earlier definitions of the genre. Botting (1996) singles out Poe as one of Gothic literature's major figures in his chapter on "American Gothic." Andrew Smith (2007, 63) supports this view, stating that "Poe's contribution to the development of an American Gothic tradition cannot be underestimated."

Poe can therefore undoubtedly be seen as a major figure of Gothic literature.

Animated adaptations of his works are ideally suited to be examined in this context.

The author formulated a set of key research questions to investigate all of the following case studies:

- What has been changed in the adaptations versus the original story or poem?
- How is the mood evoked in the literary source re-created in the animated adaptation?

Responding to this question will enable more concrete answers to the often referred to necessity of retaining the "spirit" of the original, if not all plot details.

- What has been added through the means of filmic language (visuals, music, sound, and narration)?
- What are the visual means of interpretation that define visual equivalents of literary concepts?
- Which of these concepts are unique to animation (from the specific vocabulary of animation), and why do they relate so well to the narrative demands of Gothic literature?

Let's take a look now how two animated short films answered to these specific requirements in adapting two classic works by E.A. Poe.

Adapting E.A. Poe for Animation: *The Tell-Tale Heart* (1953) by Ted Parmelee and *The Raven* (1999) by Hannes Rall

I chose these two works for several reasons: First of all, they adapt two of the most popular works of Poe that also cover different aspects of his work: One is a short story, and the other is a poem. Second, these choices combine a groundbreaking work from the 1950s with a much later interpretation that can almost be seen as contemporary.

Lastly, I gained extraordinary insight into the artistic creation process—in the case of Parmelee, through access to his production notes.

For *The Raven*, I can rely on my own recollections and production documentation.

I do complement these documents with secondary sources and peer review.

Both works have received wide acclaim in terms of critical reception and can be justifiably established as examples for successful adaptations.

The Tell-Tale Heart

The Tell-Tale Heart, one of Poe's best known short stories, is a frightening first-person account of an objectively senseless killing of an old man, narrated by the murderer himself. The tone of this telling is factual and devoid of emotion and, therefore, all the more horrifying. The narrator strives to explain his rationale for the cruel deed and permanently insists on his mental sanity, which makes the entire lack of it completely obvious. The reader becomes complicit with the protagonist and is literally entering the head of a madman, a psychotic killer. Any adaptation for an audiovisual medium has to face the challenge to define an appropriate way to recreate this highly individualized reading experience through other means.

Figure 4.1: Animation background painting by Paul Julian from Ted Parmelee's *The Tell-Tale Heart* (1953). (From *The Tell-Tale Heart*. ©1953 renewed 1981 Columbia Pictures Industries. All rights reserved. Courtesy of Columbia Pictures.)

World-renowned animation historian Giannalberto Bendazzi (2015b) writes about Ted Parmelee's adaptation in his *Animation: A World History*, Vol. 2 (2015, p. 11):

> "*The Tell-Tale-Heart* was innovative by virtue of being a noncomical cartoon.
>
> (…) it emphasized the nightmarish qualities of the story and was a first example of an animated horror movie. The staff included star voice actor James Mason, director Ted Parmelee (1912–1964), scrlptwrlter Blll Scott and especially scene designer Paul Julian, one of the best of American animation ever."

The artistic excellence of the film and its unique and innovative approach to adaptation were immediately noticed through its critical reception. The film was nominated for an Academy Award in 1954 and was later included in the book *The 50 Greatest Cartoons* by the renowned animation historian Jerry Beck (1994). This book presented the titular most popular cartoons, as selected by 1000 animation professionals—a clear verdict through peer review.

Despite the fact that the film is correctly credited to Ted Parmelee as director, one could arguably identify the ingenious designer and background painter Paul Julian as the major artistic force behind the film. His inventive staging elevated the film to artistic heights that perfectly express the tense atmosphere, as Brandie(2013) concurs: "Paul Julian crafted the eerie, gorgeously animated backdrops for the action (with Pat Matthews contributing the character animation), which set an immediate tone of dread and despair."

Giannalberto Bendazzi (2015a) states: "In my opinion animation is an ace up your sleeve, because animation can invent things that you don't have to look for in the reality, in the real world. So the language of animation is physically based on the possibility to invent, to paint, to mold, to create the things that you are filming. Therefore, the style of the painter or the draftsman is fundamental for telling a story."

Readers of this book are already familiar with Julian's outstanding work through Giannalberto Bendazzi's critical praise of his work for *The Hangman* (Goldman, Julian 1964) in the introductory interview—another adaptation that is much elevated by the visual contributions of Julian. *The Hangman* carries noticeable Gothic elements and can be seen as a continuation of the previous groundbreaking work with the earlier Poe adaptation.

On *The Tell-Tale Heart*, Bendazzi comments that "(…) not by chance, the drawings, the paintings of Paul Julian had been used for illustrating the famous *Tell-Tale Heart* made by UPA. So the style, the language of animation in this sense is very important because that drives you to a special world. That is not any available world. It is the world which is within the head of the artist."

Figure 4.2: Animation background painting by Paul Julian from Ted Parmelee's *The Tell-Tale Heart* (1953). (From *The Tell-Tale Heart*. ©1953 renewed 1981 Columbia Pictures Industries. All rights reserved. Courtesy of Columbia Pictures.)

In animation, the term staging describes the placement of character against background in a way that directs the attention of the audience to achieve the strongest emotional impact through the visual storytelling. The interior of the house in which the story takes place in *The Tell-Tale Heart* is heavily stylized to resonate with the dramatic developments in the story.

Ted Parmelee (1953) describes his approach to the background design in meticulous detail: "We decided not to set the stage in a modern environment. We found, to our own amusement, that the black walnut furnishings of the houses of the 80's presented an inherently disturbing stage in themselves." Parmelee fully realized the central importance of the house's design for the artistic success of the work: "The house that appeared normal to the madman could not be an ordinary house for anyone else."

Figure 4.3: Production still from Ted Parmelee's *The Tell-Tale Heart* (1953). (From The Tell-Tale Heart. ©1953 renewed 1981 Columbia Pictures Industries. All rights reserved. Courtesy of Columbia Pictures.)

Bendazzi offers an interesting analysis and, if you will, criticism of the narrative point of view applied for *The Tell-Tale Heart:*

> "So let us make a comparison between the *Tell-Tale Heart* and *The Hangman*. They are painted by the same person and the animation is relatively limited in both cases. What is the limitation of *The Tell-Tale Heart*? It is the fact that you see the face of the old man. Of the victim. You never see the face of the killer, which is good. But you see the face of the victim, which is not good, because in this case, you have an individual, you recognise those features, so this special person is the victim, and you don't care very much about him because he is not you. If you wouldn't see his face, you would care for him, because it could be you."

I would not entirely agree with this opinion, as I recognize a narrative necessity for showing either the victim or the murderer. In other words, it is highly doubtable that the storytelling without showing either would work at all. But what the remarks really tell us is the high relevance of visual storytelling decisions in relation to the original story.

What exactly do I show visually? What angle precisely is taken, which perspective and point of view? How do I select the images to demonstrate my choice?

As the film starts to move towards its climax, animation and background elements become increasingly nonrepresentational to illustrate the protagonist's dramatic descent into madness, taking the spectator through an "area of complete sound and graphic abstraction." This animation can therefore be seen as a prime example of Paul Wells' theory about the strength of animation to express atmosphere and internal mental, which states: "Animation accentuates the intended 'feeling' of the text through its very abstractness in the use of colour form and movement" (2002, 208). The film excels at creating visual equivalents for the Gothic elements of the source material by a perfectly matching use of animation techniques, as the "rational self" of the spectator is facing the "malign environment," which is visualized through the expressively lighted and highly stylized background design. The film's exploration of humanity's psychological limits is specifically addressed by "establishing a point of view for the madman" (see Parmelee) and therefore forcing the audience to take on his persona (Rall, Jernigan, ibid, 43)."

In summary, the visual choices, particularly in staging; limitation of movement; and color, all serve the storytelling in an almost-perfect way. They are deliberately selected to enable the narrative purpose—being eyewitness, if not accomplice for a murderous crime.

Subsequently, I want to investigate further examples of the closely linked relationship between narrative intent and visual storytelling choices. In 1999, I adapted Poe's still-highly-popular poem *The Raven* as an animated short film. At that point in time, I only knew about the legendary reputation of Paul Julian's work for *The Tell-Tale*

Heart, yet I had not even seen the film. In fact, my major inspiration for creating an animated adaptation was its musical adaptation as a pop song by the Alan Parsons Project (*The Raven* on *Tales of Mystery and Imagination*, 1974). Its haunting use of a repetitive knocking pattern opened my eyes to the rhythmic qualities of the poem, and a plethora of images unfolded in my imagination. Ultimately, my adaptation bore little resemblance to the narrative and flow of the Alan Parsons version, yet it had sparked my creativity.

Moreover, the fact that there was a highly successful pop-music adaptation of his major works in the 1970s proves that Poe's writings continue to inspire artists from diverse fields in the modern age.

The Raven by Hannes Rall (1999)

Figure 4.4: Production stills from Hannes Rall's *The Raven* (2009).

Taylor (2009) states that "Poe's most famous poem, *The Raven*, with its echoing refrain of 'Nevermore', is a haunting hymn to lost love and the finality of death, tinged (as is so much of Poe's writing) with the sense that madness is waiting round the corner and there's nothing we can do to avoid it. In this sense he is a very modern writer."

The Raven enjoys enduring popularity in pop culture to this day. It has been frequently adapted and parodied for different media such as films, animation, and comics. Such parodies include the comics produced for *MAD* magazine. *MAD About The Raven* examines the 11 times when *MAD* magazine uses *The Raven* as a vehicle of parody either against something external to the poem or to parody Poe and/or his most famous work (Eddings, 2013).

When it comes to film and animation adaptations, spoofs and parodies also outnumber straightforward or faithful adaptations, taking significant liberties with the source material:

The Simpsons episode *Treehouse of Horror* (dir. Archer 1992) parodies the poem as well: In the third segment, a satire of Poe's *The Raven*, a grief-stricken Homer, is tormented by bad bird Bart. (Banks, nd)

Roger Corman directed a (1963) adaptation, starring the horror icons Boris Karloff and Vincent Price, again not exactly replicating the melancholic tone of the original poem: "In this tongue-in-cheek movie inspired by Poe's poem, Dr. Craven is the son of a great sorcerer (now dead) who was once himself quite skilled at that profession, but has since abandoned it. One evening, a cowardly fool of a magician named Bedlo comes to Craven for help—the evil Scarabus has turned him into a raven and he needs someone to change him back. He also tells the reluctant wizard that Craven's long-lost wife Lenore, whom he loved greatly and thought dead, is living with the despised Scarabus." (Yousten, nd)

One of the major reasons for the frequent deviations from the content of the poem is the difficulty in transferring the short and relatively open narrative to the needed complexity of a feature-film plot. That is why, serious and faithful interpretations are rather found in adaptations as comic short stories or short films. American comic artist Richard Corben (1974) has repeatedly adapted *The Raven* in comic form, first, in issue #67 of *Creepy* (1974, later collected in 2005's *Edgar Allan Poe: The Fall of the House of Usher and Other Tales of Terror*) and later in *The Raven and the Red Death* (2013). In his 1974 adaptation, Corben creates wonderfully atmospheric imagery in his trademark style, while sticking relatively closely to the openness of the narrative in the poem. He adds only subtle interpretation and succeeds in keeping the haunting mood intact. In the newer 2013 version, he strays further from the original:

> "This time around, Corben is a little looser in his adaptation. When we first see the protagonist, he appears to be actually with Lenore, holding her in his arms as he hears the 'tap, tap, tap' on his chamber door. The embrace soon becomes hot and heavy, and then right after another series of taps, we realize that it is the memory of Lenora that the man now holds, not the actual woman. It would appear that Corben has shifted back to focus of Poe's original narrative poem, if not for the abrupt change in paneling style four pages from the end. This is the climax of the tale, where the protagonist directly, and violently (another liberty Corben takes with the original), confronts the mysterious bird. Given the story's earlier shifts in psychological perspective, one isn't sure if this final confrontation is actually occurring, or if the change in paneling is indicative of yet another state of mind."
>
> (Royal 2013)

Interestingly, the author has created a similar plot twist in his own animated interpretation of "The Raven" (1999), preceding this comic adaptation by 14 years: The unnamed protagonist attacks the bird, violently demanding to be told about Lenore's whereabouts. In his rage, he finally kills the titular raven, only to see the bird transforming into the long-lost Lenore before his very eyes. However, this change from the original was met with critical approval: "Rall doesn't stick entirely to the poem, giving it a twist that Poe himself would certainly have approved. Excellent and striking." (Zimmer, 2000)

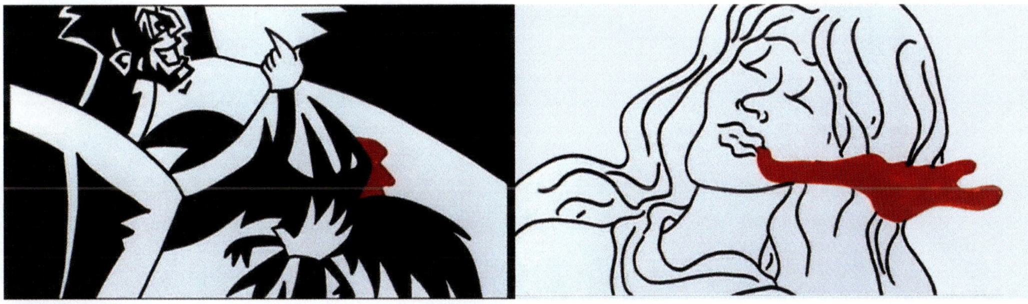

Figure 4.5: The new ending from Hannes Rall's adaptation of *The Raven* (1999).

Both adaptations (Rall 1999, Corben 2013) can be seen as further proof for the theory that an expansion of the narrative content of the adapted material can be successful, if these are in tone with mood, atmosphere, and artistic intent of the original author.

These two examples substantiate the rather-vague idea of keeping the adaptation in line with the spirit of the adapted original work: The reviewer (Zimmer) can very well imagine that Poe himself could have come up with a similar idea.

> Hughes (2001) concurs: "It's a very loose interpretation of Edgar Allan Poe's poem made in stark black, white and red images that are evocative of expressionist woodcuts. *Der Rabe* is kinetic and fluid all at the same time and though Poe's lines are essentially abandoned, the dark and disturbing feel of his poem remain."

These opinions further strengthen support for the theory that a change of the narrative for adaptation in another medium can work to the advantage of the emerging filmic work.

Zimmer (ibid) has also something to say about the specific graphic and cinematic qualities of the film, elements he obviously approves of in the context of adapting the poem for the screen: "Rall's intriguing variation on the famed poem *The Raven* gives us black, white and red animation, rendered in a highly angular German expressionist style, combined with sweeping vertiginous motions."

Figure 4.6: Collage of images from *The Raven* (Rall 1999).

> "The expressive graphics and brilliant animation give the film its intense atmosphere."
>
> (Ade 2004)

As rightfully pointed out by the reviewers, I chose German expressionism as my major source of inspiration for the art style. I have always been an admirer of the work of the German expressionist artistic group *Die Brücke*. Of special note for me was the work of Ernst Ludwig Kirchner (1880–1939). I wanted to transfer the raw power of his woodcut work to the moving image and was striving to emulate the aesthetics of woodcut through drawings with ink on paper.

Figure 4.7: Evident stylistic influences of expressionist woodcut in *The Raven.*

But I also combined these influences with my own, unavoidably more modern artistic sensibilities. My fascination for visual storytelling had been sparked by my fascination for comics, particularly the avant-garde works of the artists published in Art Spiegelman's and Francoise Mouly's magazine *Raw* (1980–1991).

Artists to mention as major influences from that magazine are definitely the brilliant Argentinian artist Muñoz and the Italian artist Lorenzo Mattotti.

My intent was to evolve a new and unique art style through the amalgamation of these different elements that reflects the influences but also develops them significantly beyond a mere pastiche. It is further important to mention that any artist cannot help but bring their own (and highly individual) artistic "signature" to the table, particularly in an immediate reflection of artistic handwriting through drawing.

In the case of the cited influences from comic artists, I was also able to add the element of motion to whatever I chose to adapt from these sources for my own style.

Similar to the adaptation of a purely written text, a cinematic adaptation offers something that a comic cannot: time-based storytelling through movement and sound.

Figure 4.8: Collage of images from *The Raven* (Rall 1999), demonstrating the kinetic energy of animation drawing.

> "Definitely one of the highlights of the collection, this animated adaptation of Edgar Allan Poe's classic poem is striking and powerful. German voice-over star's Hans Paetsch low, raspy narration perfectly accompanies writer/director/animator Hannes Rall's bold, looming images."
>
> (Bozdech 2000)

Zimmer (ibid) agrees: "The animation is bold and confident, and perfectly married to the monotone narration by Paetsch."

Bruno H. Piché (2009) also mentions the importance of Hans Paetsch's contribution: "*Der Rabe*, an animated short film by the animator and illustrator Hannes Rall, with the participation of one of the most popular German voice actors over decades, Hans Paetsch. Through the basic markmaking, the bold drawing, and by employing the colours black and red, through the fatal swell of the musical soundtrack, in the agonic and desperate cadence of the brittle and nocturnal voice and the fragmented recitation from the poem: In all of that you can recognize a sovereig reflection of the oldest expressionist esthetic bursting out with renewed vigor in 1998."

Piché describes in suitably poetical fashion how the diverse elements of cinematic adaptation come together to create a whole that is bigger than the sum of its parts:

> "Through the choice of the fine arts inspired graphic style, the colour design, the voice of the narrator and last but not least the musical soundtrack a new piece of audiovisual art is created that strongly reflects yet ultimately transcends the literary source material."

In the case of *The Raven* I had decided to commission a soundtrack that is entirely composed of music and suggests sound effects through accents in the music itself.

The score was created by Eckart Gadow, who has now become my most frequent longtime collaborator for soundtrack. As diverse reviewers have attested previously, his work was very successful in adding to the dark atmosphere of the film. It also supported the dramatic arc of the story perfectly through its wide range of dynamics and symphonic opulence.

Gadow also remained on board for my following adaptation, as did the famous voice actor Hans Paetsch. This film once again reflected my fascination with dark and haunting topics, not the least because I feel that these themes can strongly correspond with my artistic style(s).

In 2003, I chose to adapt another poem, or, more precisely, a very popular ballad, a German "Volksballade" with strong Gothic elements: *Der Erlkönig* (*The Erl-King*) by Johann Wolfgang von Goethe.

Two other animation directors of renown adapted the same source material in 2002 (Benny Zelkowicz) and 2015 (Georges Schwizgebel), respectively. Therefore, this poem provides the ideal subject for an expansion of this study through a comparative examination of all three adaptations. Before we take a closer look at these adaptations, a deeper insight into the tradition of supernatural ballads will provide the necessary context.

Classic Ballads, the Supernatural, and Animated Storytelling

While ballads formally resemble poems (i.e., employing verse, stanza, rhymes, and a metric), they tell stories in a condensed form by using scenic settings. A ballad is often narrated by several protagonists; parts of the action can be conveyed through dialogue sequences.

Classic ballads can offer short and concise linear narratives, often with a surprising twist in the end. This category of poems can therefore deliver a strong structure for animated storytelling, adding dramatic weight to (potentially) strong visuals.

That is one of the key reasons why they are very suitable for adaptation for an animated short film: They can provide an ideal match in length and narrative structure.

Examples are rather rare in modern poetry, but there are plenty of historic examples:

Historically, a major distinction is made between the folk ballads of the fifteenth and sixteenth centuries and the artistic ballads of the following centuries. The authors of these simple folktales are usually unknown. From then, nineteenth century on, prestigious writers would dedicate themselves to the genre:

Prominent literary figures such as Robert Burns and Sir Walter Scott in Scotland wrote their own ballads, using the form to create their own artistic product. In England, William Wordsworth and Samuel Taylor Coleridge compiled a collection of lyrical ballads in 1798, including Coleridge's "The Rime of the Ancient Mariner." Others include Friedrich Schiller's "Bürgschaft" and "Der Handschuh" in Germany; Clemens Brentano's "Lore Lay"; Ludwig Uhland's "Des Sängers Fluch"; Annette von Droste-Hülshoff's "Der Knabe im Moor" and "Der Schlosself"; Conrad Ferdinand Meyer's "Die Füße im Feuer"; Theodor Fontane's "Die Brück' am Tay" and "John Maynard"; and Johann Gabriel Seidl's "Die Uhr." One of the most famous collections of classic German ballads is the "Romanzero" by Heinrich Heine—in his time, the term "Romanze" was synonymous with "ballad".

Supernatural ballads emerged from the time of Goethe onward, a tradition primarily started by himself through his ballads "Der Fischer" ("The Fisherman" 1778) and "Erlkönig" ("The Erl-King" 1782).

Diane Long Hoeveler reminds of scholarly opinions to include classic German ballads in the Gothic canon or to define them as important precursors of the genre in her essay *Gothic Ballads* (2012). She explicitly names *The Erl-King* as an example for such consideration (ibid, 505).

In the romantic era, a lot of ballads were created, which were negotiating the magical forces in nature and the supernatural. The romantics such as Wordsworth, Coleridge, and Keats were attracted to the simple and natural style of the traditional folk ballads, encouraging them to imitate the style.

The ability of animators to depict the fantastic and magical through the specific toolset of their art form naturally led to a comparatively high number of adaptations from that field: The famous adaptation of Goethe's *The Sorcerer's Apprentice* in *Fantasia* (1942) might come to mind first, but there have been many other examples over the years.

The Erl-King Animated: A Comparative Study

Der Erlkönig (The Erl-King) was written by Johann Wolfgang von Goethe originally for the musical *Die Fischerin* (1782) and has over the years become one of his most popular ballads. It was used as the basis for several "Lieder" (songs) by German composers, the most popular one certainly being Schubert's composition *Der Erlkönig*:

> "Erlkönig, also called Erl-King or Elf-King, song setting by Franz Schubert, written in 1815 and based on a 1782 poem of the same name by Johann Wolfgang von Goethe. 'Erlkönig' is considered by many to be one of the greatest ballads ever penned. The song was written for two performers, a singer and a pianist, and it packs a remarkable amount of tension and drama into a mere four minutes. Its effectiveness is doubly impressive because Schubert was only 18 years old when he composed it."
>
> (Schwarm 2014)

The poem has remained highly popular as a source of inspiration for musicians up to this day. The 2002 German singer and songwriter Achim Reichel released a rock version on his album *Wilder Wassermann*, while the pagan folk project *Falkenstein* released a song version of the poem in 2008.

The Erl-King has been adapted three times as an animated short film, in different animated techniques: By Benny Zelkowicz as a sand animation in 2002, by the author of this book as a hand-drawn animated short in 2003, and by Swiss animator Georges Schwizgebel as painting under camera in 2015.

The reason for the fascination the poem exacts on animators quickly becomes obvious when looking at the original:

The Erl-King

by Johann Wolfgang von Goethe (1782)
Translated by Edgar Alfred Bowring (1853)

Who rides there so late through the night dark and drear?
The father it is, with his infant so dear;
He holdeth the boy tightly clasp'd in his arm,
He holdeth him safely, he keepeth him warm.

"My son, wherefore seek'st thou thy face thus to hide?"
"Look, father, the Erl-King is close by our side!
Dost see not the Erl-King, with crown and with train?"
"My son, 'tis the mist rising over the plain."

"Oh, come, thou dear infant! oh come thou with me!
For many a game I will play there with thee;
On my strand, lovely flowers their blossoms unfold,
My mother shall grace thee with garments of gold."

Figure 4.9: Illustration to Goethe's "Erlkönig" by Moritz von Schwind (1917).

"My father, my father, and dost thou not hear
The words that the Erl-King now breathes
in mine ear?"
"Be calm, dearest child, 'tis thy fancy
deceives;
'Tis the sad wind that sighs through the
withering leaves."

"Wilt go, then, dear infant, wilt go with me
there?
My daughters shall tend thee with sisterly
care;
My daughters by night their glad festival
keep,
They'll dance thee, and rock thee, and sing
thee to sleep."

"My father, my father, and dost thou
not see,
How the Erl-King his daughters has
brought here for me?"
"My darling, my darling, I see it aright,
'Tis the aged grey willows deceiving thy
sight."

Figure 4.10: "Der Erlkönig" (ca. 1910), Illustration by Albert Sterner.

"I love thee, I'm charm'd by thy beauty, dear boy!
And if thou'rt unwilling, then force I'll employ."
"My father, my father, he seizes me fast,
For sorely the Erl-King has hurt me at last."

"The father now gallops, with terror half wild,
He grasps in his arms the poor shuddering child;
He reaches his courtyard with toil and with dread, –
The child in his arms finds he motionless, dead."

Several observations can be made to connect the inherent narrative qualities of the poem with its specific suitability for animated adaptation.

First of all, "Der Erlkönig," as many poems, will leave spaces that the reader has to fill with his own imagination.

- It remains unclear why the boy knows about the "Erl-King" and why he is immediately afraid of him, despite the Erl-King's initially friendly demeanor.
- It is never explained why the narrative tense changes from the present to the past at the

end of the poem. Logically speaking, the opposite would make sense: Beginning in the past, arriving in the present. However, great dramatic effect is achieved by this reversal.

- Finally, the actual reason for the death of the child is never explained concretely. Was he sick to start with? Has the Erl-King actively killed the child ("And if thou'rt unwilling, then force I'll employ")?

Any adaptation for a visual or audio-visual medium can address these deliberate gaps differently, without ever raising any questions about faithfulness, as the original does not provide answers. This openness is freeing as well as challenging at the same time.

Many decisions must be taken: One possible solution could be to explain the child's immediate fear of the Erl-King by a particularly terrifying look of the supernatural being.

The lack of a concrete description of the outer appearance of the mysterious Erl-King invites and opens up for a wide variety of visual interpretations, without ever contradicting the source material. There is a strong narrative structure and a "twist" ending, which can be perfectly adapted for the medium of animated short film. On the practical side, the length of the poem will not exceed 8 minutes, even when narrated completely, and still leave room for purely visual sections without any voice-over.

Moreover, the story is driven by perpetual motion and an increase of drama toward the end. That begins with the motif of the father riding with the son and escalates into a wild hunt and attempted escape of the father to save the son.

This emphasis on movement is of course perfectly suited to be transformed into animated visuals, as motion is the very heart of animation and a major distinction from static illustration.

The boy sees the Erl-King and becomes increasingly frightened, while the father does not recognize any visible threat at all: To him, the Erl-King remains invisible until it is too late. This continuously present conflict between the subjective views of the father and the son also plays to animation's strength: the expression of inner states of mind through external appearances and limitless possibilities of stylization.

Closely connected with this subjectivity in the reception of the surroundings is the implication of a continuously evolving and changing form that the Erl-King is taking on. Again, a narrative component that can be extremely well addressed through one visual tool unique to animation is metamorphosis.

Paul Wells (2002, p.136) defines: "The ability of a figure, object, shape or form to relinquish its seemingly fixed properties and mutate into an alternative model. This transformation is literally enacted within the animated film and acts as a model by which the process of change becomes part of the narrative of the film. A form starts as one thing and ends up as something different."

The resemblance of this description with the story idea of an ever-elusive mythical creature in a magical forest is striking. This finding might have instigated similarities in adaptation approaches: When looking at all three animated adaptations of the poem, as stylistically different and narratively diverse they might be, metamorphosis is a visual "trademark" of all of them.

These adaptations will now be negotiated chronologically and discussed with the directors directly. The discussions offer deep insights into the process of creative decision-making and production techniques. First and foremost, however, they can demonstrate how the same source material can be adapted differently yet successfully with diverting adaptation strategies and animation styles.

Interview with Benny Zelkowicz

The ErlKing 2002

Hannes Rall (interviewer)
Benny Zelkowicz (interviewed)

What inspired you in the first place to adapt Goethe's poem *Der Erlkönig (The ErlKing)* as a short animated film?

I first heard the song when I was probably about 10 or 12 years old. My father is a musician, and he played me the song and told me the story—it was most likely a version sung by Dietrich Fischer-Dieskau. I was completely captivated by the way the piano painted a clear image of the horse, the urgency, and the darkness. I was always drawn to dark stories—even at that young age, I had a fondness for Poe, Stephen King, the un-sanitized Grimm Brothers stories, and monster movies of every stripe, so the macabre elements of the song stuck with me. In college, I encountered the version sung by Bryn Terfel and fell in love with it again. Terfel's version is incredible for the shadings he brings to each character, making them each distinct and emotive. The chilly flatness he imbues in the ErlKing is especially effective.

Figure 4.11 : Film still from *The ErlKing* (2002) by Ben Zelkowicz.

Although I was not studying film, I made a few short clay animations in college, including a crude adaptation of Poe's *Tell-Tale Heart*. I wanted to do something with *Der Erlkönig*, but I couldn't think of how to do it in stop motion, which was the only medium I knew at the time. I took some time off after my first year at grad school for animation and moved to Oregon for a TV job. While there, I was eager to start a short film on my own time, and I borrowed a Bolex 16mm camera, built a lightbox, and started work on the *ErlKing*, which had never been far from my mind.

You are using the famous musical version of the ballad by Franz Schubert as the soundtrack for the movie. How did you work to relate images and sound?

I was working to the Bryn Terfel recording, but I knew that there was a good chance that I would not be able to secure the rights. Since I knew I might have to re-edit the film to pair it with another recording, I didn't want to match the timing too exactly. Lines and phrases should sync up, but I didn't want to match particular movements to particular beats. That way, I could make some adjustments to the editing of the film and have it match another recording. Also, I always liked the serendipitous alignments that come when you play any video to any piece of music. I found that by shifting the timing of the recording and by swapping out one singer's take for another's, different bits of the animation would be emphasized. It was like discovering things in my own animation I had not noticed.

I kept a copy of the score next to me, while animating and made notes in it as to where I wanted transitions and key actions. When the film was nearing completion, I contacted Deutsche Grammophon to see if it would be possible to license the Terfel track. They offered it to me at a reasonable rate, but I was advised that it could complicate sending the film to festivals and securing distribution, so I set out to find another recording. I found versions that were free of licensing issues, but none that I thought captured the drama or intensity I wanted. Then, I attended a concert of Mahler songs at CalArts, where I was in graduate school. The singer was Paul Berkholds, a member of the faculty, and I was impressed by the dark timbre of his voice and invited him to record for my film.

He was terrific to work with. We discussed the aspects of the Terfel recording that I liked. He was not particularly fond of the character voicings Terfel did, and I told him to interpret according to his own instincts and not attempt to mimic. He brought Peter Miyamoto aboard as pianist, and we recorded three takes. I opted to not have them perform to a screening of the film in progress, as I wanted them to be able to focus on their own performances and not get caught up in trying to match the timing of the visuals. After the third take, we figured Peter's wrists had enough of triplets.

Figure 4.12: Film still from *The ErlKing* (2002) by Ben Zelkowicz.

What I find extremely interesting is the fact that you actually use the original German Schubert song, only preceded by a few lines in English, to introduce your audience to the topic (I assume). You are not using subtitles in further course of the sung narrative.

Your thoughts?

As a huge fan of silent cinema, I think the images should be sufficient to convey emotion, mood, and narrative. And in this case, I have the added benefit of the Schubert score. I had several people to tell me in the course of making the film that I needed to subtitle it, but I was opposed. Text would draw the eye away from the image, and since the image is constantly shifting, I wanted it to be the sole focus. Also, I think the story is simple enough and is told so clearly through the music and (hopefully) the images that there is no need for the details of the words themselves. Probably, the most common reaction I get is "I didn't understand that at all. I mean, I get that it's a kid who is seeing this weird king figure and is scared and the dad doesn't believe him and at the end the kid is taken away and is dead... but aside from that I didn't get it." People think that there must be more to it than that, since they don't understand the words, but I think that most follow it more than they think they do.

I saw that Raimund Krumme, the famous German animator, was teaching at CalArts at that time. Did that influence your decision in any kind of way?

No, but Raimund was a terrific guide. Both in conversation and by the example of his films, I think I learned a lot about depth from him, about exploring three-dimensional space within the confines of a two-dimensional (2D) film frame. His films are among my favorites, and he was a very inspiring teacher. The last time I saw him was at the premiere of *ErlKing* at Annecy in 2003. Unfortunately, the video dub I had for the screening had a terrible glitch in the sound. I was heartbroken that in front of such a large crowd of peers and fans, the film was deeply compromised! I don't know if he ever saw the film after that. I hope he doesn't think that it was actually the sound I wanted on it!

How did you work out your visual style, which was finally used in the film? What was the visual development process?

I think that a lot of it developed by working in the medium. What always attracted me about sand is that it's a negative medium, meaning the imagery is created by subtracting darkness to create light, rather than traditional pencil animation, which is creating dark lines against a white background. It's also a very physical medium, using my fingertips, palms, heels of my hands, and even my forearms, to create certain effects. In some cases, the particular shape left in the sand by my palm would become the basis for a design. Sand is not generally a good medium for highly detailed images (though I found that Oregon beach sand was incredibly fine, almost a powder, and allowed for much finer lines than the coarser sand found in California beaches), and so, things were conceived in broad shapes, with large areas of dark and light. This was especially true for the *ErlKing* himself (see the answer to your next question below). I originally conceived the film as a sort of moving tableau, like an illustration with small moving pieces at a time, but the music is so driving that I felt the film needed constant motion in order to really mesh with the score.

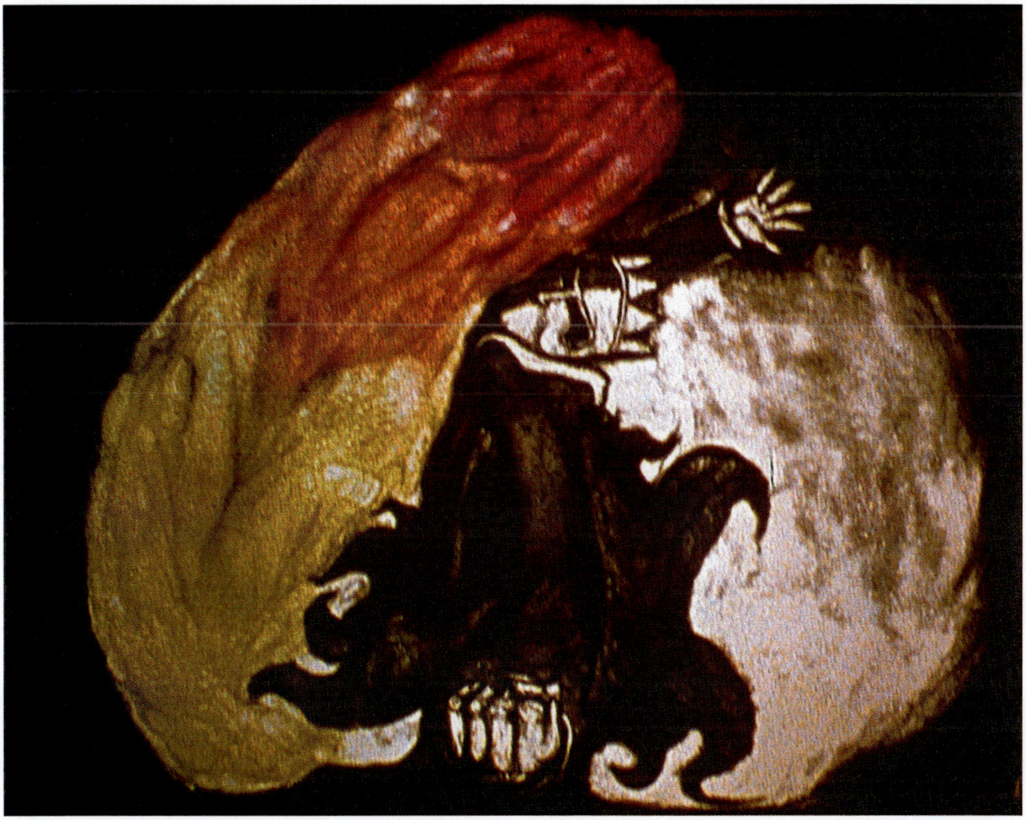

Figure 4.13: Some sparser color touches in *The ErlKing* (2002) by Ben Zelkowicz.

I really wanted to fully exploit the tactile quality and unique textures of this particular medium, which allows for flowing, organic movement that is never quite perfect. If a hand, say, passes in front of the face, the face will need to change, as the frame of the hand in front of the face necessarily erases the image. Objects leave ghostly "trails" across the sand, like incomplete erasures. I find it a very dream-like effect.

My intention was to create the whole film as a single unbroken shot, as if you were looking at a frame that was constantly evolving. All edits would be achieved by animated transitions (although I eventually decided to include a few hard cuts at the climactic moment before the final verse). Production ended up spreading over a number of years and locales, though, and of course, a glass plate covered in sand is not exactly easily transferrable from one state to another, so I included several transitions to black, which I cross-faded in post-production. This gave the effect of a single take, even if not a seamless one.

Was there any research into other visual artists' interpretations of the mysterious "ErlKing" involved?

If so, which ones were you looking at?

Did you get visual inspiration from elsewhere? If so, can you name the artists?

The sand animation is beautiful and reminiscent of woodcuts or linoleum cuts in movement—artists of German expressionism or the famous Munch paintings come to mind.

Possibly also an artist like Käthe Kollwitz?

I did not look at any other artists' interpretations of this poem, in particular, but there were several artists whose work was deeply influential. Kollwitz was indeed one of these, and I kept a book of her drawings near me throughout the production. The bold contrasts of light and dark in her drawings were very instructive, and I have always been drawn to the intensity of the emotions she manages to convey. The filmmaker Caroline Leaf was also a tremendous influence. Her sand adaptation of Kafka's *Metamorphosis*, as well as her paint-on-glass version of Mordecai Richler's story *The Street* are brilliant masterclasses in using animation to convey literary truths, as well as tremendous examples of space, timing, and economy. I was also profoundly affected by Carl Theodor Dreyer's 1928 film *The Passion of Joan of Arc*, which breaks almost every rule of narrative filmmaking and manages a power that few films achieve. By focusing almost exclusively on faces, Dreyer seems to illuminate thoughts and emotions within his characters, so we have an experience akin to witnessing minds at work. It was an effect I desired to emulate by working in extreme facial close-up for a good portion of my film.

Let's talk a little bit more about the storytelling aspect—how you actually combine words and images in your film? For example, you do not show the ErlKing's daughters at all in your film, while they are clearly mentioned in the lyrics. Instead, you have the ErlKing offering the son a place beside him as his potential heir or successor.

I find that a very interesting (and successful) choice in your version. Can you explain how you arrived at this specific decision?

Ah, but I *do* show the ErlKing's daughters! Look again at the moment set to the line "Mein Vater, mein Vater, und siehst du nicht dort Erlkönigs Töchter am düstern Ort?"

I was stuck for a while on how to show the ErlKing's daughters. I did not want to create feminized versions of the simple graphic shapes I used for the ErlKing, as I thought they might be unintentionally comic. The ErlKing's words are alluring, but there is a frightening menace to the promised encounter with the daughters. I decided to start the verse with a literal invitation in, flying past the dancing figure of the ErlKing, through a darkened castle, and eventually, as you say, to the empty throne beside the ErlKing, leaving the daughters hinted at but not seen. I wondered if I should leave it at that, but that felt like a missed opportunity to see a truth about the ErlKing that is revealed by his words. Since the child tells his father that he can see the daughters, I decided I needed to reveal them in some capacity. When I struck on the idea of what they would actually be, it instantly felt *right*, as the ErlKing is a forest spirit, and I felt he should be unique and not one of a community of similar beings. That meant that his children should be creatures of the real world, of the forest itself, and not additional spirits like him.

You use color in a very sparse and well-considered way to support the dramatic arc of your film. Can you elaborate on that?

My original conception was to always have the ErlKing associated with some color, so that the monochromatic "real world" would be touched with a spot of color when the spirit invades. I attempted to achieve this by applying paint to acetate and sliding pieces of the acetate between the light and the underside of the glass on which the sand was arranged. While you can see hints of this in the finished film, the color was muted and not very effective. For the climactic moment, I knew I needed to punch up the film with a new element, something not seen previously. The first part of the story is a repetitious variation on a theme, with the child crying for help and the father ignoring him, but the music climbs in pitch and volume with each iteration. I wanted to intensify the visuals to parallel Schubert's musical peaks and the poem's emotional crux at the moment of death. I found some colored sand at a craft store and was pleasantly surprised to see how translucent it was, almost like stained glass.

Figure 4.14: The use of the color in *The ErlKing* (2002) by Ben Zelkowicz.

Did you "see" the images of your film already while you were listening to the Schubert song or reading the poem? Did some of the visuals arrive during the process of making the film?

Almost all of the visuals arrived during the process. I did rough storyboards for large sections but invariably threw those out and just "went with the flow." I frequently did thumbnails of upcoming scenes and moments, so I could anticipate what needed to be moved in the transitions.

Some technical glitches forced me to rethink for several moments. The original conception for the opening was to begin the film with a first-person point of view (POV) of racing through the forest and trees appearing in the distance and whipping by to either side of the viewer as the first blast of triplets sounded. Over the course of 3 months, I animated the entire opening, including the first appearance of the carriage and the child's first sight of the ErlKing, in a style much more akin to the "moving tableau" mentioned above (similar to the pinscreen films of Alexeieff and Parker). However, the film lab screwed up the processing, and I lost all of that footage. I had to re-shoot it, which turned out to be a blessing in disguise, as I reimagined it in a much grander, more cinematic style that was 100 times more difficult to achieve but was also a vast improvement. Something similar happened with the climax, where I lost a month of work due to a camera malfunction (since sand is such a slow medium to shoot, it made sense to send film to the lab only every month or so). Rather than attempt to recreate the animation of my first pass, I reconceived the staging and the direction of the scenes and created something much more dramatic and effective.

Looking back on my own thought process when creating an animated adaptation of "Der Erlkönig," I remember that the visualization of the mysterious and elusive "ErlKing" himself was quite the challenge.

Luckily, the original ballad offers next to nothing in terms of a description of his actual appearance, allowing for a maximum of freedom in the visual interpretation.

Can you describe how you answered to this enigma in your own filmic version?

To be honest, I didn't know what he was going to look like until the moment he appeared. I had established such detailed looks for the father and son, and I knew that I wanted the ErlKing's animation to be much broader and freer than the other characters. This necessitated a relatively simple graphic that could be easily manipulated. The mask-like face of black and white turned out to be ideal, as it made for a shape that was easy to rotate in space. The crown, hinted at by the character's name, also made for an easily manipulatable landmark.

Figure 4.15: The ErlKing, as he appears in the film. © Ben Zelkowicz.

His robe became tentacle-like, as I animated it, which was a pleasant surprise. In the end, I thought the iconic contrasting of white and black in the figure suited the nature of the character well, since he is making sweet promises and delivering darkness and death. The empty eye sockets also hint at the promise of death, though I wanted to avoid making him too obviously a skull-like "grim reaper" figure. The idea of having the dead child's face echo the ErlKing's was a happy discovery in the final stages of shooting.

I understand that this was your graduation project at CalArts. Can you tell us more about the way your project developed under the guidance of a teacher in an academic environment?

How were you mentored? What input did you receive from your professor(s)?

Was it helpful to you and, if so, in which way specifically?

I went to CalArts directly from undergrad, where I had studied neuroscience and English. I was not happy during my first year at art school and produced nothing that I was pleased with. My classmates were making marvelously inspired films, and I felt I was way out of my league. Then, I got a job animating on a TV show at Will Vinton Studios in Portland. While I was there, I decided I wanted to start making a short film in my spare time. Since I would be shooting in my apartment, sand animation made sense, as it requires limited space. I borrowed a Bolex 16mm camera from a colleague, bought a heavy desk, and built a lightbox. When I returned to CalArts the next year, I had shot about 2 minutes of footage. The response when I screened it was greatly encouraging, and I felt like I was on to something. Raimund Krumme helped push me further in terms of imagining space and encouraged me to visualize the end of the film in more dramatic terms. The great Jules Engel was the head of the department at the time, and though he was teaching only minimally, he was a tremendous inspiration as well. You always knew you were onto something when you got Jules to swear, which wasn't often. I remember, one teacher told me that the animation moved too slowly, and I needed to accelerate it to match the music. Another teacher said that it moved too fast, and I should slow it down to contrast the music. Then, I showed it to Jules, and he said, "Son of a bitch! It's perfect!" I decided to stick with his advice!

Was there an animatic stage before you started the actual sand animation?

Did you use a sound breakdown to be able to (roughly) time your images to the music?

No, I timed things very roughly to the Terfel recording and the written score.

The technique used is sand animation animated directly under camera (correct me if I'm wrong). Can you explain your reasons for choosing this specific and rather-difficult animation technique? (Talking about metamorphosis as an artistic tool specific to animation).

Can you go more into the process of shooting your movie?

Can you explain your technical setup? (Ideal with a little (very) rough sketch).

Did you draw templates for the different stages of your sand animation to guide you along?

The technique involves a wooden box with a light inside and a sheet of translucent milk-glass on top (it has to be glass rather than acrylic, since plastic builds up a static charge and makes the sand dance around undesirably). The camera is suspended above, pointing down at the glass. A layer of sand is spread across the glass, so that it blocks the light. By varying the thickness of the sand by using fingers, brushes, and other tools, it is possible to create a full range of tonalities from black to white. I create an image, photograph it twice, then alter the image in some way, and take another frame. Sometimes, these alterations are slight, leaving most of the frame untouched, but often (especially on this film), the entire frame is changing. It took anywhere from 5 minutes to more than an hour and a half per frame of film, depending on the complexity of the movement. The most challenging sections were those involving the horse, especially the opening "camera move," trying to create the sense of a moving perspective. Since sand is so tactile and idiosyncratic, the perspective shifts did not need to be perfect in order to register and look cool—it is rather forgiving in that way.

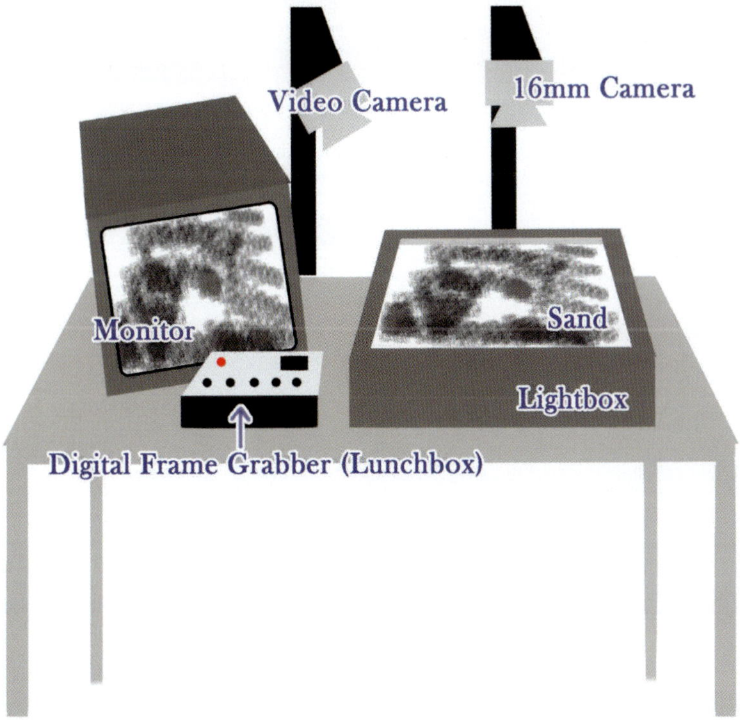

Figure 4.16: The technical setup for Ben Zelkowicz's animation of *The ErlKing*.

I first experimented with the technique in an "introduction to experimental techniques" class at CalArts and instantly fell in love, even as all my classmates hated it. I found it incredibly absorbing, a sort of zen-like trance state that was very conducive to creativity. Most of my animation experience is in "straight ahead" techniques, especially stop-motion clay and puppet animation. Traditionally drawn animation and contemporary computer generated (CG) animation are done pose to pose—that is, the key postures and poses are set and timed, and then, the animator goes back and adds in between frames and breakdown poses, refining the timing as they go. I think of those techniques as comparable to film acting, where the performer gives multiple takes and variations, and then, a complete performance is created and shaped in the editing process. Straight-ahead animation is much more like a stage performance, where you walk out before the lights, with a good idea of where you are going, but every moment has the opportunity for surprises and unexpected shifts. Every frame has to be shot in sequence, and there is no going back (Okay, that's not quite true. You can always cut back a number of frames in stop motion, so long as you repose the puppet to match the action. This is not the case in sand, where it is of course impossible to put every grain of sand back where it was. Once something is changed, it is changed forever.) It's a sort of tightrope walk, where you must keep moving forward. It is a very different experience for the animator but also gives a different quality to the animation.

Figure 4.17: Benny at work on his film.

I think there is also a parallel between sand animation and music. A piece of music has a careful structure, and if you pause at any given note, you can orient yourself in the piece of music based on this architecture. It is always clear what is behind you, but you can only move forward, and the next note is dependent on the previous ones. The attack of one note is affected by the harmonic decay of the previous. Sand animation is like that, where each image is affected by the previous (often to the point where there are ghosts of previous frames visible in the sand). Each frame exists only because of what came before. It creates a unique dynamic flow and a sort of tension, as the viewer sees one single performance, a single stream of ideas uninterrupted by cuts, one idea becoming the next.

Was there any digital support used in the actual production (as it was very early in the digital era, the production time itself, probably around the early 2000s or even in the old millennium)?

I did have digital assistance. I began the film by using a product called a "Lunchbox," which was a digital frame grabber. The actual film was captured on 16mm, but I had an additional video camera set up nearby, also pointing at the lightbox. This video camera fed into the Lunchbox and from there to a TV monitor. With it, I could capture a low-resolution video still and play it back at speed. This allowed me to see the animation as it progressed, as well as compare the previously captured frame with the frame in progress.

Eventually, I found some programs for my computer that did the same thing and switched to those mid-production.

How long did the actual production process of the film take, and can you point out the different stages?

I began the film in Portland in 1999 and completed it at CalArts in 2002. Each time I moved, I needed to get myself to a totally black frame, so that I could dissolve in post-production and create the illusion of a single unchanging image.

Your film was very well received at the festival circuit, with even a Sundance acceptance, and is obviously very popular on YouTube. Can you tell more about the general feedback to the film—maybe even curious and interesting things nobody has heard of before.

The film played at numerous festivals and won several awards. It was nominated for a Student Academy Award and was actually eligible for the Oscars that year as well (though it did not make the shortlist). My favorite screening was the very first one on the festival circuit, as part of the prestigious New York Film Festival at Lincoln Center. It is extremely rare for them to screen animated films. It showed before a packed house, paired with a documentary about Hitler's secretary. To see it on a massive screen in front of a thousand enthusiastic people, while sitting in a private box, was truly special. It received a massive ovation.

A few years ago, a heavy metal band called "Hope Lies Within" asked if they could pair the film with their rendition of the song. I gave them permission, provided they did not change the timing of the film. You can find that version on YouTube as well.

There have been a few performances of the film with live musical accompaniment, although I have been unable to attend any of them in person.

Were there any specific reactions from literature or music scholars to your animated version of the poem and/or the musical version of the ballad?

I've heard from some music teachers that they use the film in their music appreciation classes but not too much beyond that.

I understand that you are very busy these days with all kinds of commissioned creative work as well as writing books. Are you planning to ever go back to creating your own independent animated shorts, possibly even a new adaptation?

And, if that would be the case, what would you be interested in? What fascinates you in the world of literature?

I've made a few other short films, some in collaboration with my writing partner Cam Baity and some on my own. I was working on a 10-minute-long sand film that has sort of fizzled out due to my own dissatisfaction with its progress, but I edited some of the footage from that into a brief film called "Terrible Things (Happening To People Who Aren't You)," which can be seen at my website, camandbenny.com A number of years ago, I was eager to adapt a Ray Bradbury story called *The Scythe* in sand animation. It is a terrific mood piece, involving a man who comes upon an abandoned farm and takes up the work of harvesting the grain, only to discover that he has become the Grim Reaper. I put together some sketches and sent them, along with a copy of *ErlKing*, to Mr. Bradbury, requesting the rights to the story. He replied with a very kind letter that explained that the rights were held by someone else and were part of a proposed TV anthology of his stories. That anthology never came to be, so I don't know what happened to the rights of the story. Perhaps, someday, I will find the time to dedicate to that.

Since I have been focusing most of my creative energy as of late on writing fantasy novels (my series *The Books of Ore* is published by Disney-Hyperion. The second volume came out in April 2016), I've been more invested in creating original ideas rather than in adaptation. But there are plenty of pieces of art that inspire me and excite me. Adaptation is a way of engaging with an admired piece, like dancing with a master. It's risky to harness your creativity to someone else's work, since the goal is neither to repeat what they have said so well nor to subsume their artistry with your own but to symbiotically create something new that provides insight into the original.

Finally, any thoughts about what type of written source material is suitable (or non-suitable) for an animated adaptation?

Generally, what are major mistakes or shortcomings of non-successful animated adaptations?

I think being too literal is a major risk. As with any illustration, you need to add to the text, providing something that is not in the original. I think any type of material is adaptable, though sometimes, you need to really approach the work abstractly, responding to it rather than trying to re-create it in another medium. My favorite adaptations find a mood within the text and manage to breathe it onto the screen in a way that opens up the words and allows us to enter them anew. Animation creates a unique perspective, allowing us to see through the eyes of an artist who has complete control over everything that flows across the screen. Caroline Leaf's films do that. Frederick Back's marvelous *The Man Who Planted Trees* is perhaps my favorite example of a film that absorbs us into a subjective reality and bursts out the edges of the words.

Adding additional dimension to the original text was certainly also the main goal of my adaptation.

Hannes Rall: *Der Erlkönig* (2003)

I started work on *Erl-King* from ca. 2000 onward, which resulted in a finished animated short in 2003. As can be easily deduced from the dates at hand, Benny and me, both, didn't know that an almost simultaneous adaptation of the same source material was happening. I only learned of his film shortly after I had started submitting my version to festivals, while Benjamin didn't know about my version until I contacted him for this book. In retrospect, this provides a unique chance for a comparative study of both pieces in an almost identical temporal context.

In the next section, I will take a closer look at my own artistic process and explore potential similarities as well as the strong diversity inherent to the two adaptation concepts.

Figure 4.18: Film still from *The Erl-King* (Rall 2003).

The main differences clearly present themselves in two major areas: the aural aspect of the film and its process of creation.

Before delving deeper into the details of these varied approaches, I want to quote some peer review.

> "The Goethe-poem narrated by the late 'fairy tale-voice' Hans Paetsch, but this adaptation succeeds way beyond a mere recitation of this poem, which is well known to every German school-kid. With simple means and a reduced use of color, the highly creative animation achieves a unique filmic interpretation. Erl-King's daughters for example differ visually from their menacing father, the dead child in the father's arm is depicted in surprisingly simple yet entirely moving ways. Reminiscent of the tradition of Lotte Reiniger as well as of Japanese manga, the images resemble silhouette-and woodcut-styles and keep moving constantly. The music supports this rhythmic flow, the film arrives safely at the yard of highest distinction."

(Jury commentary [translated from German] on rewarding *Der Erlkönig* the "Seal of Approval: Highly Recommended" (2003) by the Film-und Medienbewertung Wiesbaden (FBW), an official German institution, which rewards films on artistic merit).

Figure 4.19: Film stills demonstrating the continuous flow of motion and transformation of backgrounds in the film.

Music and Sound

Legendary German voice actor Hans Paetsch was indeed once again a key factor in determining my approach to adapt *The Erl-King*. After my previous collaboration with him for my Poe adaptation *The Raven* (1999, as discussed in the preceding section), I wanted to use his magical voice again. Therefore, I decided early on not to use one of the many musical versions of *Der Erlkönig* but instead opt for a recitation of the poem accompanied by an original soundtrack. It was ultimately composed by my longtime collaborator Eckart Gadow after the completion of the actual animation.

On the contrary, Hans Paetsch's fabulous voice performance was recorded before the animation started, to provide a guide track for timing and inspire the visual approach.

Here lies one of the fundamental differences to Benjamin Zelkowicz's adaptation, for which he could turn to the musical ebb and flow of Schubert's song to provide inspiration for the pacing and general flow of his film.

Narrative and Plot

In terms of the narrative itself, I struggled initially with the idea of adding a new, "twist" ending, which would deviate from the original. This was largely inspired by my adaptation of *The Raven*, where I had added a more concrete ending, as opposed to the open-ended lyrical abstraction of the original.
It took me a while to finally figure out that, contrary to *The Raven, The Erl-King* already offered a perfect twist in the end, and no addition or change was necessary:

> "He reaches his courtyard with toil and
> with dread, –
> The child in his arms finds he motionless,
> dead."

The reader is made to believe that father and son have escaped the evil Erl-King.
Then, suddenly and brutally, the disaster reveals itself.

A master piece in building a sense of relief for the reader, before he is unexpectedly confronted with the tragic turn of events. Yet, and that might be the true stroke of genius here, a sense of foreboding doom permeates the whole poem, which only becomes fully evident at the very end.

In fact, it became very clear to me that any narrative addition would probably have weakened the adaptation. Instead, I added a visual commentary on top of the original ending:

As the camera pulls back from the devastated father holding the dead child in his arms, we see the Erl-King hovering above them.

The house was not a safe place after all; the demonic creature had been "along for the ride" all the way—there is no escape.

Figure 4.20: The ending of *The Erl-King*.

In general, I decided to stay entirely faithful to the given plot structure and to concentrate primarily on visualization and dramatic pacing for my film.

Visual Development

Defining the right style for an adaptation project (particularly an author-driven one) is often based on an interdependency between individual artistic style or preferences and the chosen source material. In other words, if given the choice, an animation director would look out for material that can match his own style. Vice versa, the original text might provide inspiration or require a certain artistic style for adaptation.

If there is only a small team or the animator does every part of the movie himself, he would naturally be on the lookout for a topic that they design and animate all by themselves convincingly.

In this specific case, I was indeed drawn to the poem, because I identified it to be suitable for my own artistic abilities. The supernatural elements resonated with my usually highly stylized approach and constant use of metamorphosis.

My choice of a woodcut resemblance in mark-making and initial drawing on paper responded to the main theme of an enchanted forest.

Strong use of silhouette and a reduced color palette allowed me to infuse the shapes with demonic similitudes and dramatic accents.

Character Design

This artistic approach corresponds well with the requirements of a character like the Erl-King, a mythical forest creature. It is implied by the poem that he might be shapeshifting constantly, once being a part of the forest and once taking on the form of a human-like figure. I answered to this idea by defining a character design that stays recognizable for narrative purposes yet allows for flexibility to transform into a part of the environment. The long cloak can flowingly transition into tree branches or wind; the simplified black silhouette allows negative-positive interplay of shapes.

Throughout the film, the character morphs in and out of different incarnations, always returning to his identifiable design to keep the audience connected.

Figure 4.21: Character design of the Erl-King by Hannes Rall (2001).

At the same time, this ambivalent idea of character design answers to the differing points of view of father and son:

> "My father, my father, and dost thou not
> see,
> How the Erl-King his daughters has
> brought here for me?"
> "My darling, my darling, I see it
> aright,
> 'Tis the aged grey willows deceiving thy
> sight."

Figure 4.22: The shifting shapes of the Erl-King's daughters.

Filmic montage technique presents the boy's vision of the figurative appearance of his tormentor and his daughters, while the hybrid shape of daughters and trees represents the inability of the father to detect the looming threat.

Different from a static medium like illustration, animation can add time as a tool to add the story: According to the perception of father and child, respectively, the appearances alternate between tree-like and humanoid forms.

Color Design

Similar to the Zelkowicz film, I employed color primarily to support the dramatic arc of the film. His most striking use of color is primarily in one shot; I used a very limited and restricted color palette for dramatic effect and accents throughout.

As he reveals in his interview, Benjamin had a similar approach in mind, which did not quite work out, owing to some technical difficulties.

Interestingly though, this does not hurt the artistic impact of his film at all but might even heighten it by creating a huge effect for the one moment when he actually uses full color.

This provides further evidence for my thesis that there is not only one "correct" approach for adapting a specific piece of literature but many artistic options.

For my film, I combined flat colors with huge areas of black and white: This creates a bold, poster-like graphic look. This is very different from the earlier film, which naturally possesses a more painterly and textured quality, owing to its production technique.

The idea of local color was almost completely neglected in favor of creating a mood and directing the attention of the spectator through color. For example, there was no skin color per se, and large portions of the image in each frame were left white. To differentiate and identify shapes, an interplay between the negative and positive shapes with contrasting scale was often used.

In addition, I chose a few primary colors, which could provide strong contrast and make important elements stick out: the huge yellow eyes of the Erl-King, when father and son enter the forest; crown and cape, when the son is crowned by the Erl-King; and the "lovely flowers their blossoms unfold."

Figure 4.23: Crown and cape, lovely flowers unfold.

The dramatic arc of the film displays a constantly increasing tension until the full horror of the Erl-King reveals itself not only to the son but also to the father.

To reflect this, a complete and very abrupt change of the dominant color from blue to entirely red happens in that very moment.

The color mood remains the same until father and child are literally "out of the woods."

The color returns to a predominant night blue, with a few sparse touches of local colors, corresponding with the final rescue in a safe harbor.

This use of color therefore supports the narrative goal to lull the audience into a false security, before the final twist is delivered.

Figure 4.24: The dramatic turning point of the movie, reflected through a sudden color change.

Animation Technique and Production Pipeline

The previously defined artistic look of my adaptation led directly to the choice of production pipeline. I was trying to achieve a very graphic and 2D look, with a very crisp quality of lines and absolutely regular and flat look of the color areas.
What half a decade before still would have been a difficult task to achieve (the film was produced between 2000 and 2003) was now comparatively easy, owing to the dawning of the digital age: It was created by combining a traditional hand-drawn process for the animation with digital coloring of the scanned black and white cleanup drawings.

The cleanup turned out to be rather laborious and slow because of the varied thickness of the characters' outlines, which was necessary to create the "woodcut-look" and the subtly "boiling" line quality I was after.

The digital coloring was also entirely done by me with CTP, an easy-to-use ink and cel paint program on a computer entirely dedicated to it.

It is typical, if not even a trademark, for my animation style that, often, characters and backgrounds are not treated as separate entities but interwoven as a seamless whole.

This allows me to work with both to create an overall artistic impression, which contributes to the mood conveyed by each frame in the film.

Backgrounds are in constant movement and transition from shot to shot through metamorphosis rather than hard cuts.

This technique is specific, if not unique, for animation and requires a lot more work than the more-labor-efficient separation between static backgrounds and animated characters, as each background as well as the characters need to be redrawn (in traditional 2D animation).

For sand animation (like in the 2002 *ErlKing*), it is usually the only option. Looking back on Benjamin Zelkowicz's comments on his film, he states:

> "My intention was to create the whole film as a single unbroken shot, as if you were looking at a frame that was constantly evolving. All edits would be achieved by animated transitions."

This demonstrates that, evidently, the content of the poem had led us both to the same conclusions to employ this very typical tool from the "vocabulary of animation" (Wells 2002, p. 37). Yet, the very different animation techniques lead to an entirely different outcome:

- Ben Zelkowicz sometimes had to revert to a fade into black and subsequent cross dissolves of connected scenes to achieve the idea of a seamless whole. He was working from rough guides only for the look of his final animation. With sand animation, "happy accidents" and "going with the flow" add an element of improvisation through his under-camera animation technique.
- The traditional 2D animation with digital post-production approach of my film allowed for a precise planning of each shot transition through storyboard, layouts, and keyframes. It was possible to correct drawings, where needed, and refine everything through several passes, until the animation appeared perfect to me.

Both approaches have their advantages and disadvantages, and it is largely up to the preferences of the artist and tastes of the audience that will be favored in the end. Apples and pears!

Soundtrack Composition

The sound components of the two films are equally hard to compare. The re-recording of the famous "Lied" "Der Erlkönig" by Franz Schubert for the 2002 *ErlKing* stands in stark contrast to the full symphonic soundtrack—composition by Eckart Gadow for my 2003 version combined with Hans Paetsch's atmospheric narration.

Again, the fundamentally different approaches prevent easy comparison and allow each version to stand on its own.

On the one hand is the intimacy of a small group of performers, which creates an eerie and quietly intense atmosphere.

On the other hand is the accompaniment of a full (synthetic) orchestra, with a wide dynamic range, precisely accentuating the action onscreen.

Further adding to a completely different experience is the fact that, despite the later re-recording, Benjamin Zelkowicz was reacting to the music that he already knew, whereas Eckart Gadow composed his soundtrack entirely on the basis of an already-existing animation.

In the older film, the musical sound elements dominate, but traditional sound effects are used in the very beginning and very sparsely throughout.
I decided to completely forego a traditional sound design approach in favor of the music providing the emotional sound beats and "illustrating" the visuals.

Eckart Gadow has made it a trademark of his collaborations with me to mimic classic sound design through a simulation of sounds using instruments.

Sound design elements become an integral part of the soundtrack, if you will.

To me, the rationale behind it is the chance to completely immerse the audience in a pure combination of music and visuals, without a distraction by sound effects.

This can only work in my opinion if the music carries a strong emotional quality, which supports the visual narrative.

One option to achieve that is the use of strong melodies and character-driven leitmotifs, two concepts Eckart Gadow excels at.

The completion of the soundtrack and the final mix completed the production of the film, and it was released for festival distribution in early 2003.

Reception and Feedback

The critical reception proved to be generally favorable, with the initial distinction of the FBW "Seal of Approval: Highly Recommended," as previously quoted. Naturally as an animated short film, the distribution was primarily limited to film and animation festivals between 2003 and 2005. But the film even saw a DVD release in Germany by Matthias-Film.

It was screened at 26 international festivals, including Seminci in Valladolid, Santa Barbara Film Festival, Odense, Brooklyn International Film Festival, Foyle Film Festival, Anima Mundi, and Melbourne Animation Festival. The crowning achievement was certainly the win of the "Goldener Reiter" as best national animation at the Filmfest Dresden in 2004.

More than a decade passed until the next animated adaptation of *Der Erlkönig/The Erl-King* was created, this time by the famous Swiss animator Georges Schwizgebel.

Interview with Georges Schwizgebel

Erlkönig (2015) by Georges Schwizgebel

Hannes Rall (interviewer)
Georges Schwizgebel (interviewed)

Der Erlkönig or *The Erl-King* has (to my knowledge) been adapted twice before you created your version: by Benny Zelkowicz in 2002 (as *The ErlKing*) and by me in 2003.

I am fascinated by the fact that each of these three versions is very different yet artistically valid in its own right. And still they are all created from precisely the same source material.

What aspect of the *Der Erlkönig* inspired you in the first place to create your film?

I have always loved this music that my son played *(editor's remark: the solo piano version of Schubert's "Erlkönig," transcribed by Liszt)*, but I didn't know the poem.

One day, in China, the organizer of a concert asked my son to explain the background of the piece he had played to the audience. He told the story of the poem to the audience and explained the interpretation of the four voices that are present in this poem and in the music.

This inspired me right away to come up with a visual interpretation of the music that tells that story. Subsequently, I discovered that there were already several animated films, which had chosen to adapt this theme, with words or without.

Figure 4.25: Film still from *Erlkönig* (2015). © Georges Schwizgebel.

You are using the *Erlkönig* by Franz Schubert, but in the version transcribed for solo piano by Franz Liszt, as the soundtrack for the movie. Therefore, very different from the aforementioned previous animated versions, you do not use the actual text of the original poem for your film. Still, all the drama is there, as it is inherent in the music itself, and the visuals do fully communicate the story.

I would like to hear more about this decision, as it differentiates your film strongly from the preceding adaptations.

Why did you choose to work with the Liszt–Schubert version, instead of commissioning an entirely new soundtrack? Do you have a special relation to this piece of music?

Yes, I absolutely wanted to use the Liszt–Schubert version despite contrary opinions on the matter, which were stating that non-German spectators would not understand the story.

Finally, I decided to include a very short synopsis in three languages in the opening credits of the film to provide a minimum of information on the topic.

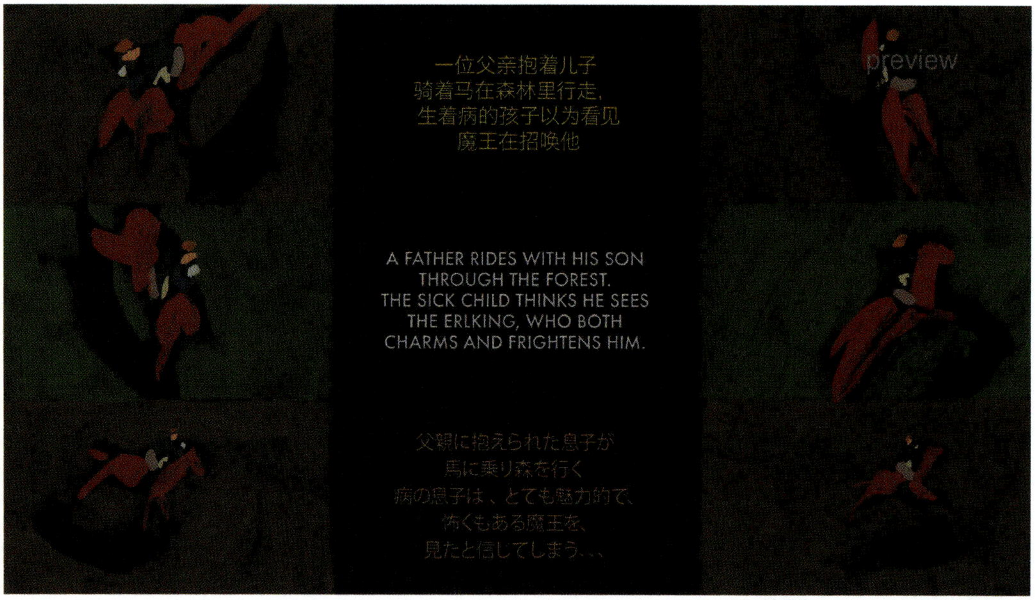

Figure 4.26: Short synopsis in the opening credits. © Georges Schwizgebel.

I have always made short films without dialogue. And in this film, despite the magnificent sung versions that exist, it would have not improved the comprehension of the story without using subtitles.

With subtitles (and in which language?), however, much of what is happening in the image would get lost. I have also read that this version *(editor's remark: the solo piano version)* is considered as equal, if not superior, to the sung version by musicologists.

I am very interested in the relation between narrative content and visual style in an animated adaptation. How did you work out your visual style, which was finally used in the film? Was there a specific visual development process? Alternative versions or stylistic approaches to visualize the poem?

I used an animated loop for the narrator at the beginning and at the end of the film (a cycle of 20 images and then 52 images for the end). One enters the cycle at the beginning and leaves it at the end of the film. The "voice" of the king is visualized with vibrant colors on a blue background and that of the son with pastel drawings on papers, which are slightly reminiscent of children's drawings. The animation for the son's sequences is created with only six drawings per second and therefore looks a little bit more jerky.

The answers of the father are illustrated with the same colors as those of the narrator.

Figure 4.27: The different drawing and painting styles in the film. © Georges Schwizgebel. *(Continued)*

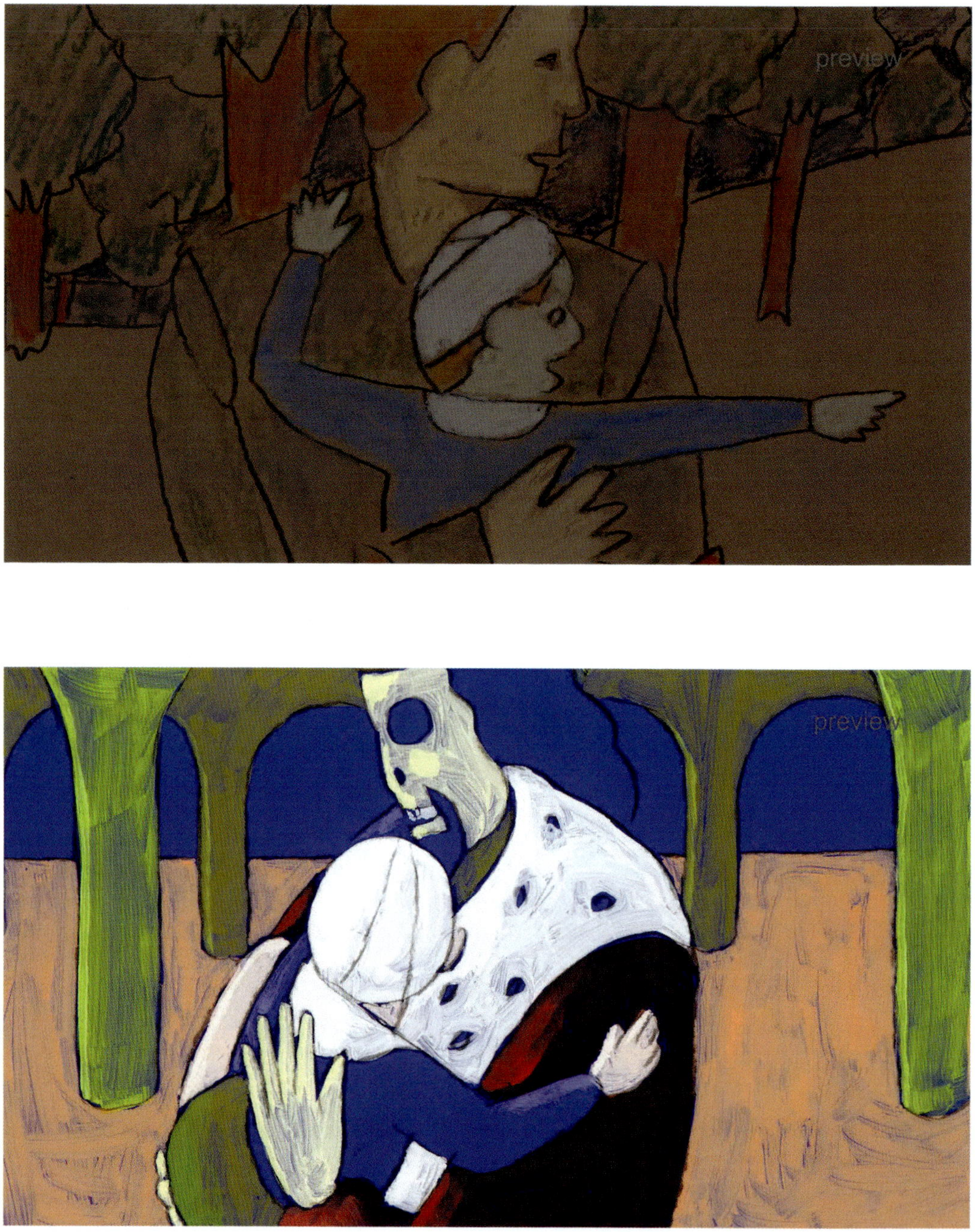

Figure 4.27: (Continued) The different drawing and painting styles in the film. © Georges Schwizgebel.

Did you "see" the images of your film already while you were listening to the Schubert song or reading the poem? Did you meticulously storyboard the film? If so, did you largely stick to that storyboard, or was it changed drastically? Or did some of the final visuals arrive during the process of making the film?

Of course, I have created several animatics (or line tests) before creating the storyboard and, once again, several afterward. There are several sequences that divert from the animatic.

The reason for that is that some ideas actually came along while I was already working on the film and also because I showed the animatic to people without prior knowledge of the story to test the comprehension. If you work with an existing soundtrack, it will provide the rhythm and the pacing of the film, and all the editing will already be decided before you actually create the images.

One of the major narrative aspects of the poem is the different point of view of father and son. You skillfully employ different styles to differentiate them. Am I right to assume that you were inspired by children's drawings for the visions of the son?

The brushstrokes do also take on a very different quality whenever the threat by the supernatural creature becomes imminent.

Can you explain how you developed these two styles (father and son), respectively?

I think I already answered this before; in effect, I was inspired by children's drawings.

And for the king, despite the bright and happy colors, I have progressively increased the sense of menace projected by him.

Your masterful use of a constantly changing perspective without traditional cuts is one of your "trademarks," and you arrive at new heights with this film. Dou you ever use any reference to create this amazing animation, or does it all emanate purely from your own imagination?

I have always aimed to find solutions that are specific for animation (metamorphoses and spatial movements), which avoid cutting from one place to another but instead resemble a continuous dream where no cuts take place. (Even if you suddenly re-awake, that seems to be the logical consequence of a dream that you quit.)

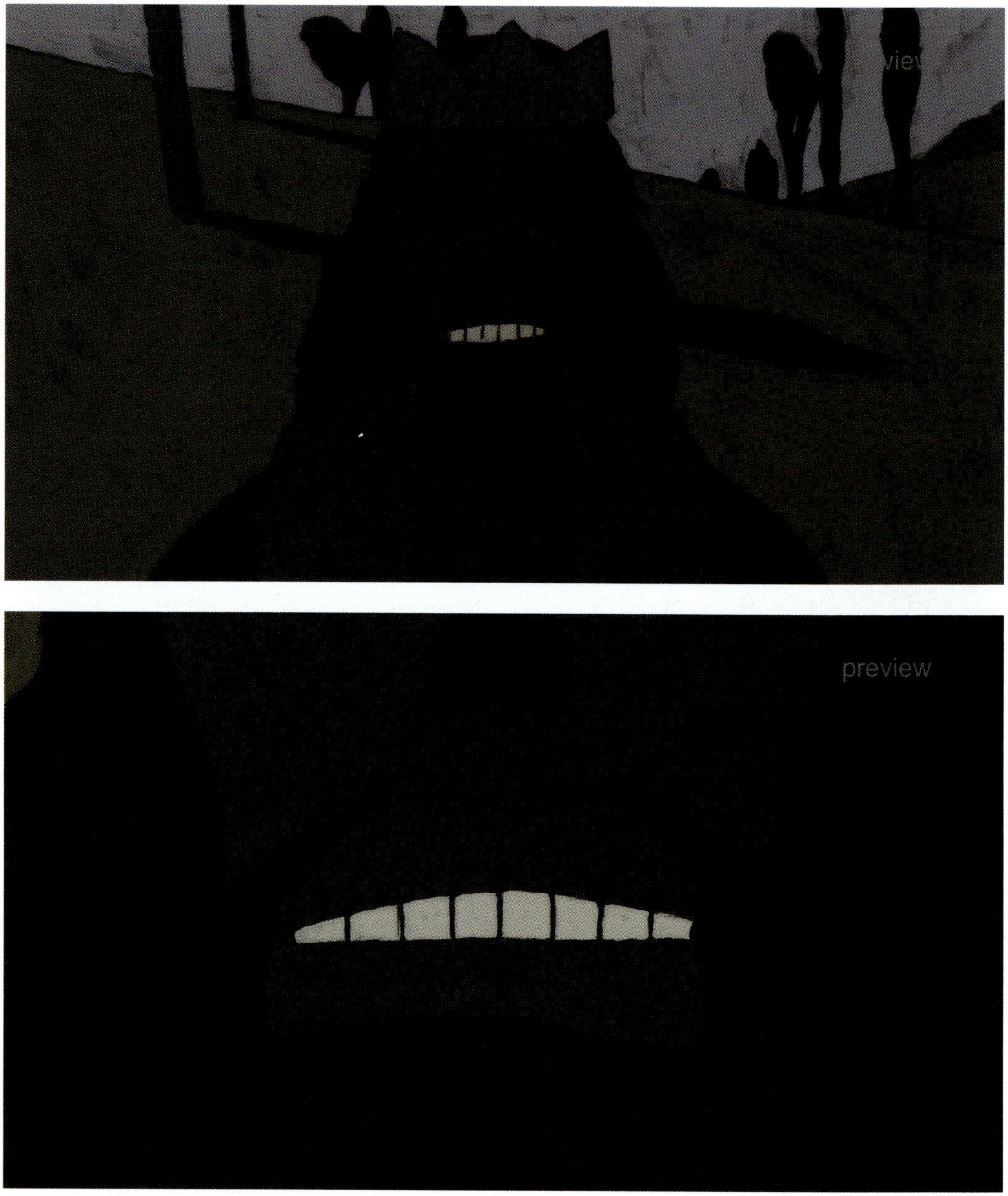

Figure 4.28: Masterful use of metamorphosis. © Georges Schwizgebel. *(Continued)*

Figure 4.28: (Continued) Masterful use of metamorphosis. © Georges Schwizgebel.

Obviously, you have always been able to achieve just the right amount of "flickering" of your expressive brushstrokes to keep the image lively yet not overwhelm the actual animation. Another strikingly beautiful component is the lighting, as you use shadows to great effect.

Can you further elaborate on your technique(s) to achieve the look of an animated painting?

Contrary to a white piece of paper or canvas on which one can apply the colors, a cinema screen is black and animated by light. That gave me idea to paint on a black surface or with a dark color, which also unifies the tonality of the acrylic color and enhances the light transparency. Before painting, I sketch the images for the animation with crayon precisely enough to allow me the liberty to execute the paintings. The shadows allow me to give weight, achieving a sense of reality for the objects and there is a marvelous sentence by de Chirico: "On the earth there are much more mysteries in the shadow of a man who walks under the sun than in all the religions past, present and future."

One of the most compelling sequences of your film is the final "dance of death," which alternates and transitions between images of the father and the Erl-King, respectively, holding the (dying) child. This negotiates the tension of the scene perfectly, until it closes the film narratively with the inevitable. It is a perfect ending.

Did you have this approach in mind from the start, or was it developed through different versions?

Figure 4.29: The final "dance of death" in the film, and its connection to the initial animation cycle. © Georges Schwizgebel.

Yes, it was my intention to come full cycle for the end by (re-)using my first sketches, since it was the technique provided for the narrator. But I have restarted several times (three) before I achieved the imagery for the king, the son, and the father in the order of appearance, as in the poem. The idea was also to achieve the visual equivalent of a musical fugue (i.e., a "drawn fugue") for the finale, by bringing all the different elements of the story together again.

Can you go more into the actual process of animating your movie?

Do you work with extremes or keys?

Can you explain your technical setup?

Was there any digital component used for the production, or was the film shot under camera, that is, using traditional equipment?

I draw my sketches beforehand in a very small format (3 per second), and I film them; after that, I do the inbetweens. That is what I call the line tests or animatics. Then, I do the key drawings in a normal format (a little bit bigger than A4) and then the inbetweens to have the animation timed precisely at 12 drawings per second. For the loops, the format is much bigger, because I also use the details of the cycle. Finally, I paint with acrylic colors on cels. I use a traditional camera setup now with a digital camera instead of a 35mm camera, which I used for my previous films.

How long did the actual production process of the film take, and can you point out the different stages?

It takes me in the area of about 2 years to realize a film of about 5–6 minutes in length: 2 months to prepare the dossier; 1 year for the diverse try-outs, line tests, and the animation; 8 months to paint; and 2 months to shoot and for the post-production.

Your film has already been hugely successful at the festival circuit; it was selected for competition by the major animation festivals (and beyond) and won multiple awards. Can you tell us more about the reaction to your film—maybe even curious and interesting things nobody has heard of before.

I was very pleased to be selected for important festivals, and, of course, I was very happy to win awards. But I was also rejected by other festivals; everything is relative, and it is important not to attach too much importance to it. After one screening, one spectator asked me:

"But in the end, is the child really dead?"

Were there any specific reactions from literature or music scholars to your animated version of the poem and/or the musical version of the ballad?

German spectators would almost always know the whole poem or in any case at least the first and the last sentence, and those who have learned that language have frequently also learned this poem. Some people have expressed their regret that I did not choose the sung version of the poem.

Finally, any thoughts about what type of written source material is suitable (or non-suitable) for an animated adaptation? Do poems offer specific opportunities or challenges for animation? (In my opinion, change is inherent and even necessary, if you are transforming a poem into an animated adaptation.)

Generally, what are major mistakes or shortcomings of non-successful animated adaptations?

Important is the "mise en scène," finding a (visual) way of narration that adds to the original itself, to make a different choice. I have often let the visuals dominate through creating non-narrative films or chosen a well-known story (*Cendrillon*) to be able to come up with variations. Moreover, if one utilizes an existing piece of music, it is difficult enough to narrate something precisely in one way, as each spectator will let his imagination wander in a different way. In the case of the *Erlkönig*, if you assume that the music tells the story, it is a little bit easier. But it is important to be careful not to explain too much to the spectator but to allow space for his own imagination. If one achieves to create an emotional response from the audience, this comes close to success.

These closing remarks of Georges Schwizgebel provide an ideal connection to the next case study presented. Maria Lorenzo has created beautiful imagery in her adaptation that strongly evokes atmosphere of time and place, yet remains open enough to allow ample room for the imagination of the audience.

Adapting H.P. Lovecraft and Robert Barlow: *The Night Ocean* by Maria Lorenzo

The popular American horror author Peter Straub has a clear opinion on H.P. Lovecraft.

> "I think Lovecraft has a permanent place in American writing (...) He stands next to Poe as the high-water mark in 19th- and 20th-century American gothic. His influence on other writers, which was immediate, has proved to be unending and fruitful."
>
> (as cited by Dziemianowicz 2010)

Other scholars such as Hudson (2013) are more ambiguous toward the matter of counting Lovecraft's works as "truly Gothic" but ultimately advocate for his inclusion in the canon. In any case, there is no denying the strong Gothic elements in Lovecraft's works and that fully qualifies this adaptation to be examined in this chapter, even more so, as *The Night Ocean* is actually a co-authored work with the author Robert Barlow.

That leads to a different writing style that diverts significantly from other Lovecraft tales, as Lorenzo explains further in her interview. What Hudson (ibid) criticizes as potentially non-Gothic about Lovecraft's style are "his sometimes frustratingly methodical descriptions, ostensibly for the sake of accuracy, separating him from Gothic writers whose narrative is perhaps more emotional or character driven."

In Lorenzo *The Night Ocean* (1972), a far more subjective voice emerges, one that embraces the unreliable accounts of the narrator as a crucial element to the story.

The story is told in the first person. The narrator, an unnamed artist, has retreated to the seaside, a quiet beach town, where he encounters and remembers strange events. These are rather being hinted at than fully explained, the reader being left to guess what is real or imagined. Much of a parallel can be established with the similar perspective of the narrator in *The Tell-Tale Heart*. Here, the reader (and later, the watcher of the adaptation) is also entering the head of an obviously disturbed person.

Ultimately, the events described in *The Night Ocean* turn more concrete, and the appearances of strange monster(s) emerging from the sea suggest an imminent threat lurking in the ocean.

Figure 4.30: Development sketches by Maria Lorenzo for the monsters in her animated adaptation.

The magic of the story is very much defined by the fact that the writing style manages to suggest that the events reported could be entirely real.
This creates a menacing atmosphere and finally leaves the reader with an uneasy feeling, a genuine scare.

In my interview with Maria, I was interested to learn how she discovered this rare and unusual story and how she encountered this little-known collaborator of Lovecraft.

Figure 4.31: Development art for *The Night Ocean* (2015), as adapted by Maria Lorenzo.

Interview with Maria Lorenzo

Hannes Rall (interviewer)
Maria Lorenzo (interviewed)

How did you learn about Robert Barlow, his fascinating biography, and his very special relationship with H.P. Lovecraft?

I found *The Night Ocean* very different from other tales by H.P. Lovecraft, and I found it captivating because of the love for the landscape, the unreliable narrator, and the depictions of the seaside, which reminded me so much of my own city, a Mediterranean place called Torrevieja. I even used to see a half-abandoned, mysterious small house in front of the sea, near to the populous beach. Unfortunately, when I used to spend my holidays in Mallorca, I also saw some drowned people, owing to the strong winds and high waves. It is terrifying how a space for solace and enjoyment, such as the beach, may turn into a deadly place. It is twofold, like our relation with nature and especially with the sea.

I did not realize that the tale was also written by Robert Barlow until I started to consider it for adaptation (by 2003). I found his name in a really small footnote stating that the tale was published by Barlow, on his own, by 1936. Lovecraft had passed away time enough to not worry about right holders, but Barlow was unknown for me. Then, I started to look for information on the Internet, and I found some hints about his life in Wikipedia and on a portrait photograph.

Figure 4.32: Robert Barlow (second from left) with his family.

When I first read about his early suicide, it really moved me. Actually, he was a child when he first met Lovecraft, and apparently, he did not have recognition as the legitimate Lovecraft's literary executor by most of his friends. But the fact of being blackmailed by one of his anthropology students just for being homosexual was the saddest thing of all, something that probably wouldn't happen in our society today.

So, later, by 2011, I had to research about who could retain the copyright of this story, and then asking from different Spanish publishers that had published the tale before, I discovered that they had never paid for these rights. Hippocampus Press, the American publisher that published Barlow's entire fiction work, and also a very interesting study on Barlow (by Massimo Berruti) suggested me to contact "a Barlow expert," a person called Vance Pollock, who kindly replied to my emails, and he assured me that the tale hadn't any copyright holder. However, since I needed special permission for its further transformation as an animated film, Vance kindly directed me to Donna Leach Canfield, the closest surviving relative of Robert Barlow, his cousin. This lady is nearby 80, but she uses Facebook (FB). We had a short talk by FB, and we're in touch since then.

Even after finishing the film, I haven't stopped learning things about Barlow. He was a person of many talents, something that impressed Lovecraft very much. It is a pity that none of his drawings and sculptures made when he was young were preserved. Massimo Berruti's essay, *"Dim-Remembered Stories: A Critical Study on R. H. Barlow"*, which I didn't read after completing the film, helped me understand many interesting things, for instance, how came his unexpected love for Mexican anthropology: It was the logical consequence of his fascination toward the mystical, the ancient, and fearsome in H.P. Lovecraft literature, transposed to a likely, historical scenery: a language and a history that he could decipher and enjoy.

What made you consider this story for an animated adaptation?

When I first read the book by 2002, I was 24, and I was immersed in another project, *Portrait of D.* Its main character was also a painter (with sort of existentialist issues), and somehow, *The Night Ocean*, whose narrator is also a painter—with a notable neurosis and paranoia—made me believe that it could be a kind of second part of my first film or an alternative adventure with a similar character. In any case, the story was familiar to me.

Moreover, with its hint to the end of life and the sea moving for all eternity, surviving any human being, the tale recalled a certain sensation to me, something from my childhood that I had forgotten: Carl Sagan depicting the end of life on Earth in his memorable series *Cosmos* (1980). It frightened me so much when I saw it as a child that I ran to hide myself into my brother's closet. My brother had to convince me to get out of there, saying that the end of the world would happen in a very far future…

When one reads *The Night Ocean*, it becomes evident that the narrator isn't sure of what he saw, or he thinks he saw; thus, he is unreliable. The fantastic is suspended in the air. But the end of life, at least as we know it, is unavoidable. This double sense, this feeling of making you think about it is what I wanted for the film.

However, the most difficult of all was to decide the focus for the story. Who could be this intriguing narrator? I even considered the possibility of transforming him into a child, to play with his special understanding of things. At the end, I decided to return to the source, though taking seriously the possibilities offered by the character as a painter. The tale doesn't mention that he makes any drawing during his holidays, though he is a "very imaginative person." But, after seeing Bastien Dubois' *Madagascar: carnet de voyage* (2009), I realized that the narrator being a painter provided a very good pretext to suggest some double meaning and that the film could develop entirely like his own drawings, like his subjective voice.

Your adaptation incorporates parts of the original text. How did you select these? What was your criterion for what to put in and what to leave out?

The text was so inspiring, so poetic, and so rich in images that it was very easy. I read it several times, and then, I used two color markers. I marked in orange what I wanted for the voice-over and in blue everything that I could just show in the film. This way I arranged a first script with depictions.

However, when you develop the animatic and while you progress in the film production, you tend to leave things out: you simplify scenes or you need to invent new things. The voice-over was reduced to its very basics to follow the story. From the beginning, I renounced to one of the most shocking scenes from the tale, when he finds in the beach something that remains to a human hand chopped and bitten and that simultaneously seems like an octopus. It really marks a point of no return in the obsession of the main character, but I didn't need it, since the scene during the storm, when he first sees strange creatures in the waters, was enough to suggest such turn of events.

Also, I needed to suggest through images the idea of the narrator as a very imaginative person, so I invented a new situation at the very beginning: When he examines the cabin at his arrival, he finds a graffiti in one of the walls, the drawing of an octopus. Then, he slightly transforms the drawings into a mermaid-octopus. This should suggest the idea of his capability to see the human into the animal—or his obsession with the fantastic. At the end, we return to that image to recover this idea.

Figure 4.33: Various explorations of sea creatures through different stages of visual development. © Maria Lorenzo.

In my opinion, your film works particularly well on a multitude of visual levels and that helps to make your adaptation artistically as successful as it is.

You are masterfully building up the dramatic tension by letting the otherworldly and weird only creep in subtly until it builds toward the final climax.

That is reflected in the use of sunlit imagery of beaches and ocean in beautiful watercolors and other techniques until slowly but surely the colors and images change to communicate darker moods.

You are (more or less) going from light to dark in a sophisticated artistic transition. Was that your intention?

If everything you said was true, I would feel very happy. I took many photos and videos between 2011 and 2012, to have images that inspired me. This way, I started the film as a series of landscapes. I had just a few sketches for the storyboard, some videos, and those concept art paintings to compose the story and build the rhythm. So, these images found their place almost from the beginning, before animation began. I believe that, in this process, sound and music had a leading role. I had a provisional recording of the music, composed by my musician, Armando Bernabeu Lorenzo, who is from my family. The music is tender at times, very moving, but it also becomes dark and disturbing. In addition, I found some sound tracks by Martí Guillem, which were very suggesting, and I also used them from the beginning. At the end, Martí arranged the complete sound effects and abstract sounds that you can hear in the film, especially in the climax scene.

Second, what struck me as particularly effective is the visual storytelling tool to depict some of the drawings and sketches as journal or diary notes. This suggests an authenticity, implying to read through found records of a real person. This approach makes the impending "horror" or "weirdness" that follows extremely believable and allows the audience to empathize strongly.

Can you talk about your visual storytelling concept, and how you related it to the source material?

Actually, I would like that this resource, the "animated diary," was as effective with everyone as it has been for you! Well, sometimes, the viewers like the changes in the techniques (an artist's sketchbook is supposed to show some variety of approaches), but, at the same time, some people find them so striking that they get distracted from the main narration (however, they don't mind if they have to see the film a second time, that's good). As I have explained before, the tale itself, with the main character as a painter, provided the context for this visual experimentation. I would have liked to give a step forward and have included marginal notes, written lines, and words, like in *Madagascar: carnet de voyage*. It would have been perfect. But it was a bit late when I realized about this possibility. I also had a powerful voice-over, and I didn't want to renounce to it. Maybe it would have been too much information together.

Figure 4.34: Examples for the sketchbook/diary styles employed for the narrative. © Maria Lorenzo.

Concerning the "horror," I really needed to give a visual shape to the monster, which is scarcely depicted in the tale, just as half human, half dog… "but it swam with a horrible ease…" The monster, supposedly male, entered the earth to return to the sea, carrying a human corpse. But there was too much to imagine. One night, when I was breastfeeding my daughter, I thought that the monster could be a female: a mother that feeds her spawn on earth. This allowed me to establish connections with the scene with the little creature (a scene that I had to rewrite to make it more visual) but also a stronger relation between the Sea-Mother and the mermaid-octopus. It is funny how things come to their place when you develop a project for so long. For me, every project is like a puzzle to complete.

Figure 4.35: Stages of visual development for the fantastic sea creature(s). The wide variety of artistic styles is evident, ranging from light pastels to the darkly painted monochromatic images at the bottom—reminiscent of the great German expressionist artist Käthe Kollwitz (1867–1945). © Maria Lorenzo.

Another "meta-approach," if you will, is the fact that you are telling the story of a painter through different painting techniques, very much in line with the aforementioned "diary-concept"?

Probably, I have elaborated enough, but I must remark the difficulties that apply to changing the aesthetic from scene to scene. It makes any attempt of artistic direction impossible. As well, at the very end, I realized that if you want to have a film with different aesthetics, you need to involve more people to create the concept. In my case, except those scenes where the sea foam is animated, and also the main titles, everything is animated, scanned, cleaned with the computer, and composed by myself. I animate quickly; I sketch just a few key frames, and then, I draw directly the entire animated scene with a good-quality paper. If you have a beautiful drawing, probably you only need to test it once or twice before you go on with compositing. The fact is that I could animate an entire scene during only one evening, but I could be editing it on the computer for a week, making decisions all the time…

My favorite scene is the "happy Twenties" diary, with the jazz music, developing as a series of animated illustrations from old photographies and films… I really enjoyed making that fragment, and I need to make more of this.

Figure 4.36: Study for the dance scene. © Maria Lorenzo.

As you describe in your previous essay, you have recorded and used live-action footage as reference for your film. Partially, it is also integrated directly into your film. What impressed me in both cases is the seamless artistic integration you achieve: The rotoscoped action has none of the usual sterility but looks organic and well timed, and the live-action footage fits in seamlessly through the choice of color and style.

I would be interested to learn in precise detail how you achieved this.

Figure 4.37: Imaginative use of rotoscoping for the film. © Maria Lorenzo.

Well, rotoscopy doesn't have to create such sterility if you use the frames just as a reference, not to trace over them. The only rotoscoped scenes in the film are the animated waves and the main titles, because they needed to be as much realistic as possible. Concerning the animation of animals and humans, I had many recordings taken at oceanographic parks, and I also used the Internet to find more videos. The main character is entirely animated, with my husband as a reference: I asked him to perform, and I recorded my videos in the moment I needed them. Then, I analyze the videos to find the key frames; I decide the timing, and then, I start in-betweening. It is simple and saves time. Some "difficult" scenes, like the protagonist swimming in the beach, came from suitable films such as *Gattaca*; the dog running came from the French film *A Man and a Woman*, and probably, the aspect of my animation that comes the closest to a rotoscopy, but I just copied the frames by hand, looking at the computer.

In the film, some live-action scenes appear, just to give more variety of approaches. I especially like the Super8 scene of the coast, which was recorded by my father in the 1970s. A friend of mine suggested to apply a filter to transform that lovely take into the two-color film system from 1920s, and we did it. Some other scenes come from Super8 family films, such as the women walking into the water (they were my mother and oldest sister). Finally, the scene with the sketches of the monsters, just before the climax, they're just photographs of my own production sketches, when I was trying to give form to the monsters. So, there's a lot of self-referenciality in them. Ah, after that, we can see the main character almost as a photographic one, because I transferred frames to the pages of a sketchbook: So, anybody who knows my husband can recognize him in that scene.

Finally, related to the previous question, can you explain how and why you selected a particular technique for a particular part of your film?

Can you tell us about the connection between narrative function and artistic style?

Figure 4.38: Further examples of the wide variety of artistic styles developed for and used in the film. © Maria Lorenzo.

I believe that, at many times, I wasn't aware of this connection. I would have developed more scenes with just a few drawings, very sketchy drawings, but finally, I tended to animate everything, or almost, at 12 images per second. In my own sketchbooks, I had some very stimulating drawings that didn't find their place in the film. As well, I had many folders with thousands of art references that were extremely interesting, but finally, I selected only a few as a model for certain scenes. Probably, when you have so much in your head, at the end, you select the options that seem more natural. Having the entire project in the timeline, with music and sound, introducing new scenes on it as soon as they're finished, helps you to make decisions. The last scene I animated was the most crucial: the encounter with the monster. I used a lot of pastel painting, not only because it needed to be very shocking, very expressive, but also because I missed this technique in the entire project. Then, I tried to introduce more scenes painted with pastels, where I needed it. Pastels also allowed me to create some scenes like seen "from under the water," because I could draw and change the drawing many times, and I recorded the changes by using the scanner (I also had video reference for this: video recordings that I created with a special technique, using a water container). Another technique, watercolor, was used when I wanted to create the sensation of movement, especially with the water, or to give color very fast to a scene (it was easy, since I was using a good-quality paper for the animation). But, most of the film is developed like line drawing and a (painterly) texture in the background, which are the simplest, nicest forms to give some life to a scene.

Summary of Case Studies

I consider it essential to go back to the primary sources, the films themselves, and gain insight into the creative process by entering into conversations with the filmmakers, particularly when it comes to a subject like adaptation, where it is crucial to understand the rationale behind the creative decisions in correspondence with the source material. Coming back to the initial research questions, the previous interviews have offered ample responses.

As we have learned through the various statements, there is certainly not one but multiple possibilities to approach the adaptation of Gothic writing for animation.

This is to be expected, because artistic research must embrace the artistic individuality and subjectivity as an element: Different artists can come up with equally viable solutions when approaching the same challenge. The three different versions of *The Erl-King* demonstrate this convincingly, as all of them succeed on their own (and different) artistic terms.

Yet, communalities can be detected: For one Bendazzi's mention of the necessity (and advantage) of animation to create its very own world—a "world that does not exist in reality".

From *The Tell-Tale Heart* through *The Raven*, the three versions of *The Erl-King* up until Maria Lorenzo's *The Night Ocean*, the artistic handwriting becomes evident and central for the creation of an atmosphere that responds to the literary source.

Paul Wells (1999) notes that animation constitutes "a distinctive film-form which offers to the adaptation process a unique vocabulary of expression unavailable to the live-action film-maker" (199) and that "animation (...) provides a vocabulary that enables the most sensitive response to literary texts" (212). Wells further claims that "the openness" of the animated vocabulary is especially conducive to fantastical or supernatural contexts" (210).

Three main levels of such artistic interpretation can be identified:

1.) Static: The look development of the films corresponds to the needs of establishing visual equivalents that can successfully re-evoke feelings that the reader might experience in the source material. This involves various techniques and methods, as it should be to respond to different source materials. Drawing and painting, digital and tradigital, create visual styles for characters and environments:

The wood cut leanings and bold designs in *The Raven* and *The Erl-King*.

The variation between elaborate painting and child-like drawings in Schwizgebel's "Erlkönig" to illustrate the different perspectives.

The wider variety of painting and drawing styles chosen by Maria Lorenzo for *The Night Ocean*. Very strikingly, her artistic reminiscences to a sketched diary suggest the idea of an authentic account of incidents. This aspect greatly adds to the perceived scariness of the film, as the horror becomes "real."

In all examples, the animators/designers were striving and ultimately succeeding to find and formulate the correspondence between the adapted material and its visual counterpart(s).

This is of essence, as there is a lot of room for misguided choices here, sometimes driven by commercial considerations (for feature films) but sometimes equally by artistic misjudgment. An example for such a mistake is a failure to come up with an original artistic voice that rises above a mere replication of the narrated events.

The animated interpretation must transcend the original, add to it, and reinterpret it for animation, as Bendazzi and Schwizgebel have previously confirmed in this chapter. These includes the following aspects:

2.) Dynamic: Once the design is found, the next level of finding the right choices for the adaptation comes with setting the previously static images into movement.

The choices to be made: The supernatural is a central motif in the Gothic and it contains many related narrative elements that are particularly well suited for visual interpretation through animation's specific vocabulary; for example, transformation and the Other in Gothic writing correspond strongly with the animation technique of metamorphosis. In the final twist of *The Raven*, the formerly menacing titular raven transforms into the dearly missed Lenore.

The atmosphere and mood prevalent in Gothic architecture, such as haunted houses, can be translated by creating highly stylized backdrops, as shown in *The Tell-Tale Heart*.

3.) Audiovisual: From the interviews, it became very clear that the role of sound cannot be underestimated for the success of an adaptation. The triptych of narration and dialogue, music, and sound design can elevate the quality of a film greatly and even become the defining element. The masterfully laconic narration of James Mason for *The Tell-Tale Heart* lets the audience enter the mind of a murderer. The moody narration of Hans Paetsch in *The Raven* and *The Erl-King* contributes greatly toward re-creating the atmosphere suggested by the respective poems. Music speaks on a direct emotional level to the audience and is a match for animation in answering to the Gothic: Menace and drama, threat and murder can be greatly enhanced through contrasts between harmony and dissonance as well as dynamic range and tonal choices. In combination with sound design, it will go a long way toward adding to the spooky atmosphere, establishing the lurking threat.

This becomes immediately apparent when imagining *Jaws* (dir. Spielberg 1978) without the menacing theme created by John Williams for the approaching shark or the shower scene from *Psycho* (dir. Hitchcock 1960) without the shriekingly dissonant violin sounds created by Bernard Hermann.

Conclusion

Gothic literature in particular is known for evoking strong images in the mind of the reader, and any adaptation for animation has to be extremely careful to define the visuals and construct the storytelling in such a way that it successfully reimagines the suspense, building the pacing and environment of the original (Edwards 2007).

When the artistic means employed to connect to the central Gothic elements of the source material are well chosen, the feedback to an adaptation is frequently positive.

We have also seen that there are multiple "right" ways to approach the same source material artistically.

But there is a potential danger of failure, when making the wrong choices.

Failure occurs when the visual storytelling techniques of animation are not used to enhance this connection. If, on top of that, the narrative decisions are equally misguided, an artistic disaster is waiting to happen.

A good example for this presents itself in Disney's adaptation of *The Hunchback of Notre Dame* (Trousdale, Wise 1996). For one, the ugliness of the titular hero was significantly toned down to achieve a more family-compatible look that would not frighten children. Second, the tragic ending of the original novel is replaced by a completely unmotivated (if not for assumedly commercial reasons) happy ending (Laster 1997).

In my opinion, this signifies not only a slight modification but also a complete contradiction to the Gothic concepts of the source novel (Brew 2011). The ugliness of Quasimodo is supposed to express his status as the Other, the outcast, the monster. Even more significantly, the happy ending is violently drawing the narrative from darkness into light—the tragedy that is inherent to the Gothic concept is entirely ignored.

We have looked at a different approach in our case studies: the animated short film directed and often also completely created by an independent director. Commercial considerations are certainly not the driving impact of such artistic exploration. Arguably, this will heighten the chances for (artistic) success, as the artist can fully concentrate on expressing the source materials through his own means. But the essential challenges remain just the same:

What to keep and what to change from the narrative of the original text?
What to show and what to deliberately leave offscreen?
How to design the visuals in a way that represents the source material well?

"Doing so in a way which resonates with the artistic intention of the author of the original source can prove uniquely difficult given how much the Gothic is defined by such intangible characteristics as mood, ambience, and atmosphere". (Rall, Jernigan 2015, 39). From this angle, what is possibly most important, then, is that such works display what Fred Botting observes in his description of Gothic literature as "a writing of excess, an exploration of physical, psychological, and social limits and boundaries" (1996, 1).

Moreover, in addition to capturing excessive and extreme states, the animator would also be well advised to consider Saloman's (2002) keen observation on how Gothic literature produces additional anxiety in its readers by gesturing toward "extreme thresholds" as "some spook invades our commonplace reality, or our apparently sane and rational self enters a categorically malign environment" (2002, 9). Therefore, I propose that the artistic success of adaptations of Gothic literature for animation depends on convincingly defining a corresponding audio-visual language. This audio-visual language needs to employ the visual vocabulary of animation for expressing the uniquely Gothic features represented in the source material. If the animation director understands and applies this underlying concept, he will create an appropriate artistic representation instead of a mechanical replication.

References

Ade, Albrecht. 2004. *Review: The Raven*. In: *Animated Film from Germany 2004 Exhibition Catalogue*. Stuttgart, Germany: Institut für Auslandsbeziehungen (IFA).

Archer, Wes, dir. 1992. *Treehouse of Terror*. Episode from animated TV series *The Simpsons*, season 2. Los Angeles, CA: Fox Television Animation.

Beck, Jerry. 1994. *The 50 Greatest Cartoons: As Selected by 1,000 Animation Professionals*. Atlanta, GA: Turner Publishing.

Bendazzi, Giannalberto. 2015a. Interviewed by *Hannes Rall*. Singapore.

Bendazzi, Giannalberto. 2015b. *Animation: A World History: Volume II: The Birth of a Style—The Three Markets*. Boca Raton, FL: CRC Press.

Botting, Fred. 1996. *The Tell-Tale Heart. The Gothic*. London, UK: Routledge.

Bozdech, Betty. 2000. *Review the raven*. DVD Journal website. Accessed June 19, 2016. http://www.dvdjournal.com/reviews/s/short9.shtml.

Brandie. 2013. *The beating of the hideous tell-tale heart*. Accessed March 26, 2014. http://trueclassics.net/2013/10/31/the-beating-of-the-hideous-tell-tale-heart-1953/.

Browning, Tod, dir. 1931. *Dracula*. Film. Universal City, CA: Universal Pictures.

Butt, Richard. 2012. *The classic novel on british television*. In: *A Companion to Literature, Film and Adaptation*, edited by Deborah Cartmell, 163–164. Chichester, UK: Wiley-Blackwell.

Columbus, Chris, dir. 2001. *Harry Potter and the Philosopher's Stone*. Film. Burbank, CA: Warner Bros. Pictures.

Columbus, Chris, dir. 2002. *Harry Potter and the Chamber of Secrets*. Film. Burbank, CA: Warner Bros. Pictures.

Corben, Richard. 1974. The raven. In *Creepy* #67. New York City: Warren Publishing.

Corben, Richard. 2013. *The Raven and the Red Death*, Issue # 0, Milwaukie, Oregon: Dark Horse Comics.

Corman, Roger. 1963. *The Raven*. Film. Alta Vista Productions (studio); American International Pictures AIP.

Cornwell, Neil. 2012. *European gothic*. In: *A New Companion to the Gothic*, edited by David Punter, 64. Hoboken, NJ: Wiley-Blackwell.

Cotte, Olivier. 2007. *Secrets of Oscar-winning Animation*. 1st ed. Waltham, MA: Focal Press.

Cuarón, Alfonso, dir. 2004. *Harry Potter and the Prisoner of Azkaban*. Film. Burbank, CA: Warner Bros. Pictures.

Disney, Walt, dir. 1929. *The Skeleton Dance*. Burbank, CA: Walt Disney Productions.

Dziemianowicz, Stefan. 2010. *Terror Eternal: The enduring popularity of H. P. Lovecraft*. Accessed June 19 2016. http://www.publishersweekly.com/pw/by-topic/industry-news/publisher-news/article/43793-terror-eternal-the-enduring-popularity-of-h-p-lovecraft.html

Eddings, Dennis W. 2013. MAD about the Raven. *Edgar Allan Poe Review* 14 (2): 144–162. Poe Studies Association, Pennsylvania State University.

Edwards, Paul. 2007. *Adaptation: Two theories. Text and Performance Quarterly* 27 (4): 369–371.

Elliott, Kamilla. 2008. *Gothic—Film—Parody. Adaptation* 1 (1): 24–43. doi:10.1093/adaptation/apm003.

Goethe, Johann Wolfgang von. 1782. *Der Erlkönig*.

Hand, David, dir. 1937. *Snow White and the Seven Dwarfs*. Film. Burbank, CA: Walt Disney Productions (production). New York: RKO Radio Pictures (distribution).

Hillard, Tom J. 2009. *Deep into that darkness peering: An essay on gothic nature. Interdiscip Stud Lit Environ* 16 (4): 685–695.

Hitchcock, Alfred, dir. 1960. *Psycho*. Film. Shamley Productions (production). Paramount Pictures (distribution).

Hoeveler, Diane Long. 2012. *Gothic ballads*. In: *The Encyclopedia of Romantic Literature: Re-Z, Volume 3*, 505. London, UK: Wiley & Sons.

Hudson, Kathleen. 2013. *Lovecraft Reads a Story: The Gothic Manuscript*. Accessed June 19 2016. http://sheffieldgothicreadinggroup.blogspot.sg/2013/11/foreshadowings-hp-lovecraft-as-gothic.html.

Hughes, Chris. 2001. *Review The Raven*. DVD Talk (website). Accessed June 19, 2016. http://www.dvdtalk.com/reviews/print.php?ID=1632.

Jackson, Peter, dir. 2001. *The Lord of the Rings: The Fellowship of the Ring*. Los Angeles, CA: New Line Cinema.

Jackson, Peter, dir. 2002. *The Lord of the Rings: The Two Towers*. Los Angeles, CA: New Line Cinema.

Jackson, Peter, dir. 2003. *The Lord of the Rings: The Return of the King*. Los Angeles, CA: New Line Cinema.

Julian, Paul, dir. 1964. *The Hangman*. Animated short film. Los Angeles, CA: Melrose Productions.

Kaye, Heidi. 2012. *Gothic film*. In: *A New Companion to the Gothic*, edited by David Punter, 239–251. Chichester, UK: Wiley-Blackwell.

Laster, Arnaud. 1997. *Waiting for Hugo*. Accessed August 31, 2014. http://www.awn.com/mag/issue1.10/articles/laster.ang1.10.html.

Logan, John, creator. 2014. *Penny Dreadful.* TV series, 3 seasons, 25 episodes. Desert Wolf Productions; London, UK: Neal Street Productions.

Lorenzo, Maria, dir. 2015. *The Night Ocean.* Animated short film.

Mamoulian, Ruben, dir. 1931. *Dr. Jekyll and Mr. Hyde.* Universal City, CA: Universal Pictures.

Marciniak, Małgorzata. 2007. *The appeal of literature-to-film adaptations. Lingua ac communitas* 17: 59–67.

Melani, Lilia. 2002. *The gothic experience.* Accessed June 18, 2016. http://academic.brooklyn.cuny.edu/english/melani/gothic/gothic.html.

Méliès, Georges. Dir. *A Trip to the Moon.* Film. Star Film Company, 1902.

Méliès, Georges, dir. 1904. *The Impossible Voyage.* Film. Star Film Company.

Murnau, Friedrich Wilham, dir. 1922. *Nosferatu—Eine Symphonie des Grauens.* Film. Film Arts Guild.

Murray, Elizabeth. n.d. *Harry Potter and the Gothic Novel.* Accessed June 18, 2016. http://www.the-leaky-cauldron.org/features/essays/issue8/gothicnovel/.

Newell, Mike, dir. 2005. *Harry Potter and the Goblet of Fire.* Film. Burbank, CA: Warner Bros. Pictures.

Oxoby, Marc. 2003. *Review: Harry potter and the chamber of secrets (2002) & The lord of the rings: The two towers (2002) (Film). Film & History,* 33 (1): 67–69.

Parmelee, Ted. 1953. *Production Notes for The Tell-Tale-Heart.* United Productions of America. New York: MOMA Archives: 2–3.

Parmelee, Ted, dir. 1953. *The Tell-Tale Heart.* Film. Los Angeles, CA: Columbia Pictures. Produced by United Productions of America.

Piché, Bruno H. 2009. *Versiones del Cuervo de Poe.* Accessed July 3 2016. http://www.letraslibres.com/blogs/versiones-del-cuervo-de-poe.

Poe, Edgar Allan. 2004. *The Raven.* In: *The Selected Writings of Edgar Allan Poe*, edited by G. R. Thompson, 57–59. Norton Critical Edition. New York: Norton.

Rall, Hannes, and Daniel Keith Jernigan. 2015. *Adapting gothic literature for animation.* In: *New Directions in 21st-Century Gothic: The Gothic Compass*, edited by Donna Lee brien and Lorna Piatti-Farnell. London, UK: Routledge.

Rall, Hannes, dir. 1999. *The Raven.* Animated short film. Meier & Rall Animation.

Reiniger, Lotte, dir. 1926. *The Adventures of Prince Achmed.* Animated feature film. Berlin, Germany: Comenius-Film Berlin/Louis Hagen (production).

Rowling, J.K. 1997. *Harry Potter and the Sorcerer's Stone.* New York: Arthur A. Levine Books (Scholastic).

Rowling, J.K. 1998. *Harry Potter and the Chamber of Secrets.* New York: Arthur A. Levine Books (Scholastic).

Rowling, J.K. 1999. *Harry Potter and the Prisoner of Azkaban.* New York: Arthur A. Levine Books (Scholastic).

Rowling, J.K. 2000. *Harry Potter and the Goblet of Fire.* New York: Arthur A. Levine Books (Scholastic).

Rowling, J.K. 2003. *Harry Potter and the Order of the Phoenix.* New York: Arthur A. Levine Books (Scholastic).

Rowling, J.K. 2005. *Harry Potter and the Half Blood Prince.* New York: Arthur A. Levine Books (Scholastic).

Rowling, J.K. 2007. *Harry Potter and the Deathly Hallows.* New York: Arthur A. Levine Books (Scholastic).

Royal, Derek. 2013. Review: Richard Corben's *The Raven and The Red Death.* Accessed March 10, 2019. http://comicsalternative.com/review-raven/.

Saloman, Roger B. 2002. *Mazes of the Serpent: An Anatomy of Horror Narrative.* Ithaca: Cornell University Press.

Schwabe, Claudia Mareike Kathrin. 2012. *Romanticism, Orientalism and National Identity: German Literary Fairy Tales, 1795–1848.* PhD diss. University of Florida. Accessed March 23, 2014. http://ufdcimages.uflib.ufl.edu/UF/E0/04/39/60/00001/SCHWABE__.pdf.

Shelley, Mary. 1818. *Frankenstein or the Modern Prometheus.* London, UK: Lackington, Hughes, Harding, Mavor & Jones.

Smith, Andrew. 2007. *Gothic Literature.* Edinburgh: Edinburgh University Press.

Spiegelman, Art, and Françoise Mouly, eds. 1980–1991. *Raw.* Comics anthology. New York City: Raw Books & Graphics (1980–1986). London, UK: Penguin Books (1989–1991).

Spielberg, Steven, dir. 1978. *Jaws.* Film. Universal City, CA: Universal Pictures.

Stoker, Bram. 1897. *Dracula.* London, UK: Archibald Constable.

Taylor, Andrew. 2009. *Two Centuries Have Not Aged Poe's Writing.* Accessed March 19, 2014. http://www.theguardian.com/books/booksblog/2009/jan/19/edgar-allan-poe-bicentenary.

Tolkien, J.R.R. 1954–1974. *The Lord of the Rings* (Vols. I–III). New York: Ballantine Books.

Trousdale, Gary, and Kirk Wise, dirs. 1996. *The Hunchback of Notre Dame.* Film. Burbank, CA: Walt Disney Feature Animation.

Wells, Paul. 2002. *Animation: Genre and Authorship.* New York: Wallflower Press.

Whale, James, dir. 1931. *Frankenstein*. Universal City, CA: Universal Pictures.

Wells, Paul. 1999. *Thou art translated: Analysing animated adaptations*. In *Adaptations: From Text to Screen, Screen to Text*, edited by Deborah Cartmell and Imelda Whelehan, 199–213. London, UK: Routledge.

Wiene, Robert, dir. 1920. *The Cabinet of Dr. Caligari*. Film.

Yates, David, dir. 2007. *Harry Potter and the Order of the Phoenix*. Film. Burbank, CA: Warner Bros. Pictures.

Yates, David, dir. 2009. *Harry Potter and the Half-Blood Prin*ce. Film. Burbank, CA: Warner Bros. Pictures.

Yates, David, dir. 2010. *Harry Potter and the Deathly Hallows— Part 1*. Film. Burbank, CA: Warner Bros. Pictures.

Yates, David, dir. 2011. *Harry Potter and the Deathly Hallows— Part 2*. Film. Burbank, CA: Warner Bros. Pictures.

Yousten, Ken. n.d. *The Raven plot summary*. IMDB.com. Accessed March 19, 2014. http://www.imdb.com/title/tt0057449/?ref_=nv_sr_3.

Zimmer, Mark. 2000. *Review Short 9: Trust*. Digitally Obsessed. Website. Accessed June 19 2016. http://www.digitallyobsessed.com/displaylegacy.php?ID=163.

As You Like It

Adapting Shakespeare for Animation

Why Shakespeare?

The reasons to discuss adapting Shakespeare for animation are manifold, but one clearly stands out: Shakespeare is the writer who has been adapted the most for the screen worldwide (Young 1999). If that is the case, there is also clearly a reason for that:

Roberta Pearson (2004) says: "The humanist Shakespeare, set free from the stifling historicism of a particular English heritage is a transcendent genius who wrote of universal themes and emotions and created emblematic characters recognized by all." Pearson further cites Fiona Shaw (2002), "His plays can be reset in any time and any place because what we recognise in them isn't the dates and the towns, it's the emotions and the experiences, and the personalities familiar to everyone everywhere." Pearson (ibid) concludes: "A humanist Shakespeare is a cosmopolitan who speaks to all the world in contemporary terms."

If an animation director wants to maximize his or her audience and yet desires to be able to add local flavor to his adaptation, Shakespeare offers the ideal source material.

This, in return, provides an explanation for the high number of filmic adaptations.

Shakespeare is by far the most popular author for filmic adaptations. In 2011, Forrest Wickman conducted an analysis of IMDB data to identify the most adapted author. With 831 adaptations that credit him as a writer, Shakespeare came out on top, followed by Chekhov (320), Dickens (300), and Poe (240). His work can therefore stand as "pars pro toto" in terms of representing models for transforming classic literature from page to screen.

His plays have also been adapted for the screen all around the globe, making it particularly suitable to examine transcultural interpretations. This aspect will be more closely explored in the next chapter.

The relatively low number of animated Shakespeare adaptations compared with the far higher count of live-action versions can be attributed to various factors. For a long time, animation was foremost regarded as a medium that addressed children or family audiences.

Certain Shakespeare plays, with their high amount of adult content, were therefore excluded from any serious consideration for adaptation. The other aspect is clearly the initial hesitance to adapt a "high brow culture" author, possibly the most admired playwright in history, for a "low brow medium"-like animation.

Early pioneers in establishing more mature content for animation content were the productions of United Productions of America (UPA) in the early 1950s (Bendazzi 2015). Ted Parmelee's adaptation of Edgar Allen Poe's *The Tell-Tale Heart* (1953) was an example of brilliantly adapting classic literature with darker content for animation. This film is more elaborately discussed elsewhere in this book.

From the late 1960s onward, independent animation started to flourish (Bendazzi 2015), and independent animation authors introduced more adult-oriented themes and daring graphic styles to the medium that allowed for a much greater variety in the choice of source material for adaptations. Still, the strategies for adapting Shakespeare require different considerations compared with the methods of adaptation for live action.

There is more liberty in being able to express the narrative through seemingly limitless imaginative visualization. But the necessary considerations in relation to the economic realities of the extremely labor-intensive animation process demand constraints of different sorts. If there is no budget for a full feature film in a high quality, this can be solved by using a shorter form for the adaptation. Laurie Osborne (2003) compares animated adaptations of Shakespeare with silent films, stating that "the similarities in necessary abbreviation, the dominance of visual images, and a radically new presentation of Shakespeare's plays ally the two forms." She states that "animation offers its own radical innovation by mixing the still-image with frame-by-frame motion in ways which can preserve both media in tension-painting and film."

In her detailed analysis, Osborne focuses on the two BBC series *of Shakespeare: The Animated Tales* (Grace 1992 and 1994, respectively). The film series was produced for TV and employed a variety of animation techniques to retell some of the most popular Shakespeare plays in abridged versions of 30-minute-length each.

The adapted works included *Macbeth*, *Romeo and Juliet*, *A Midsummer Night's Dream*, *Twelfth Night*, *The Tempest* and *Hamlet* in the first series (1992). The second series (1994) consisted of adaptations of *Richard III*, *The Taming of the Shrew*, *As You Like It*, *The Winter's Tale*, *Othello* and *Julius Caesar*. All episodes used abridged scripts to fit the thirty-minute format of the series and employed a variety of animation techniques including traditional cel animation, stop motion and painting on glass. *Hamlet* was awarded an Emmy.

It was produced in the quite unique constellation of a "multinational combination of Welsh producers, English actors and Russian animators (…)" (Osborne 2003).

She further says that the second series particularly "has developed dynamic relationships between Shakespeare's texts and the several distinctive styles of animation."

Michael Dobson (2016) confirms the outstanding quality of the series: "There was that very successful series (...) made by Channel 4 in Wales and a team of Russian animators, *The Animated Tales* (...) and they are really good. It's a handling that suits Shakespeare better than orthodox cine film I think." Bendazzi (2015, 198) concurs: "Many films carried the traces of the Russian school and showed genuine artistic ambition along with masterful execution." In his seminal 1999 article on animated adaptations, Paul Wells also refers to this series by comparing three animated adaptations of *A Midsummer Night's Dream*: John Canemaker's animated short *Bottom's Dream* (1989), Jiří Trnka feature length *A Midsummer Night's Dream* (1959) and Robert Saakyants' version, an episode from the aforementioned BBC/Christmas Film TV series *Shakespeare: The Animated Tales* (1992).

The second series also included an adaptation of *As You Like It*, directed by Alex Karayev (1994). *As You Like It* (Shakespeare 2005) is certainly one of Shakespeare's better-known comedies and contains the famous monologue *All the World's a Stage* narrated by the cynical character Jaques, who serves as a commentator on the events of the play.

The play is a comedy of errors but underplayed with notably darker undertones:

The evil usurper Duke Frederick has exiled his older brother Duke Senior, the rightful ruler, to the forest of Arden. There Duke Senior sits and waits with his fellow band of merry men.

Duke Senior's daughter Rosalind gets banned from court as well and disguises herself as a man by the name of Ganymede to hide. Orlando, a young nobleman, who is in love with Rosalind, has to flee from court and seek refuge in Arden as well. However, he is not able to recognize Ganymede as Rosalind in disguise. Reported comedy of errors ensues—not only for the aforementioned couple but for many more: Oliver and Celia, Phoebe and Silvius, birds and bees, and so on. Only poor Jaques has nobody to quarrel with but himself.

In the end, not only the love-related entanglements resolve, but also, the supposedly evil Duke Frederick suddenly gets reformed, without any concrete reason given.

Numerous weddings happen all at once initiated with a cameo from the deus ex machina marriage god Hymen. Duke Senior is returned to his throne, while Duke Frederick seeks to live as a lonely hermit to repent for his sins.

If this sounds rather random and playful, the author can reassure the reader that it is. And then some. But this seemingly wild abandon is also the great strength of the text: The playfulness of the narrative, the multitude of characters, and the diversity of moods all offer many different options for any director—be that a director of a stage performance or a filmic adaptation. The contrast between shadow and light and occasional melancholy and lively comedy creates an appealing dramaturgical tension that helps to keep the audience engaged.

Juxtaposing the BBC's animated adaptations of the tragedy *Richard III* and of the lighter play, Osborne says "*As You Like It* uses watercolors (...). As a consequence, the comedy offers both more color and more extreme variations in visual style. Both tales, however, incorporate a striking degree of self-consciousness about the dependence of their animation upon stained glass, painting and etching."

In other words, the films move deliberately away from the idea of a suspension of disbelief as a narrative necessity to engage the audience. The authors do trust in the possibility to create empathy for their characters, although these are not perceived as "real" but as literally moving drawings or paintings.

This marks a significant departure from animated films that try to establish a caricatured realism as the mode of delivery, like most of the Disney or Pixar feature films—a stylistic choice that is still pertinent in most contemporary mainstream feature animation and that has even grown with the introduction of computer animation since the early 1990s.

Yet, it is of note that, while unconventional in its visual depiction of characters and scenery, Karayev's version still firmly approaches *As You Like It* as a period piece. The costumes, armory, and architecture reflect a time period that could vaguely be defined as later Renaissance. Karayev set the adaptation roughly in the time period when it was originally written.

A possible reason for this concept might lie in the fact that the BBC series was supposed to primarily educate younger students. The rather modern visualization style might have been considered daring enough. An additional relocation from the traditionally associated time period could have been seen as a step too far. For educational purposes, it is safer to let the play itself remain in the life and times of Shakespeare.

Figure 5.1: Francis Hayman. Ca. 1750. *Shakespearean Scene: As You Like It.*

This classic depiction of the wrestling scene from *As You Like It* (Figure 5.1) demonstrates the more conventional approach defined by a historical setting between the Renaissance and the Early Modern Age. The original text, however, does not suggest this at all.

The lack of an animated version that relocated *As You Like It* to a different place and time inspired the author to create an interpretation of his own (2013–2019).

This idea was first suggested by Assoc. Prof. Daniel Keith Jernigan, a colleague from the department of English literature at Nanyang Technological University in Singapore. Jernigan had previously engaged with abridged versions of Shakespeare plays in his research. He was eager to try his hand at such a shortened version and was fascinated by the artistic options animation could offer. Jernigan came on board the project as the screenwriter and co-producer.

Hannes Rall was supervising the artistic process, which included storyboarding, visual development, and production design, further encompassing character design and color design.

The whole project was developed in the framework of the research project *Wayang Kulit As You Like It: Transcultural Adaptation of Shakespeare for Asian Animation*, with the author as principal investigator (PI). As the title suggests, the idea was to contextualize the creative production within a research framework that investigated the possibilities of employing a traditional Asian art form for adaptation. The research team also included the computer scientists Prof. Seah Hock Soon and Dr. Henry Johan. They supported the development of new software that would simplify the process to animate in the style of Wayang Kulit (Indonesian/Malaysian shadow puppet play).

Hannes Rall also approached one of the world's leading scholars on Shakespeare, Prof. Michael Dobson, with a request for collaboration. Prof. Dobson is the director of the Shakespeare Institute in Stratford-upon-Avon. By accepting the invitation, Prof. Dobson contributed immensely to the project and gave it the much-needed foundation in Shakespeare studies.

All researchers agreed that it was necessary to address the most crucial research questions with Prof. Dobson first. By doing so, all narrative and (visually) artistic decisions would be informed by an expert view on animated Shakespeare adaptations in general and on *As You Like It* in particular.

The authors/researchers were interested in understanding the narrative essence of *As You Like It*. The goal was to find the universal topics that can allow a wide audience to empathize with the characters in the narrative and make it communicate across cultural barriers.

The team wanted to create an abridged version and still capture the essence, the "true spirit" of the Shakespearean source material, if this elusive term could be defined appropriately. For this purpose, it was necessary to identify one or two major themes that could guide the shortening of the source material and still leave the spirit of the original text intact.

The authors were also thinking about the tone of the adaptation—should the creative team even consider creating a spoof or parody of *As You Like It*?

The shorter version would make omissions and shortening of the full dialogue necessary. It was crucial to develop meaningful strategies to make the "right" choices:

Should a shortened version of the original dialogue be used? Which parts could be left out?

Could the adaptation include newly written material for dialogues or even a voice-over narration for certain sequences? These were the major questions about the adaptation at hand when entering into a first conversation with Prof. Dobson and actress Pippa Nixon at the Shakespeare Institute in Stratford-upon-Avon.

An Interview with Prof. Michael Dobson and Pippa Nixon

As You Like It: Core topics and universal themes

The following interview with Prof. Michael Dobson and Pippa Nixon was conducted on June 17 and 18, 2013.

Hannes Rall (interviewer)
Prof. Michael Dobson, University of Birmingham, Director of the Shakespeare Institute Stratford-upon-Avon (interviewed)
Pippa Nixon, actress, performed as "Rosalind" in the 2013 production of *As You Like It* by the Royal Shakespeare Company (interviewed)

Figure 5.2: Prof. Michael Dobson, director of the Shakespeare Institute in Stratford-Upon-Avon.

I spent a great deal of my artistic life adapting classic literature for animation. I am hoping to continue this string of well-reviewed films with a new adaptation of a major Shakespeare play: *As You Like It*. I intend to come up with something interesting but also an animated version that captures the very essence of the play. So, what is for you at the very center of the play?

Love.

That is a perfect answer.

Love, yes.

The reason why I consider this to be a very intriguing answer is that there are indeed many themes and topics in *As You like It*, but it is true, everything is related with or rooted in love somehow. It talks about people being rejected and unrequited love.

And, in some ways, it is also about marriage, because it is not good enough just falling in love with someone, but it is like what are you going to do with it?

Reasonable or entirely unreasonable choices.

Commitment, because, I think, at the beginning of the play, there is quite a strong residue of melancholy between Rosalind and the Duke; her father has been banished from the court, and even though it says that Celia wanted her to stay behind, perhaps there is a feeling of abandonment, and therefore, it is then difficult to trust that someone is going to stay. And so, perhaps that leftover residue comes into her testing Orlando in an extreme way. Can she really trust that someone is not going to leave her? So, perhaps it is about love, but maybe it is about commitment too, or marriage.

I completely agree, but for us, there is also another challenge: Looking at the production realities of our animated adaptation, we will have to come up with an abridged version. We will be required to focus on a certain aspect of the play. And it certainly helps that you are identifying a central topic so clearly. Would you think that focusing, for example, on the relationship between Rosalind/Ganymede and Orlando could be an option to consider? What is your thought about even neglecting some supporting characters?

To be honest, Maria (Aberg), our director has probably focused the play around the Orlando and Rosalind relationship. She has not really cut much of the play, but it has been centered around that. When it came to the previews, the very first shows, it became necessary to shorten the performance. I actually did propose to cut some time from my and Orlando's scenes, and she said, no, because it is the heartbeat of the play. So, I think if your animated adaptation is about half an hour long, you have to center it on that relationship.

Figure 5.3: **Pippa Nixon performing as Rosalind in the 2013 Royal Shakespeare Company Production of *All the World's a Stage*, directed by Maria Aberg. (Courtesy of the Royal Shakespeare Company, Stratford-upon-Avon 2013.) Photographer: Keith Pattison.**

I am also convinced that it is necessary to find a specific focus.

But also, the theme of love in all of its complexity needs to be considered. So, Rosalind and Orlando is the central relationship of love, because it also has its complications. Then, you have Silvius and Phoebe, which is unrequited love, and then, you have Touchstone and Audrey, which is lust. Then, you have Oliver and Celia, which is love at first sight, immediately going to get married, which in some ways, I think, propels Rosalind to marry Orlando. So, you need those four couples, but you could just do a two-dimensional storytelling of those three other couples, if you focused it on Rosalind and Orlando. But I think you would need to have a little strain of each of the other themes.

Absolutely. I was watching that one adaptation that was already done, by the BBC, produced in the early 1990s.

Was it a cartoon?

Yes.

Because I remember seeing them when I was younger.

Sylvestra Le Touzel does Rosalind's voice, and Stephan Bednarzyk, who I used to be in revue with, when we were students, did the (sound) ambience and the music for it. It is done in a style strongly reminiscent of children's picture books and using a watercolor technique.

When considering the narrative aspects only, every adaptation will probably have its shortcomings in that shorter version. But what I found quite well done there is that they also somehow established a focus. You can understand the story completely, even in that shorter version, which is difficult enough. With *As You Like It*, you encounter such a huge sprawling epic, and there are so many almost-anecdotal themes going on, branching off in so many directions. They are all connected, but it is very hard to get all of this into a more condensed format. Actually, these are similar problems like I faced in my last film *The Cold Heart*. The richness of the source material there also would initially be more suitable for a feature-film format than for 30 minutes. Your analysis of the central themes of *As You like It* will therefore prove very helpful going forward: It will help us center our version around these focal points and condense the narrative, without neglecting the essence of the original.

Another important topic I was discussing with my screenwriter Daniel Keith Jernigan is related to the tone of our adaptation. He was proposing to possibly explore a parodistic approach there, basically a spoof of the original play. Or just to make fun of it. I personally do think this would probably be quite difficult, because *As You Like It* is this comedy of errors by and in itself, with many humoristic elements already inherent to the original. I would be interested in your thoughts on this consideration.

Yes, the characters talk in very different styles, which send each other up, as it is: Phoebe, who quotes Marlowe, and Touchstone, who takes the mick out of Corin, and Jaques, who wants to criticize everybody and makes himself ludicrously funny in the processes, by mistake. The question is, how closely the dialogue is going to be based on the original, whether you are simply going to abridge the Shakespeare and leave little bits of the unaltered script or whether you are just going to tell the story and completely rewrite and use your own language, I would have thought.

I feel, the way in which we do it, and the way in which to develop the character, our version is not a spoof or a send-up, even though the situations and the circumstances are very funny. And I think, in Shakespeare's comedy, there is also so much darkness and tragedy, even in *A Midsummer Night's Dream*: It happens at the beginning, at the court, that Hermia, if she does not marry Demitrius, is going to be punished to death. And it is the same with Rosalind and the court. She is now banished or if she does not leave within ten days she is going to be put to death. And when they escape to the forest of Arden, the idea of dressing up as a man is purely for survival rather than any comic foresight. But obviously, when she finds herself in the forest as a man and her lover is in the forest as well, hey presto, comic situation then gets out of control. But I would say that the comedy is born out of necessity and need.

And out of a character development.

Yes, and out of a tragic situation. So, in some ways, I think you would lose the heart of *As You Like It*, if it was sent-up.

Things that ask to be sent-up are things that are solemn and things that are very straight-faced; they make out that they are terribly important, and they make out that the plot is really realistic and gritty, whereas the plot in *As You Like It* is beside the point. As I say, once you have got everybody in the forest, the plot stops, while we just enjoy listening to everyone in the forest talking to each other, flirting with each other, and seeing what happens between them. There is not really anything much to send-up that the play does not already think is funny.

Yes, that is my feeling too. I would be hesitant to go for a pure spoof, because it probably would ultimately fail for the reasons you mentioned. What I find very interesting is precisely the contrast between these darker aspects and the relief and the hope and the ultimate salvation. In some of your interviews about *As You Like It*, you were quoted saying that it is one of a few plays you have been in where nobody dies.

Yes, that was actually a quote from Maria, my director.

Your director said it, yes, I remember. And I find that very interesting in that sense, but I think it probably works as a relief only if you have some menace preceding that outcome. Obviously, here we have not a very happy situation to start with.

Yes, and one of the advantages of doing an animation, rather than a realist movie, is that the forest can be very different things to different characters who arrive in it. For Duke Senior, it seems to be really uncomfortable and difficult; he has got to survive, and he finds moral lessons, and maybe, it represents winter for him. But it seems to be spring for Rosalind; one minute you see Celia saying she is dying of starvation, the next minute she thinks, oh this is great, let us buy a holiday cottage. And sometimes, it is very literal, and sometimes, it is very pragmatic, and there are agricultural people who are worried about the price of sheep, and there are others to whom it is allegorical. And you can do that in a non-realist mode like animation in a way that you cannot do it in a realist movie.

I think that characterizes the big fascination of animation that you can really show different viewpoints by employing different settings and diverse styles with alternative techniques.

And you can have a god turn up, and nobody is going to be bothered; supernatural things will just happen or not happen, and it is not a problem.

In the programme note, there is an essay by Jay Griffiths on the forest of Arden. She also wrote a book called *Wild* (2008) that we used a lot in rehearsals, or we had already read it before. She talks about that kind of spirit of coming back to our own natural wildness and human temperament that is untouched and has not been affected or corrupted by institutions and belief systems. She describes the forest of Arden very similarly to you, that it is a forest of the heart, that they find themselves the forest what it is to them. Because also, on stage, it is very difficult to make a decision about how to do that, because there are also snakes and lions, so it is a dangerous place, but it is also a place where there are no rules.

That is a great inspiration: This narrative property of the forest of Arden forest could be represented by corresponding visual ideas in our adaptation: One would be to explore what this forest is to different people. Maybe it is also like an internal place in a way, and second, also the forest, this wild medicinal place. We were always thinking about this as one of the approaches to visually narrate the forest throughout the whole play. But there is also the aspect of two very different main locations: one is a castle, one is the forest. Most of the story is taking place in the forest, of course, but there is also the castle that could be treated in a very different visual style.

Absolutely.

I am just thinking about this line that Rosalind says when Oliver reveals about the handkerchief, and she faints, and the first thing she says when she awakes is, "I would I were at home." I was just thinking of that now; I could make a totally different choice there at the performance. But the way I have been doing it is just saying that to Celia. It is a very vulnerable, open moment, and her response is 'We'll lead you thither.' Celia interprets that as, right, we will take you back to the cottage. But it could mean, I just want to be the person I have been created to be now. I just want to be myself, I just want to be in a place that is completely safe. And that made me think, because you mentioned of the forest being interior. I think the forest needs to be a place where it displays a sense of coming home for the characters as well. In our version, we feature people who have been living in the forest for years. They have found stuff from the outside world and just brought it in, as we have used car seats and a fridge that still works, a hammock, a deckchair. There is a sense of relaxing outside, and inside. And I like the idea that the forest can be that as well.

Figure 5.4: Pippa Nixon (right) in *As You Like It.* (Courtesy of the Royal Shakespeare Company, Stratford-upon-Avon 2013.) Photographer: Keith Pattison.

It is really good to have all of that input, and I think there are a lot of options here. But some things are clear to me already, where to go and where not to go in the adaptation. What I really liked about your first comment is that you identified love as the central theme. Second, it is about these different couples; they all represent very different ways how love can play out and what to expect from love—what I found particularly engaging is this whole idea of unrequited love and then the attraction to Ganymede. Both narrative elements are funny, because particularly, the unrequited love seems to be very current somehow. It is so typical and so true to be drawn to somebody who actually rejects you and just like to be drawn to that person.

And Orlando enjoys it so much. "I am a lover, and I do not have to do anything about it except tell everybody that I am a lover. It is not as if I actually enter into a relationship or do anything complicated, like getting a mortgage", and poor Rosalind has to spend a lot of time, saying it is not about" you writing poems on trees. How are you actually going to live, how are you going to cope with a wife?", he has to be much more pragmatic and domestic about it. I remember Sam Troughton doing that terribly well, when he played Orlando, and when he turned up in the forest, having decided he was a great, unrequited lover; he went in for some Jack Sparrow eye makeup, had more jewelry than he had before, and was terribly vain about what a great, unrequited lover he was, and Rosalind had to get him down from there somehow. That was great fun to watch.

That is good.

I want to get back to another aspect of adaptation you already touched upon shortly. Can you further elaborate on your opinion about how to work with the original text? In most of the adaptations I did myself, I always left the dialogue in its original version. I selected only parts from the original text, because I could not use everything, but when I used it, I really stayed true to how it was written. And with Shakespeare on top of it, the rhyme form, I think this is even more critical. What would you say, or how do you feel about that—about basically keeping the original, maybe not using the complete text but keeping what you use intact and not change it? What about the option to rewrite dialogue in your own words?

I think, personally, it would be interesting to do it in an abridged version with the original text, to do a 30-or 45-minute version of *As You Like It*, using the actual text. That is very hard as well, because you need a very good editor and dramaturg in some ways.

In part, it is a pragmatic decision about what market you are aiming for.

That is true.

If you are trying to pitch it to an educational market, you want to set it to people who are teaching Shakespeare. Then, they are going to want the original text abridged, I would have thought. If you are trying to sell it to people whose first language is not English, then obviously, you want to do it in translation, and that really frees you up to do those other things.

At this point, we are purely looking at the research aspect of it, which is, in our case, to go for the best artistic option, without any commercial considerations. That is, of course, also relative, because clearly, it is related also to who you are talking to. Are you talking to children? Are you talking to all ages? What is the target audience there?

It is basically what voice do you want to give to the characters, because even in an abridged version, if you give them Shakespeare, you are either giving Shakespeare's voice or you are giving an interpretation of Shakespeare's voice.

A very practical problem is, how can you ever combine that in production?

Edit.

Yes, that is one possible approach, but how can you ever match the beauty of his writing with something else?

There are plenty of filmmakers who really do want as few words as possible distracting people from what they are looking at, for the story. But *As You Like It*, as we have been saying, is not a particularly story-driven piece; the main point is these really interesting things they say to each other and sing to each other and the effect those words have on one another; so yes, you are better off getting people who can speak it.

It always remains a big challenge when you are creating text for anything that is already there and then writing additional text or changing the original or interpreting it—it is always difficult to match. You would have to come up with something on par with some of the greatest writers on earth ever. Therefore, it remains difficult to create something adequate or appropriate: This will mainly be the screenwriter's job, but I will, of course, have an ongoing conversation with him to inform which script finally emerges. That brings me to the visual aspect of the adaptation: I saw that, in the current version of the play, you use these vertical cardboard pillars moving around.

Yes, they are made out of wood, so they are a bit like beams, so they double the court and pillars within a court, and they are on a revolve. Actually, we have a circle with the pillars, and then, there is a square in the front for the court. And then, when we go into the forest, that square is taken away, and there is mud everywhere, and then, the pillars revolve. So, it has a sense of changing location and with the way the light goes, time of day, and things like that.

That I also found quite appealing, because I would also like to bring some kind of level of abstraction, a similar concept to the animated version. I think that there is always a big temptation to be very literal, and this approach completely avoids falling into that trap.

Figure 5.5: Layout drawing by Hannes Rall for the final scene of his *As You like It* adaptation. It shows how stage-like elements are combined to create a theatrical setting.

There was a beautifully spare and stylised *As You Like It*, in the Complete Works Festival, the one that Sam West brought down from Sheffield, with Eve Best and Lisa Dillon. The inhabitants of Arden had the day-job of maintaining the forest of Arden, bringing on the tree, hoisting up the sun, which was this big Habitat lampshade, and there was a big plastic robin which I do not think there is a picture of, it looked slightly like a rather up-market shop window display, and there was a dressing up box, pretty much in view of the audience, in which they kept getting into different hats for different parts of the play.

That leads to another theme, or that, I think, is important to capture, the role of magic in *As You Like it*. When Rosalind improvises in the first wooing scene with Orlando, she talks about an old religious uncle. At the end of the play, when Duke Frederick comes into the forest, he meets with an old religious man as well. I think it is supposed to be the same person. So, there is always this aspect of uncertainty; even though she is improvising, is there truth to what she says? When Ganymede speaks to Orlando and Ganymede says that he will reveal Rosalind to Orlando tomorrow, he also says that since he was 3 years old, he has conversed with a magician most profound in his art. And so, we *(the actors)* were thinking that perhaps, when Rosalind was in the court, and probably incredibly lonely and feeling abandoned, she had this sense of something or someone being with her. So, it could be like an imaginary friend, or it could just be like a guardian angel or somebody that she talks to, that has talked to her about love. So, she has this understanding of love that is rooted in this magician. And the chain that I have *(in the role of Rosalind)*, which I give to Orlando: We talked a lot about what the pendant was, and to us, it is a feather, and that also feels like something quite magical to me; it also feels like bird flight, but it also stands for a magician. And I feel like she had this chain, that this represented her magician. And then, at the end, when Hymen comes (in our production Corin plays Hymen) and when Rosalind first enters into the forest, Corin is present, almost watching her or leading her in. He happens to be the first person that she encounters, who provides a home. Jo Walton, who plays Celia imagined so that when we are getting ready for a wedding, that we go back and tell Corin, this is who we are, but he knew all the time, and in some ways, he is my magician. That is what I always thought.

That is also a very good point for you to look into.

No one in the audience would know that. And so, right at the end, when Jaques, the other son of Sir Rowland de Bois, comes in and says.

'Let me have audience for a word or two'

Exactly, and says about the old religious man that Duke Frederick meets, he and the actor who plays Corin, who is also Hymen at that point, look at each other and perhaps just communicate through his fingers and his lips not to tell anyone. So it is just a tiny thing.

But that is also such an interesting new theme to touch upon or also to think about, because that is also very animatable.

Exactly, that is what I mean.

In terms of atmosphere and in terms of looking at subtle suggestions through gesture and movement, another typical trope of animation obviously is transformation.

Transformation: The duke beautifully talks about tongues in trees.

Books in the running brooks.

And for animation, I just wonder about the aspect that there is life in the tree, there is life in the land, a bit like in a Disney movie, when Orlando is carving in the tree. Because, as Ganymede, I say: "he abuses our young plants." I just feel like that in the original version as well; Orlando and Rosalind are looked out for, that there is something, a sense of fate that happens in that relationship.

I was also thinking a lot about to really understand the forest as a character in itself.

Yes, because the forest responds to the characters; it makes visible what they are feeling, and it also enables what they need to do. Everybody who comes to Arden finds himself interacting with it, in really intriguing ways. The forest responds to peoples' desires—they all seem to meet what they need from it.

This combines well with the main narrative thread of love and these three couples going through the whole narrative. Their stories could be supported by the approach to really have the forest react or maybe even act out some wishes and perceptions of the animated characters. The more I engage with the topic or try to explore adaptation options, the more I think it is actually pretty well suited for an animated adaptation. Usually, I always have people dying in my films. In my last film *The Cold Heart*, the love interest Lisbeth dies, but she gets resurrected, so she lives again in the end. Therefore, I was initially very much drawn to the darker Shakespeare plays such as *Macbeth* and *Hamlet*. But I like *As You Like It* very much in the sense that it is all about balance between light and dark. As you said, there is menace, and then, there is comedy playing against it, but the comedy would not be strong enough if there would not be something like the darker elements in contrast. And I think we should reflect that in the animation.

Figure 5.6: Celia and Rosalind (disguised as Orlando) in the new adaptation.

And also that melancholy is a definite theme that manifests through Jaques, in our version as well, when Jaques and Rosalind meet each other. I think Rosalind knows melancholy, but she chooses not to live her life that way. And when Jaques talks about it, he thinks it is the experience of the world that has made him sad. Rosalind says: "I would rather have a fool to make me merry than experience to make me sad." And I think she knows experience to make her sad, and that is why, she has chosen the fool to come with her, but if you have too much laughter, or too much sadness, you are both as bad as each other. You need the balance.

I think it is the same with everything; it is also the same with animation. If you only have a slow movement or you only have fast movements, it does not work at all. Because you need the contrast to create some tension.

One of the things you will find, when abridging the play for the script, is that *All the World's a Stage* is the one speech from this play that a lot of people still know by heart, and therefore, you would possibly have trouble cutting it.

Exactly, what I took from the older animated adaptation was that, obviously, this specific monologue was one of two sequences where they actually employed a different visual style, a more graphically sparse style. Obviously, what *All the World's a Stage* says about the seven ages of men is pretty much what everybody would recognize from the longer play. And I agree with that—that is probably a simple way to connect to people. When looking at this, another thought crossed my mind: When you look at the history, of how Shakespeare has been staged over the years, overall in modern theatre, is there a little bit of a return to more visual opulence displayed on stage?

It depends on the budget. It varies, different plays have very different performance traditions, and different companies too.

Looking specifically at *As You Like It*?

With *As You Like It*, for much of the twentieth century, there was a default setting of rustic, where you have real trees, and Rosalind always wore green tights, and in Stratford, they had the same dead deer in every single production, which probably received a round of applause when it came on. They would drag on the same dead stag out of the cupboard, and everybody would be very pleased to see it. But the forest was literal, for a lot of the time, even right down to Vanessa Redgrave (1961), who was probably the best Rosalind until Pippa Nixon, by all accounts.

I saw this stated somewhere in a recent review actually.

You cannot get away from it. And yes, I do not know if it has become more opulent. There have been more fanciful Ardens, but there has also been a tradition of pretty depressing *As You Like It*. There is an awful lot of fake snow in the forest of Arden the last couple of years.

Did you see the one that Dominic Cooke did?

Yes, where they all sang the twenty-third psalm in the end, it was rather pious. It was freezing, and they were bare-footed in the forest, and they were dying of exposure, poor devils, the Duke could fool nobody but himself that he was able to have a nice time in the forest. Quite often, again it has become a kind of cliché saying that there is winter in the first half and summer in the second half. It all changes miraculously during the interval while you are not looking. There is nothing to cue that for you in the text.

Although I just wonder that, in some ways, time bends in a forest.

Exactly, which is the first thing Rosalind talks about.

Yes, exactly, about time. Time means different things to different people, and I wonder whether you can get that in there as well. Because if you start looking at it literally and linearly, it makes no sense; it is almost like I am sitting here 1 minute, and I move over there, and it changes season. And in some ways, to accept that is beautiful, and it is almost like no one ever ages or something.

Yes, and I remember that from watching, in the wings, the 1985 Royal Shakespeare Company (RSC) *As You Like It*, with Juliet Stevenson, because Fiona Shaw used to play snooker with Hilton McCray in the green room. And so I would be watching on the monitor and trying to think through the play, not in terms of what had to happen next and the action, but when were Celia and Orlando next going to be neither of them on stage, so they could get on with the snooker game.

Yes, because Celia is on most of the time.

She is on an awful lot. And when you watch the movement of the characters, in terms of when the actors are coming off-stage, rather than what they were doing on stage, then there is no structure to this play at all, it is just a matter of, who has not had a conversation with who yet, in front of the audience. So whose turn is it with the snooker table next? It is quite different. This is one of the plays where you can put scenes in a different order and hardly anyone notices it, because it is not one of the tight-structured ones like *Much Ado About Nothing*, or *Romeo and Juliet* or *Othello*, where this has to happen so that this happens, and as a result that happens, and we in the audience always know what time it is.

But I wonder whether maybe there was method in that madness, because with our set at the beginning, with having this square court in front of the circle, the court is all about edges and sides, and contained boundaries, whereas in the forest, this is a circle, so there are no edges.

I always love these lead ideas, where the visual is informed by the content in such a way that the design really supports the narrative. That is really crucial in my opinion, and it is very important to get that right. Because if you do not, then it just becomes decoration, in a way, and you want to avoid that. But there is also the whole idea of timing—that is another beautiful aspect of animation to consider.

And it is one of the ways in which Jaques is such an important counterpart within the play. He is the person who says, not only that he met a fool in the forest, but he had a watch. For him, we only get seven ages, we are running out of time.

This is also something that can be represented very nicely and beautifully in animation. Very often, what you can do in animation becomes interesting, if you go against the expectations: Frequently, animation just follows the idea of a logical, linear, storytelling; one thing leads to the other, but alternatively, there could be a sudden change in the narrative. You can do that easily in animation, but a lot of mainstream animation never does that, because it is a little bit more challenging to the audience. But if you dare to do it, the audience often completely buys into it.

So, Pippa, did you look back on previous performances, or did you stay away from them completely?

Stayed completely away. It is funny, I am playing Rosalind and I am playing Ophelia. For Ophelia, I looked at previous performances, I did not have any problems with that. I looked massively so, because there are so much missing scenes; Rosalind, I do not want to go near anybody. This is the first time, I am like, oh, suddenly I start to feel like I can now. I really think I will pay a visit to you at the Institute in August or September and say, right, show me all you have got. I feel so strong in what we have done over there. I think I have worked with the director a number of times before, and I trust her, and I love her exploration of character, and I just wanted to start it fresh.

I read about her approach actually, which I found very interesting, that she leaves the actors a lot of room to develop; she actually creates only the parameters of the basic.

Yes, she lets you play a lot. Ideas come, and she never fixes the stuff until right at the end, where she fixes a lot or will tidy up. But what she will always do is when you veer away from the truth, either in the text or of the character, she will bring it straight back, and she will make you look at it in a very different way. I remember the first scene as Ganymede with Orlando, it is very tempting in those scenes, because she is very clever, and she is very quick-witted. I think she runs circles around Orlando anyway, but for it to feel like 'I know it all,' or just being bossy, or irritating, Maria said to me, you have to bond with him. That is your one action with this scene; you have to bond with him. So, whatever you say, it is always for him to want more. And actually, the charm comes out of that. If my main aim is to become his best friend, and in a way, to woo him, to get him to come to my cottage, I have to work very hard at leaving little bits of bread crumbs for him to gobble up. If I become really quite hard, and cold, then people would be like, why does he even want to become friends with this person?

That is exactly what Rebecca Hall did as Rosalind, she was much too controlling.

That is a curiosity to me.

She is the only Rosalind I have ever seen who I actively disliked throughout; she just knew better than everybody else.

Exactly.

She was a private-school girl on holiday, telling the locals what they should do.

It can be read like that, with Phoebe, when she comes in. But the heart of this person, she is unbelievably in love with this man, and she manages to play that scene by keeping the disguise. And with Phoebe, when Ganymede talks to Phoebe, it is because Silvius is the first person that she has seen in the forest that has gone. Oh, I get that feeling of love, that unrequited feeling, not being able to stop talking about it. She wants to help him, and that is why she is tough on Phoebe. I cannot remember what your question was, but I did not look at anybody's previous performance. And what I feel pleased about with that is that with finding Ganymede, I went through a bit of a journey of…

That is also another question, what would have to be my last, to look at that whole concept of…

Dressing up.

Yes, exactly.

The first thing I thought about was the film *Boys Don't Cry* that featured Hillary Swank. It is an amazing film, and she plays a boy like I have never seen before, and I watched that with Maria, the director, and we both thought this was fantastic. But it is for different reasons that this woman, as a boy, wants to go through a whole gender transformation and that is not what Rosalind does yet. I did not want to play Ganymede, like I have seen so many, of a girl, just literally tying her hair back, wearing an open shirt —, you are so clearly a girl.

That reminded me of the German actress Liselotte Pulver. I am quite sure you would not know her. She is in *The Spessart Inn* (dir. Hoffmann 1958), a German film from the 1950s. She was a really big star in Germany after the war, in mainstream movies. She did exactly that—she was also playing a guy.

Exactly. And I just thought, whatever happens, the reason why Rosalind has to dress up as a boy is for their safety—of hers and Celia's—and it has to cost her something, and I thought, as an actress, it has got to cost me something, so my hair had been long; I thought I cut it off. I think she would have cut her hair off, and would be very much disguised by it, and then, I wear a body stocking to be bound down, and then, we put something down my trousers—that is invasive as a woman, but it just centers you as a man differently, and that is all we did really. And I also thought, I want to go for, I think you talked about it with the hermaphrodite, I thought I want to go for androgyny. So, unlike Tilda Swindon, David Bowie, and Ben Whishaw, we have these actors, who have a mercurial quality; that is something else that has both feminine and masculine, and going for those things helps to create Ganymede.

Figure 5.7: Early designs for the film exploring Ganymede as a hermaphrodite. Jochen Rall, digital, 2013.

Do you apply particular acting methods to achieve this? Special movement patterns or just special ways to move? How you change coming from one to the other?

Yes, in some ways. In court as Rosalind and I have this very elegant black dress; in court, it is a very feminine and masculine world, where the women have to perform their sexuality in a sense, so it is very sexualized, and the men are very sexualized with our wrestling; it is bare knuckle fighting; guys' tops are off, and they are very tough. And then, in the forest, it is a free for all. But our movement director is fantastic, and she said, as women, we self-groom quite a lot; she said, let us cut that out for the man, as a woman, we protect here; [*gestures to her crotch*], for guys it is much more open. And they are protecting.

That is very interesting, because the famous animation director Richard Williams talks about exactly the same things. He has created this tutorial series (2008) about animation, which also addresses the different ways of man and women walking.

I have seen it, because we watched something about the different gaits.

It also shows that, different from men, women are "protecting their business" during a walk.

Yes, and also that men can take a lot more space. And actually, as Ganymede, that started to happen naturally, because there is an energy about him, and so, I take more of the space. The thing is, that can be difficult; Rosalind in the first half of the play and in the second half of the play can seem like a very different character, and so, there has to be elements in both. So, whenever Orlando would go off the stage, and I was with Celia, I would drop back into the feminine, and then, when a man came on, the hands go back in the trousers, and it becomes a lot more masculine. This is very subtle.

Figure 5.8: Rosalind and Ganymede in the new adaptation. Character design by Hannes Rall and Lim Wei Ren Darren.

Now, I am sorry I did not record your visuals, because you are so expressive. There is so much going on when you speak in terms of gesture and everything, a real inspiration for an animator. There are a lot of things I really can take with me for input into the script or the visual development. I was never a big friend of the idea of a parody or spoof, so it is good to hear you concur with this. Why would I want to do a send-up if I can do something much stronger, if it is being played straight, in that sense, and humor and darkness can be balanced like in the original play.

Just on that, there is still some great comedy or playing up in the Rosalind and Orlando scenes, where he might have moments of going, is this Rosalind, and then disappearing. Because I played it as well in the second wooing scene, that in some ways, Ganymede wants him to know that it is Rosalind, but then, he just does not get it. So, there is a lot of comedy to be had.

Definitely. The other challenge we are facing in that very stylized approach we use is the technically limited expressiveness of the characters. That is because we will use less-detailed and less-animatable facial features for the characters. So, you have to come up with equivalents for expressing moods and subtle emotions.

Figure 5.9: A model sheet from the adaptation that showcases the limited variation of facial features in the chosen animation style of digital cutout animation. Model sheet by Lim Wei Ren Darren, character design by Hannes Rall and Lim Wei Ren Darren.

But I think we can solve this problem, because, in animation, a lot of these things can be expressed through the image as a whole. As already mentioned, most of the traditional Disney animation or most computer generated (CG) animation is using a caricatured realism approach for the character design and animation. That means exaggerating the acting like it would have been done by real-life actors and then adding some other level to it. When you use a more stylized approach, you have to replace this approach by other means, in a way. And I usually try to do a balance of both, in my films. But, certainly, if we would have just visually recorded you during the interview, that would have resulted in some amazing reference. Just observing your eyes, it is amazing how they just become wide and how you play with your eyes, which, in a theatre, you would notice only if you had had these theatre glasses or would be sitting in the first rows. But your bigger gestures are also so animated, very fascinating. Thank you very much. (End of interview).

This interview with Michael Dobson and Pippa Nixon answered to a lot of questions about the concept and narrative mode of the new adaptation. Based on this input, the authors Hannes Rall and Daniel Keith Jernigan decided to definitely forego the option of a parody. Michael Dobson's information about the highly eclectic approach inherent in Shakespeare's original itself encouraged the production team to approach the adaptation more freely.

Narrative choices: script and storyboard

Daniel Jernigan came up with a first draft of the screenplay. It turned out be a strongly abridged version that focuses mainly on the love story between Rosalind/Ganymede and Orlando, in line with what Pippa and Michael had identified as the essence of the play. Along with Rosalind and Orlando, the romantic entanglement (or non-entanglement) of Phoebe and Silvius offered contrast and reflection.

Daniel also changed the sequence of some scenes and dialogues within the play. For the dialogue, he almost exclusively relied on a selection from the original Shakespeare text. For an introduction and some transitions, additional text for a voice-over narration was written. It serves as a summary of events that cannot be shown in full, owing to time constraints. Great care was taken to match these few additional lines to Shakespeare's original in tone.

For the abridged version, anecdotal episodes, storylines of lesser importance, and the number of characters were reduced significantly. It was important to always consider the relevance to the central theme of love as the guiding line for what to eliminate and what to keep. The highly complex original text was restructured into a total of eight scenes that were feasible to produce at a ca. 25-minute running time:

Introduction: An introductory scene that familiarizes the audience with the main situation: Evil usurper Duke Frederick has exiled his brother and rightful regent Duke Senior, who had to flee to the forest of Arden.

Figure 5.10: Visual style: A flat, more painterly introduction to the main characters that distinguishes this scene as an introductory sequence from the rest of the film. Concept drawing by Hannes Rall.

Scene 1. The wrestling match between Orlando and the Duke's wrestler. Orlando wins and leaves the court after upsetting Duke Frederick. Celia and Rosalind are also being exiled from the palace by Duke Frederick.

Figure 5.11: Visual style: This scene introduces the main style of the film: A layered 2.5 D digital cutout technique that creates depth of field and dimensionality through virtual lighting. This is used for dramatic effect in this scene that takes place at night. A dark atmosphere is established to communicate the menace present by the evil usurper. Film still.

Scene 2. Escape to the forest of Arden: Rosalind, Celia, and Touchstone.

Figure 5.12: Visual style: Continues the previously established 2.5 D digital cutout animation style. But the scene changes to brighter daylight colors and shows the transition from dawn to dusk as the refugees travel to the forest of Arden. Concept drawing by Hannes Rall.

Scene 3. All the World's a Stage.

A "film within a film." Thematically and artistically different from the other scenes.

Initially planned as a part of *As You like It* - it ended up as an animated short film on its own.

Figure 5.13: Visual style: Intentionally different from the rest of the film, stark black and white, with only red as color added. Highly abstract and stylized. Film still.

Scene 4. Love letters in the forest: Flirtatious scene between Orlando and Rosalind disguised as Ganymede.

Figure 5.14: Visual style: The forest of Arden is introduced as a tropical rainforest that reminisces the rich and vibrant colors from the paintings of Henri Rousseau. Extended background drawing by Hannes Rall and Lim Wei Ren Darren. Film still. Painting *Il sogno* by Henri Rousseau (1910).

Scene 5. Rosalind and Celia, Phoebe and Silvius: The trials and tribulations of the complicated relationship between Phoebe and Silvius are explored in dialogue. This gives Rosalind some second thoughts.

Figure 5.15: Visual style: A parody of classic pastoral paintings combined with the tropical setting of the film—an intentionally eclectic mix that fuses influences from Western and Eastern artistic traditions.

Scene 6. Duke Senior and foresters at the banquet: Orlando enters with dramatic pose, tells a story, and is invited for dinner.

Figure 5.16: Visual style: Dramatic lighting through torchlight enhances the spooky atmosphere of the scene. The design fully embraces the idea of a stage performance by having Orlando appear on top of a moveable stage prop. Rich and vibrant colors of the characters provide contrast to the darkness surrounding them. Layout drawing by Hannes Rall and film stills. Art by Lim Wei Ren Darren and Hannes Rall.

Scene 6a. Orlando narrates how he rescued a man from a tiger.

Figure 5.17: Visual style: An entirely different color scheme of very muted colors is used for this scene to distinguish it as a dream-like flashback sequence. This also suggests that this tale could be entirely invented by Orlando. (Art by Lim Wei Ren Darren and Hannes Rall.)

Scene 7. Orlando and Rosalind meet and make up, same as Phoebe and Silvius.

Figure 5.18: Visual style: A return to the pastoral setting of scene 5. This scene once again provides contrast to the preceding scene: A sunny day and the bright atmosphere reflect the impending resolution of the complicated relationships. It serves as a more neutral optical "palate cleanser" before the visually indulgent finale. (Art by Lim Wei Ren Darren and Hannes Rall.)

Scene 8. Initiated by the deus ex machina love god Hymen, a sudden mass wedding occurs. Happy ending.

Figure 5.19: Visual style: An intentionally over-the-top parody of the classic Busby Berkeley musicals, abundant in richness of characters, color, and elements. Film stills 2019. Hannes Rall (design and cleanups), Khoo Siew May (digital painting, color design and postproduction/rendering).

Figures 5.20 through 5.22 show a good example of the process of narrative development. They display the progression from original text through the screenplay and finally the storyboard of a section of Act III, Scene 2. We christened this particular scene "Love Letters in the Forest," due to its main content: Rosalind (disguised as Ganymede) finds love letters pinned on trees, singing her praises. Orlando (who is the culprit behind these) and later Celia enter the scene. An amusing conversation ensues as Orlando is unable to recognize Rosalind in her disguise and vice versa; Rosalind is not revealing herself to Orlando as being in love with him as well. Despite Orlando's non-awareness of who that mysterious Ganymede actually is, a heavily flirtatious conversation between both plays out with witty wordplay. On top of it all, foolish Touchstone, turned into a monkey for this version, delivers satirical comments.

AS YOU LIKE IT

ACT III. Scene II. The forest.

Enter ROSALIND, with a paper, reading

ROSALIND
From the east to western Ind,
No jewel is like Rosalind.
Her worth, being mounted on the wind,
Through all the world bears Rosalind.
All the pictures fairest lined
Are but black to Rosalind.
Let no fair be kept in mind
But the fair of Rosalind.
TOUCHSTONE
I'll rhyme you so eight years together, dinners and suppers and sleeping-hours excepted: it is the right butter-women's rank to market.
ROSALIND
Out, fool!
TOUCHSTONE
For a taste:
If a hart do lack a hind,
Let him seek out Rosalind.
If the cat will after kind,
So be sure will Rosalind.
Winter garments must be lined,
So must slender Rosalind.
They that reap must sheaf and bind;
Then to cart with Rosalind.
Sweetest nut hath sourest rind,
Such a nut is Rosalind.
He that sweetest rose will find
Must find love's prick and Rosalind.
This is the very false gallop of verses: why do you infect yourself with them?
ROSALIND
Peace, you dull fool! I found them on a tree.
TOUCHSTONE
Truly, the tree yields bad fruit.
ROSALIND
I'll graff it with you, and then I shall graff it with a medlar: then it will be the earliest fruit i' the country; for you'll be rotten ere you be half ripe, and that's the right virtue of the medlar.
TOUCHSTONE
You have said; but whether wisely or no, let the forest judge.
Enter CELIA, with a writing

ROSALIND
Peace! Here comes my sister, reading: stand aside.
CELIA
[Reads]
Why should this a desert be?
For it is unpeopled? No:
Tongues I'll hang on every tree,
That shall civil sayings show:
Some, how brief the life of man
Runs his erring pilgrimage,
That the stretching of a span
Buckles in his sum of age;
Some, of violated vows
'Twixt the souls of friend and friend:
But upon the fairest boughs,
Or at every sentence end,
Will I Rosalinda write,
Teaching all that read to know
The quintessence of every sprite
Heaven would in little show.
Therefore Heaven Nature charged
That one body should be fill'd
With all graces wide-enlarged:
Nature presently distill'd
Helen's cheek, but not her heart,
Cleopatra's majesty,

Figure 5.20: Act III. Scene II. The forest: Excerpt from the original Shakespeare text of *As You Like It*.

Enter ORLANDO, with love letters in his hand. Using his arrows, he pins these love letters to the trees in the forest. A TIGER stalks ORLANDO. The TIGER pounces and misses ORLANDO, who climbs a tree to pin yet another love letter. In the meantime, the NARRATOR continues.

NARRATOR
We find Orlando fixed in the third stage
His love blazing a trail of poetry
From tree to tree a path for Rosalind
The forest proves a tonic to young love.

ORLANDO
O Rosalind! these trees shall be my books
And in their barks my thoughts I'll character;
That every eye which in this forest looks
Shall see thy virtue witness'd every where.

The camera shifts to the left, away from ORLANDO. Enter ROSALIND and TOUCHSTONE. Rosalind plucks one of the love letters and reads it.

ROSALIND
From the east to western Ind,
No jewel is like Rosalind.
Her worth, being mounted on the wind,
Through all the world bears Rosalind.

TOUCHSTONE
I'll rhyme you so eight years together (*pause*)

For a taste:

Sweetest nut hath sourest rind,
Such a nut is Rosalind.
He that sweetest rose will find
Must find love's prick and Rosalind.
This is the very false gallop of verses: why do you
infect yourself with them?

Truly, the tree yields bad fruit.

Enter CELIA, with a writing

ROSALIND
Peace you dull fool! Here comes my sister, reading: stand aside.

Exeunt TOUCHSTONE

CELIA
Didst thou hear these verses?

ROSALIND
O, yes, I heard them all, and more too; for some of
them had in them more feet than the verses would bear.

CELIA
Trow you who hath done this?

ROSALIND
Nay, tell me who it is.

CELIA
It is young Orlando, that tripped up the wrestler's
heels and your heart both in an instant.

ROSALIND
Orlando?

CELIA
Orlando.

ROSALIND
What makes him here? Doth he know that I am in this forest
and in man's apparel?

CELIA
I found him under a tree, like a dropped acorn.
He was furnished like a hunter.

ROSALIND
O, ominous! he comes to kill my heart.

CELIA
Soft! comes he not here?

Enter ORLANDO

ROSALIND
'Tis he. [*Aside to CELIA*] I will speak to him.

There is a man haunts the forest, that
abuses our young plants with carving 'Rosalind' on
their barks; hangs odes upon hawthorns and elegies
on brambles, all, forsooth, deifying the name of
Rosalind: if I could meet that fancy-monger I would
give him some good counsel, for he seems to have the
quotidian of love upon him.

ORLANDO
I am he that is so love-shaked: I pray you tell me
your remedy.

ROSALIND
But are you so much in love as your rhymes speak?

ORLANDO
Neither rhyme nor reason can *express* how much.

ROSALIND
Love is merely a madness, and, I tell you, deserves
as well a dark house and a whip as madmen do.
Yet I profess curing it by counsel.

ORLANDO
Did you ever cure any so?

ROSALIND
Yes, one, and in this manner. He was to imagine me
his love, his mistress; and I set him every day to
woo me.

He was, to forswear the full stream of
the world, and live in a nook merely monastic.
And thus I cured him; and this way will I take upon
me to wash your liver as clean as a sound sheep's

Figure 5.21: The same scene in the animated adaptation by Rall (screenplay by Daniel Keith Jernigan 2013.)

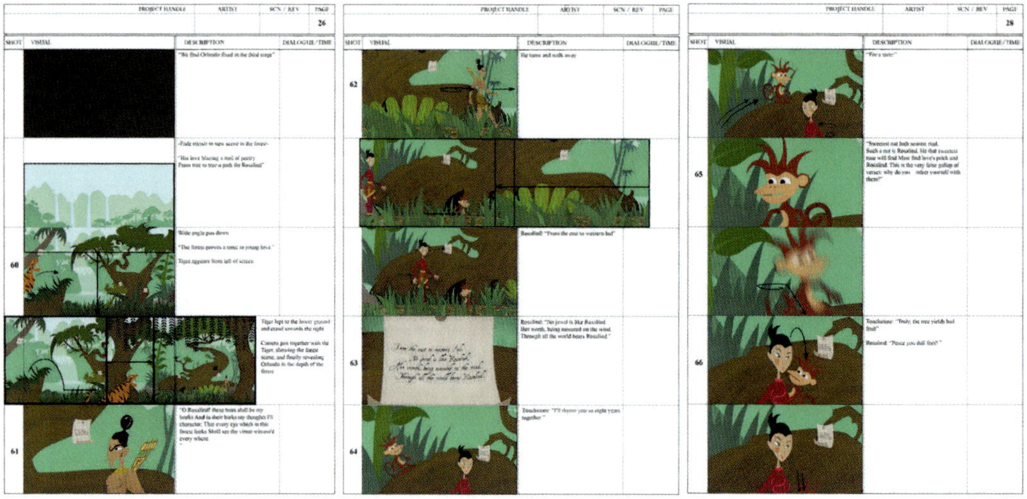

Figure 5.22: The storyboard for the same scene in the animated adaptation, edited by Lim Wei Ren Darren, based on characters and environments created by Hannes Rall and Darren Lim.

A major challenge for the adaptation was to keep this dialogue-heavy scene engaging enough for the audience. In other words, how to avoid a mere sequence of talking heads and enable the spectator to empathize with the characters on play?

This proved all the more difficult, as the chosen digital-cutout animation technique limited the animation and excluded subtle expressiveness of the facial features.

For the lip syncing, our digital models allowed only for a minimal variety of mouth positions, basically mouth open and mouth closed.

The proposed and ultimately executed solution consisted of two main components.

First by taking good care that the editing provided a variety of shots that allowed the audience to indulge in the richness of the virtual environment with long shots and focus on the characters in medium shots and close-ups.

Second, through relying on bigger theatrical expressions and body language for the dialogue animation. This worked well and superseded the problem of the limited lip-sync animation.

Mark Hendry (2016) provides a great example of how such a strategy can work extremely well for animation in his thoughtful essay on Richard Williams's unfinished masterpiece *The Thief and the Cobbler.* An example of dialogue animation for the sultan is shown that succeeds in being highly expressive, despite only using two mouth positions: open and closed.

What greatly inspired our dialogue animation was the lively voice acting provided by a number of well-known Singaporean actors. These recordings took place ahead of the animation in 2014 (which is the usual process).

Figure 5.23: Singaporean actress Julie Wee recording the voice for Rosalind/Ganymede (2014). Julie Wee went on to perform as the character Miranda in the 2015 staging of *The Tempest* in the *Shakespeare in the Park* series at Fort Canning Park in Singapore.

Once again, the team referred back to Prof. Dobson for advice on the artistic direction the voice recordings should take. The decision to work with local actors made it necessary to decide to which extent local accent(s) should also be used for the dialogue.

Michael Dobson considered that as a possibility but ultimately recommended a different and more complex solution: The main characters would speak in a classical Shakespearean English voice, with barely the hint of an accent. This was a real possibility, because the main local actors had performed in Shakespeare plays in a classical mode before.

The artistic reason was to avoid a clichéd "exoticism" and to deliberately push the artistic contrast between the clearly localized design style and the classic British Shakespeare voice.

One notable exception was the character of Touchstone: He stands out in the adaptation, because he is the only anthropomorphosized character. His acting is intentionally over the top. He provides a satirical voice, more commenting on the events than acting in the play. Therefore, the initial plan was to have him voiced by a local voice actor, with a strong local flavor in his dialogue.

Figure 5.24: Model sheet of the Touchstone character, designed by Hannes Rall and Lim Wei Ren Darren.

The design of Touchstone (Figure. 5.24) anthropomorphosizes the character as a monkey wearing a jester's cap. The jester's hat references many previous visual interpretations. The monkey character is vaguely reminiscent of the Monkey King—the iconic and irreverent hero known from the Indian national epic *Ramayana* (Arya 1998) as well as the Chinese *Journey to the West* (Wu, Cheng'en, and Anthony C. Yu 1980).

All the World's a Stage

The famous monologue *All the World's a Stage* forms a part of the much longer play *As You Like It*. In this well known speech the character Jaques ponders the 7 ages of men. Prof. Michael Dobson, Director of the Shakespeare Institute in Stratford-upon-Avon notes (2013): "Jaques is such an important counterpart in the play, (…) he says not only that he met a fool in the forest, but that he had a watch. There are only seven ages of man, we are running out of time."

The immense popularity of this poetic treatise might very well have its cause in the universality of its topic: the seven ages of man. In very short and concise terms, the tragicomedy of human existence unfolds. It ends with the bleakest of outlooks, with no hint at otherworldly bliss or deliverance. The final lines are matter of fact at least, if not downright sarcastic in the end. This modern point of view gives the writing a timeless quality. Details of the described life periods may vary today, but the overall sentiment still stays the same.

Narrator

All the world's a stage,
And all the men and women merely players:
They have their exits and their entrances;
And one man in his time plays many parts,
His acts being seven ages. At first the infant,
Mewling and puking in the nurse's arms.
And then the whining school-boy, with his satchel
And shining morning face, creeping like snail
Unwillingly to school. And then the lover,
Sighing like furnace, with a woeful ballad
Made to his mistress' eyebrow. Then a soldier,
Full of strange oaths and bearded like the pard,
Jealous in honour, sudden and quick in quarrel,

Seeking the bubble reputation
Even in the cannon's mouth. And then the justice,
In fair round belly with good capon lined,
With eyes severe and beard of formal cut,
Full of wise saws and modern instances;
And so he plays his part. The sixth age shifts
Into the lean and slipper'd pantaloon,
With spectacles on nose and pouch on side,
His youthful hose, well saved, a world too wide
For his shrunk shank; and his big manly voice,
Turning again toward childish treble, pipes
And whistles in his sound. Last scene of all,
That ends this strange eventful history,
Is second childishness and mere oblivion,
Sans teeth, sans eyes, sans taste, sans everything.

The monologue can also stand well on its own. It does not relate to the bigger narrative of *As You Like It* at all; it neither propels the story nor comments on the plot itself. Instead, it transcends the narrative framework to offer a more general comment on the human condition.

As mentioned previously, a widely known series of animated Shakespeare adaptations was commissioned by the BBC in the early 1990s. *All the World's a Stage* was also adapted in this series as a part of the full episode *As You Like It* (Karayev 1994). This earlier adaptation was examined by the new adapters to identify artistically successful elements as well as less-convincing stylistic approaches. The age of the earlier adaptation (1994) also meant that it could not use digital production methods at all, because they simply did not exist at that time. This previous version was produced in black and white, to stand out from the rest of *As You Like It*—an idea that seemed worth considering for the new adaptation as well. The older piece featured representational yet stylized imagery that was reminiscent of renaissance woodcuts. Hannes Rall decided to replace this historical setting with a less-representational style to emphasize the timelessness of the topic.

For his new adaptation, the author intended to reflect the specific qualities of *All the World's a Stage* in the visual design for the sequence. It was supposed to be significantly different from the rest of the film and also visually express the universality of its theme.

Both aspects were addressed by choosing a highly abstract style that creates characters from basic geometric shapes such as the circle, the triangle, and the square.

The colors are restricted to black and white, with red serving as the sole "real" color to accentuate certain elements in the scene.

The sobering description of man's life cycle finds its equivalent in the puristic design approach.

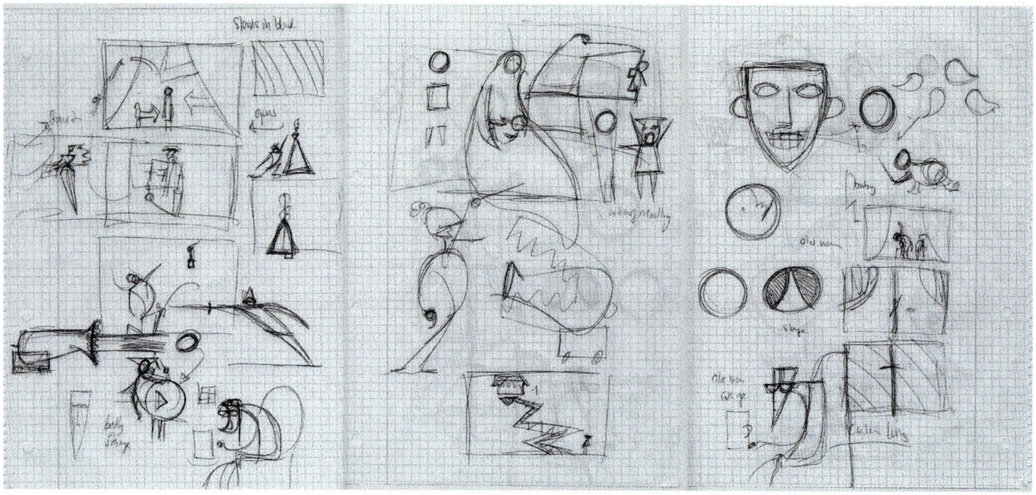

Figure 5.25: The initial development sketches by Hannes Rall that already laid out the narrative and visual flow for the whole short film. They also reveal how characters are constructed from very simple geometric shapes. Ink on paper, 2014.

Narratively, the sequence was constructed as one continuous long shot, for which different perspectives and camera angles are created through animated metamorphoses.

Metaphorically speaking, it used a visual storytelling method that reflects life as a constant flow progressing from one stage to another until it reaches an abrupt halt.

The curtain falls.

This style is entirely different from the rest of the film, it was initially planned for: *the new As You Like It* adaptation—that works more with techniques reminiscent of live action by employing virtual sets and classic editing.

In the 1994 Karayev version of *All the World's a Stage*, single characters are fully animated within bigger tableaus of figures and settings. Some characters are not animated at all.

The 2016 version focused on one constantly transforming character that was fully animated throughout.

Figure 5.26: Film stills from *All the World's a Stage* (Rall 2016). Directed by Hannes Rall. Animated by Hannes Rall and Andre Quek.

The resulting 1 minute and 30 seconds version of *All the World's a Stage* was considered artistically so successful by the production team that it was finally decided to release a modified version as a standalone film (instead of integrating it into *As You Like It*).

But this required a different strategy in terms of narration and soundtrack for this form of release: Without the context of the narrative from *As You Like It*, it didn't seem appropriate anymore to use the voice of Gene Shah Rudyn—our "Touchstone" in *As You like It*—for the narration. Without being introduced to the character of Touchstone and his incarnation as a monkey, the highly localized and stylized voice-narration style would have seemed out of place. Instead, an authoritative reading of the text in classic Shakespearean fashion would ease the audience into the more abstract imagery through a familiar mode of delivery.

Through Michael Dobson, the chance arose to ask the renowned Shakespeare actor and director Samuel West to collaborate in the project. Most fittingly, West had also directed *As You Like It* as part of the Royal Shakespeare Company's (RSC's) Complete Works Festival in Sheffield in 2007 (Spencer 2007). He recorded the voice-over narration of the basis of the already-completed animation. This was possible because there was no lip sync involved. Samuel was therefore able to react to the animation that he was seeing onscreen. He delivered an excellent narration, combining the requisite gravitas with ironic wit.

Figure 5.27: Samuel West (*Howards End*, Ivory 1992; *Notting Hill*, Michell 1999.)

Figure 5.28: Daniela Martella, soundtrack composer for *As You like It* and *All the World's a Stage*.

The young German composer Daniele Martella had already come up with a musical concept for the whole adaptation of *As You Like It*, but for the short-film version of *All the World's a Stage* by itself, he had to reconsider his approach. He needed to subtly balance his musical score with the constant presence of Samuel West's strong voice-over narration.

He used a small chamber music ensemble to weave string instrumentation around the voice and comment musically on the events onscreen. Sound effects were also used sparsely throughout to accentuate strong actions in the animation.

Independent critical review of *All the World's a Stage*

Right after the completion of the film, *All the World's a Stage* was submitted for review to the Deutsche Film und Medienbewertung (FBW). This is a German federal authority for evaluating and rating film and media. Its two "seals of approval" for outstanding quality are "Recommended" and "Highly Recommended." *All the World's a Stage* was awarded the highest distinction "Highly Recommended" in 2016.

This award is highly competitive, as it also helps to qualify toward receiving governmental film funding grants for future projects.

The jury statement (2016) says about *All the World's a Stage*:

> "It is one of the best known monologues in the history of theatre. "All the world's a stage. And all the men and women merely players. "It is an excerpt taken from the play *As You Like It* by William Shakespeare and its central theme is the life of man. According to the narrator a human life unfolds in seven phases or acts, from the cradle to the grave. The animation artist Hannes Rall has now adapted the famous speech written by Shakespeare in a 2-minute- film. The individual figures and forms are artfully transformed and connected through metamorphosis; black, white and red are dominating in a highly purist approach. A baby grows to become an adult, a proud man turns into a dodderer. All of this happens in fluent animation movements, which together with the subtle observations result in a wonderful rhythm. The spectator cannot help but follow it intuitively with great pleasure. The British actor Samuel West further adds to the charm of the play by narrating the story with his sonorous voice. With *All the World's a Stage* Hannes Rall has fully succeeded in creating a congenial adaptation of one of the most famous monologues from the history of theatre. A pleasure for eye and ear!"

This quote demonstrates that the chosen adaptation approach has worked well. There is further evidence available that the combination of scholarly research and artistic creation resulted in an artistically successful outcome.

All the World's a Stage was released for the public in April 2016 at the Stuttgart Festival of Animated Film. It was selected for official competition in the world's biggest Poetry Film Festival ZEBRA in 2016 (out of 1100 submissions, only 120 films were selected for competition according to festival administrator Denise Rietig). As of September 2018, the film has been selected for 135 international festivals and won 7 awards.

Based on the immense popularity of the film with festivals, the authors decided in 2017 to omit the *All the World's a Stage* sequence entirely from their *As You Like It* adaptation.

This decision was also supported by the fact that the famous monologue is not crucial to the overall plot of the play at all. Instead, it rather pauses the narrative, providing a moment of reflection delivered by the "melancholic Jaques" in the original text. An omission also provided the chance to advance the story uninterruptedly and support the focus on the theme of love unfolding between the various couples.

A central aspect of this new animated *As You like It* is the relocation of the play from its usual Western setting to an imaginary Southeast Asian location. The specific challenges of transcultural adaptation for *As You Like It* in particular and animated adaptations in general will be discussed in the next chapter.

References

Arya, Ravi Prakash, ed. 1998. *Ramayana of Valmiki: Sanskrit Text and English Translation.* (English translation according to M. N. Dutt, introduction by Dr. Ramashraya Sharma, 4-volume set). New Delhi, India: Parimal Publications.

Bendazzi, Giannalberto. 2015. *A World History of Animation, Animation: A World History: Volume III: Contemporary Times.* Waltham, MA: Taylor & Francis (CRC/Focal Press imprint).

Bendazzi, Giannalberto. November 8, 2014. Interview with Hannes Rall. Nanyang Technological University, Singapore.

Dobson, Michael. Interview with Hannes Rall. June 18. 36 minutes. Shakespeare Institute, Stratford-upon-Avon, England.

Dobson, Michael, and Pippa Nixon. June 17, 2013. Interview with Hannes Rall. 36 minutes. Shakespeare Institute, Stratford-upon-Avon, England.

Dobson, Michael. December 12, 2016. Interview with H. Rall. Shakespeare Institute, Stratford-upon-Avon, England.

FBW Film und Medienbewertungsstelle Wiesbaden. 2016. *All the World's a Stage.* Accessed May 14, http://www.fbw-filmbewertung.com/film/all_the_world_s_a_stage.

Grace, Christopher. 1992–1994. *Shakespeare: The Animated Tales. 12 episodes.* Moscow, Russia: Soyuzmultfilm (production). Cardiff, FC: BBC Wales (distribution).

Griffiths, Jay. 2008. *Wild.* London, UK: Penguin.

Hayman, Francis. Ca. 1750. *Shakespearean Scene: As You Like It.* Oil painting on canvas.

Hendry, Mark. 2016. *Notes on Animation: The Thief and the Cobbler.* YouTube video. Accessed September 24, 2016. https://www.youtube.com/watch?v=zUt423CFVgw.

Karayev, Alexei, dir. 1994. *As You Like It.* Animated adaptation. Moscow, Russia: Soyuzmultfilm (production). Cardiff, FC: BBC Wales (distribution).

Osborne, Laurie. 2003. *Mixing Media and Animating Shakespeare Tales.* In: *Shakespeare: The Movie II: Popularizing the Plays on Film, TV, Video and DVD,* edited by Richard Burt and Linda Boose, 140–153. New York: Routledge.

Parmelee, Ted, dir. 1953. *The Tell-Tale Heart.* Animated short film. Los Angeles, CA: Columbia Pictures. Produced by United Productions of America.

Pearson, Roberta. 2004. *Heritage, Humanism, Populism: The Representation of Shakespeare in Contemporary British Television.* In: *Janespotting and Beyond: British Heritage Retrovisions Since the Mid-1990s,* edited by Eckart Voigts-Virchow, 91–92. Tübingen, Germany: Gunter Narr Verlag.

Rietig, Denise. 2016. E-mail message to author. September 12.

Shakespeare, William. 2005. *As You Like It.* In: *Complete Oxford Shakespeare,* 2nd edition, edited by Stanley Wells and Gary Taylor. Oxford: Oxford University Press.

Shaw, Fiona. 2002. *Great Britons.* TV mini-series, season 1, episode 10. London, UK: BBC. Quoted in Pearson, Roberta E. 2004. *Heritage, Humanism, Populism: The Representation of Shakespeare in Contemporary British Television.* In: *Janespotting and Beyond: British Heritage Retrovisions Since the Mid-1990s,* edited by Eckart Voigts-Virchow, 91–92. Tübingen, Germany: Gunter Narr Verlag.

Spencer, Charles. 2007. As Shakespeare wouldn't like it. *Telegraph* (UK), February 9, 2007. Accessed September 25, 2016. http://www.telegraph.co.uk/culture/theatre/drama/3663035/As-Shakespeare-wouldnt-like-it.html.

Wells, Paul. 1999. *Thou Art Translated: Analysing Animated Adaptations*. In: *Adaptations: From Text to Screen, Screen to Text*, edited by Deborah Cartmell and Imelda Whelehan, 199–213. London, UK: Routledge.

Wickman, Forrest. 2011. *The Most Adapted Authors: Revised and Expanded Edition (INFOGRAPHIC)*. Posted March 23. Accessed July 13, 2017. http://www.slate.com/blogs/browbeat/2011/03/23/the_most_adapted_authors_revised_and_expanded_edition_infographic.html.

Williams, Richard, dir. 2011. *The Thief and The Cobbler Original Cut*. Posted November 30. Accessed September 24, 2016. https://www.youtube.com/watch?v=bggDbbKyuXk.

Remark: This is an unauthorized compilation of scenes in different completion stages to assemble a version of the movie that reflects Richard Williams original artistic intention.

The Thief and the Cobbler was released commercially only in a version that was disowned by the famous animation director, because he considered the film not finished at the point of release. Therefore a release date of this particular version cannot be provided.

Wu, Cheng'en, and Anthony C. Yu. 1980. *The Journey to the West*. Chicago, IL: University of Chicago Press.

Young, Mark, ed. 1999. *The Guinness Book of Records*. New York: Bantam Books, 358.

Sushi on Sauerkraut? Transcultural Adaptation

Unexpected combinations can be thrilling. They can prove exciting and adventurous and rather tasty in the world of fusion food, where ingredients and tastes from different cultures and cooking traditions are combined to often amazing results. However, when not done right, such combinations can leave a bad taste in the mouth.

The author proposes that similar conclusions can be suggested for transcultural adaptations of written literature for film and animation. To see a well-known Western novel adapted and visualized in the historical setting and cultural context of an Asian culture can provide the thrill of the new. It can also demonstrate the universality of a topic that is able to transcend cultural barriers.

At the same time, a lack of respect for local traditions and cultural codes might lead to misinterpretations, misunderstandings, and rejection by cultural communities.

To avoid such missteps, well-informed creative decision-making is of the essence.

This brings us back to the further production process of Hannes Rall's animated adaptation of *As You Like It,* which employed the idea of transposing the forest of Arden to a Southeast Asian jungle setting. The challenges posed by this transcultural adaptation led the author to seek further advice from Prof. Dobson, particularly on the aspect of Shakespeare adaptation across cultural barriers.

The following portion of the interview with Prof. Dobson (and Pippa Nixon) addresses this specific aspect.

Interview with Prof. Michael Dobson and Pippa Nixon (Continued)

"Humanity Is the Same Wherever It Is"

Hannes Rall (interviewer)
Prof. Michael Dobson, University of Birmingham, director of the Shakespeare Institute Stratford-upon-Avon (interviewed)
Pippa Nixon, actress, performed as "Rosalind" in the 2013 production of *As You Like It* by the Royal Shakespeare Company (interviewed)

I would like to discuss the transcultural aspect, because that is actually one of the central ideas of our animated adaptation. And it is something we are looking toward with a conceptually very open approach. I have to explain where this is coming from: In Wayang Kulit, the Indonesian shadow puppet play, one of the most performed plays, is actually the *Ramayana*. We found it visually interesting, to also mirror some of that narrative concept stylistically in the visual development, to work with something that would integrate Indian influences.

Figure 6.1: Height comparison sheet of all the main characters from *As You Like It* (Rall 2018). Character design by Hannes Rall and Lim Wei Ren Darren.

Still, we want to keep the major themes of the actual Shakespeare play and leave those completely intact. All of these themes (we discussed) are so beautiful, and they center the narrative. At the end of the day, it is always important to me that the content drives the design, that form follows function in a way. I think there are two main choices. Choice number one would be to say: We go toward something that takes the idea of the silhouette, the very stylized and the not too literal, and work with that concept, not necessarily really pushing it toward a specifically Asian version. The other one would be to think about how to employ the idea of a different setting, of a different culture, in the context of a play as it stands, without losing any of the beautiful topics you were referring to: the idea of the forest as a different perception of a forest in animation, the theme of love, those conceptually really strong ideas.

For the point of view of the stage tradition of Shakespeare, this is a complete non-problem. The most famous and most influential Shakespeare production of the last 50 years was Peter Brook's last *Midsummer Night's Dream*, which was completely borrowing things from Oriental theatre and doing circus languages and not having a real forest, just having a blank white box and bringing in the fluffy things as you needed them and juggling plates on sticks. There is a very widespread tradition of interrelationships between Oriental theatre forms and Shakespeare performance, sometimes done in the East, sometimes done in the West, borrowing both ways, just as there are Korean companies that hybridize the plots with bits of Korean mythology and bits of Korean history, from time to time, as they see fit. In a way, there is not anything authentic to go back to; Shakespeare was not authentic. It was a rather short-lived theatre he was involved in—that mixed stuff from Italy, and France, and anywhere he could get a hold of it. And that then went out of fashion again and was felt to be obsolete and foreign. *As You Like It* got rewritten a couple of times in the eighteenth century, because it obviously made no sense to anybody the way it was.

It does feel like a play that you could stretch, it really does. And last year, *Much Ado About Nothing* was here, and that was set in Bombay, and it worked fantastically well. I think you could put *As You Like It* anywhere, because ultimately, it is dealing with humanity, and humanity is the same, wherever it is.

These universal themes should always take center stage, because they are what an audience can relate to. If you do not do that, it becomes pointless, in a way. And the theme of love will resonate across all cultures. Maybe it would even be an option to really consider: We were just discussing the different perceptions, different people, and different styles. Something of that could also be employed in the service of universal appeal. It is a very simple idea, but sometimes, the simple ideas are good ideas. One of these ideas was, for example, that the original Wayang Kulit puppets are colorful when you look at them in a normal light, and then, you see them backlit in performance, as a silhouette; they are, of course, completely black. It could be very appealing to work with these two aspects. We have not even gotten there to develop that aspect of a colorful design versus the stark silhouette. That also definitely could be an idea I can take from our conversation and integrate in our further visual development. This would obviously really quote from the real Wayang Kulit culture, but at the same time, it would add an additional level of abstraction closely related to the adapted narrative.

Yes, that is a lovely idea.

Figure 6.2: The images from the visual development for the new version of *As You Like It* demonstrate the dual versions developed for each character: One almost entirely in silhouette, resembling the look of Wayang Kulit puppets when backlit during performance. The two designs of Celia on the right demonstrate variations of the idea to mirror the colorful look of Wayang Kulit puppets under normal lighting conditions. During the film, the respective use of either version is used to express the emotional state of the character or the general atmosphere of the scene. Character design by Hannes Rall and Lim Wei Ren Darren.

Yes, it is.

My wife and I have a couple of Wayang Kulit puppets: the prince and the princess from the *Ramayana*. I always felt a bit guilty, because they are in a frame on a neutral background, so we never do actually move them. You never see them as the silhouette. They are so beautiful. They have got this almost-jeweled type of patterning on them.

There is also a 2011 film *Ulek Mayang (Spirits of the Sea)* by the young Malay animator Hajar Aznam. She did exactly that. She did a computer animation, but very stylized, very nice, very graphic in style, and she employed the original Wayang Kulit puppet design by showing all the colors, not working with the silhouette only. This approach is very powerful in its own way. Within animation history, there is also the prominent figure of the German animation pioneer Lotte Reiniger, most famous for her 1926 animated feature film *The Adventures of Prince Achmed*. This was a silhouette film. She was already inspired by the Wayang Kulit tradition herself, first by Chinese shadow puppet play and later by Wayang Kulit. So, it is interesting, there is also a subtext of silhouette inspiration in animation history. What very often comes up when you are collaborating in interdisciplinary research is the concept that any adaptation of an artistic tradition should first and foremost be "authentic," whatever that can really mean in an artistic context, particularly when you are working with colleagues who are coming, for example, from anthropology, or working in visual communication. You might encounter a very rigid research approach that says, any use of indigenous art concepts should be completely true to the source in the first place. And everything has to be "true," meaning unchanged, like it has been done for centuries; otherwise, you are disrespecting: You are coming as a new colonialist, and you are "stealing" from the respective culture. This does not quite apply in our case, because there are so many people from the Southeast Asian region employed or actually working on the project. But my personal take on it is different. As you said, at the end of the day (referring to Shakespeare and also to the Wayang Kulit), there is nothing purely authentic—both are also evolving in the sense of a living art form, constantly developing and ultimately changing.

Figure 6.3: **Film still from *Ulek Mayang* (2011) by Hajar Aznam.**

Yes, if artists are not free to "steal" stuff...

I always get these big eyes from my students when I tell them, you have to "steal." And, of course, when you explain to them what "stealing" means in that context—that you have to transform any influence in such a way that it ultimately becomes your own—they understand. But it is also an illusion to think that anybody is completely free of influences anyway. Probably, it is the same with an actor.

The link between content and visuals is crucial to me when adapting literature for animation. You already mentioned the Korean examples, with their integration of a local culture and mythology in their versions of the Shakespeare plays. Another important example that comes to mind are the Shakespeare adaptations by Akira Kurosawa, for example, *Throne of Blood* (1957, a *Macbeth* adaptation) and *Ran* (1985, a thinly disguised adaptation of *King Lear*), possibly some of the best known Asian adaptations for film. What are your thoughts on those?

He is a useful precedent. I like *Throne of Blood* as a movie. I do not very much like *Ran*, but then, that is a personal preference. I find it rather overblown, and I just keep imagining the logistics involved in moving all those extras around, instead of concentrating on the story. But the scripts of Shakespeare's plays are quite old. They were local in some ways of the time. There are conventions that have died out. You always have to hybridize them with what is happening in the present to make them live, and there is no geographical limit on that. It does not have to be hybridized with stuff that is currently happening in London or stuff that is currently happening in Stratford, who knows. And it is always intercultural: when you are dealing with a script written 400 years ago, you are "stealing" stuff from a foreign culture already.

I believe throughout art history, you can observe a tradition of taking influences from other cultures, then merging them, and in the process, something new will come out.

Exactly. *As You Like It* is apparently set in France and also apparently set in Warwickshire. I do not remember the French having sued for copyright over the mention of the forest of Arden; it is not a problem, as you say.

It is also hugely popular among Indian filmmakers to adapt Shakespeare.

There is wonderful stuff. I am supervising a doctorate on some of them. I have an excellent student from Kerala who is working on southern Indian Shakespeare and brings in these wonderful DVDs. An *Anthony and Cleopatra*, in which the battle scenes are cockfights, set in villages with these real cockfights, so Anthony has to kill himself by fixing the spurs to the ankles of his favorite cockerel and putting his hands behind his back and provoke it, so that it kills him—the only Mark Anthony I have ever seen killed by a chicken, and it is astonishing. The film is called *Kannaki* (2001), directed by Jayaraj. Yes, there is loads of it. And, sometimes, it is being done by people who know they are adapting Shakespeare, and sometimes, it is just that the stories are common currency, and there are lots in Indian stage versions, at several removes, of *The Comedy of Errors*. It is because *The Comedy of Errors* got translated and got used in the Indian school system in the nineteenth century, and people have forgotten that these two pairs of twins were ever Shakespeare's.

Sometimes, a purely research-based approach and the artistic approach may collide: Frequently, one is faced with the discussion, if you are "entitled" as a Western artist to just take some elements of the respective local culture(s) and use them for the purpose of exactly creating such a kind of artistic fusion, even when you collaborate with Asian colleagues—like we do. Something that, the other way around, people in the Western world, for most of the part, would feel rather flattered when that happens, when somebody references or acknowledges their style by integrating it into their own artistic approach.

Yes, absolutely. And after all, it is not as though there was a monoglot culturally pure single spectator who was only going to understand everything in relation to the *Ramayana*, and one who was only going to know about Shakespeare. Presumably, one is aiming at audiences who know a little bit about each and who can appreciate the codes that are being played off against each other.

Particularly in the case of Singapore, because it is so cosmopolitan and it is so multicultural. When I look at my students, it would be a different type of so-called colonialism to tell them, well, you have to be purely authentic, you are not allowed to take influences from any other culture than your own.

As in: You are only allowed to do folk dances, and no, you cannot come to the disco, it might corrupt you. That is awful. Somebody we would talk to, if she was in today, is Erin Sullivan, because she worked a lot on the World Shakespeare Festival last year and actually brought out a very nice book called *A Year of Shakespeare* (2013), which is partly about all that happened at the Globe, where they had performances of Shakespeare's plays and each one in a different language, and so, 36 plays, 36 languages.

She is interesting on the subject of intercultural performances and what happened there, where different language communities in London came to see different plays: They wanted the thrill of seeing something in their own language, but it is something definitively that was not theirs, in some sense, or that was, to a different degree, as being internalized as part of their culture. So obviously, the Germans knew that Shakespeare belonged to them much more than he does to the English and were very happy to see Shakespeare in a proper language, done at the Globe. There was a Punjabi production, where Christie Carson went along to see it, standing in the yard at the Globe, and it was completely full of Indian diaspora people, and an Indian woman turned and said to her, 'You do know this is *our* show? You will not understand what is going on,' which of course, you know, is fair enough. It is a very well-worn topic among Shakespeareans, the plays being translated and so much being the occasion of hybridization. And half the point of Shakespeare's stuff is that it is a very impure art form, which is why the French cannot stand it. It is not classical. Shakespeare does not say it is all going to fit this one set of codes absolutely to the letter but incorporates stuff from clowning and stuff from Morris dancing and stuff from all over the place. It is a plural, voracious type of theatre already. So, it naturally invites more stuff to come in and join from elsewhere.

That is encouraging to hear. Another question I have in that context is: Would you say that there is any adaptation of *As You Like It*, or Shakespeare in general, to film, animation, or even comics that you consider particularly successful?

There are some of the movies that I am very fond of: But most Shakespeare movies I do not much like, because I do not like realist Shakespeare. In these the scenes are somehow all about the fact that the main character is riding a horse past a castle, in spite of the fact the dialogue never mentions a horse or a castle, I find it distracting. But I like the adaptations by the Russian director Kozintsev. I like the Kozintsev of *Hamlet* (1964) and the Kozintsev of *Lear* (1971). I like the Richard Loncraine version of *Richard III* (1995), which is quite free and uses very short scenes, which has a quite imaginative visual concept and a very strong cast and is not just a pageant; not 'this is what it would have looked like in history,' or, 'this is what it would have looked like in Shakespeare's time,' because Shakespeare is an anachronistic writer, and trying to tie things down to a single time period is going to mess him up anyway. It is all about the interplay between the present and the past and the future, as it happens. I think the comicky things and visual things, *As You Like It* has not attracted that much with this kind of interest. It is the more plot-driven plays, which tend to spurn adaptations. I like the visuals, I like the visual style of the *Animated Tales Hamlet*, which was painted very quickly on glass, as I remember, as a swirly and cloudy and rather gloomy effect, it is quite attractive to look at, as they go. There is a series called *Classics Illustrated* (various authors 1941–1971), done in the 1940s and 1950s, of very literal-minded comics, that are just funny. They are unintentionally funny, because the heroes are so square and heroic and muscle bound, and the villains are so villainous, and it is so literal-minded about what clothes they wear; it is unbelievable. They are a good example of how not to do it. I do not really know enough about Manga to read its codes, but there is a whole series of Manga Shakespeare, which sells in quite large quantities, at the Birthplace gift shop and down at the theatre.

Because *As You Like It* is so loose and meditative and playful, it tends not to produce this kind of work. There is no opera of *As You Like It* that I know of, whereas there are lots of others, some better than others. And obviously, there are any number of spin-offs from *The Tempest*, which lie behind so much science fiction, *The Forbidden Planet*, (dir. Wilcox 1956) and all that stuff, and many others besides, and lots of baroque operas based on *The Tempest*. But no, there is no singing Rosalind that I know of yet, and the earlier adaptations of *As You Like It* are versions that try to flatten it out and simplify it for realist theatre. There is an eighteenth-century play that tries to straighten out *As You Like It*. It just calls it *Love in a Forest*, and there is very little character development, and nobody converts from being bad to being good. Jaques marries Celia because Oliver is killed off. You do not want to deal with him.

I like the title; it is actually quite funny, *Love in a Forest*, it is just like…

You get what it says on the tin, with that one. Whereas *As You Like It* is such an open-ended title—it could mean anything, and yes, it is such a playful thing.

This is also what we wanted to hint at by choosing the title of our research project that will ultimately deliver the animated adaptation: *Wayang Kulit As You Like It*. A wordplay, if there ever was one. We wanted to clearly flag our intention that this is not about authenticity in the first place but about a more playful approach instead, in the sense of being merely inspired by the South Eastern tradition of shadow puppet play in place of painstakingly recreating its conventions. An "all by the book adaptation" of Wayang Kulit as a tradition would have to consider certain formal rules that would have to be absolutely obeyed to. We are also taking the freedom to abridge the original Shakespeare play in that context. So, let's go deeper in that discussion as well.

Yes, and again, it is a very long tradition. There already were abridged versions of Shakespeare in the mid-seventeenth century: there is all your favorite bits from *Henry the Fourth part one*, retitled 'The Bouncing Knight.' The plays were always cut for performance. Shakespeare delivered more text than the actors could use in any single performance. There are shortened versions being taken on tour in Shakespeare's time. There are shortened versions being taken on tour around Europe and adapted into local languages, in Shakespeare's time. So, yes, it is a very long-established tradition.

What about the idea to go toward either abridging using the original text or alternatively creating a shorter version with adding new or changed text? You were basically saying that, depending on the target audience, both approaches could be legitimate in their own way?

Yes, it is not as if every time you cut a speech out of *As You Like It*, it vanishes from all the existing copies of the play—it is not going to hurt anything. But yes, and actually, some of the most interesting and sometimes some of the most radical rewrites of Shakespeare have simply put speeches in a different order or reassigned them to different people rather than actually writing new material. Charles Marowitz is a very famous exponent of this, he used to do these collage versions of Shakespeare, where you just move speeches around and make it turn out totally differently, and they are really interesting. Yes, you can have great fun interpreting a play just by leaving in the bits that you think really matter and transposing enough material around them to lead up to them and give them something interesting.

I tend to be more drawn toward the idea of using the original text for our abridged version. In any case, it is very interesting to hear about the many creative possibilities that can actually open up through that approach. On another note, I think it is probably almost unavoidable, particularly in the case of *As You Like It*, to work with some narration, if you want to condense it into the 20 to 30-minute range. Do you know of any other adaptations that try to blend similar narratives, such as we hope to do with the *Ramayana* (Arya 1998) and *As You Like It*?

Well, there is the Mokwha Repertory Company's *Tempest*, which came over last year to the Edinburgh festival and has been touring around a bit. They are an interesting company. Oh Tae-Suk is their main director, who has worked on those shows.

This is a very helpful information, as we are clearly looking at another precedent of an Asian adaptation of Shakespeare that takes in local traditions and visual styles.

Well, of course, Kurosawa's *Ran* does that to some extent, in that there is this historical setting which is given in which, it is sons rather than daughters, who are being rival warlords, and gives it a kind of historicity somewhere else.

That is true. Like Kurosawa does that quite a bit that, at least he is definitely integrating some very Japanese conventions or Japanese ways of acting.

Yes, as does Ninagawa on stage. The Ninagawa *Coriolanus*, though, that was absolutely wonderful, which was very much influenced by martial art movies as much as anything else.

This closes that chapter of the discussion. Let's switch to another important topic to consider. About that whole aspect of the gender-changing roles: I could imagine, somebody could choose that as a focus, but Pippa did not do that at all. I found that very interesting, and because it indeed proves dangerous to go down that path too much, because you might be slipping into some kind of politically correct agenda.

That is true, or one might be treating it as a realist play, in which Ganymede absolutely has to look exactly like what a boy really looks like. Whereas, actually, for it to work, you have to be able to see that she is not a boy, in the conventions we have got now anyway. It is a play written for boys actually to act, so the gender conventions are out of whack with ours anyway. You are always going to be using it within whatever framework; it is going to make some sort of sense in now. But yes, it is not *Tootsie* (Pollack 1982), it is not a study in accurate drag.

Yes, because what is, at the same time, so fascinating about it and also makes it probably so difficult to adapt the right way, is that there is so much on offer; it is like almost an endless array of possibilities. What we were discussing this morning is already one way out of this, in order to find the right thread to go to connect the pieces there. But, obviously, it is so much going on. I have to admit, I was trying to wrap my head around what is going on. I felt like, wait a minute, it was too much, too many characters, but I guess, if you make the right choices, you could get out of that trap.

Yes, it is not as if it matters, that is very much part of the mood of this play. People come on and come off, and it is not a problem really; it is not a play where the payoff depends on you following every single word until you reach the climax. There are some characters that wander in and wander out again, and it does not seem to matter. Adam does not have any lines after the first half of the play. A bloke called William turns up for one scene, and he is never seen again. It is all the sense that this is just life, and people turn up—some stick around and some of them do not. For the formality of the ending, though, where it finally resolves, it helps if you know who all these couples are.

I was also thinking that, in a way, the reformation of the evil duke is almost anecdotal. It is not really like you cut back and forth permanently, and there is a huge amount of character development.

We are having the happy ending, and the bad character is gone. It is not a problem, let us get on with it. And that is it. It is very throwaway. And it is very anticlimactic, that is one of the effects this play uses, it is deliberately interested in bathos. It calls a character Orlando, and he is not a great chivalric hero who has to fight against paladins or anything. He is not pulling up trees in despair like Orlando in the *Orlando Furioso*, he just writes graffiti on them. And the scene where he meets the Duke at the picnic, he comes rushing in with his sword, saying, give me food. And the Duke says, yes, fine, help yourself. And he says, oh I am terribly sorry, I did not mean to be rude, I thought you were all going to be savages. It is that way, even where you get a big plot motive of the evil duke and these awful things that might happen; by the end of the play, you forget about that.

I think it might be still well advised for any adaptation, as also Pippa was touching on, to take the menace in the beginning to make it very real. Because that incredible tension that is built up there finally then leads to the escape.

There has to be mortal danger, but over the course of the play, rather slowly, the sense you get is that the real risk is not that you might be killed by an evil duke. It is that you might get old, or you might get bored, or you might get disaffected. Those are the kinds of everyday problems of jealousy and boredom and cynicism that you are actually set close to looking at. That is why Jaques takes over, this miserable, self-important person who cannot get over himself enough to enjoy the party he is in.

Yes, that is also a very interesting aspect, which is also very unusual from the point of view of classical Hollywood plot building, in that sense. It is not really plot building.

Yes, and Jaques is such an unusual and useful character who just does not want to be in a comedy. He cannot believe, of all the plays to find himself in, it is *As You Like It*; 'Oh god, why are you so in love? Could you not be melancholy instead?' A great dialogue that he has with Orlando, but Orlando is just not interested.

As I said, there is so much on offer that you really have to choose—to decide on a focus. Let us put it this way: you have to know what to pick to succeed. We basically already talked about the almost accidental reformation in the end.

Yes, the comicky off-stage crisis.

Yes, it arrives, and then, oh well. So, I think we pretty much have covered what I thought was most important to talk about in this stage. Just one final question: You already mentioned, in passing, about the possible different target groups for the play, or for the adaptation. That is, at least not in that stage, really something we are already looking toward. However, I am sure you have a lot to do with all different things, keeping on radar what is going on in terms of Shakespeare adaptations. Would you actually see a certain target group to favor a market out there that might be interested in such a type of adaptation, or is it hard to say? Of course, this is a short film with limited potential in terms of distribution outlets, maybe TV at best or educational distributors. Any thoughts on that?

There is a huge educational market, obviously, schools. The *Animated Tales* (1992–1994) is still on sale. We notice when we go to the gift shop at the Birthplace, people are still buying that as Christmas presents, probably for hapless nephews and such like. And because it is animated and because it is short, because it is based on a Shakespeare play, this is bound to be mentioned in the same sentence as the *Animated Tales*. And the fact that it is being made in Asia, and incorporating Asian imagery, I think it is going to be very important to it. I would have thought that a Shakespeare festival in the Far East is going to be where it is going to be screened, where you could have events to launch it, and indeed, where you could sell DVDs of it. And to Asian universities, since there is not a good movie based on *As You Like It*. There is the Kenneth Branagh one (2006), which is pretty terrible. I should not say that, but it is. And there is the old one that Laurence Olivier was in, pre-war, which was an extraordinary thing, with the Scandinavian actress as Rosalind, replicating the performance she gave on stage, clearly in a very big theatre, and Olivier came skulking in the background with a few real sheep. But nobody watches that anymore, except as a historical curiosity. I think it is bound to be a university- and schools-dominated market, and now, it is more likely to be distributed on DVD than screened on screens, I think. That is what I would imagine. I am trying to think of an analogy. I was involved a bit with a documentary film, called *Shakespeare High*, that was made in California by a Romanian friend of mine called Alex Rotaru; it is a documentary about a school's Shakespeare competition. It was in California, and Kevin Spacey came out and a few other actors. And I have been at screenings of that at theatre festivals, and it sells on Amazon. It has its own website. It is about *Othello* actually.

What I hope we can achieve in this research project is really to find the best possible script, find the most suitable style, and do test animations first. Then take it to the next stage and explore different ways of approaching it. What do you think about exploring a wider palette of ideas first, branching out in different directions? We could really find different ways to link content and visuals and then see what happens, talking about experiments and outcomes.

I think that is an excellent idea, and experiments in what you do with the dialogue, experiencing what voices you have and how Asian you make it look, if you have indeed sound, what kind of soundtrack it has, which is something we have not talked about, whether it has some incidental music or anything.

That is also a very good point what you bring up, because, as everybody knows, sound is sometimes 50 percent of a movie. Therefore, that is a very important component to experiment with: How do you work with all of these combinations—what images, what kind of sound would you use, along with different combinations? I imagine, for example, a very interesting contrast between very classical Shakespearean voices in the most traditional Shakespearean English you can imagine and then having very different images. But then, you could also try to go the other way and move away from the traditional text and even use, in the outmost extreme, an entirely different language. I think we will probably stick with the English, but we could also really move away from the "normal" modus operandi. So, I think you have your option to match dialogue and images, but you could also create something interesting by creating a strong contrast between these elements. So, that is a very good result to go forward with the adaptation. I think we really covered a lot of ground today. There is actually a lot of new input that was not there before, and that is just great. Thank you very much for that!

Transcultural Aspects of Hannes Rall's *As You Like It* Adaptation

The outcome of the author's conversation with Prof. Dobson had already encouraged the team to address the adaptation with a freely eclectic approach. This was clearly found to be the continuation of an established tradition in Shakespeare adaptation with a significant number of precedents. As Dobson had further pointed out, it also resonated well with Shakespeare's own approach of drawing from very diverse cultural influences from different countries. Even more so, if one considers the eminently playful character of *As You Like It*: Wouldn't the play's title itself strongly imply an adaptation liberated in spirit and freedom of choice?

Figure 6.4: An illustration of the *Ramayana* on the left (author and date unknown) in comparison with a design for Hannes Rall's *As You Like It.*

Therefore, the *As You Like It* adaptation at hand was conceived by integrating several influences drawn from different cultural backgrounds:

The character and production design reflected the similarity of certain story elements to the famous Indian national epic *Ramayana* (Narayan, Kampar 2006).

This visual idea was further motivated by the fact that the *Ramayana* is one of the most played tales performed in Wayang Kulit, the Southeast Asian shadow puppet play. Wayang Kulit became a major design inspiration for the film.

On the other hand, the whole global tradition of animated silhouette film (as begun with Lotte Reiniger and inspired by Asian shadow puppet play itself) played a huge role in determining the final designs. This demonstrates that our choices were, while eclectic, still interrelated and connected to the demands of the adapted narrative.

Case in Point

The standalone character of the *All the World's a Stage* sequence within the original Shakespeare play and our animated adaptation was addressed through a design style influenced by the work of the American designer Saul Bass (1920–1996) and the Russian painter Lazar Markovich Lissitzky (1890–1941).

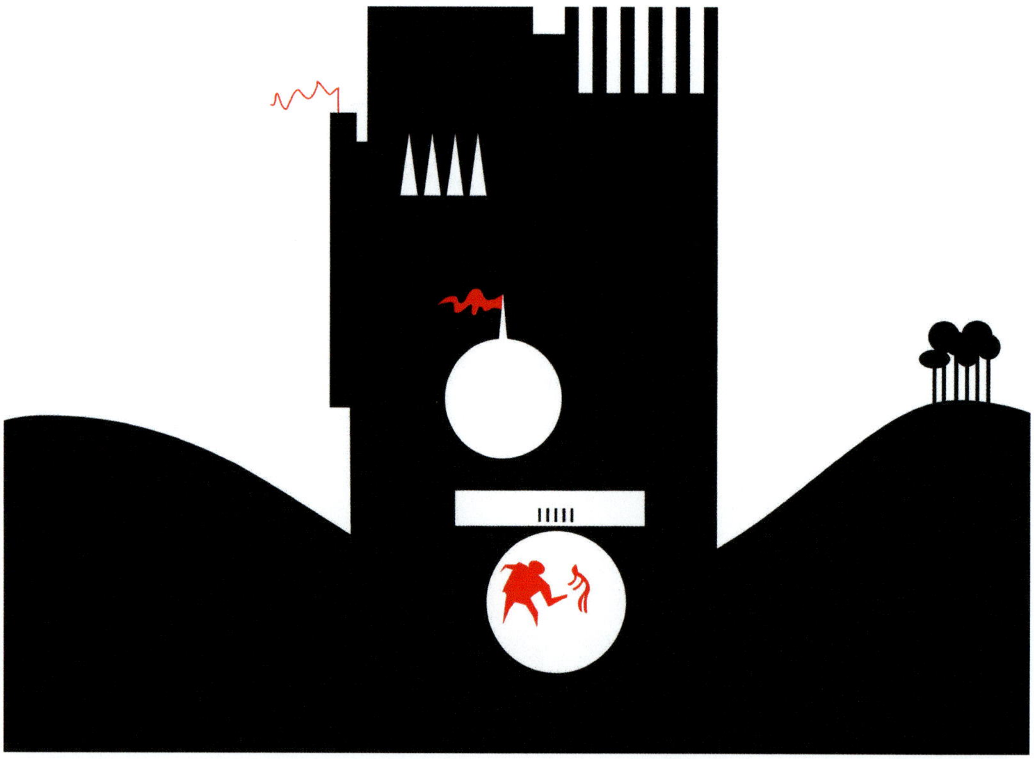

Figure 6.5: This more abstract design style, influenced by Saul Bass and Lissitzky, was first considered as a general approach for the whole adaptation of *As You Like It*. In the end, it was specifically used for the *All the World's a Stage* film adaptation. (Courtesy of Hannes Rall.)

As a Western narrative adapted by an international team in a Singaporean university, the transcultural component was not only evident in the adaptation itself but also represented by the culturally diverse production team. It featured collaborators from Singapore, the United States and Germany. One collaborator came from France but is of Asian heritage. This also allowed for an immediate feedback on narrative and design-related concepts in terms of their cross-cultural appeal and suitability.

The eclecticism of choices still was to be confined by the need to create a conclusive visual narrative. This limits the number of visual options. The film must still be able to relate a story to a stylistically cohesive universe.

Figure 6.6: Early design studies for *As You Like It* that finally developed into the final style for *All the World's a Stage*. Hannes Rall, digital ca. 2014.

It must ultimately succeed in integrating all the initially differing elements into a new and seamless whole. Or, any remaining or deliberately used stylistic discrepancies must be justified by special requirements of the story. For the major part of the film, this means a cohesive design, with a clearly visible influence of traditional Indian and Southeast Asian art styles.

As it serves a different purpose and stands out from the rest of the narrative, the introductory sequence of the film is depicted with a different stylistic approach. The characters remain recognizable, but the richly detailed textures of figures and backgrounds are relegated in favor of a simplified painterly style. Extremely limited animation further helps to clarify that this is different from the following: a mere introduction preceding the main events.

By visually depicting the figure of Robin Hood in an intentionally clichéd way, the authors intend to wink at the audience: This idea signals to the spectator that the overall concept of this adaptation is playful inspiration by the source text instead of authentic replication.

Figure 6.7: Development art for the prologue sequence by Hannes Rall (top) and for the love letters sequence (bottom) by Hannes Rall and Lim Wei Ren Darren.

With this approach being justified through our discussion with Prof. Dobson, the authors felt liberated to combine culturally diverse influences, whenever it enhanced the artistic quality of the adaptation. But anytime the team decided to quote a specific local artistic tradition, the intention was to get this reference right.

When showing Balinesian architecture, it was supposed to be based on or at least inspired by the look of buildings in Bali. The artistic concepts of the Southeast Asian puppet play Wayang Kulit remained another important influence on the film, and Wayang Kulit itself has a very strong tradition in Bali.

Case Study: Developing the Palace

The renowned anthropologist Prof. Stephen Lansing was part of the research team, and his expertise on Balinese culture and art proved tremendously helpful to refer the creators to authentic sources for the adaptation.

The following sequence of images from the visual development process demonstrates how the palace from *As You Like It* evolved: It transformed from an initially conceived fusion between a Western design concept and a vaguely Oriental inspiration toward a more Asian influenced architectural approach that concretely references original Balinese temple designs.

Figure 6.8: Development sketch by Hannes Rall (left), production painting by Lim Wei Ren Darren (right).

The initial design approach for the palace in *As You Like It* was supposed to combine Western ideas of a castle with Oriental architectural concepts. What looked good in initial sketches didn't work out sufficiently in more finalized design stages. Therefore, the research team reverted to a very different design approach.

Figure 6.9: From historic photographs of Balinesian temples (author unknown). Hannes Rall analyzed the basic shape structure through simplified drawings.

Figure 6.10: Development art by Hannes Rall/Lim Wei Ren Darren.

Based on the research on authentic Balinese temples, Hannes Rall created design suggestions for the palace. Darren Lim integrated these influences into a first production design and developed it further into a final version for production. The lighting played an important role to evoke an atmosphere of menace for the darker tones of the palace scenes and created a strong contrast to the lighter atmosphere in the forest.

Figure 6.11: The final version of the palace in the film. Production designs by Lim Wei Ren Darren.

Other Influences from Southeast Asia

Early experiments were also carried out with inspirations from Indonesian landscapes, patterns, and fabrics. Although the style ultimately did not materialize in this form in the final film, the visuals show the many possibilities that emerged throughout the development process.

Figure 6.12: Visual development art based on Balinesian landscapes, handicrafts, and Wayang Kulit by Tran Nguyen Tuan Anh. The art was created in the framework of an undergraduate research project (Undergraduate Research Experience on Campus, URECA) at Nanyang Technological University, under the supervision of the author.

Figure 6.13: Lineup of characters from *As You Like It* (Rall) in their silhouetted/colored versions. Top row: Hymen (god of love), two lords/merriment. Bottom row: Phoebe, Silvius, anonymous sheep. Character design by Hannes Rall and Lim Wei Ren Darren.

This line up of further character designs demonstrates the playful diversity in approaches that is still unified by a common visual vocabulary: reduction to basic shapes and the duality of silhouetted and fully colored versions of the characters. The character of Phoebe on the lower left in Fig. 6.13, for example, displays traces of Indian influences, combined with a visual parody of the idealized romantic image of a shepherdess in pastoral painting.

Figure 6.14: *A Shepherdess with Her Flock.* A classic pastoral painting by Eugène Joseph Verboeckhoven (1871). Compare with the character design for Phoebe.

Figure 6.15: The animated version of the author simultaneously quotes and parodies the well-known cliché. Layout drawing designed by Hannes Rall and Lim Wei Ren Darren.

The previous examples have shown that the authors deliberately gave up on the idea of "authentic representation" of any single "pure" culture but instead embraced the idea of cultural fusion. This is an approach and cultural fact that is increasingly recognized by scholars in transcultural studies as well.

Within the context of visual culture, Wofgang Welsch (1999, 194–213) believes that the concept of "transculturality goes beyond the seemingly hard alternatives of globalization and particularization." He denotes that the concept of "culture has changed with the growth of communication and stresses that" (…) "cultural determinants today—from society's macro level through to individuals' micro level—have become transcultural."

In other words, cultures today are interconnected and entangled with each other. They are, in general, more characterized by a fusion and mix of cultural influences. The intercultural connectivity through the Internet certainly furthers this development, and it becomes evident in the stylistic eclecticism students display in their work on a global scale: Manga and anime mix with Western drawing styles; stories from the West are adapted in Asia, and vice versa.

Julia Binter (2013, 183) also insists that "getting at the transcultural does not necessarily entail the sacrifice of cultural differences in favor of a notion of abstract shared humanity." Andrew Irving (as cited by Suhr and Willerslev 2012, 296) states about transculturality that "strangeness, diversity, and otherness are not the opposite of mutuality but the conditions that bring it into being."

This means that it is not necessary to give up individual voices to create a globally appealing vision—the opposite is the case. The dialogue between different artistic traditions can result in the creation of something new and entirely original—something an artist is always striving for. In the next section, an animation director who has succeeded at the highest level will grant a deeper look at his process.

Ishu Patel—insights from a master animator

There probably couldn't be a more suitable candidate than Ishu Patel to discuss the complex matter of transcultural adaptation. He can share the unique point of view of one of the most achieving independent animators of all time. Owing to his cultural background and his longtime affiliation with the National Film Board of Canada, all of his films could be defined as transcultural art. Ishu was born in Gujarat, India. A Rockefeller Foundation Scholarship brought him to the National Film Board of Canada, where he developed innovative animation techniques, producing and directing 11 award-winning films.

Figure 6.16: Ishu Patel working in his studio at the National Film Board of Canada in the 1980s.

He is an acclaimed animation film director and producer and educator whose films have received theatrical and television distribution worldwide. His many international awards include two Oscar nominations, a Silver Bear at the Berlin Film Festival, a British Academy of Film and Television Arts Award (BAFTA), and the Grand Prix at both the Annecy International Animation Film Festival and the Montreal World Film Festival. From 2011 to 2017, Ishu became a visiting professor for animation at the School of Art, Design and Media at Nanyang Technological University in Singapore. With faculty from 16 different countries in the school and in the cosmopolitan and multicultural environment, transcultural art creation is not mere theory but daily practice.

During this 6-year sojourn based in Singapore, Patel took the opportunity to follow his mentor, photography legend Henri Cartier-Bresson's footsteps, with whom Patel had worked as a photo assistant many decades ago, when he was a student at the National Institute of Design in Ahmedabad, India. Adhering to Cartier-Bresson's mantra to "photograph the truth," Patel embarked on a photographic journey in Southeast Asia from 2011 to 2016. Abandoning his moving images for still images that capture a human story while he prowls both urban and rural areas armed only with his Leica M9 and 35 mm and 50mm fast lens. The result is a collection of illustrative photographic images that tell a story, seize a moment, witnessing joys, struggles, and human dignity. A 200-page hardcover photography book, entitled *Asian Lives: A Closer Look*, was published by Thames and Hudson in July 2016.

This is a further testament to his ongoing fascination and engagement with local communities in Southeast Asia and brings him back to his roots. His awareness and continuous negotiation of Western and Eastern art traditions make his points of view particularly valuable.

In the following interview, Patel starts discussing his animated adaptations in general, but the conversation later turns toward the challenges of transcultural adaptation in particular.

Interview with Ishu Patel

Conducted in 2015 at Nanyang Technological University Singapore

Hannes Rall (interviewer)
Ishu Patel (interviewed)

Ishu, you are one of the most renowned independent animation directors living today, and your films have won many international prizes throughout your long career. Some of these films were inspired by narrative sources from written literature or oral tradition. That is why, I want to talk with you about your very own experiences with transforming such material for animation. You told me there is a total of three works for which you have worked with some form of adaptation.

Yes, that is correct.

Can you please name the three works and then explain more in detail about each of them?

Okay, the first film, most closely matching a traditional definition of adaptation, is *Paradise*. The second one is called *Top Priority*, adapted from an actual "true-life" story, written by an author from Egypt. The third film is called *Divine Faith*. It is based on a dialogue between my father and me. We adapted the dialogue for the film. These are the three main films and three very different types of adaptations.

Let's begin with *Paradise*. When I was a little boy in school, we used to learn a poem. It's in my language, Gujarati, which is a provincial language.

Figure 6.17: Two film stills from the Academy Award–nominated short *Paradise* (1977). (From *Paradise* ©1977 National Film Board of Canada. All rights reserved.)

This poem was very important. When I was about 13 or 14, we used to read the poem. One of our teachers also used to sing the poem quite nicely. I don't exactly remember the poem, but you can still find the source of it. The poem was about an old lady who owns a beautiful bird, but it's in a cage. Every morning, she'll take the cage with the bird and hang it outside on the porch.

At night, she'll take it inside, but in daytime, she'll put it outside on a porch. This was going on every day, and she would feed the bird nice food, and she would give water and sit on a rocking chair and watch the bird. She was an old lady. Then, every day, a blackbird would come from the forest and hang on the outside of the cage. This poem was about these two birds conducting a dialogue. The one bird inside the cage would say, "what a wonderful life you have outside. You can fly through an open sky. You can do whatever you want. You can eat the berries and the fruits, and look at me, I'm spooked up here. I can't fly. My wings are tied."

Figure 6.18: Layout and final color drawing for a background element in *Paradise.* (*Paradise* ©1977 National Film Board of Canada. All rights reserved.)

Then, the other one would say, "Yeah, but look at you. You don't have to worry about the danger. I have to constantly worry about the danger. I can't sleep at night. I can't order good food. You're being given water. You're given all the food and all this stuff." That was the poem or back-and-forth dialogue. Each stanza, the blackbird would say something. The bird in the cage would answer to it. That's basically the story.

Now, how do you create an idea for an animated short film from this poem? These are the stanzas. Here's the poem. I want to adapt the poem. When I looked more closely for a possible visual narrative, I realized that it was not a very good idea to have two birds, talking birds, back and forth, back and forth.

Then, we took it from there and said, "How do we adapt it more elaborately and differently?" There was a solution: The bird on the porch could be one character, and the bird in the cage should be another character, but the bird in the cage would be a bit more artificial looking and more elaborate. We called it the "divine bird." Then, there is a blackbird, which is very small, black, and scruffy; it is called a yellow nose. We made the divine bird the extraordinary one. Then, we were wondering, "Well, where would the divine bird stay?" The blackbird would stay in a forest. But where would the divine bird stay?

We talked about many different ideas. Of course, it will be in a cage, but where is the cage? Is it in the house? Somebody's house? We decided that it had to be next to the emperor. Some emperor owns the bird, and because it's a divine bird, it could do amazing things. That's how we started. That's the adaptation. We took it from there, and then, we turned it into a narrative we could use as a starting point for the animated short film.

Once we had these two elements, which were the combination of a black ordinary bird in a forest and a divine bird owned by the emperor, we were able to apply all kinds of contrast. The idea was to be able to achieve a contrast between two different situations, between two birds and two environments. It was very easy to have a bird in a forest. There wasn't a big problem, because this is how you would imagine it to be. How can you imagine anything else than a contrast if you combine the little bird with the background of the natural forest?

Figure 6.19: Inspirational drawing for the enchanted forest. (From *Paradise* ©1977 National Film Board of Canada. All rights reserved.)

The idea appealed to me to create a very strong contrast instead of a small difference. You really should push things in that respect—make it as effective as possible. We started working on the idea of the palace, and we started to research all the reference on palaces, and interiors, and so on. After that, we even started coloring it. But then, I started asking myself, "Would that be enough? If I color it by hand. If I color it with watercolor. If I use pastel chalk." I didn't like the artwork. I didn't like the concept of producing actual artwork for the palace. I liked the idea of creating artwork for the forest, but I didn't want to produce any artwork in terms of creating a palace. How would I be able to solve this problem? I wanted to make it look so different, and I didn't know how.

This is where the innovation started coming in, by looking for a solution. What kind of solution could we come up with? We sketched and sketched and sketched and kept exploring the idea, and then, at some point, I was just thinking, "What can I do?"

And I finally thought, "So what about, if we do not use traditional backgrounds?" I know it's a very simple answer, but then, how are you going to do it? We thought we'd do it in sand, maybe. Something like that. We create the background in sand, and so on, but then, how to compose the divine bird coming in and dancing? We also thought that we need color for this. Without color, it just wasn't very impressive. Because you wanted to have the huge dance before the black bird comes and watches it. That was the original idea, as you have heard from the original story.

Figure 6.20: Sketch and color development studies for the forest. (From *Paradise* ©1977 National Film Board of Canada. All rights reserved.)

At some stage, it gets to the point where it is just a question of observing things around you. I think it was during Christmas time. Around that time, while I was looking for ideas. Christmas time in Canada. One night, I went outside and looked at all the Christmas lights—beautiful lighting everywhere. You see the trees and people, decorate all kinds of things with lights. If I could make the palace look like this, then it would be wonderful. Because the city hall was decorated with lights, so I said, lets make the palace just like that, that would be wonderful, because then you see painting with light." I said, "Okay, how to go about it?" It was ultimately very simple.

Then, I also saw the whole picture: What if I draw everything and put holes in a black paper and then light it from behind? I immediately went in the next morning and made some tests to explore and try that technique. They looked pretty nice, and then, we thought about star filters and similar devices to achieve a more natural look, so that the environment wouldn't look too sharp, too much in focus. That way, there is a little bit of fuzziness in it, a little blurriness. Okay, so that was one thing solved. That was working just fine. We could do that, but how could we put the colored characters inside? We had to use a matting process, which meant that each character had to be drawn separately. Every character had to be matted, and the matting had to be overlayed on the background to block the lighted pin holes coming through the character.

Figure 6.21: Development sketches of the palace. (From *Paradise* ©1977 National Film Board of Canada. All rights reserved.)

We shot a first pass only of the background with little holes lit from under-light, combined with the black painted matte of the character over it. We then made a second pass of the color character with a top light on pure black background. The results were amazing. All animation that was supposed to appear in the film was created in two forms. One is the color drawing of that particular character and also the exact matte of precisely the same drawing. That became very costly and very laborious. We had to hire people just to create all the matching black mattes. Once the animation was finished, somebody would make a matte of it. That matte had to be opaque, so it could cover the whole pin holes.

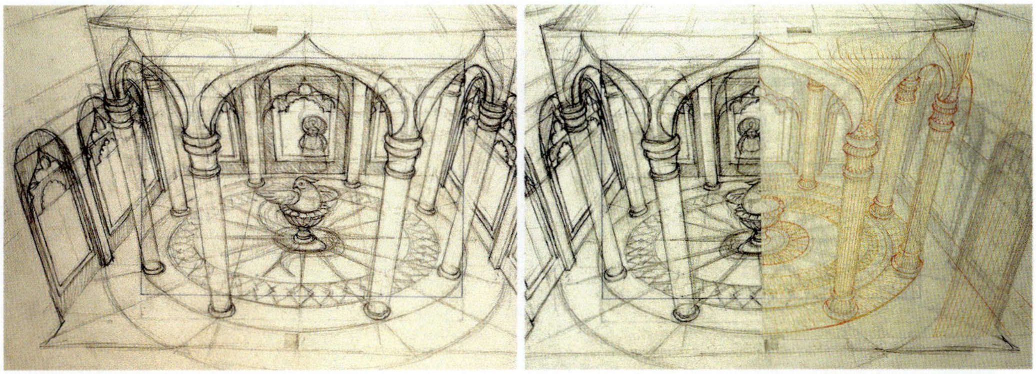

Figure 6.22: Interior sketch and architectural drawing of the palace. (From *Paradise* ©1977 National Film Board of Canada. All rights reserved.)

Figure 6.23: The animation technique and shooting process for *Paradise*. (From *Paradise* ©1977 National Film Board of Canada. All rights reserved.)

1. Preparing perforated artwork for the crystal palace.
2. Overlaying black cardboard.
3. On the black cardboard, overlaying a cleanup drawing.
4. Puncturing holes though the drawing and black cardboard.
5. Punctured black cardboard with top lighting.
6. Punctured black cardboard with bottom light.
7. Fine tuning of the punctured holes in the black cardboard.
8. Final film still.

That's the general process, and that is how we produced the entire film. It was actually a lot more complex than that, because each scene consists of multiple layers and so on. But that was the basic principle we used to shoot the film. Simultaneously, we had to think about the music; the music was very important for the film. In the beginning, I thought I should use some melodic Indian music, because of the source of the main poem. It didn't work. Then we tried something else. I tried the sitar. I tried the flute and many other musical instruments and elements. It just wasn't working. It's just somehow that it was getting too..., it was becoming too identifiable. In terms of cultural context, the Film Board wasn't very happy. *(Remark of the editor: The National Film Board of Canada, where Ishu Patel was making the film*). The people, the practitioners in the film board kept saying: "Make it more international. Don't make it too Indian."

I finally agreed with that point of view. Then, I heard Georghe Zamfir's panpipes flute, and I immediately knew I had found what I was looking for. I started shooting the film. But then, I had to clear the rights for using his music.

I was looking for him, trying to contact him. I couldn't find him. On and on it went, and we were trying to find him through the Romanian Embassy. We looked in France, where he was living before. In those days, there was no Internet, so you never knew where people were. Your only option was to find sources from the official government offices or people who knew about him. Anyway, finally, it just wasn't going anywhere. What I decided then was, "I am going to take panpipes flute music straight from the record and worry about the rights later."

Figure 6.24: Music recordings with Georghe Zamfir. (© National Film "Board of Canada." All rights reserved.)

The first passage, the first track is the *Lonely Shepherd*, which is composed by James Last, a famous German composer, and so, we wrote to this German composer. He gave the permission. Then, we wrote to the German company that had published the *Lonely Shepherd*. They both helped me. They gave me permission, and so, we started animating the first sequence with that. Then I thought: If nothing else works, then we'll find a composer who will do the rest of the music for us. Just then, one day, I saw an announcement in the newspaper: Zamfir in concert in Montreal. As soon as I saw he is somewhere around here, I knew I had to meet him. I was finally able to meet him in person right after the concert.

He was very tired. He came from Mexico and did the concert. They were going somewhere else in a few days. I introduced myself and said that I'm from the National Film Board. I'm making a film. I'm using his music. He said, "Okay, I don't have much time. I have to leave, but I can give you a little time." I said, "Well, I have something to show you. If you look at the Animation I have done, you might be interested in doing the music for the film." He said, "Okay, but you have to wait for few more days after I come back to Montreal from my concert trip."

That night, after the concert in the middle of the night Zamfir agreed to come to the National Film Board studio and I was able to show him the opening sequence of the dancing bird in the palace.

I showed the entire segment to him. He then said, "I will do the music for you. Because I love it the way you've done it. I will also do all the other pieces." Then, about 3 weeks later he came back to the Film Board recording studio and around 11 o'clock we started recording his panpipes music. We recorded all kind of variations and combinations of his flute including various types of bird sounds. He was known for making great bird sounds with his panpipes. We recorded about 3 hours of music that night.

What I find actually very interesting is that the original poem was, in this case, more like a starting point or a springboard for the final animated short.

Yes. The springboard, and you'd sort of departed from it but kept the same basic idea. The concept remains the same: that each bird tries to imitate each other. The black bird meets the divine bird and gets into trouble. Then, it goes into the palace, gets caught, and then is thrown out, and then learns the lessons, and goes back to the forest and finds out that, "Oh my gosh. My world is better than that." That was the underlying concept, the general idea.

Right. It works, but it illustrates very well that although the concepts stayed the same, the narrative still undergoes a transformation for the adaptation—in a way, staying true to the original concept through adapting but also demonstrating the requirement to change when you take it to a different medium.

It changed after all, because it's animation. It has to be fantastic. It has to be imaginative. It has to have a certain kind of motions and moves and music and so forth. Then, at that point, although the divine bird became an important element, the blackbird was the winner in the end.

I would also like to reiterate what you were already talking about. For the animation, there was a need for visual contrast, right?

Absolutely. That contrast component is important, and the palace has to feature the strongest contrast. Athough the palace was all dark it was lit up with pin hole brightness while the characters are acting out. Then, there is the lush green forest creating contrast between the natural environment and the artificial environment of the place. So that was the idea and it worked very well.

Out of the requirement for this particular adaptation grew this completely new technique, right?

Yes, that was the reason, because I was forced to come up with something new. I was determined not to paint the background. Because as soon as I painted it, it didn't look different than the paint it was. It just looked like an "ordinary" palace. It just didn't look like the environment that I wanted. Then, it became a question of how to achieve this through entirely new ideas. But this is how this whole new process came about—the lighting technique and everything else. I think that it apparently became a new impressive method. When the palace sequence opens and the audience sees it for the first time, it has a dazzling effect on them.

It still does. The combination with the music is also very important.

At the time, when it came out in 1985. It's dated right now, but when I finished it in 1984, it was quite a sensation—immediately, because digital technology wasn't there. When you make something like that, people say, "How did you do it?" That's the first question people ask. Today, people all over the country thought that we used computers to do it. You can do complicated things in a simpler way now with digital tools, but in those days, it had to be created through a complex process like this. People really always asked, "Well, how did they do it?" That was always the first question they asked. That was the strongest part of the film.

The film did very well commercially. The music was also very popular at the time. It's a very pleasant piece of music. Right after that, Tarantino used the same music in *Kill Bill Volume 1* (2003).

He used exactly the same music.

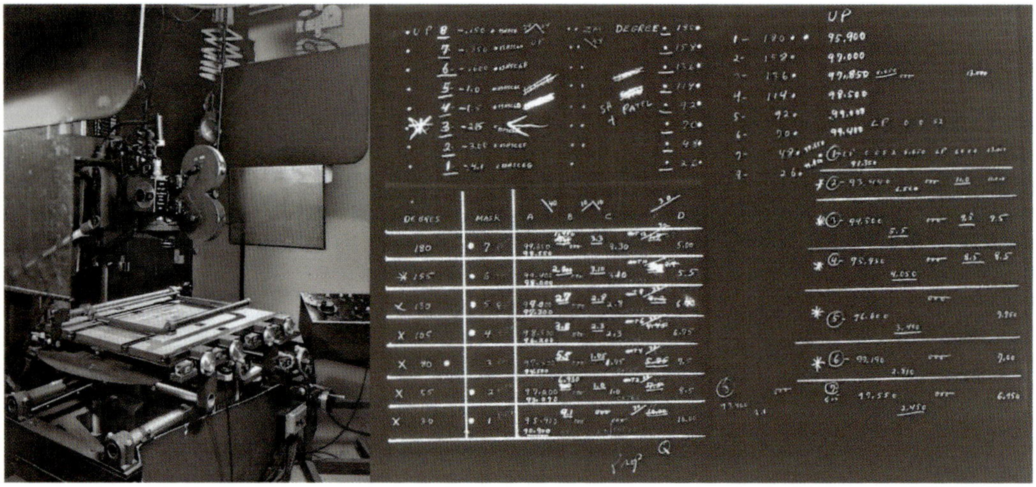

Figure 6.25: The computerized Oxberry camera setup and an example of the multi-level background calculations used for the film. (© National Film Board of Canada. All rights reserved.)

Let's talk about the second example of your adaptations now. It would be good if you could say something about how that was different in terms of the original source material and also in terms of the adaptation method.

Okay. Let's discuss the second story. I read it once in one issue of a magazine called *Internationalist*. It was written by the Egyptian writer Enver Carim. It's a short story called *Top Priority*, about a family that is stuck in a remote desert somewhere. It's an absolutely true story I adapted completely the way it was written. I did not change much in the story but reduced the number of characters to one family unit since I am working in the animation medium. But I kept the story intact. I also made a choice of how many characters I should have in the family. In the original story, there was a large community of people, which would have been hard to deal with in animation film.

Figure 6.26: Film still from *Top Priority* (1981). (From *Top Priority* ©1981 National Film Board of Canada. All rights reserved.)

Because the whole village was affected by the lack of water, the drought. But I took the village out and turned it into a family. That was the situation—a story that is about a whole village, a small community was transformed into just one family unit. There is one hut, one little broken pump, and three or four people from the family. The family should have a father and mother obviously; and a boy and a girl, which we kept; and a grandfather. These were all the characters.

What would they have in terms of their possessions? Because in the village, there were many different things. They were worried about it. They worried about their farming. The crops were not growing with all the consequences from it. We said, "Well, that is too much. Too difficult to do it in animation, because it will require to be done as a live action film." Go there and do on-location shooting. We had to simplify all the complexity for animation. That is why, we decided that they should have only one hut, in which they were living. There should be a broken pump, and there should be a cow, which is their only possession. It was early on based on that. We thought, "Had the cow come into trouble?" That became the critical point. That gives an idea why the family has a problem.

If the cow dies, they die. Because the cow is very important. That was for the audience. The adaptation sort of pared it down, pared it down to something very basic and clear in communication. How would I want to do it? I just thought about the technique I used for *Afterlife*. *Afterlife* is backlit, but everything was black. Pretty much black, and the color is very vibrant. I used opaque plastic to create a white background and animated the color characters shaped out of flat plasticine. Since there were many colors in each character, the film turned out to be the hardest one I ever did. When I took some tests, it worked beautifully, but took a lot more time to do each frame under the Oxberry animation camera stand.

Figure 6.27: The backlit plasticine technique used for the film. (From *Top Priority* ©1981 National Film Board of Canada. All rights reserved.)

It looked like the background is in light mist. You didn't know where from, of course. It's hot and arid. When the colors were added to the characters, it looked like a hot country. It really looked like some kind of different kind of desert environment, where the colors were brighter and the darker is darker. There were no in-between extra tones, so that's exactly the color scheme, the atmosphere I wanted. The third problem was how to create movement with that technique. What part should you animate, and what part shouldn't you animate? We looked and tried. I looked into the story. It was a very desperate situation described in the story.

I think it could be compared to a post-war situation, all kinds of people scattered somewhere. They're totally desperate. They are demoralized, and they have no money. The same thing happens here in this story. They have nothing left. There's only one choice: to die. They just sit. They're very desperate. They have no energy left. They can't run around, doing things.

We were trying to figure out how to animate this film. A long time ago, I had seen a Polish Film. A long, long time ago. But that film stayed in my mind. I don't remember the name of the title. In that film, the character never moved, but the camera moved around and took shots, giving you the kind of motion that was matching the story it was telling.

I thought this could be the solution, if I created the characters in such a technique, but I really wanted to avoid animating jumping up and down or similar movements. Because they can't. They're in a desperate situation. Then, we thought about moving everything instead. I just moved the camera—move it so we can achieve a real motion. You can't create an animated film by just showing still frames, not until you make the whole filmic environment move. I used a constantly moving camera. Things were moving. I'll just go around the character if I wanted to go around it. If something came closer, I animated those things, and within that, there was a little bit of limited animation. The hands were moved. Mouths were moved. A little gesture here, a little gesture there. The characters did not do anything else.

I spent a lot of time on designing the characters, and I gave each character a distinct pose. They would stand in a certain way, or they would sit in a certain way. A mother has a certain pose. A grandfather will sit in a certain way with the stick and his hand on it. The father will be a little bit more energetic. The kids were a little bit mischievous from time to time, because they still could run around and do things. We used that as I saw fit, but the rest of the time, it always kept at the basic poses. They would all stay in that pose. Within that pose, I would move around the whole thing and tell the whole story about how the water was coming there.

Figure 6.28: Film still from *Top Priority* (1981). (From *Top Priority* ©1981 National Film Board of Canada. All rights reserved.)

One day, they're all waiting, and then, you think you already know the story. When the truck comes in, it's a surprise for them. It's not a truck that they're looking for, instead an army comes in. They tell them all kind of nonsense. The army says one thing and the people are saying one thing, and nobody's really talking to each other. That's pretty much the situation. The original story was about the whole village. We turned it into a family unit. The story was about where they were going. In the story, they were taking the cattle. They would walk her in the river. A lot of narrative elements were in the story, which I could not adapt for animation. I didn't want to do it.

We sort of turned everything into a steady situation instead. Then, we added a little bit of a dream sequence. One dream sequence was put in for the men, so that the audience gets an idea why water is so important to them. He's sleeping, hallucinating, and he's thinking that all of his surroundings have come alive. It turns out that the rain has come, and everything is turning green. Then, it turns out it is just a dream, and he finds out that the cow has died. It just gives us an idea to say how important the water is at that point. That was that particular film.

In the case of that story, did you have to ask the writer for permission?

Yes. We had to clear the rights for the story. I also added an agreement with the writer that the film would be just (freely) based on the story. It's not exactly this story. We based it freely on the story, which means I was allowed to change it, and he agreed.

I explained that it would be an animated film, so that it cannot be made exactly faithful to the original story. Some people thought this could have been easily made into a short film with live-action actors and everybody else. I think it works better for me the way I did it, and I was also exploring the techniques at the same time—the same technique we already had developed for *Afterlife* but taken a step further and developed it into a more realistic kind of style.

In this case, the animated adaptation added some narrative focus, didn't it? Because you'll bring it down from a larger community to really just a core group of people.

I can focus on the character, and each character had a different kind of attitude about life and death. Father was adamant about it. Kids were kind of not sure. Mother was always cautious and warning everything. The grandfather was always a wise man saying, "No, no, we should live stay here blah, blah, blah, and so on, so forth."

Figure 6.29: Film still from *Top Priority* (1981). (From *Top Priority* ©1981 National Film Board of Canada. All rights reserved.)

You concentrate, you bring together, make it more focused. It was a tool.

In animation, it becomes more powerful actually. When you condense the content, it becomes much more powerful. You had to condense it in such a way that it doesn't get too complicated for the audience to perceive it, understand it. The audience will still understand it. By using symbols and by using certain metaphors, you can build those back up. Like, for example, a skinny dog howling. It gives an idea that is originated by that. You don't let them talk, make them look like they're not eating. Showing the dog gives an idea. Dying, a cow dying gives a certain idea. There's a danger present.

Those kinds of metaphors you can use.

Then, there is a third example of adaptation I can talk about. The third example is *Divine Fate*. This is interesting, because most of my films have come from my childhood memories. All of them pretty much, including my first film, second film, and third film. All pretty much comes from what I learned and what I knew. This is the nice thing for me, a nice thing that worked for me at the National Film Board of Canada, too. Because, by then, everywhere, somebody was making films in a certain way. I would follow all the rules and regulations and understood the structure and learned from the other filmmakers and seeing other films.

Figure 6.30: Film still from *Divine Fate* (1993). (*Divine Fate* ©1993 National Film Board of Canada. All rights reserved.)

The content I would use would hail from my childhood, from my own history, and I would present it in my very own way. That made me different from the others. That's the only way I could differentiate myself from everybody else. Otherwise, if I copied other people, with the same idea, it would have never worked. *Divine Faith* emerged like that. Back then, when I was a 7- or 8-year-old boy, we used to have a huge mango tree in our farm. I grew up on a farm, so I was used to helping my father ever since I was 7 years old. I would get up in the morning at 6 o'clock, going to help my father. I had chores to do. It was all decided. We didn't speak much, but I had to do it.

It was a hard life, so in those days, agriculture wasn't all that productive as today. Everybody had to work twice as hard. Everybody in the family. I worked. My sister worked. My mother worked. My father worked. We all worked. Including the bullocks. They all worked. This mango tree was always providing the most pleasant situation for the family, because we loved having mangoes. That was our treat. Because most of the time, we ate ordinary food, day after day after day, we ate the same things. Then, the mango season would come, especially for the kids. They got excited because they went, "Oh, wow. We got a lot of mangoes to eat."

Mango trees were for all villagers, everybody had one or two mango trees. We had a huge one there. Every year, it was a normal process. During winter months, it would bloom, and we would have lots of mangoes. At the end of May, we had to harvest the mangoes. I went with my father to pull out the cart and everything else. We harvested the mangoes. For many years, I didn't pay any attention, but one year, I remember, when I was 8 or 9 years old, we met, and that particular year, the mango tree had bloomed so much for some reason, with many mangoes. We went and harvested. I climbed the tree, and it was a wonderful time for the boy. That was all great. We finished everything, and we loaded the bullock cart full of mangoes.

We headed home on the bullock cart with mangoes but then I looked back and I saw so many mangoes still left on the tree. I asked my father. I said, "Hey, you forgot the mangoes. How come there's so many mangoes left?" He said, " Son, learn, never to rob the nature entirely. Never take too much from nature. Always leave something behind for others." I remembered this so well. When I was looking for new ideas, I came up with this. I remembered his words saying that. Take only what you need and leave something good behind, for other people. That became the start. I took that as a basic idea and turned it into my own little story afterward. That's the original philosophical thinking coming from an old farmer, my father, who I still remember to this day.

Figure 6.31: Cutout replacement artwork for *Divine Fate*. (*Divine Fate* ©1993 National Film Board of Canada. All rights reserved.)

Because for him—he understood the nature, because he lived with it. Not philosophical at all in that regard. He simply knew how to behave, where the connection was, between the tree, himself, and the mango. He left it for the birds and animals to eat it basically.

That it was not only about him. The tree wasn't for him alone just because he owned the tree. That's the idea. The idea is that because the monkeys will carry the fruits somewhere else, a new tree will grow and influence the whole environment around him. When we received a brief from NFB to create some films that address environmental concerns, this is where this one came from. The basic Idea of the environment was there but how could we make a film out of that/ what kind of story could we develop?

Do I exactly describe what I experienced with my father? Can I have me in there? The story about the tree and all what he told me? This was all very realistic and straight forward. As usual, we decided that we must do some creative transformation of the original concept of "take only what you need and give something in return." Can we take this concept and turn it into a mythological kind of story rather than making a realistic story? Because if you look at all mythological stories, they have big messages. They give nice messages, but in a very soft way, and not "in your face." I finally realized that that was a good approach. Mythology always interested me. I decided to create a mythological story here:

You take something, you put something back in its place. You cannot take anything without putting something good in return. That was the original idea I thought about. On and on it went, and we discussed it. We had some producers and some people in the studio. At the Film Board, we talked. We talked about the ideas, and we finally came to the conclusion that it'll be nice to use a different setting. Take the whole story to another planet, a good place somewhere, imaginary, not on Earth. We used this kind of divine land we made up, and on that land, there were gates. Each gate would offer something special. You could take everything from the gate, but you had to put something good back in return.

Figure 6.32: Film still from *Divine Fate* (1993). (*Divine Fate* ©1993 National Film Board of Canada. All rights reserved.)

There are no people there, only the spirits who can live there. Sprits who meet other spirits and they take whatever they wish from the divine gates but always return some thing good back into the gates. Then, one day, for some reason, two human-like creatures fall from the sky. They fall on the land, and all the spirits are wondering who these people are. They help them out, and they come alive. Well, if you want to stay, you can stay here, but there's one rule on our land. On this land, the rule is that you only take what you need from this land, but you also have to return something good. In other words, take something but always return something good.

That was the idea. Based on that, the whole film starts, and then, as usual human nature takes over. In the beginning they comply with the rules of the divine land but slowly one of them decides to cheat. One of them thinks that the other one is following the rule so he does not have to obey the rules of the land. It starts from there. Then, it turns into a competition between those two humans while the spirits are watching that this land is being turned into a small currency. Then, at the end, the gods get angry, because the humans have behaved badly, so the gods punish them. They close all the gates totally, and they (the humans) can't get anything out of them anymore.

At the same time, they start pulling back and start crying and so forth, until the supreme god agrees to give them one more chance. The god said: "You can not stay here you must leave." With his two divine hands he gathers some soil from the land and turns it into a ball and presents it to the humans with a warning: "Take this, it has every thing you need and more, but remember, take only what you need and give something good in return." The ball turns into a blue planet as it moves away to the stars. This is how I adapted this original concept of my father into an animated short film.

Figure 6.33: Film still from *Divine Fate* (1993). (*Divine Fate* ©1993 National Film Board of Canada. All rights reserved.)

In this case, the adaptation was actually first going back to your childhood memory and what your father was telling you.

Yeah, that's right.

That is basically only one sentence of basic concept.

One sentence that turned into the foundation for the film. Then, the challenge was how to illustrate that sentence in an animated film. I mean, that was the central message. That message is very powerful, because that describes the general problem. We all exploit resources and nature, basically without thinking about it. That was the idea. The idea really went down hard on the people there, considering that you put in a factory here, a factory there. Again, what is the essence of the whole story? The essence of the whole story is to find some way to convince the audience that it's important to take what you need and give something back in return.

That was the idea. And the challenge was: How to transform it for an animated short film? We just found this mythological way of showing something. It's happening somewhere else, but there's (still) a lesson for us there, I think.

The interesting thing is that this is something that really related to a very universal topic of the human condition. That's why it works, right?

Exactly. That's why it works.

This demonstrates some similarity with the previous examples of your adaptations. Because there's something you can relate to, and an audience can relate to.

Exactly. That's is the reason. The idea is not to make it too complicated. At the same time, when you watch a film, it has to be enjoyable, through the use of new techniques and how you put it together. You need to make it dazzling. You must have that cinematic element.

The language for animated short films is different, right? First of all, the cinematic language, and, on top of that, the specific animation language.

Also animation. Everything animates only correctly in a specific matching style. Because for me, the choice of animation style is always important. It doesn't mean that you need to animate everything fully all the time. But it has to be done in a certain style. As the visual style. The style of motion. Each film requires a specific style of motion. It can be fast-paced. *Afterlife* is all different melting motion. Each story requires a different type of animation—you simply cannot say, "Well, that's the only way to animate." From the ideas, visual style and motion come film structure and clarity.

Figure 6.34: Film still from *Divine Fate* (1993). (From *Divine Fate* ©1993 National Film Board of Canada. All rights reserved.)

You must know how the motion style matches your visual style. Then, when you will know the motion style, you will subsequently be able to animate in an innovative style. Some kind of new structure emerges, and that structure becomes the kind of a new way of thinking of filmmaking. That's how you get to stand out from the crowd.

In your films, you have almost always introduced a new style for a new film.

Because of the changing requirements of the new story.

For me, it's about the new requirement. It's not the same requirement, because I have chosen this particular story. I cannot use the same style, the same with learning with the second film or the third and the fourth. It has to be different, because I'm choosing a subject matter far apart. Far and wide, I don't mix my former styles with this new film. I don't rely on the writing, lines, dialogues, and so on. The subject matters there range from death to life, to environment, to human conditions, and so on. They are changing and so should the (visual) styles of the films with them.

In all of these cases of adaptations, this always meant bringing something else to the plate, right?

Yeah, adding to it. Also, for me, adaptation is important, because if I see something in a story, it's important to find a certain way to adapt it. But while you adapt it, the good thing about the films is that they often require you to find new ways of doing things. The reason often was a lack of budget. For example, when I was making *Paradise*, the rule came that you will not be allowed to use cels anymore for film, because they (the National Film Board of Canada) could not afford cels anymore. In other words, we could not make cel animation anymore.

Maybe one film, maybe one in a couple of years, because each cel cost about 75 cents, and I would have needed thousands and thousands. Somebody said: "No, we're not going to do it." We said okay. How do we do it then? "Okay, well how do you do it now?" Then, we had to figure out those things. Okay, no cels. Fine. We'll use paper instead.

Limitation…

Triggered creativity.

With *Afterlife*, it was exactly the same situation. I just created that technique because there was nothing else available, as they say. At that time. The interesting thing was that they were saying that film should not cost so much money. We cannot afford too much costs, because our studio budget was reduced actually. As for some reason, a bureaucratic reason, they had to fight for those things. The budget was reduced, and they gave us 1.6 million for the studio for the whole year for 10 filmmakers. We all wanted to make films.

How much money would we have each month? We all struggled. How did we do it, then? We all gathered together. We agreed we should all do it; we should all be able to make films. Then, I came up with this idea, and I worked on it and figured it out. I said, "Okay, I have a film here, where the material costs only $50. Would you program it?" They were all saying why don't you let us see all the figures. I said, "Yeah, I'm just telling you. I only need $50. If I spend more than $50, don't fund me again. Ever again." In those days, plasticine cost only 50 cents for each package. I bought $50 of material. I made the whole film from that budget.

These kinds of solutions help. Sometimes, they would help. We complained quite a bit, but I thought about it. You can complain. I mean, I complained. I said, "This is ridiculous. How are you going to say you cannot make things you cannot have. I want to have materials. How could you stop all art supply and stuff like this?" They were just doing it, because they were cutting down the budget. The government was cutting their budget, so they cut all the budget. We needed money for the music and everything else. We couldn't really afford to overspend. Then, it became a necessity to say to find a solution for this situation, just on my own. I didn't have any assistant. The camera was already there. They could be in danger, because when there is too much spending, they sometimes consider throwing out even somebody senior. It does happen. I've been in storms like this sometimes, because of sometimes having too many things. This is not always necessary, because once you start making things, solutions will emerge.

So, I thought twice, and I was not against it. I'm sure if somebody gave me a lot of money, I would have been fine with that, too. But I prefer to be less complicated. I prefer simplicity in a process, so then, I put more effort into creativity and getting new ways of putting the films together. I find the new structures, I find a new way of looking at a subject.

We have already talked about the fact that, very often, adaptation for animation actually requires change.

Yes.

Because you're going to a different medium, you have to create a different artistic vision. You have to define the visual language first.

Absolutely.

Because before that there is none. Now, let's go to a topic that is sometimes quite sensitive: adapting indigenous art forms or also traditional stories from other cultures. Very often, there is this debate about how much are you allowed to change when it comes to art, to adaptation, for example, for animation. What is your point of view on this topic?

I understand what you mean. I know what you're trying to say. I made my first film called *How Death Came to Earth*. It's an Indian film. I wanted to do it with that kind of cultural motives. But I think, if you have to stay true to each and every image, you look at what is already illustrated on that particular subject matter by somebody, it can become a problem. For example, if you have a story, and it's a story told in a temple-cloth, the whole story is told in a temple-cloth, with all the characters designed by that particular artist or a folk artist or a folk person. Then, you start from there, and you try to develop it for animation.

And that is when people often get very sensitive about it. You're taking that story, and you're not using exactly the same style of drawing like in the original illustrations or patterns. Those drawings would not animate properly for us. You still have to adapt them. Even the visual aspect has to be adapted, as long as you stay true to the feeling of it. It cannot be exactly the same way. Just like what you have done with shadow puppets. A shadow puppet is a shadow puppet. When you have to animate it, maybe there are some changes to be made to it, as long as the look is the same. I think it's very hard to convince people sometimes. If you get too close to the actual subject matter and the actual pictorial presentation done on that particular situation, your animation and story suffer.

Because it's a different medium. That's why they told a story on the temple-cloth, and they hold the whole temple-cloth. You can see the images. If you want to put the same story into their animated form, then the story has to have some changes to take place, and the visual has to change. You can take those references as inspiration and the whole character of it. To keep exactly the same style. In some cases, it works. Most of the times, it can get very difficult to animate a certain image without any changes. For example, let's look at Inca drawings. If you tried this and you wanted to animate the whole film like the start, you will see that, in some points, something would be working, other parts would not be working at all.

You have to come up with some decisions in the end. You basically get inspiration from those original drawings, the original indigenous designs. The structure, the look, the size, the forms, as shown, and then create your own little thing, which resembles that but not necessarily exactly replicates it.

Sometimes, I would also assume that artistic exchange between cultures has been a very natural thing throughout the centuries.

Sure.

It's not something that needs to be necessarily connected with negative implications.

That's right, absolutely.

Because if you look at the Silk Road or all kinds of different adaptations of different art styles, even the nineteenth and twentieth centuries, early twentieth century. Like looking into aboriginal art and how it inspired expressionism, so it could possibly also be seen as a sign of artistic respect.

Yes. We have one good example for that. It is called *The Owl Who Married a Goose*, which is actually a perfect example. It is a film by Caroline Leaf. Originally, it's an Inuit story. It's told, but it's not exactly the Inuit drawing. Because the goal is drawing into sand animation. Silhouette, like in the Inuit drawings, but not simply replicating it. The animation drawings are not done exactly the way the Inuits draw it. Because Caroline Leaf had to move them. You still get the feeling that, in this case, it's an Inuit story, done in the same way. It's a silhouette design still but transformed for a completely different medium. Once such a medium is used, then, of course, the design is slightly going to change, and the motion is going to change.

Figure 6.35: Film still from *The Owl Who Married a Goose* (Leaf 1974). (From *The Owl Who Married a Goose* ©1974 National Film Board of Canada. All rights reserved.)

Some point is often forgotten. You don't mind that she is not entirely faithful to the story actually. She's true to the story. The silhouette is there but not exactly using the same design (the Inuit) would do. Because she has to animate something—the story too. She has to change it, because the story is so bizarre that sometimes it doesn't make sense if you follow exactly the way it is narrated in the original source material. But that is okay. Here, it is better. Some good things from the original to start with, but then, on top some connections, we can make by adding some extra character or something else to it. Which you put in and which is not from the original story.

When I look into adaptation(s), I keep coming back to the fact that the final work must convince in its final form and stand on its own and by itself.

Absolutely. I agree with you. It has to stand on its own, but people can still feel well, you can see it's from a particular culture. That's okay. Nothing's wrong with that. Look at Disney. Disney has taken German fairy tales and all this, and look what Disney has done. They have Americanized the whole thing, but these old stories are from German tales and originated from the old world. They're not American stories, but today, nobody knows that they're German stories. They think, "Oh, this is all American." Because he did it the way he wanted and then added characters there as well. All kind of changes were made. Even (more) for feature films.

Any of the old tales were taken. The same thing with *Pinocchio* and a lot of other stories. The stories are taken and changed into something else, because an adaptation for feature film requires even more changes.

I think that we also have to think about something else. Artists very often naturally don't look at such considerations from any ideological point of view. They just love to create and see something that they find inspiring and interesting and then combine it with their own styles, and then, something new emerges.

I have encountered artists who prefer criticizing me by saying, "You're not true to what you are adapting, to the original source." I answer, "Well, but it's not the same thing." A fresco is painted on a wall. If you ask me to animate that character for some reason, let's say a commercial company came and said, "We're going to use Mona Lisa as our character. But you have to do something with it." It's a part of a commercial. If I had it animated, then I'm not going to do the same way as she is shown in the painting. That remains possibly close to the original, but you have to adapt it to the medium, because Mona Lisa will turn into a (different) Mona Lisa there. How would I move it, and what do I do with it?

It's the same thing. People have taken Piet Mondrian paintings and animated them, and it changes. It always changes. It has too. My film *Perspectrum* is pretty much based on Victor Vasarely's paintings. That inspired me. Am I doing the Victor Vasarely in there? No, but I'm using his inspiration and transparent colors and hues of colors and so forth. Then, how to adapt it? It's technically an interpretation. I make my own version of these designs, but that's the inspiration. That's the origin of the story. Doesn't mean I have to exactly do it like Victor Vasarely. He did the paintings, and I'm making a film.

Any folk story and any kind of folk character that approach can be hard to explain to people. Sometimes, people don't understand it. I just ignore it.

Also, sometimes, the interesting thing is that many folk stories have been delivered through oral tradition always, and they were basically supposed to change.

That's right. They moved it. Exactly, so if the story changes, then I'm allowed to change the story too, because I'm part of the folk story—storytelling person.

Yeah, so it's more like a dynamic process.

That has become common knowledge. That's why the people who write the original material usually never write the screenplay for the adaptation. Somebody else writes the screenplay based on their knowledge of filmmaking. It will be written by somebody else. Very rarely you find the person who wrote the original story or book who would also write his/her own screenplay. It happens but is rather rare, generally speaking.

It's rare.

Very rare. The reason is because a novel is a novel, and then, it has to be adapted for the screen. If you adapt a scene that is written, the opening sequence will be the first funny page, not the actual first page from the novel.

It goes back to what you said before that, in an animated film, to keep it interesting, you cannot have talking heads all the time.

You got to find a way to make it interesting. How do you open the film? Like a live action film? The same problem. You compare with the novel. It starts differently. The animated film opens from the middle of the chapter, sometimes in some cases, and then goes back an hour and so on. There are many, many different reasons for that. I think the filmic language is only understood by the people who make the films, not necessarily by the people who look at the films or not by the people who criticize the films. I generally ignore the comments by the non-filmmakers about that. I'd rather discuss with a fellow filmmaker, because I know he would have a different opinion about the same thing.

Now, that doesn't mean I don't think. I just get stopped and I go, "It's okay. I listen to you. But I've got a language too—the filmic language." It's like asking a writer to say, "Well, why are you writing the words? Let me draw a picture there." He would answer, "No. I've got to write the words. That's my job. That's what I do."

Bibliography

Arya, Ravi Prakash, ed. 1998. *Ramayana of Valmiki: Sanskrit Text and English Translation.* (English translation according to M. N. Dutt, introduction by Dr. Ramashraya Sharma, 4-volume set). New Delhi, India: Parimal Publications.

Aznam, Hajar, dir. 2011. *Ulek Mayang (Spirits of the Sea).* Animated short film. Malaysia.

Binter, Julia. 2013. *Radioglaz and the Global City.* In: *Transcultural Montage*, edited by Christian Suhr and Rane Willerslev, 183. New York/Oxford: Berghahn.

Branagh, Kenneth, dir. 2006. *As You like it.* Live action feature film. London, UK: BBC Films (production). Santa Monica, CA: HBO Films (distribution).

Brook, Peter, dir. 1970. *A Midsummer Night's Dream.* Theatrical production. Stratford-upon-Avon, England: Royal Shakespeare Company.

Jayaraj, dir. 2001. *Kannaki.* Live action feature film. Kerala, India.

Kozintsev, Grigori, dir. 1971. *King Lear.* Live action feature film. St. Petersburg, VA: Lenfilm.

Kozintsev, Grigori, dir. 1964. *Hamlet*. Live action feature film. St. Petersburg, VA: Lenfilm.

Kurosawa, Akira, dir. 1985. *Ran*. Live action feature film. Tokyo, Japan: Nippon Herald Pictures; Tokyo, Japan: Herald Ace; London, UK: Greenwich Film Productions (production).

Kurosawa, Akira, dir. 1957. *Throne of Blood*. Live action feature film. Tokyo, Japan: Toho Studios (studio).

Leaf, Caroline, dir. 1974. *The Owl who Married a Goose*. Animated short film. Montreal, Canada: National Film Board of Canada (studio).

Loncraine, Richard, dir. 1995. *Richard III*. Live action feature film. London, UK: Mayfair Entertainment International (production).

Narayan, R. K., and Kampar. 2006. The Ramayana: A shortened modern prose version of the Indian epic (suggested by the Tamil version of Kamban). New York: Penguin Books, 243.

Patel, Ishu, dir. 1978. *Afterlife*. Animated short film. Montreal, Canada: National Film Board of Canada (studio).

Patel, Ishu. 2016. *Asian Lives-A Closer Look*. London, UK: Thames & Hudson.

Patel, Ishu, dir. 1993. *Divine Fate*. Animated short film. Montreal, Canada: National Film Board of Canada (studio).

Patel, Ishu, dir. 1974. *How Death Came to Earth*. Animated short film. Montreal, Canada: National Film Board of Canada (studio).

Patel, Ishu. 2015. Interview with Hannes Rall. April 7. 50 minutes. Nanyang Technological University, Singapore.

Patel, Ishu, dir. 1977. *Paradise*. Animated short film. Montreal, Canada: National Film Board of Canada (studio).

Patel, Ishu, dir. 1981. *Top Priority*. Animated short film. Montreal, Canada: National Film Board of Canada (studio).

Pollack, Sydney, dir. 1982. *Tootsie*. Live action feature film. Los Angeles, CA: Mirage Enterprises (production). Los Angeles, CA: Columbia Pictures (distribution).

Rotaru, Alex, dir. 2011. *Shakespeare High*. Documentary feature film. Beverly Hills, CA: Ifavor Entertainment (production). New York: The Cinema Guild (distribution).

Shakespeare, William. 1896. *As You Like It*. Boston, MA: Allyn and Bacon.

Shakespeare, William. 1864. *Coriolanus*. London, UK: J. R. Smith.

Shakespeare, William. 1968. *Hamlet*. Cambridge, UK: Cambridge U.P.

Shakespeare, William. 2007. *Coriolanus*. Performed by Ninagawa Company (April 25). London, UK: Barbican Theatre.

Shakespeare, William. 1899. *Shakespeare's Othello: The Moor of Venice: With Introduction, and Notes Explanatory and Critical for Use in Schools and Families*. Boston, MA: Ginn.

Shakespeare, William. 1992–1994. *The Animated Tales*. Animated TV series. Adapted from William Shakespeare by Leon Garfield. Moscow, Russia: Christmas Films (production).

Shakespeare, William. 1958. *The Tempest*. Cambridge, MA: Harvard University Press.

Shakespeare, William. 2011. *The Tempest*. Performed by Mokwha Repertory Company (August 2011). Edinburgh, Scotland: King's Theatre.

Suhr, Christian, and Rane Willerslev. 2012. *Can Film Show the Invisible? The Work of Montage in Ethnographic Filmmaking*. In: *Current Anthropology*, Vol. 53, No. 3. Chicago, IL: The University of Chicago Press. June 2012, p. 282–301.

Sullivan, Erin. 2013. *A Year of Shakespeare Re-living the World Shakespeare Festival*. London, UK: Bloomsbury.

Tarantino, Quentin, dir. 2003. *Kill Bill Volume 1*. Live action feature film. Los Angeles, CA: A Band Apart (production). Miramax (distribution).

Various authors. 1941–1971. *Classics Illustrated*. Comic book series. New York: Elliot Publishing (1941–1942); New York: Gilberton (1942–1967); New York: Frawley Corporation (1967–1971).

Verboeckhoven, Eugène Joseph. 1871. *A Shepherdess with her Flock*. Oil painting on canvas, 113 × 161.3 cm (44.5 × 63.5 in). Source/Photographer: Sotheby's, New York, November 8, 2012, lot 34.

Welsch, Wolfgang. 1999. *Transculturality: The puzzling form of cultures today*. In: *Spaces of culture: City, nation, world*. edited by Mike Featherstone and Scott Lash, 194–213. London, UK: Sage.

Wilcox, Fred M. dir. 1956. *Forbidden Planet*. Live action feature film. Beverly Hills, CA: Metro-Goldwyn-Mayer (studio).

Visual Poetry and Experimental Adaptation

Rhyme with Reason

Introduction

Exploring the art of adapting Gothic literature, the previous chapter has already included two adaptations of poetry for animation: *Der Erlkönig* by Johann Wolfgang von Goethe and *The Raven* by Edgar Allen Poe. That investigation focused on the aspect of transforming the supernatural elements from the written page to the filmic version.

Moreover, both poems largely offer a traditional linear narrative, a plot more easily transferable for an animated short film:

Der Erlkönig is an example of a classical ballad and was published in 1782. Goethe was inspired by a translation of a Danish folk-ballad by Johann Gottfried Herder (Bormann 1996). The slightly more modern *The Raven* (1845) by Poe also offers a very concrete storyline at first, before it veers off into a more ambiguous and dreamlike storytelling with a somehow open ending. In my own adaptation of Poe's poem, I added a more concrete ending to fulfill the needs of a traditional climax and plot resolution.

Moving toward more modern poems, such linear storytelling, concrete plotlines, and easily ready narratives for filmic transformation become less and less frequent.

Metaphorical description, atmosphere instead of concrete plot, moods and emotions, and increasing abstraction become prevalent.

Therefore, the investigation in this chapter is now examining the very specific demands of adapting poems with varying degrees of narrative linearity and nonlinearity.

How can an animated adaptation answer to such challenges presented by the source material?

Is it possible to enhance narrative linearity while still preserving the artistic intent of the author of the original piece?

Or, should the animated adaptation fully embrace a less sequential (non-sequitur) structure of the poem and create an animated equivalent?

Why and how does the rhythmic nature of (most) poetry favor animation as the medium for animation?

Is animation possibly even particularly well suited for adapting fragmented, nonlinear narratives by employing its unique means of filmic expression?

Can experimental animation serve as an audiovisual equivalent to adapt abstract poetry adequately?

Accordingly, the chapter also follows a chronological structure moving toward modern and contemporary poems and their adapted animated versions.

The three case studies move increasingly away from traditional linear storytelling and demonstrate the development over time in terms of the chosen adaptation material: *Seemanstreue* (1924) by Joachim Ringelnatz, adapted by Anna Kalus-Goessner in 2008; the poem *A Lost and Found Box of Human Sensation*, developed by Martin Wallner from 2005 in various versions and then adapted by himself together with Stefan Leuchtenberg in 2010; and finally, the poem *The Great Escape* (2012) by contemporary Singaporean writer Alfian Sa'at adapted by Tan Wei Keong as an experimental animated short in 2015.

Preceding this triptych of modern poetry animation will be an in-depth interview with the director of the ZEBRA Poetry Film Festival, who has curated animated poetry for many years and therefore acquired a high expertise in the field.

But before moving forward, a look backward will help to gather a better understanding of the foundation: the definition and history of poetry. The intention here is not to provide a complete history of poetry—this is not an investigation from the point of view of literature studies. Instead, the following paragraphs will selectively highlight facts that are relevant in the framework of adaptation studies for animation.

And one of these questions is certainly what distinguishes poetry from other forms of literature, because this carries a multitude of implications to define a narrative approach in the animated adaptation.

Oxford Dictionaries (2015) offers the following definition of poetry:

> "Literary work in which the expression of feelings and ideas is given intensity by the use of distinctive style and rhythm."

Poetry, from the Greek poesis, meaning "making" or "creating," has a long history.

The oldest surviving poem is the *Epic of Gilgamesh* (Sandars 1972). The poem, based on the history of King Gilgamesh, was written around 3000 BC in Sumer, Mesopotamia in cuneiform script on clay tablets. Hess (n.d.) states that "as an art, poetry may out date literacy itself. In prehistoric and ancient societies poetry was used as a way to record cultural events or tell stories. Poetry is among the earliest records of most cultures with poetic fragments found on monoliths, rune stones, and stelae."

Aristotle's Poetics (Halliwell, Aristotle 1998) defines three genres of poetry: epic, comic, and tragic. Aristotle's writings were highly influential in the whole Middle East during the Islamic Golden Age and then further in Europe during the Renaissance. Later, aestheticians described poetry to have three major genres: epic, lyric, and dramatic, with dramatic holding the subcategories tragic and comedy. The telling of stories about history have been used up until the twentieth century, and in some cases, it is still in use today. During the Middle Ages, ballads were a common way of doing just this, and it was also a way to pass along news throughout the kingdoms. Today, ballads are not used in the same way.

During early modern Western tradition, poets and aestheticians sought to distinguish poetry from prose by using the understanding that prose was written in a linear narrative form and used logical explication, while poetry was more abstract and beautiful. (Rexroth n.d.)

The more traditional understanding of poetry as written literature has been questioned in modern times. Recently, it has become increasingly difficult for scholars to agree on a common definition for the wide variety the art form has to offer: How to compare contemporary slam poetry to a classic ballad from the 19th century? Tatarkiewicz (1975), a Polish historian of aesthetics, notes that "poetry expresses a certain state of mind." This viewpoint has been growing in popularity every year. Today, even media that doesn't involve words has been called poetry, for example, paintings and classical music.

"Modern theorists rely less on opposing prose and poetry, focusing more on the poet as an artist. Intellectual disputes over the definition of poetry had erupted throughout the twentieth century, resulting in the rejection of traditional forms and structures of poetry, and coinciding with the questioning of traditional definitions of poetry and its distinction between prose. More recently, post-modernists have begun to embrace the role of the reader and highlight the concept of poetry, incorporating its form from other cultures and the past." (Hess, nd)

However, for the purpose of clarity, I limit the definition of poetry largely to its more commonly known form as written literature. This is of particularly importance, because the focus of this investigation clearly lies with the transformation from writing to screen adaptation and from words to filmic translation.

Poetry can provide an excellent source of inspiration for animation filmmakers, in particular for directors of animated short films. There are several reasons for that:

The majority of contemporary and classic poems are short. This answers to the requirements of the equally short form in animation.

Short animated films though have, different from their feature-length counterparts, struggled to see any distribution at all, to reach audiences. A champion for bringing animated short films that adapt poetry to the public is Thomas Zandegiacomo Del Bel. As the artistic director of the ZEBRA Poetry Film Festival, he has seen hundreds of animated poetry adaptations since 2006. In his curatorial position, he had to decide about the criteria for selecting animated short films over other, artistically less-qualified submissions.

I therefore chose him as a highly suitable expert to examine more closely what makes an animated adaptation of a poem work (or not).

Interview with Thomas Zandegiacomo Del Bel, Artistic Director of the ZEBRA Poetry Film Festival

Hannes Rall (interviewer)
Thomas Zandegiacomo Del Bel (interviewed)

Dear Thomas, you have been the artistic director of the ZEBRA Poetry Film Festival in Berlin since its inception in 2002. This is one of the very few film festivals in the world that is wholly dedicated to screen adaptations of poetry.

What gave you the idea in the first place, and how has the festival developed since its start?

Honestly, I am the artistic director of the ZEBRA Poetry Film Festival since 2006. Dr. Thomas Wohlfahrt, the director of the Haus für Poesie (formerly Literaturwerkstatt Berlin) had the idea in the year 2001, after he was visiting the poet Bob Holman in New York. Holman has shown him some poetry clips with American poets performing their poems in front of the camera. It was more a filming of poets who read their poems than poetry films. But these videos gave Thomas Wohlfahrt the idea to search for more films based on poems: poetry films. Back in Germany, he opened a submission for the best poetry films. Together with Heinz Hermanns, the festival director of Interfilm Berlin, he organized, in the year 2002, the first ZEBRA Poetry Film Award, which took place as part of the Poesiefestival Berlin.

Every 2 years since 2002, the ZEBRA Poetry Film Festival has been presenting the current state of this dynamic short film genre located between poetry, film, and the new media. The first of its kind, it is the largest international platform for short films that deals with poetry, in their content, their aesthetics, or their form. It offers poets and filmmakers, as well as festival organizers, a lot of space for coming together with their audience and exchanging ideas and experiences. With exhibitions, readings by poets, and performances, it creates new impulses and inspirations, while aesthetic questions are discussed in colloquiums; retrospectives, talks, workshops, and film programs with various focus topics supplement the competition to find the best poetry films from the whole world. Originally part of the Poesiefestival Berlin, which is a project of the Literaturwerkstatt Berlin, the ZEBRA Poetry Film Award quickly grew so big that it needed a festival of its own: the ZEBRA Poetry Film Festival. From the films that are entered, a program commission selects the films for the competition, and a jury then chooses the winners. Both the program commission and the jury include internationally renowned figures from the worlds of film, poetry, and media.

In 2010, it was possible for the first time to hold a film workshop, Poetic Encounters: Filmmakers from Tel Aviv met with poets from Berlin to create a joint concept for poetry films and then make the films, which premiered at the ZEBRA Poetry Film Festival before being shown in Israel. In 2012, the results of the second cross-border Poetic Encounters workshop were presented at the festival. Polish filmmakers have worked with Berlin poets to create film scripts based on their poems and then realize them jointly. They have shown the results in the festival and talked about working together.

In the year 2012, for the first time, the Literaturwerkstatt Berlin invited filmmakers from all over the world to make film interpretations of the poem *[meine heimat]* by Ulrike Almut Sandig. Thirty-three filmmakers from 13 countries followed the call. Thirteen of the films have been selected for the festival. In the year 2014, the festival had invited entries of films based on the festival poem *Love in the Age of the EU* by Björn Kuhligk. The directors of the three best films were invited to Berlin to meet the poet and have the opportunity to present and discuss their films.

In the year 2010 started ZEBRINO—the program for poetry films for children and young people, with its own prize. The young viewers selected the winner of the ZEBRINO, the best poetry film for 8- to 12-year-olds. An extensive children's program was an integral part of the festival, exciting an interest in poetry in children and school pupils through play. The Duden textbook publisher has released a DVD featuring a selection of films from the ZEBRA Poetry Film Festivals for use in schools.

In the year 2014, for the seventh time, the ZEBRA Poetry Film Festival had invited entries for the competition to find the best poetry films. The total value of the prizes in the competition was € 13,000. From among the films submitted, a program committee was nominated for the films to be entered for the competition and selected the films for the various sections of the festival program. The winners were chosen by an international jury.

Do you see any specific trends and/or developments in current years or since the start of the festival? Is there an increase or decrease in the number of adaptations and submissions?

In the last years, we got more and more very professionally made poetry films: animations, experimental, and feature films. The film schools sent us very beautiful and excellent poetry films. And professional filmmakers and poets sent us their adaptations of poems. Of course, the poetry films react to the political and social events in the world. And we have got a lot of contemporary poetry and spoken-word poetry. Nearly every year, we get a collection of poetry films, like *Dicht/Vorm* from The Netherlands, *Poem* by Ralf Schmerberg from Germany, *Black Ceiling* from Estonia, poetry films by S.O.I.L. from Belgium, by Autour de Minuit from France, or by Motionpoems from the USA. *Dicht/Vorm* is a series of 25 animated poems. The short films were distributed in cinemas and were part of a very successful educational project. *Black Ceiling* is Estonia's first animated selection of poetry. Seven short films illustrating works by Estonian poets. *Motionpoems* catalyzes the remix of poetry with other forms to create compelling hybrid artworks. In 2008, animator/producer Angella Kassube animated one of Todd Boss's poems. The results were so compelling that Boss and Kassube began introducing other poets to other video artists. A year later, a public screening in Minneapolis drew a crowd. Since then, motion poems have appeared in mainstream media; blogs; YouTube; international film festivals, including the Hammer Museum's Flux Series; classrooms; art galleries; and their website. *Poem* by Ralf Schmerberg shows film stars interpreting famous poems by Hermann Hesse, Ernst Jandl, Heiner Müller, Johann Wolfgang Goethe, Mascha Kaleko, Ingeborg Bachmann, Kurt Tucholsky, Erich Kästner, Else Lasker-Schüler, Heinrich Heine, Paul Celan, Rainer Maria Rilke, Friedrich Schiller, and others. The quality of all those films is very high. The trend is also a technical trend, because we have got a lot of digital films with amazing special effects and beautiful animations. The new films can answer to the complexity of the poems.

Even for the very first ZEBRA in 2002, 610 films from 35 countries were entered for the competition; by 2004, this had grown to more than 800 films from 57 countries, with entries topping 1000 from 58 countries, for the first time in 2008; filmmakers from 69 countries participated in 2010. Eight hundred and seventy films were entered for the sixth ZEBRA Poetry Film Festival from 63 countries, and for the seventh edition, 770 films from 77 countries were submitted. We changed the submission form in the year 2004, because there were a lot of films older than 4 years. Now, a film should not be older than 3 years and not longer than 15 minutes. And we ask for the publishing house of the poem that was used for the film. Maybe that's the reason for a decrease in the number of submissions.

What are the general challenges of adapting poetry for the moving image?

The general challenges of adapting poetry for moving images are to transform a very complex text into another media, without illustrating the text. Otherwise, the film is just a simple reflection of the text. The filmmaker should answer of the poem with his film. So, it is very complicated to create your own pictures or filmic metaphors. It is more a translation or a transformation into another art form.

As the director of the festival, you see a lot of adaptations of poetry. Naturally, you must also have seen submissions, which didn't quite succeed artistically, or to put it more bluntly: bad films. Can you think of general and common mistakes, which let filmic adaptations of poetry fail in the artistic sense? What can go (terribly) wrong?

A lot of mistakes can be made, like bad acting, bad sound, or cinematography. Mostly, the less successful films are just an illustration of the poem. They are really well made but boring. Or the filmmakers work together with bad actors/actresses, narrators, and musicians. Or the films are too long, because the filmmaker would like to show us many beautiful pictures or shots. In the first instance, poetry films have the demands like all movies. Especially, the editing and the sound are very difficult, because the poems seldom have a narrative structure, besides ballads, maybe. And often, the poems are whispered, which is not necessary.

I believe that animation and poetry have a lot in common in several aspects. Therefore, it seems to me that animation often is very well suited to adapt poems for the moving image. Do you agree with that opinion, and can you share your reasons for that?

In our archive, we have over 5000 poetry films: 900 of them are animations, 1100 are feature films, and over 700 are experimental films. It takes a long time to make a good animation, so maybe that is the reason we have more feature films than animations. But yes, the animation can answer very well to the poetic structure. Maybe that is also the reason that we have a lot of experimental films in our archive. Both experimental films and animation are very well suited to adapt poems for the moving image. Feature films are mostly suited for novels, short stories, etc. In the last years, we have got a lot of very-well-done computer animations with visual effects or mixed with real settings.

Expanding on my previous questions, there is a very concrete fact that further supports the implicit connection between poetry and animation: Poetry often presents itself in the short form, which qualifies it as an excellent source material for animated short films. Can you point out the parallels?

I would say that poetry often presents itself in a highly compressed form, which qualifies it as an excellent source material for short films in general. Maybe that is the reason why we find a lot poetry films in social media channels like YouTube or Vimeo. Parallels are music videos. Animated short films can answer to the complex structures of the poems, because there are no limits for the fantasy of the filmmaker. He can change the situations and the pictures as often as he likes. The filmmaker can answer to the poem with poetic pictures.

Do you know of any adaptations of long-form poetry for animation?

Oh yes. The most popular adaptation of a poem is *The Nightmare Before Christmas*, a 1993 American stop-motion musical fantasy film directed by Henry Selick and produced and conceived by Tim Burton. The animation is an adaptation of the poem *A Visit from St. Nicholas*, popularly called *The Night Before Christmas* (1822), by Clement Clark Moore. One of the first poetry films was *The Night Before Christmas*, made by Edwin S. Porter in 1905 in the studios of Thomas Alva Edison. Another example is *Beowulf.* It is a 2007 American 3D motion-capture epic fantasy film directed by Robert Zemeckis and written by Neil Gaiman and Roger Avary; it is inspired by the Old English epic poem of the same name. The cast includes Ray Winstone, Anthony Hopkins, Robin Wright Penn, Brendan Gleeson, John Malkovich, Crispin Glover, Alison Lohman, and Angelina Jolie.

But these movies are longer than the original poem they are based on, of course.

One might even go so far as to qualify outstanding abstract animated work (I am thinking of the films of Oskar Fischinger, for example) as "visual poetry"—even if they are not based on any literary source material. Can you explain what might lead to such a classification? What are the concrete communalities between written poetry and abstract animation (particularly "visual music")?

It is the rhythm. Visual poetry and abstract animation often work with musical structures, for example, the films made by Gerhard Rühm and the visual poetry by Eugen Gomringer. Oskar Fischinger works with the rhythm of music. The first forms of poems were mostly songs or orisons, which work also with rhythm. The filmmaker takes the rhythm of the poem and transforms it into motion. One of the most popular forms is the *Silly Symphonies*, which is a series of 75 animated short films produced by Walt Disney Productions from 1929 to 1939 animation. Best example is Mickey Mouse as *Sorcerer's Apprentice (Zauberlehrling)* in the 1940 American animated film *Fantasia* produced by Walt Disney and released by Walt Disney Productions.

Another part of the *Silly Symphonies* series was *The Night Before Christmas*, which is a 1933 American Pre-Code animated short film produced by Walt Disney Productions and released by United Artists. The film is an adaptation of the aforementioned poem *A Visit from St. Nicholas* by Clement Clarke Moore. The film was directed by Disney animator Wilfred Jackson.

Like the music or modern form of poetry, like spoken word or even rap work, works with loops. So, abstract animation, visual music, visual poetry, and sound poetry are very similar in their structures, for example, rhythm, loops, and composition. The concrete communalities are the rhythm and the loops and not narrative structure. Hans Richter (1971) said: "I would describe the exploration into the realm of mood, the lyrical sensation as ›poetry‹. I would call all experimental films 'film poetry.'"

A very specific topic is the use of the original text in the adaptation, and there are plenty of options to choose from: The completely unaltered text could be narrated throughout the film by a voice actor; it could be expanded upon or even completely omitted. Alternatively, the poem itself could also show up only visually, leaving the audience to read it. The creative possibilities are seemingly endless. Can you provide examples for either approach?

Most popular form to "bring" the text into the film is a voice-over or actors who recite the poem. Sometimes, the text appears at the beginning or the end of the film. Beyond these possibilities, there are a lot of forms of typography in the movies, or type is image in motion. (There was an exhibition with type in movies at the ZKM – Centre for Art and Media). In the archive of the Haus für Poesie, there are a lot of poetry films with typography. This form of animated poetry films started very early. Charles Sheeler and Paul Strand, with their futuristic adaptation of Walt Whitman's city melancholia in their film *Manhatta* (USA 1921), put the poem into the intertitles and set standards that still apply today. *Combat de Boxe* (B 1927) by Charles Dekeukeleire is a timeless interpretation of a poem by Paul Werrie. In *L'Etoile de Mer* (F 1928) by Man Ray, lines from Robert Desnos' 1928 poem *La place de l'etoile* are faded in on boards. Later, Gerhard Rühm worked with typography in his film *3 Kinematograhpische Texte.* In the year 1971, Klaus Peter Dencker made a series of TV-poems for German television: *Starfighter (Geschichte eines Fronteinsatzes)* (D 1971), *Rausch (Buchstabiertafel mit anschließender Diskussion)* (D 1971), and *astronaut (Deutscher Film mit Untertiteln)* (D 1971). These are only some examples of the early poetry adaptations. In the last year, we have got a lot of animations with "type-motions" by Ottar Ormstad or Kristian Pedersen from Norway, Erica Scourti from the United Kingdom, Dave Hemmingway and Nirit Peled from The Netherlands, and Susanne Wiegner from Germany. In the poetry animations of Susanne Wiegner, the letters are divided into layers, which become spaces, streets, and falling rain, or it is a mental journey through personal spaces, images, letters, and words. In her poetry animation *Just Midnight* (D 2010), a three-dimensional word structure is formed by letters, crossed and circled by the camera before disappearing again in a sheet of paper.

Figure 7.1: Film still from *Just Midnight*, director: Susanne Wiegner, DE, 2010.

Do specific forms of poetry lead themselves to particular modes of adaptation in this respect?

Yes. Sound poetry is mostly transformed in animation, like the poetry animation *Bestiarium* (D 1989) by Eku Wand, based on the poem by Ernst Jandl, or the visual poem *Bebe Coca Cola* (BRA 1957) by Décio Pignatari.

So concrete, pattern, or shape poetry; visual poetry; sound poetry; and digital poetry were often transformed into animations. The last form, digital poetry, is transformed into interactive installations or apps for mobile devices, like the works by Jörg Piringer from Austria. The pioneers of this scene were, among others, Paulo Aquarone, Caterina Davinio, Loss Pequeño Glazier, Eduardo Kac, Theo Lutz, Philip M. Parker, and Gianni Toti.

The adaptations of spoken-word poetry are often poetry clips and sometimes animations, like *Der Conny ihr Pony* by Robert Pohle and Martin Hentze, based on the same-named poem by Gabriel Vetter. Ballads or plays are often transformed into animations and feature films.

Can you talk about what makes them work?

The feature films that are based on ballads work, because the texts of these ballads are narrative. These poetry films are more like normal short films based on short stories, which are represented by entertainment films, or reportages, which are represented by documentaries. The animations based on sound, visual, concrete, or digital poetry transform the non-narrative structure of the poem very well. These animations can react to any kind of meanings or sounds. The experimental films do very well with modern poems, too. They are very free and do mostly not illustrate the poem in any way. It is very important for the nonnarrative poetry films that they don't illustrate the poems but work with their own pictures and visual metaphors.

How do you feel about shortening or expanding the original poem in an adaptation?

Sometimes, it works when you repeat the very essential lines of the poem. Shortening the poem is not so good, because something gets lost in the adaptation. But if the poem is too long for the film, it would be better to choose another poem. In principle, the short films should be short. That means don't make a film of 20 minutes when you can tell the same story in 5 minutes. And if you choose a poem, make sure that you really like it. The best poetry films I have seen were made with poets or based on poems the filmmaker really liked.

How should the visual style of the adaptation and the literary tone of the original poem correlate? Are there different possible strategies to define the visual approach?

Not really. The filmmakers should be free to select their own visual style. More important is that the filmmaker reacts to the structure and the rhythm of the poem. The animation, experimental, or feature film should be a real animation or a good film and not just a slide show with some visual effects. The text should be one of the essential parts of the film and not just the inspiration for the film. Sometimes, the feature films are visual one-to-one translation of the original poem, but these films are not really the best films. The films should be more than a visual interpretation.

Let's talk about visuals and narrative now. Again, a multitude of approaches are thinkable. The visual storytelling might closely reflect, if not illustrate, the actual content presented by the poem. Or, it might strongly expand on it, comment, or even deliberately contradict it. Each approach can succeed on its very own terms. Your thoughts? Examples?

Your structure of the poem can be reflected in the film, like in the poetry film *Love Is the Law*, in which the director Eivind Tolås works with and sometimes against the rhythm of the same-named poem by Ole Mads Velve. The film is made as a news broadcast, and the newsreader recites the poem like a rap but a little bit slower than the pictures are. A very good poetry film was *One Person – Lucy* (NL 2005) by Taatske Pieterson based on her same-named poem. The director combines the words and the rhythm of the poem with pads or more little windows of cardboards and the face of the speaker Lucy Gold very impressively. The audience can feel the power of this poem. Another example is the poetry film *15th February* (UK 1995) by Tim Webb, based on the same-named poem by Peter Reading. Tim Webb has chosen the images very good and combined real images or feature film with animation. This enforces the words of the poem and the inability to communicate. There are so many good examples, but these are only three of them.

There often is also a necessity in filmic adaptation to successfully balance a triptych of voice-over/dialogue, music/sound, and visuals. Poetry does very often carry rhythm and musicality within itself. Therefore, it can be very challenging yet ultimately rewarding to delicately establish the artistic interplay with sound and music. Can you first share your thoughts on this topic and support them with one or several concrete examples of outstanding animated films?

I found a successful balance of the triptych of voice-over, music, and visuals in very good spoken-word poetry clips, because they are very powerful. There are animations like the three poetry films *Poetry In Motion* (NL 2007) by Nirit Peled and David Hemmingway based on the poems *Jazz*, *Crossfire*, and *Frenzied Days* by Staceyann Chin. This animation is really remarkable. The form of the words and the movements are really in harmony with the voice-over of the poet. Another very powerful spoken-word poetry film is the spoken-word music video *Human Condition*, directed by Mark Wilkinson, based on the same-named poem by Rich Ferguson. I have to admit that this film is not an animation. Two very good animations with voice-over but without music are the films *Missed Aches* and *Dear Pluto* by Joanna Priestley, based on the poems *The Impotence of Proofreading* and *Pizza* by Taylor Mali. *Missed Aches* is about proofreading and the indiscriminate use of spellcheck. It combines animated characters with moving text. It was written and narrated by poet Taylor Mali, who led teams to four championships in the National Poetry Slam (USA). This poetry animation was made with Adobe Flash and After Effects. *Dear Pluto* was animated with Maya, 3-D Studio Max, and Flash. Sometimes, you find a successful balance of the triptych of voice-over, music, and visuals in dance films, like *The Thing with Feathers* by Rain Kencana, Miguel Angelo Pate, and Jalaudin Trautman, based on the same-named poem by Jinn Pogy. But this is not an animation. In this context, there are two very good animations with Arabic calligraphy: First, the poetry animation *Tongue of the Hidden* (UK/IRN 2008) by David Alexander Anderson, based on the poem *Peacock and Fish* by Hafez, and *The Dice Player* (EG 2013) by Nissmah Roshdy, based on the poem *La'eb Al Nard* by Mahmoud Darwish. In the first example, a hand-drawn Farsi (Persian/Iranian) calligraphy is imported into the computer and forms the basis of constructed landscapes and animals that move within landscapes. *The Dice Player* is an animated poetry film that visualizes a poem written by the Palestinian poet Mahmoud Darwish. It was recited in the live event *In the Shade of Words*, 2008, along with harmonies by the band Le Trio Joubran. The poetry film *Tongue of the Hidden* works with motion capturing for the dance movements. And last but not least, your poetry films *The Raven* (D 2000), based on the same-named poem by Edgar Allan Poe, and *The Erl-King* (D 2003), based on the same-named poem by Johann Wolfgang von Goethe.

"Poetry" is a huge generalization. It encompasses the classic ballads with a strong narrative as well a very modern, abstract, and experimental poetry. For the complete novice to poetry, can you give us a broad yet (slightly) more detailed overview of the different historical incarnations/forms of poetry, and how they have been represented in your festival?

From the beginning of the ZEBRA Poetry Film Festival, we show historical examples of poetry films. The poetry film has been under discussion as a new film genre in its own right, since about the turn of the millennium. What is not so well known is that the combination of the arts of poetry and film was already being intensively deliberated at the very beginning of the twentieth century. Luis Buñuel's statement (1960) that "the cinema seems to have been invented for the expression of the subconscious, so profoundly is it rooted in poetry" is more relevant than ever. Films by artists such as Man Ray, Maya Deren, and Peter Weibel are roots of poetic cinema and show that, since the beginning of the cinema and later of video technology, there has been strong interest by artists in creating relationships between the two arts and media.

In the three programs *Flashback*, we have shown the first poetry films (1905–1927), the avant-gardes (1920s–1940s), and video poems and TV-poems (1960s–1980s). The first *Flashback* was devoted to the first poetry films (1905–1927). In the early twentieth century, prominent poets were just as inspired by the cinema as great filmmakers were by poetry. The program has presented known and unknown gems from the earliest period of film, with musical accompaniment by André Feldhaus. A very early poetry adaptation is *The Unchanging Sea* (USA 1910) by D.W. Griffith, adapted from a poem by Charles Kingsley. Under the name Michael Curtiz, he became world famous with *Casablanca*, but one of the first works by Mihály Kertesz was a poetry film. *Jön Az Öcsem (My Brother Is Coming)*, loosely based on the poem of the same name by Antal Farkas, is an early testimony to the time of political upheaval in Hungary. The silent movie, made in 1919, had its German première at the fifth ZEBRA Poetry Film Festival. With its futuristic setting of Walt Whitman's big-city melancholia, *Manhatta* (USA 1921) by Charles Sheeler and Paul Strand sets standards even today. *L'Invitation au Voyage* (F 1927) by Germaine Dulac is a timeless interpretation of Charles Baudelaire's *Les Fleurs du Mal*. The second *Flashback* was devoted to experimental avant-garde films and animations from the late 1920s and the 1940s. *Chad Gadjo* is an enchanting animated talkie made in 1930 by Rudi Klemm and film pioneer Julius Pinschewer, based on the poem and folk song *Chad Gadya*, which is sung on Seder evening at the end of the Haggadah. As mentioned earlier, the first and probably most filmed poem is *Twas the Night Before Christmas* (1840) by Clement Clarke Moore. The Americans William Hanna and Joseph Barbera made a Tom and Jerry cartoon in 1941, using this poem, which in 1942 was nominated for an Oscar for Best Animated Short Film. Probably, the most famous American pioneer of the experimental film was Maya Deren. She is being represented by her short experimental film *Meshes of the Afternoon* (USA 1943), directed by wife-and-husband team, Maya Deren and Alexander Hammid. She used a poetic film language in her films, which was the model for later filmmakers. The third *Flashback* devotes itself to the works of the pioneers and the important early representatives of video poetry. The new medium of video allowed artists to directly reproduce what had been recorded and to experiment with, for example, loops and other technical possibilities. The Austrian art icon Valie Export, with her partly disturbing performances and videos, deals with radical questions of physical and psychic situations, for example, in 1968, with *See-Text: Fingerpoem*, a poem without words and without movement of the lips. The retrospective screens Peter Weibel's *Video Texts* (A 1975). An important representative of the early German TV-poem is Klaus-Peter Dencker. His *Starfighter* (D 1971) is among the most important works of the 1970s. Tom Konyves' video poems give an insight into the Canadian scene of the 1970s and 1980s. The outstanding poetry clip *Novalis: Walzer* by the Hungarian artist Gábor Bódy, from 1985, was also a must here.

The different historical incarnations and forms of poetry have no special places in our festival. We mix concrete poetry with classical ballads. Our festival has the international competition, which shows the best poetry films and the different programs with very good poetry films of all forms. These programs have mostly themes like "love," "city," and "conflict," or they are focused on a country. And I think it could be boring for the audience to see only ballads in one program and only concrete poetry in another program. The historical forms of poetry are very important, but in the dramaturgy of a festival, it might be better to mix the different genres and styles, like animation, experimental, feature or haiku, and sonnet. We have shown very good haikus from Israel, like the series *Imaginary Encounters* by Mysh Rozanov or sound poems by Gerhard Rühm, adapted by Hubert Sielecki (2007) from Austria. And we have shown sonnets by William Shakespeare, modern Dutch poems in the series of *Dicht/Vorm*, and spoken-word clips from all over the world.

My further question here is: Can these very different forms (of adaptations) even be assessed under the same criteria? And, if not, how are these standards different?

No, these different forms of adaptation can't be assessed under the same criteria.

Can you provide one or two outstanding examples of adaptations of narrative poems versus their counterparts from experimental/abstract source material?

Of course, your animation *Der Erlkönig* is an example of an adaptation of the narrative poem by Johann Wolfgang von Goethe. Others are *Carnivore Reflux* (*Au 2006*) and *The Cat Piano* (*Au 2009*) by Eddie White, based on the same-named poems by the director, and *Bisclavret* (*Fr 2011*) by Emilie Mercier, based on the poem *Le lai de Bisclavret*, written in the twelfth century by Marie de France. The animated film *The Lost Town of Świteź* is based on the nineteenth-century epic poem by Poland's greatest writer Adam Mickiewicz, about a ghostly town deluged after a bloody massacre in medieval times, which now lies at the bottom of a remote lake. It is an apocalyptic tale of destruction, religious miracles, and spectral visitations. The film imports oil paintings into digital 3D, combined with both CG animation and visual special effects, to create a mesmerizing aesthetic experience, set to a specially commissioned full choral and orchestral score. It dramatically merges literature, painting, music, and animation. Other examples are *La Confiture De Carottes* (*Be/Fr 2014*) by Anne Viel and *Le Parfum De La Carotte* (*B/Fr 2014*) by Arnaud Demuynck and Rémi Durin.

Figure 7.2: A collage of film stills from *Der Erlkönig*. (From Rall, H., *Der Erlkönig* (*The Erl-King*). Animated short film, 2003.)

The classic poems of famous writers have already often been adapted as animated short films. There is a very practical reason for that, as most of these works are in public domain. But I strongly believe that is superseded by the fascination of bringing the timeless narratives of authors such as Poe, Goethe, Shakespeare, and Schiller (to name a few) to life. What qualifies an artistically successful adaptation in this specific context?

First of all, it should be a good short. For the director, it is very difficult to make a good short film when he has no imaginative approach to the poem. Most of the really good poetry films underline the intellectual relationship between the filmmaker and the poet. Sometimes, they are friends, and they know each other very well. Even when the poet is already deceased, the filmmaker could have a connection with his or her poems. Most of these filmmakers make more than one adaptation of the poems of these poets. When the filmmaker believes that it would be better to make an adaptation of a famous poem, he or she often fails. In that case, it would be better to work together with a poet whom the filmmaker likes a lot.

In the case of these famous and beloved classics, can the question of "faithfulness" to the source material be of particular concern?

Yes, because it really could be a challenge to make an adaptation that shares the aesthetic of the poem. If this adaptation is being successful, it could be a masterpiece. This could be a fascinating adaptation of contemporary poems by Gerhard Rühm, Gerhard Falkner, or Billy Collins or an adaptation of classic or romantic poems by Goethe, Schiller, or William Wordsworth. In the case of these famous and beloved classics, there are some really good short films based on poems by Friedrich Schiller, like the poetry film *Die Begegnung* (DE 2005) by Andreas Pieper with Maryam Zaree, Dieter Berner, and Emanuel Peters. In this poetry film, the set is a drive-in restaurant in which the actress Maryam Zaree whispers the poem into her headset and her colleague answers her with the rest of the poem. The set is modern, but the dialogue between a woman and a man is old. This is a contemporary adaptation of a classic poem. Another example is the spooky story of a werewolf *Loup Garou* by Gordon Volk (DE 2007), based on the same-named poem by Annette von Droste-Hülshoff (1797–1848), with the actress Gesa Boysen. The set and the costume of this feature film are like in the time of the poet von Droste-Hülshoff. The animation *Bisclavret* (FR 2011) by Emilie Mercier, based on the poem *Le lai du Bisclavret* by Marie de France (1135–1200), is made like glass paintings accompanied by a music of the twelfth century.

Do you know examples of animated adaptations that did bring up controversial discussions?

There are some animated adaptations that did bring up controversial discussions, for example, when the poem is not in the film as written or spoken text, like in the really amazing poetry films *Tyger* (BR 2006) by Guilherme Marcondes, *Seemannstreue* (DE 2008) by Anna Kalus-Goessner, or *The Lost Town of Świteź* (PL 2010) by Kamil Polak. *Tyger*, based on the poem *The Tyger* by William Blake (1757–1827), won over 20 international awards, including two at Clermont-Ferrant Festival. *Seemannstreue* is about a mariner who can't accept the death of his beloved Alwine and is based on the same-named poem by Joachim Ringelnatz (1883–1934).

Figure 7.3: Film still from *Seemannstreue* (2008) by Anna Kalus-Goessner.

The Lost Town of Świteź, based on the poem *Świteź* by Adam Mickiewicz (1798–1855), "was created in an original combination of 3D animation and classic animation painted with oil paints. Specially-commissioned large-scale paintings were composited into a multiple-plane, 3D, computer-generated (CG) environment using state-of-the-art digital animation and compositing techniques. This unique artistic way creates a quality in itself and an extraordinary means of expression, which is crucial in animation, where strength of content and visual form merge into a striking and meaningful fusion. Two distinct styles of paintings were used: nineteenth-century Slavonic paintings (such as the work of Józef Chełmoński and Aleksander Gierymski), which give the illusion of perspective and use a realistic palette, combined with the much more stylized, brightly colored and iconic 2D paintings of the Middle Ages."[1]

All of these examples are without the spoken poems, and sometimes, the directors said that the films were inspired by the poems. This fact could bring up controversial discussions.

[1] http://www.switez.com/about.html.

It strikes me that there is a still-underutilized area of opportunity: collaborations between contemporary writers of poetry (poets) and animators. This could be mutually beneficial, as it will grant the works of the writers a wider exposure, along with providing wonderful source material for animators to work from. Do you know any examples?

In the year 2012, the ZEBRA Poetry Film Festival had invited filmmakers to make a film of the poem *[meine heimat]* by Ulrike Almut Sandig. The directors of the three best films were invited to come to Berlin to meet the poet and have had the opportunity of presenting their films and talking about them. Some of these films were animations, for example, the animation by Susanne Wiegner or by Ebele Okoye. In the year 2014, the festivals had invited the international directors again to make adaptations of the poem *Die Liebe in Zeiten der EU* by Björn Kuhligk. Collaborations between contemporary poets and animators exist in many countries or even across frontiers. In Germany, Austria, the United Kingdom, Italy, Norway, Estonia, Belgium, The Netherlands, and the USA, animators collaborate with poets.

Can you tell us more about how some of these collaborations came about? (Concrete names, film examples, ideally with writer/filmmaker contacts). Do you know of filmmakers actively seeking feedback from adapted authors? Do you even know of truly collaborative approaches?

In the last years, there are more and more examples of cooperation between filmmakers and poets. The Italian poet Elena Chiesa has made 10 animations based on her own poems and on poems by Felix Dennis. The Austrian filmmaker Hubert Sielecki has made different animations, together with the poet Gerhard Rühm, for example.

The British filmmaker Stuart Pound has made a lot of animations based on the poems by Rosemary Norman, since 1997.

The Norwegian publisher Gasspedal published a lot of poems, and some of them were adapted as animations by Kristian Pedersen under the label Gasspedal Animert, for example, *Viva Zombatista. De Døde Står Opp For Å Fortære De Levende* (NO 2009), based on the same-named poem by Simen Hagerup; *Bokstavene* (NO 2010), based on the same-named poem by Sigurd Tenningen; *Kliniken* (NO 2011), based on the same-named poem by Annelie Axén; *Skogen* (NO 2012), based on the poem *langsdang – et flytans habitat* by Aina Villanger; *Bølgeslag* (NO 2013), based on the poems *Where the settlement ends*, *It requires*, and *When disappearance shines brightly enough* by Tor Ulven; and *Pipene* (NO 2014), based on the same-named poem by Øyvind Rimbereid.

In other countries as well, many animations were made based on poems. The Dutch producers Arnoud Rijken and Michiel Snijders (Il Luster Productions) have made two compilations, *Dicht/Vorm Klassiekers* and *Modern*, with 22 animations based on Dutch poems. The Estonian Eesti Joonisfilm Studio made seven animations based on Estonian poems under the title *Must Lagi (Black Ceiling)* in the year 2007. This was the first Estonian animated selection of poetry.

Figure 7.4: Capture from Egidiuslied by Martin Jan van Santen. © Luster Productions 2005. All Rights Reserved.

The Belgian label S.O.I.L. (Sight of an Ignored Landscape) has made 15 animations based on different poems, and the German publisher Edition Temmen published a DVD with 27 animated poems by Michael Augustin, made at the Hochschule für Künste Bremen under the direction of the filmmaker Joachim Hofmann. The French producer Autour De Minuit published *En sortant de l'école* (2012) with 13 short animations based on poems by Jaques Prévert. The US-American nonprofit arts organization Motionpoems is a formal collaboration between different professionals. In total, this organization has made over 60 poetry animations.

The Belgian artist Marc Neys aka Swoon has made over 200 video-poems based on different poems by international contemporary poets. In his opinion, this collection is like an artistic process.

Is there an interest among modern-day poets to have their works adapted for animation? Any past or ongoing initiatives you know of? Any poems that have been written specifically with an animated adaptation in mind?

Some of the modern-day poets like Gerhard Rühm are interested to have their works adapted for animation. But I don't know poems that have been written specifically with an animated adaptation in mind.

Can you provide practical advice in how an aspiring animator can connect to the community of modern poets and writing individuals to find source material to work with or a writer to collaborate with?

One of the biggest communities of modern poets where a filmmaker can find source material to work with is the Internet platform lyrikline.org. The filmmakers can find 9396 poems (63 languages, along with 13473 translations). Lyrikline is an international website for experiencing the diversity of contemporary poetry. Here, you can listen to the melodies, sounds, and rhythms of international poetry, recited by the authors themselves, and you can read the poems, both in their original languages and various translations.

This project from the Haus für Poesie and its partners has established itself as an online cultural project, making poetry accessible and understandable for all, above and beyond national borders and language barriers. Until today, lyrikline has been visited by several million users from over 180 countries.

Navigable in various languages, such as German, English, French, Slovenian, Arabic, Chinese, Russian, Spanish, and Portuguese, lyrikline is an internationally comprehensible archive of poetry and languages and has been around since 1999. Since then, we have added, on average, a new poet every week and new translations every day.

The different features on the site allow you not only to find the poems you are looking for but also to discover poetry you never even knew you were looking for. Thematic and formal categories, a dynamic and refined search function, and various teasers and cross-references open entirely new ways to access poets, as well as single poems and translations. Registered users will also be able to bookmark poems and, for instance, set up their own lists of favorites and share them with all other users. Lyrikline thus offers a gateway to international poetry, giving rise to a worldwide poetic dialogue.

Do you know of animation directors and/or authors who write their own poetry and even do it well? Have you included any of those in ZEBRA?

Yes, for example, Elena Chiesa, an art director and videoartist based in Rome (Italy); the German artist and writer Jochen Kuhn, with his series *Sonntag*; and the Irish poet Alice Lyons, with her wonderful work *The Polish Language* (IE 2009). The Australian filmmaker Eddie White has made two brilliant animations *Carnivore Reflux* (AU 2006) and *The Cat Piano* (AU 2009), both based on his same-named poems. The winner of the ZEBRA Award 2012 was *The Lost and Found Box of Human Sensation* (DE 2010) by Stefan Leuchtenberg and Martin Wallner, based on the same-named poem by Martin Wallner, in which a young man's father dies because of pancreatic cancer, and the boy has to cope with the loss. These are some examples that the festival has shown in the last editions.

Figure 7.5: Film still from *A Lost and Found Box of Human Sensation* (2010) © Lailaps Pictures, Dancing Squirrel 2010.

Very specific forms of adaptations of poetry (if you will) are music videos. In that case, the combination of words and music is already delivered by the song—the animation just puts its own visual storytelling spin on it. Would you even qualify music videos as adapted poetry in the broader sense?

Yes, when the text was originally a poem, like in the animation *Robin* (IL 2014) by Merav and Yaval Nathan, based on the same-named poem by Emily Dickinson (1830–1886). This poetry film was running in the competition of the seventh ZEBRA Poetry Film Festival in 2014.

Did you feature any music videos in your festival? If not, why?

If they are really based on poems and they are good, I have featured them in my festival. Pure music videos I will not feature, because for these videos, there are a lot of other festivals.

Music videos are a prime example of the two different main narrative approaches for adaptations: either reflecting the "story" in the visuals or completely moving away from it. Thoughts?

This is the same situation in the poetry films. The filmmakers can illustrate the poem or can move completely away from it. Animations are often illustrations of the poems, whereas experimental films are the opposite or a free interpretation of the poem. But, sometimes, there are animators, like Kristian Pedersen, who work with their very own interpretations of the poems.

Finally, do you have any general advice for animation directors who intend to adapt poetry?

Yes, the animators should work with their own pictures and interpretation of the poem. They should try to extend (or expand) the poem with their world of images.

In summary, Thomas Zandegiacomo Del Bel makes several meaningful suggestions about the art of adapting poetry for animation:

- The variety of possibilities in adaptation of poetry for animation.
- The option to entirely depart from the source material and transcend it in the adaptation.
- The need to find aesthetically pleasing and original imagery beyond a too literal illustration of the text. The connection between the rhythmic structure of poems and the ability of animation to answer to it particularly well.

Going forward, the examination of three very different animated short films will serve as case studies to test these suggestions with examples from creative practice.

In his very insightful interview, Thomas Zandegiacomo Del Bel mentioned the multiple-award-winning animated short film *Seemannstreue* (2008) by Anna Kalus-Goessner as an outstanding example for a poetry adaptation. The morbid topic of this tale of love gone wrong offers an interesting comparison point to the previously discussed examples of the animated adaptations of the classic gothic ballad *The Erl-King* by Goethe and Poe's equally dark *The Raven*.

Moving forward toward modern literature in terms of historical chronology, this poem is also even more impressionistic and abstract than either Goethe's or Poe's pieces.

Reflecting the development toward modern poetry, it offers less of a clear plot than its earlier predecessors and might be seen as even more daring in its overt bluntness of rather graphic details in describing nothing less than a necrophilic obsession.

In my opinion, this is clearly made acceptable by the trademark quirky humor of Joachim Ringelnatz that transcends it beyond a mere description of disgusting activities and into truly surreal territory.

It remains impressive enough, though, how Anna Kalus succeeds in creating a work of otherworldly beauty with her animated adaptation. The German Film Assessment Board FBW (Film-und Medienbewertungsstelle Wiesbaden) concurs in its review and merits the film its highest distinction, the Seal of Approval "Highly Recommended."

Figure 7.6: Production still from the animated short film *Seemannstreue*. © Anna Kalus-Goessner.

The FBW (2008) states about *Seemannstreue*:

> "This is a humorously wicked homage to the poet Joachim Ringelnatz (1883–1934) inspired by his poem *Seemannstreue*," a typical, Dadaist-inspired statement about the fugaciousness of an "amour fou."

The poem contains many strange lines like, for example *(translated from German by Hannes Rall)*:

> "My bride for the longest time was Alwine.
> Her blue eyes Gelatine
> for a long time already rotten and forgotten."

Or also:

> "Day in, day out, I dug for many weeks.
> But final it started to reek.
> Nevermind: that was truly disgusting."

Figure 7.7: This image offers an impression of the tastefully morbid visual design of the film: A combination of stylization, abstraction, and surrealistic exaggeration, supported by a muted and tonally harmonic color palette. Production still from *Seemannstreue*.

The FBW does further attest that "Anna Kalus does stay faithful to the originality of the poet and develops burlesque imagery in his spirit and sense (ibid)."

This quote adds further detail for a potential answer to an important research question: How can the spirit of an author be preserved in an adaptation? Not by literal illustration and replication of the original narrative content but by echoing the inventiveness of the author in a similarly original approach for the adaptation.

The FBW (ibid) also offers equally strong praise for animation and design style:

> "Her animation is visually stunning with an anachronistic faithfulness between Botero and Picasso and a well matched musical soundtrack that allows the film to succeed without knowledge of the underlying text (…) Anna Kalus does consequently forego the use of any recitation of the poem (surprising at first), she looks at her film as a visual association though the instruments of a different medium (comparable with the free-jazz-improvisation of an existing melody)."

Figure 7.8: The design of the curls of Adeline echoes the design style of the waves and therefore contributes to a cohesive design style. Production still from *Seemannstreue*. © Anna Kalus-Goessner.

I have been a longtime admirer of the film myself and fully share the opinion of the FBW.

I was therefore highly interested to discover more about the creative evolution of the film through a conversation with the talented director herself.

Interview with Anna Kalus Goessner

Seemannstreue

Hannes Rall (interviewer)
Anna Kalus Goessner (interviewed)

Dear Anna, first of all, can you introduce us shortly to the poem *Seemannstreue (A Sailor's Fidelity)*. It certainly negotiates a very sensitive topic and it is delivered in a very morbidly humorous way...?

The general underlying concept is the idea of "letting go." In his poem, Ringelnatz describes the inability of a sailor to let go of his deceased lover Alwine. Only when this behavior finally leads to truly disgusting results, he realizes that he indeed needs to let go of her. The mode of narration makes it easy for the reader to empathize and to transfer the topic to more common problems, for example, the difficulty to let go of certain habits and thoughts, when it seems to be impossible to part from particular thoughts or perceived matters, of course.

My own filmic adaptations frequently started with a deep and longtime fascination with the adapted literary piece or the respective writer, meaning I knew the respective source material already long before I began the adaptation, and I already had some images in my mind.

Did you experience a similar fascination in the case of Ringelnatz, or did you rather discover the poem *Seemannstreue* coincidentally? How did this adaptation come about?

I already know and admire Ringelnatz's humor for a long time. Still, my first contact with this specific poem was more like a sudden strike of lightning: I didn't ponder for long, if this would be a great topic for adaptation but instead immediately started sketching right away: This very spontaneous approach also could have gone wrong after all.

I often select my adaptation material on the criterion, if it would fit my graphic style(s), if I can use my very own artistic abilities to adapt it adequately. Did such considerations ever play a role in your approach to adaptation?

For me, the decision for a literary source is largely dependent on the amount to which it touches me emotionally, how much it appeals to me, or how fascinated I actually am by it. It is more of an emotional decision. It is possible as well that a completely new graphic style emerges during the actual adaptation process.

I have been thinking, if the topics of seafaring and sea specifically proved to be visually appealing for your animated adaptation?

Yes, probably that played a role, too. The waves at the beginning of the film kept me busy for sure. They exist in countless variations, and their animation occupied long stretches of the 3-year production time.

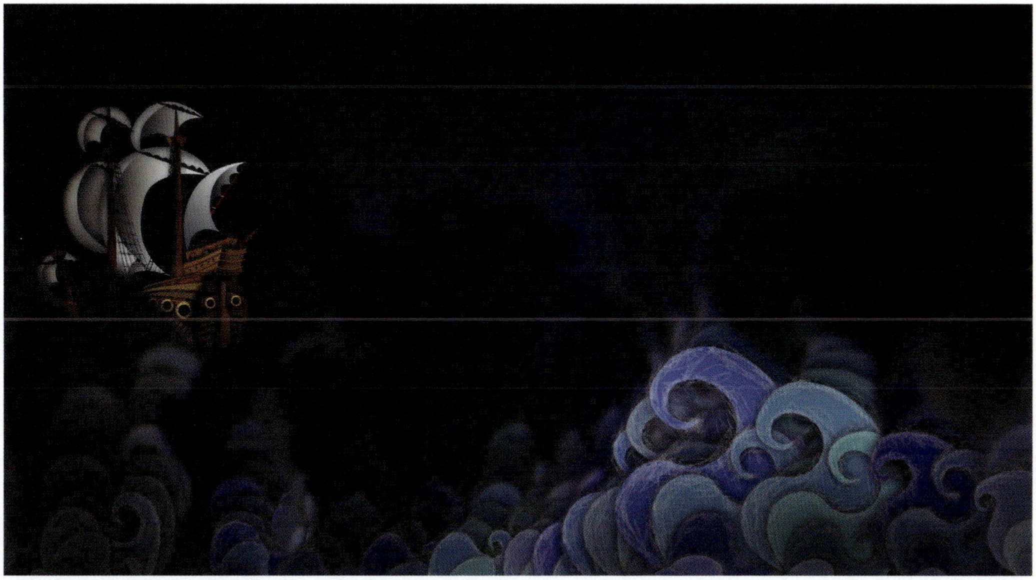

Figure 7.9: Waves in *Seemanstreue*. © Anna Kalus-Goessner.

For this book, I am particularly interested in exploring how it is possible to adapt literature for animation in different yet always convincing ways for animation.

In my opinion, a very loose adaptation can be equally successful as a very "faithful" one, as long as the resulting film can convince on its own merits.

Seemannstreue does only provide a very vague plot structure (in the traditional sense) and is therefore not easy to adapt, right? It is of further notice that you completely dispensed with any traditional voice-over narration or recitation of the original text for your film. How did this decision come about?

Initially, I stayed very close to the poem. I had a wonderful voice recording of the famous German actor and singer Ulrich Tukur, who recited the poem. That provided me with an underlying structure, a "spine" for the narrative, if you will. Only toward the end of the production process I dared to depart from this, supported by the advice of an esteemed colleague. I was ultimately able to trust in the film to communicate the narrative entirely through images and sound alone and without the help of any narration.

So, I finally did away with the voice-over and came up with the version that exists now.

That worked really well, because the spectator can probably immerse him/herself much better in the imagery without the use of any linguistic level.

That this also increases the chances for international distribution significantly was initially not on my mind at all, but this proved advantageous, of course.

What clearly distinguishes your film is the very unique and extremely appealing visual design, somehow in contrast with the rather dark subject matter but possibly even more of a fitting approach for this very reason. Can you tell us more about the development of this specific style and how it resonates with the source material?

When it comes to the design of characters and images, I want to fulfill my own high expectations for my artwork as well. It is crucial to me to be able to feel a positive sensation toward it, once it is completed. This feeling (or the lack of it) is the major criterion to either approve a visual design or not—or if I have to develop the design much more, until I can finally feel the previously described sensation.

Now, I have some even more detailed questions regarding the visual development process. This decision for a special look of your film probably also led to the decision to produce your film using digital cutout animation. Is that correct?

What kind of software did you use? How did the production process play out in detail? What kind of pipeline did you apply?

Figure 7.10: The complexity of this image from the film gices an idea of the necessity of combining animation techniques to achieve the desired final outcome. Production still from *Seemannstreue*. © Anna Kalus-Goessner.

As I have done before, I have used different animation techniques for *Seemannstreue*: For example, the unfolding rose was realized through traditional object animation (stop motion), the facial mimics of the characters in 3D computer animation, and a lot of cutout animation. This approach implied to, early on, move to the digital desktop, to combine all of these different elements through diverse digital approaches. To be able to, for example, animate all movements of the arms smoothly and not be forced to separate them into single elements, I used the software Anime Studio for the first time. Through this approach, I was able to work with inverse kinematics in a 2D environment and create softer movements.

The lighting for your film is executed with great care and contributes significantly to the spooky atmosphere of the animation. Can you familiarize us with the development story of it? Have there been several attempts and tryouts to get this right, until you found the appropriately "ghostly" lighting style?

The lighting was supposed to just focus on certain important details in an otherwise-deliberately-blurry environment. This reflects the mental state of the main character and enables the spectator to directly participate in his nightmarish situation. Because of this extremely important narrative function, I have integrated this lighting concept already in the drawn images instead of adding it later on in post-production.

Figure 7.11: An example how the lighting focuses on details in the image and directs the attention of the spectator by doing so. The overall "fogginess" of the image also succeeds in two main respects: First, to create a ghostly atmosphere, reflecting the spookiness of the original text. Second, to reference the nautical topic by implying the atmospheric effects of the omnipresent sea. Production still from *Seemannstreue*. © Anna Kalus-Goessner.

Speaking of post-production: I would imagine that compositing still played an important role to achieve the final look. Who was in charge of that, and how did you collaborate with the compositor?

Indeed, animation and compositing were created in close collaboration, often simultaneously. I have filled almost all of the required roles and responsibilities myself. I only wanted to delegate the acoustic element(s) of the film. It would have almost been impossible for me to separate the two different levels of animation and compositing, because this way, I could apply necessary changes in highly flexible ways and very quickly.

This happened correspondingly frequently during the 3-year production time.

Quite often, a certain approach proved to be a dead end or became too convoluted for production, so that I had to throw a lot of the previous material out of the window.

I couldn't have required any hired compositor to deal with this way of working.

Figure 7.12: Complex multilayered imagery from *Seemannstreue* (film production still). © Anna Kalus-Goessne.

Too often, music and sound are not considered sufficiently in terms of the immense artistic importance they carry for the final success of a film. This wasn't the case here.

With the former "Floridan Studio" composers and sound designers, Florian Käppler and Daniel Requardt, you were able to rely on a very strong team, with significant experience in the area of animation. The soundtrack of the film therefore turned out expectedly strong.

How did you collaborate as director and composer/sound designer?

How precise was your briefing for the audio team? Which ideas came from the musicians?

Were there different stages of development?

Oh yes, this constellation proved to be a very lucky choice, indeed.

Florian Käppler had come up with several proposals for the music based on a rather minimal briefing from my side. It became clear very early on that the voice of Nikolai Kinski combined with the text of his father (late German actor Klaus Kinski) would prove to be a wonderful combination with the images. The musicians didn't even shy away from recording underwater in a swimming pool! The final production once again was not easy, because the visual part of the movie and rhythm of the film were already completed entirely and the music needed to be composed to match it. Without this very strong acoustic component, *Seemannstreue* would definitely be a very different film.

Figure 7.13: Underwater scene from the film. Production still from *Seemannstreue*. © Anna Kalus-Goessner.

Was there any feedback from literature scholars or Ringelnatz experts?

So far not. But I would be very happy to hear it.

You told me that you recently have been working primarily as a motion graphics and broadcast designer, not as an animator of your own independent animated films.

If that would change in the future, would you consider another adaptation?

There are plenty of ideas in my head. Let's just wait and see what the future brings.

Finally, I would like you to tell me what you think are the major mistakes that can be made in an animated adaptation?

What to avoid at any cost?

I consider it of the highest importance to never lose sight of the initial strong passion you felt for the adapted source material throughout the whole production—with an animated adaptation that can happen easily through the long and tedious process it requires.

The FBW (ibid) also offers the fitting closing remark and summary on this fantastic animation: "This most appealing experiment of an animated fantasy inspired by Ringelnatz fully succeeds, stays faithful to the originality of the poet (...)."

A second film mentioned by Thomas Zandegiacomo del Bel is the similarly successful animated short film *A Lost and Found Box of Human Sensation* (Leuchtenberg, Wallner 2010). The FBW jury also awarded the highest distinction here and stated (2010):

> "The death of the father is simultaneously the start of a fundamental negotiation of the essential topics of death, loss and pain for the son. Martin Wallner and Stefan Leuchtenberg send us on a highly emotionally and extremely fast paced journey, garnished with innovative ideas, sometimes highly intellectualized and full of deeper meaning(s), highly confident and convincing in the filmic design. The formal structure of 4 acts might appear slightly didactic, but it also provides solid orientation for the spectator to understand the time travel of the young man on the way to discover his own true self. Designed with laborious and very original animation these 4 acts show us in quickfire pace a funeral, illness, highs and lows of a mundane existence until a paradigm shift in the last act poses existential questions about love and death through impressive imagery."

This film is of particular interest in the bigger context of this book, as it is an animated adaptation of a poem written by one of the two directors of the film himself.

In other words, he adapted his own poem.

This special case therefore can provide insight into the creative mechanics of adaptation from a very different angle. By assuming dual roles of original author and adapter Martin Wallner can reflect in unique ways on the adaptation process and how he dealt with the connected decision-making for the necessary transformation undertaken.

I had the chance to discuss this directly with the directors.

Interview with Stefan Leuchtenberg and Martin Wallner

A Lost and Found Box of Human Sensation

Interview conducted via e-mail 2015

Hannes Rall (interviewer)

Stefan Leuchtenberg and Martin Wallner (interviewed)

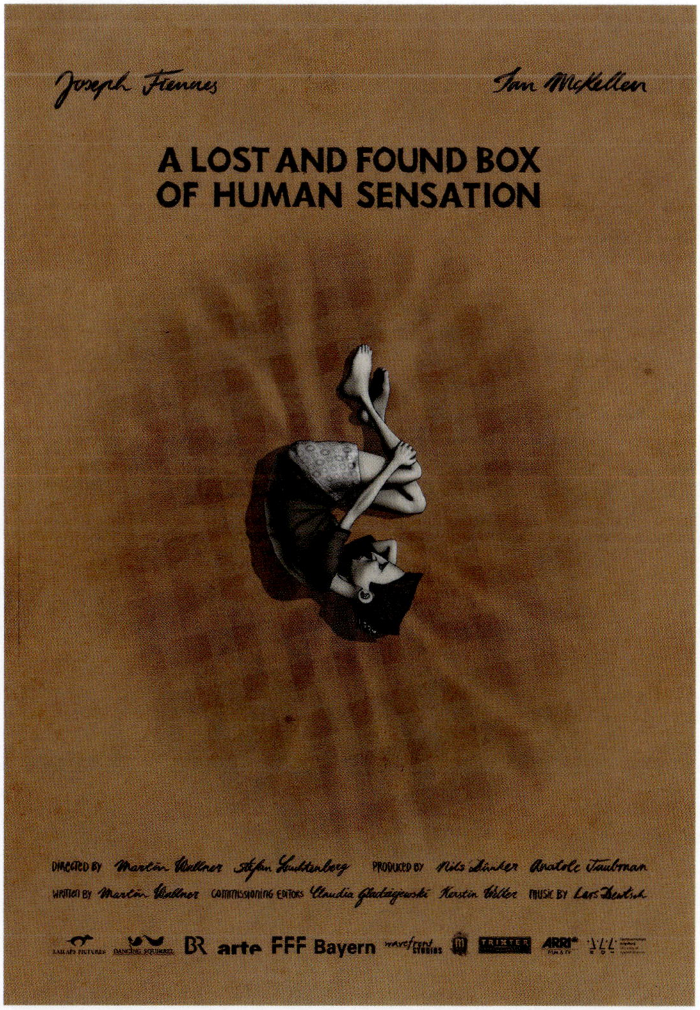

Figure 7.14: Poster of *A Lost and Found Box of Human Sensation* (2010). © Dancing Squirrel.

Dear Martin and Stefan, your film *A Lost and Found Box of Human Sensation* constitutes a very special case of adaptation: It was transformed from its original incarnation as a poem, written by Martin, into an animated short film. Can you provide a short summary of the content of your film first?

When his father dies unexpectedly, a young man seeking to cope with his grief goes on a powerful emotional journey through time and space. The film begins with the funeral and shows how feelings change throughout the years. It ends with the question: Is there a due date for grief...?

Figure 7.15: The opening sequence of *A Lost and found Box of Human Sensation*. It showcases the highly skilled and imaginatively staged use of a seamless and perspective changing transition between scenes without a cut. A typical example for the vocabulary of animation and almost impossible to achieve in traditional live action that is hindered by the limitations of real (physical) environments. © Lailaps Pictures, Dancing Squirrel 2010.

There are two parts in the movie: A poem builds the framework for the storyline and is recited by a narrator, spoken by Ian McKellen. Additionally from time to time this structure is interrupted by thoughts and experiences of the boy (spoken by Joseph Fiennes). He talks to himself and thereby gives the audience an insight into a very personal point of view.

Whereas the spoken language generally is very honest and straightforward, the visual impression of the film is rather metaphorical and picturesque. It represents the inner perception of the protagonist and his world of thoughts, a mixture between reality and imagination. The intention of this is not to dramatize but to emphasize certain emotions and sensations and to make them more comprehensible.

Figure 7.16: Film still from *A Lost and Found Box of Human Sensation*. © Lailaps Pictures, Dancing Squirrel 2010.

The prevailing mood of the movie is not grief and melancholy but an odd unstableness, sad and quiet passages take turns with anger, but also humor and self irony. All in all *A Lost and Found Box of Human Sensation* is a film about the time-consuming process of overcoming grief, with all its ups, downs, setbacks and silver linings.

The title of your film, to begin with, is a very smart wordplay by and in itself. Funnily it took me a while (actually a second viewing of your film) to "get" it and to understand how well it actually reflects the arc and content of your film. Can you explain how it achieves that?

I guess it came from the original poem?

Yes, the title came with the poem. I was looking for an image to bring all the different situations, impressions and emotions together, something to sum it all up. The image of a lost and found box seemed to be the perfect metaphor: All our sensations, experiences and memories are stowed away in the attic. They are always there but only from time to time we decide to open the box and have a look inside.

There seems to be a strong autobiographical component to both, poem and film, do you want to elaborate on that? Or is the story entirely fictional?

The screenplay is based on personal experience, although it is not entirely autobiographical. I lost my father in 2004 due to pancreatic cancer. However, it was never my intention to make the film about myself. When we started out, Stefan and I were looking for a topic we could speak about honestly and from the heart, in order to create an authentic film. So it became a film about losing someone you love, about grief and the time-consuming process of overcoming such a loss.

Figure 7.17: Stylistically different film still from *A Lost and Found Box of Human Sensation* demonstrating the transition of emotional mood reflected through visual design throughout the film. The move from monochromatic colors to a wider palette is obvious. © Lailaps Pictures, Dancing Squirrel 2010.

Can you tell us more about your adaptation process? Was the poem written with a potential film version in mind, i.e., as a special approach to scriptwriting or did it already exist on its own, before you decided to turn it into a film? Is the original poem the same as the film's dialogue (i.e., monologue)?

The original poem consisted of a number of verses which I had written over the period of a couple of years, trying to pin down certain emotions or situations. At that time I mainly tried to preserve some of my memories, without any intention of making a movie out of it. Or basically anything, for that matter. However, when Stefan and I decided to produce an animated short film during our master studies, I pitched the topic to him and he got enthused about it. From there on we collaborated, and including Stefan's more neutral, outside view on the topic I rewrote the poem and turned it into something like a screenplay.

Example: Old version of act II

Act 2: The secret art of repression

The first couple of days are like living under water
Moving slowly, vision blurred and the volume tuned down
A desperate effort to keep themselves busy
and to bear in mind not to drown

He remembers supporting his father fragile and weak
in a struggle to get him from the car to his seat
and how seeing that strong man wither away
broke something inside of him that day

He wonders why every unpleasant instant
is replayed in his head like a silent movie flick
and he gets angry
because at other times the most simple things don't stick
like names or PINs or birthdays or global politics

He gets angry because his appetite doesn't seem to fade
(apparently it often does)
and not even now he seems to lose weight
and he wonders what it might cause.

However, the days are not the problem, they go by
the images pay their respects at night
and when he finally falls asleep,
he dreams:

Dreams the same dream all alike
a slightly alternating repetition
His dad is always still alive,
and in splendid condition
The boy tries to hug him and not to let go
but it feels just utterly wrong
Tries to tell him everything he never told before
And although the movie continues at dawn
no matter how hard he tries to hold on
the prologue might be a different piece
but still the ending never is.

The result is that he feels completely alone
unable to reach the edge of his bed
his girlfriend asks him "what is wrong?"
And he says "nothing, it's just my head."

and he eats to distract himself from this sensation
and he fucks to get a different sensation
and he drinks to, well, kill the sensation
and he works to distract himself from this sensation
he works quite a lot and sometimes it works.
And sometimes he cries in awkward situations
and he can't even tell why it hurts

He gets angry at the kids in Africa
who stole his right to feel sorry for himself
since of course they are so far worse off
than anybody else

and he eats, and he drinks,
and he works, and he fucks,
and he eats, and he drinks,
and he works, and he fucks,
eats, drinks, works, fucks,
and suddenly a year is gone.
Like testing an aching tooth with his tongue
he inspects the insides of his head
For the first time he realizes that it feels just comfortably numb
and so he decides to move on.

New version

Act 2: The Secret Art of Repression

Boy:
Everyday life. Everything is so damn normal that it almost kills me.
As if nothing had happened at all. He could come through the door
any moment.
There is this lump in my throat... I feel it with every breath. I feel it
in my chest, in my head, squeezing against the back of my eyeballs.
It fucking hurts so much.
Don'tthinkaboutitdon'tthinkaboutitdon't don'tdon'tdon't

DON'TTHINKABOUTIT!!LALALAAAA....
I wish I could turn off my head

Narrator:
He gets angry.
Angry at global warming, gaining weight and passing cars
at flat beer, comforters, TV talk, bacteria
Angry at the frickin' kids in Africa
who stole his right to feel sorry for himself
since of course they are so far worse off
than anybody else

Boy:
I still see him in my dreams. Every night.

Narrator:
And every single morning with the breaking of dawn
no matter how hard he tries to hold on
the dreams fade away and all that remains
is reality and some pillow stains

and he eats to distract himself from this sensation
and he screws to get a different sensation
and he drinks to, well, kill the sensation
and he works to distract himself from this sensation
he works quite a lot and sometimes it works.
And sometimes he cries in awkward situations
and he can't even tell why it hurts

and he eats, and he drinks,
and he works, and he fucks,
and he eats, and he drinks,
and he works, and he fucks,
eats, drinks, works, fucks,
and suddenly a year is gone.

When it came to actually writing the film or creating the narrative concept, did you work with a full script or only with storyboards? Did you collaborate closely?

Starting from the original poem we began were initially very freely looking for images that would express the emotions described in words and that would ideally expand those by an additional level. From the very beginning we worked together very closely und we started equally early to define a sequential order for the images. We did this in the form of rudimentary storyboards that served as the basis for our discussions.

Figure 7.18: Example for a storyboard sequence (end scene). © Dancing Squirrel.

Two points were of central importance: For one we wanted avoid a simple duplication of words through images at any cost (with the exception of a few sections where precisely that was desirable).

Secondly we wanted to use the film-specific techniques offered by animation to create a most unique visual language.

We decided for a mixture between 2D and 3D animation because it minimized our dependency on technology and maximized our freedom for the design of the film at the same time.

- Freedom of camera: In 3D space it is easy to execute camera movements of any kind with comparatively little effort so that there were no or little restrictions expected at all.
- An economical approach: Because each new character undergoes a laborious development process in 3D animation, before it can finally be animated, we decided for a "drawn" look that allowed for a mix of 2D and 3D animation techniques. Therefore we could simply draw supporting characters of lesser importance who would appear only once and that saved us a lot of work.

I was always impressed how your film combines the technical advantages of CG animation with the limitless possibilities and freedom of stylization more inherent to traditional 2D animation.

Exactly. We decided to mix different techniques (btw. as well as to use animation in general), in order to have absolute freedom in creating the visual world of our film. Since we studied multimedia and design (in contrast to classical film studies), we wanted to use this background to our advantage. So we decided to take it as far as possible, to use farout characters, dream images, abstractions and typography, whatever comes to mind. Yes, we were young, idealistic and quite frankly, we had no idea what we were in for. It took us three years to comprehend the scale of this approach.

However, from the very beginning we were aware of the problem that all the different styles might be difficult to mix and therefore we tried to make the transitions from one to the next as smooth as possible.

Other reasons were the absolute freedom of the camera in 3D and on the other hand the possibility to blend in 2D characters, if they had only very short appearances (e.g., the pink elephant or the shadow monster).

Figure 7.19: This beautifully designed piece of development art already displays several main characteristics of the film: For one heavy stylization, more influenced by the wider variety of design approaches in independent 2D animation than the often-applied realistic look in 3D animation. It also already implies the importance of space for creating uninhibited camera movements throughout the film: An extreme "bird's eye view" is used as the camera angle. The look of the shadows themselves hints at the concept of merging 2D and 3D techniques seamlessly by choosing a design that serves the purpose well. © Dancing Squirrel.

Let's talk a little bit more about your visual development process preceding the actual production. Did it take some time to arrive at look? Were there other considerations?

How do your final decisions relate to the narrative content or the mood you wanted to create?

Because the aforementioned advantages liberated us very much for the design of scenes and environments and the staging in general, we wanted to take full advantage of this for the filmic transformation. Because essential parts of the narrative take place in the head of the boy and therefore are being expressed through distorted, exaggerated of metaphorical means, we wanted to make use of this approach for the visual design as well.

It was supposed to be absolutely clear that these images do not represent reality but the very personal view of the boy instead. By employing metaphors we wanted to avoid any direct duplications from the written word and also add new aspects that would strengthen the general expressiveness or visually define an equivalent for a very specific emotion.

Figure 7.20: Huge crosses dwarf the film's protagonist. Imaginative visual staging suggests an additional level of meaning: The situation is clearly overwhelming, menacing, if not entirely wiping out the existence of the boy as well. © Lailaps Pictures, Dancing Squirrel 2010.

Some examples for such exaggerations are the huge crosses throwing their immense shadows onto the cemetery when the boy stands in front of his father's grave or the whole scene of the doctor who delivers his diagnosis in the fashion of a musical, by plucking blossoming leaves from a flower. Such images clearly intensify the expression of the subjective perception of the boy. Our intention was to juxtapose the comical element of exaggeration with the fate of the protagonist.

That way we hoped to create a tragicomical, absurd atmosphere that would ultimately increase the severeness of the overall mood.

Figure 7.21: The doctor's scene from the film. Absurd setting and mood are created by quoting tropes of a typical showstopper scene from a musical. © Lailaps Pictures, Dancing Squirrel 2010.

Moreover we used additional characters repeatedly as metaphors for a certain emotion.

For example: the seemingly endless parade of robots, offering the boy their condolences at the graveside, express the apathy of this moment much stronger than any use of human characters ever could. Additional examples would be the shadow of the boy that projects his inner rage outside in the city environment or the "nice thoughts" that manifest themselves in the shape of pink elephants and naked girls.

Figure 7.22: The robotic parade in front of the grave. The robots are used as a visual device to express the subjective perception of the boy: In the typically endless stream of condolences at a funeral, the well meaning words of consolation cannot be truly perceived as individual human expressions anymore. For the protagonist they become deprived of any true emotional meaning. Showing robots instead of humans serves to communicate this feeling to the audience. © Lailaps Pictures, Dancing Squirrel 2010.

Did you plan systematically as in style by chapter?

No, more as in style by visual quotation, visual elements, trying to make the transitions as smooth as possible. Act I alone combines about 5 different visual styles.

I believe I detected some possible artistic influences for the character-and production design, which you masterfully transformed into your very own way of artistic expression. Can you name some of your points of reference

There have been plenty of influences on each of the different sections of our film. I'll just list a few examples:

General look and appearance: *Sin City* (Frank Miller), *Historía Tragica com Final Feliz* (short film by Regina Pessoa), *Persepolis* (Marjan Satrapi), *Waltz with Bashir* and a car commercial for the Scion Deviants done by NY agency Shilo.

Doctor's sequence: *Tim Burton's Nightmare Before Christmas*, of course. Also Terry Gilliam and Jeunet & Caro (*City of the Lost Children*). Also *Frankenstein*, bad horror movies etc.

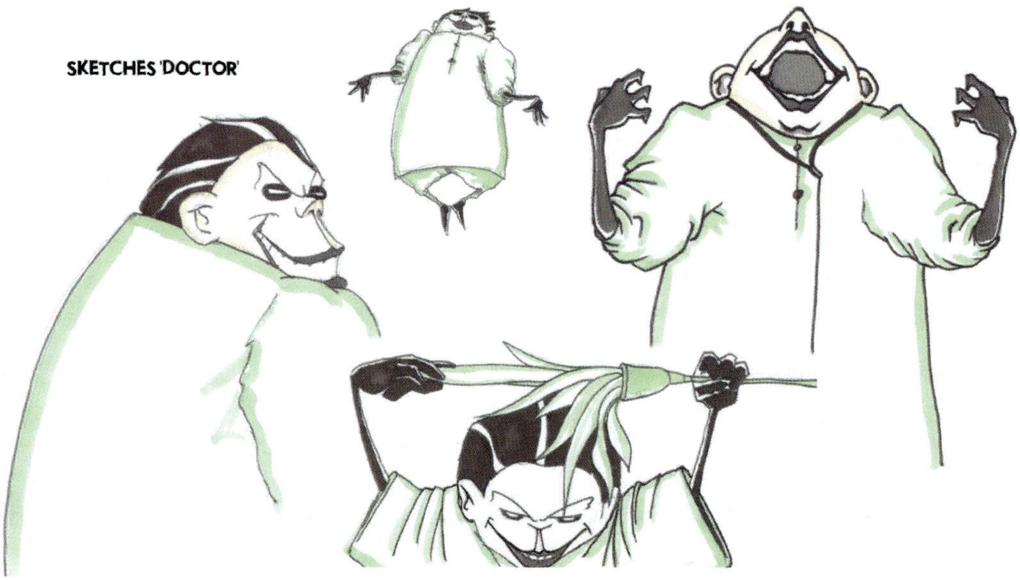

Figure 7.23: The design of the doctor can be seen as a lovingly crafted homage to Tim Burton, yet with taking its own and very distinct turn on the influences. The individual drawing style of a new designer will almost always leave its unique mark on the final design—evolving the style significantly from its original source of inspiration. An additional twist is ultimately delivered by creating the scene in 3D computer animation different from the stop motion in *Nightmare Before Christmas*. © Dancing Squirrel.

Figure 7.24: A different approach for the doctor's character design from visual development. The same set of influences are visible here, but they are applied to a completely different concept of shapes. © Dancing Squirrel.

Visual exaggerations and metaphors: Michel Gondry (as in his music videos or *The Science of Sleep*), Terry Gilliam (*Fear and Loathing in Las Vegas*), David Cronenberg (*Naked Lunch*), Guillermo del Toro (*Pan's Labyrinth*), Tim Burton (*Big Fish*).

The shadow monster: *Nosferatu* (Murnau), *Vincent* (Tim Burton)

Typography (Chemo / Prick): *The Maxx, Sin City*. Both as in the graphic novels.

Camera: *Fight Club* (David Fincher).

But there have been many more influences, whether we used them consciously or didn't even notice.

In terms of character design your main character has a very appealing yet refreshingly unconventional (for 3D animation) appearance. I assume it was your goal to define a look that resonates with the darker subject matter present in the narrative?

Yes. When we did the first concepts, we tried to feel into the emotional state of mind of the character. The idea was to give him hard edges on the one hand (nose), but also a soft and fragile appearance on the other (e.g., lips). Another reference for his appearance was Neil Gaiman's Sandman.

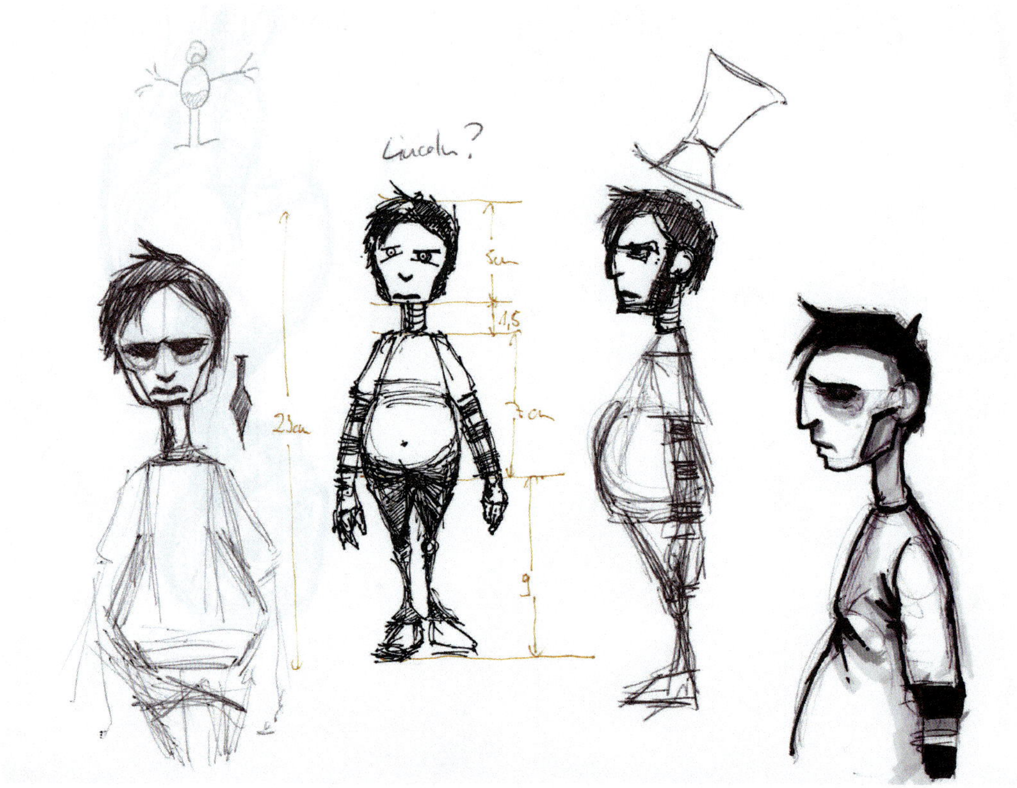

Figure 7.25: Early development art for the main character. It is very evident that the filmmakers were looking for a design style that avoids a generic 3D design approach through strong stylization, yet it remains technically feasible in 3D animation. A strong influence by German expressionism in the facial design can be detected, but the basic construction of the figure strives for a combination of simple shapes. © Dancing Squirrel.

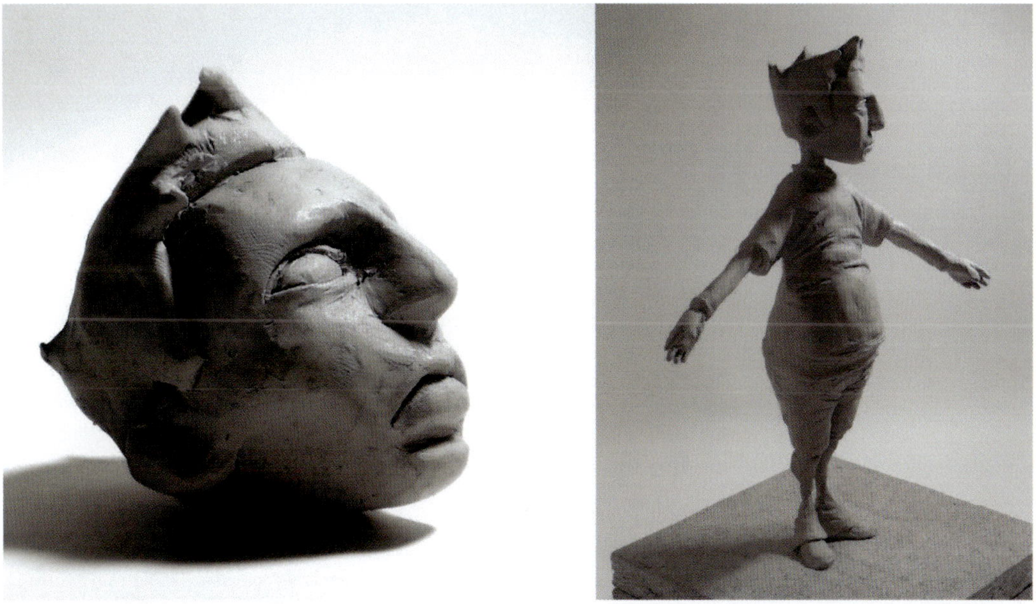

Figure 7.26: Here, it can be seen how sculpting character maquettes preceded actual 3D modeling to translate the initially drawn concept into 3D space. It is impressive how the creators managed to keep the unique approach in the 3D transformation, a most difficult process where other productions often fail. It is helpful that the underlying 2D designs are based on bold and highly diverse basic shapes, a concept that is successfully carried over into the 3D version. © Dancing Squirrel.

When it comes to the look development of the environments and props, particularly the "medical machinery," you use the vocabulary and technical tools of CG very well to create a nightmare-version of a hospital. I think that the inherent qualities of "coldness" and overwhelming complexity are very well used to recontextualize conventional 3D approaches for the purpose of creating a grotesque and menacing atmosphere. Am I right? What was your thought process to arrive at this very specific type of design?

We were looking for a Frankenstein-like look for the laboratory. First we collected dozens of images of sharp, evil-looking machinery and medical devices, which could be used to exaggerate the whole process of medical treatment and turn it into some kind of bad horror movie/musical. The intention was to make the whole sequence as over-the-top as possible, otherwise it would've been too dark and "teary" for our taste.

Figure 7.27: Development art for the lab. The imaginative staging and the exaggerated use of "crazy" machinery and equipment combines with a suitably epxressionistic sense of staging and lighting. © Dancing Squirrel.

Production-wise I'll be honest: We didn't plan very well, and to give credit where credit is due: We basically handed our mood collection over to our intern Vera Hiendl and told her to design mean-looking torture instruments. In our defense, she did seem to like this task quite a lot.

When it came to rendering and compositing however, we found that most of our backgrounds and props were barely visible due to lighting, depth of field and for other reasons. Matte paintings would've been far more economical and sufficient in most of the shots.

Another typical 3D animation trope you employ very well in the service of story is the possibility of extreme and almost unrestricted camera movements. Can you guide us through an example from your film

Regarding the camera movement, our main intention was to create a steady flow of smooth transitions from one style or time-frame to the next, and thereby connect the different parts of the film. Additionally, as we cover a time stretch of a couple of years within a 15-minute film, it was a way to display the passing of time.

Martin: A sequence I personally like very much is the beginning of Act III, where the boy leaves home and goes on a journey. In contrast to many other parts of the film, this sequence isn't very interesting in a graphical sense and at first it was quite boring visually. The challenge was to make it more special, more interesting. We started out with Guy Richie's *Snatch* in mind, where he covers a flight from New York to London in a few very quick cuts, but in the end we came up with this succession of images: A constant movement to the right (a journey toward the future) without noticeable cuts connects the shots very smoothly.

On to actual production. I know from the credits that the work was divided between the two of you and even more collaborators. I would be interested to hear about this in more detail. What was the sequence of the production?

The production of *A Lost and Found Box of Human Sensation* started in March 2007, when we began our master studies in Augsburg. Based on the screenplay we developed a project treatment, in order to gain support and a proper budget. In the consequence, our producers Nils Dünker and Anatole Taubman came on board, together with their production company Lailaps Pictures.

In January 2008 Stefan and Martin founded Dancing Squirrel, a studio for interactive media and animation, to form a co-production with Lailaps Pictures. Additionally, the Bavarian public TV station BR and ARTE, a German-French broadcaster, joined our team as financiers. The budget was completed with the support of the FFF Bayern, the Bavarian film funding.

Later on, and mainly due to our producers, we managed to win over Joseph Fiennes (*Shakespeare in Love*) and Ian McKellen (*The Lord of the Rings*) as voice actors. The recordings took place in Berlin in February 2008. The recordings with Ian McKellen were held in London in December 2009.

Moreover, a lot of notable partners and sponsors supported the production of the film: Most of the time the film team was based in the facilities of the University of Applied Sciences in Augsburg. Between October 2008 and October 2009, Trixter Film in Munich supported us with know-how and infrastructure. All sound effects, as well as the entire audio post production was done by Heiko Müller / Wavefront Studios. The score music for the film was composed by Lars Deutsch and mixed and produced by Andreas Rauscher and Audio Machinery in Berlin. Finally, a lot of the rendering and lighting process was supported by the Augsburg based animation company Meilenstein Digital.

The production of *A Lost and Found Box of Human Sensation* was realized by Martin and Stefan, with the support of several artists in specialized fields of work. Simon Leykamm worked with the directors full time for the last 12 months of the production and was responsible for the technical direction of the movie. Onni Pohl and Travis Ramsdale animated the most significant sequences of the film. Altogether, the design crew consisted of more than 15 people. *A Lost and Found Box of Human Sensation* was finished in March 2010.

Were any particular challenges encountered and how did you resolve them?

The greatest challenge was the budget. It took us three years to finish the film and more than once we ran out of money. At this point we should again mention the whole team and express our deepest gratitude: Everyone involved in the production worked either for free or earned a fraction of the money they should've earned.

During the final months of production the two of us and our Technical Director Simon Leykamm worked 7 days a week, 12 hours a day and Simon never even once complained.

The combination of 2D and 3D in the film is very well done and aesthetically pleasing. It must have been extremely well planned and included some great compositing work?

Actually it was the result of a lot of experiments. In the beginning we only had a vague idea, where we wanted to go. We had a couple of look development samples (as mentioned above), but weren't satisfied yet. We were aiming for something more special, therefore we tested a watercolor shader a team of programmers and artists at the Institute of Animation in Ludwigsburg was working on. Unfortunately the software wasn't ready for production yet and so we had to abort these plans.

In the end, we used a combination of textures, shading and a vast amount of different render layers created by our Technical Director, including edge detection, toon shaders, ramp shaders, shadows, highlights, alphas and so on. Afterwards, we blended all the different layers together in many variations until we were happy with the outcome. Lots of trial, error, aborted render jobs, cursing and sleepless nights.

Can you talk about the use (or non-use) of color in your film and how it relates to the narrative content? I think it is done brilliantly, but I want you to make us understand the "how" and "why."

Our first color concept was what turned into the movie poster later on: The boy, curled up, lying on his bed. We were playing around with brown/natural paper and drew on it with black ink for shadows and white for highlights. We liked very much, how the character stood out from the background, as he came from a different color space and tried to transfer that kind of look to the film.

Therefore, the prevailing color concept during Acts I and II are desaturated environments in sepia during the day, with a shade of blue at night. In contrast to that, the boy himself is black and white.

Figure 7.28: Film still from Act II. © Lailaps Pictures, Dancing Squirrel 2010.

The doctor sequence, as a flashback to the past and in contrast to the rest, has another tone: The doctor is black and white just as the boy, but the environment is mainly in shades of green.

Figure 7.29: Film still from the doctor's sequence. © Lailaps Pictures, Dancing Squirrel 2010.

In Act III, the boy leaves home and travels. Since his mood becomes lighter, this sequence is far more colorful than the others.

Figure 7.30: Film still from Act III. © Lailaps Pictures, Dancing Squirrel 2010.

Back home, in Act IV, he first goes back to old habits (color as in Act II). Then he falls in love (bright lights / high contrast). In the end, he crashes onto a plane of white snow, clearing a colorful spot underneath him: The flower as symbol for something new.

All in all, we used color in order to stress the emotional state of mind of the boy during the different periods of the film.

Figure 7.31: Transition from Act IV to the end of the film. © Lailaps Pictures, Dancing Squirrel 2010.

Lighting plays a big role to create mood and is often evocative of expressionist film, film noir and uses the principles of great black & white cinematography. Please explain more.

Yes, there are a couple of sequences, most prominently the doctor scene and the shadow monster, where we used light and shadow contrasts and sometimes explicitly referenced film noir and old silent movies, such as Fritz Lang's *M – Eine Stadt sucht einen Mörder* or Murnau's *Nosferatu*. However, all these references and visual metaphors are exaggerated and clearly over-the-top, meant to bring humor into an otherwise dark topic.

Figure 7.32: A still from the finished film that shows the strong influence from lighting techniques that are typical for film noir and expressionistic silent movies primarily from Germany. The lighting is also used beyond merely suggesting atmosphere. It used to beautifully frame the character against the environment: A small negative shape contrasts with a huge positive space. This lighting style can also be described as high contrast or chiaroscuro. In comics, one of the most popular uses of this technique can be seen in Frank Miller's *Sin City* (1991–2000), also quoted as an important influence by the filmmakers. © Lailaps Pictures, Dancing Squirrel 2010.

Another great achievement of your film is its excellent pacing. Did you define hat rhythm already precisely at the storyboarding stage and then transfer it into the film?
Or did you work with an editor after the actual animation production was over?

Yes, the rhythm and pacing were very important to us. This time we can proudly say that we actually did it as you should: In the animatic. We started out with storyboards, created a rough hand-drawn animatic, added sounds and refined it all the way through, replaced shot by shot with blockings, rough animations, finer animations and final renderings/comps.

A perhaps unavoidable question: you managed to get Ian McKellen on board as your narrator. I am sure a lot of young aspiring filmmakers out there are very interested how you managed to achieve this dream casting.

Here we have to hand over all the credit to our producers Nils Dünker and Anatole Taubman. Anatole managed to enthuse Joseph Fiennes for our project, who loved the script and agreed to lend his voice to the boy. Later on, we approached Ian McKellen through his agency and along with Joseph's best recommendations, our producers managed to get him on board as well.

Figure 7.33: Set photo from the recordings with Ian McKellen in London. © Lailaps Pictures 2009.

How was it to work with him, can you tell us more about the actual recording session. Was it recorded prior to animation or afterwards (possible as there was no lip-syncing necessary)?

Where did you record? Did you record several takes? How much was your input in terms of actual voice-directing?

Both Joseph and Ian have been stunning to work with and the recordings were a great and memorable experience for us as no-name directors. Of course they brought their own touch and ideas to the characters, but whenever we asked them to try a different approach they did it on the spot, never questioned our decisions (in Joe's case even when he had to sing utterly wrongly and from the top of his lungs) and always kept up an incredibly good mood. For each line and sentence both gave us a number of variations, so we had a lot of material to choose from, in order to find the perfect rhythm and intonation to go along with the animation and flow of the film.

We recorded Joseph at the BASISBerlin studios prior to the animation, as we had to do the lip-sync for the boy along to the recordings. Ian's session was recorded in London at ZigZag, close to the end of the production.

Your film was a big success at film festivals. It would be interesting to hear what the film achieved and how you managed to distribute to festivals. Did you do it all by yourself or did you have some support? What were the major festival successes and awards?

All in all the film took part in about 150 competitions worldwide and won more than 20 awards. Personally, we're most excited about the fact that we won awards in very different categories, such as Jury awards, a Youth Jury award, audience awards, an award at a horror and fantasy film festival, some animation awards and some best film awards. We did all the submissions ourselves, however the distribution of the screening copies was covered by Lailaps. We began with submitting to A-list festivals (rejected) and from there we went on to submit to all the festivals with special premiere regulations. At first we only received rejections, 18 in a row (still hurts), but all of a sudden we managed to get into competitions, starting in Palm Springs, quickly won two awards (First Steps and Best Film at Odense IFF), and afterwards the film sold itself. Among our favorite festivals were of course Annecy (animator's Shangri-La) and Tribeca, but we also went to a lot of smaller festivals which were incredibly nice and had the chance to visit cities we otherwise wouldn't have, at least for a long while. Personal recommendations are ReAnima in Yerevan/Armenia, Petaluma Film Festival in the Sonoma Valley and Poitiers IFF.

The topic is potentially sensitive and you dared to come up with an unconventional yet beautiful approach to it. To me it is great art! I am sure it was overall met with generally favorable reviews and huge support. Did you ever encounter any critical feedback?

At least not face to face. However, since the film is based on Martin's personal experience we were always concerned about the possibility, that some people might find it egocentric or even narcissistic. I think once we received a comment addressing that. But the vast majority of reviews and comments were extremely positive.

Another thing: When we started out submitting to festivals, we received eighteen rejections in a row before the first festival accepted us. Luckily, we kept going.

To end on a positive note (pun intended) I think your film concludes in a rather hopeful and uplifting way despite (or because of) its earlier realization that in real life there are no (guaranteed) happy endings. Was that your intention? Any thoughts on that?

The film displays a process that has no real ending. If you lose someone you love, it changes you as a person and stays with you for the rest of your life. But at a certain point you come to terms with it, emotions change, with the years grief becomes less and less present and eventually things are somewhat okay. Someday, there's room for something new. Our intention was to capture this process and end with mild optimism. Hence the flowers, hence the song ("I am alright, I am fine.").

Figure 7.34: The sublime ending of the film that leaves the spectator on a mildly optimistic note. The visual composition perfectly echoes that sentiment and narratively the film comes full circle through a repetition of visual motives, yet in an entirely different context now. © Lailaps Pictures, Dancing Squirrel 2010.

Finally: Any thoughts about what type of written source material is suitable (or non-suitable) for an animated adaptation?

Technically, no: Since you can do anything imaginable in animation and show whatever you're able to conceive in your head, there are little to no technical restrictions, why a story shouldn't work as animated film.

Emotionally, maybe: Adult audiences seem to relate more to real human beings than to animated characters, although many great examples prove that animated characters are able to take us on the same emotional roller-coaster ride as real actors.

Budget-wise definitely: There are a couple of financial reasons, why a certain screenplay wouldn't make a successful animation. You have to consider, that usually the budget for animation needs to be notably higher than for live-action movies. Additionally (as mentioned above), adult audiences are far more hesitant to watch animations and even more so, if it's not a comedy.

So basically: No restrictions as long as you have all the money in the world and don't bother if the film bombs at box office (might still be a great movie anyway, right?).

What are major mistakes or shortcomings of non-successful animated adaptations?

I don't think we're in any position to point out the shortcomings of others. Generally speaking it might be unwise to put a certain technique or (visual) effects first. In our opinion, it should be all about story and compelling, empathetic characters.

As a whole *A Lost and Found Box of Human Sensation* offers valuable insights into the narrative options that can be applied when adapting poetry for animation. Most importantly it stands out in terms of its storytelling approach. In essence we are looking at an interesting hybrid here: The story does follow a rough timeline, through all of the stages of loss, mourning and finally (in a way) redemption and reconnection with the world.

Within this rough structure however there is less of a strictly chronological order. Transitioning in time and space does not necessarily follow a simple sequential structure, building a classic plot-driven narrative. Instead images are freely associated, reality distorted by subjective perception, dreamlike sequences mixed with "real" facts and so forth. The narrative ambiguities of the original poem are answered to with equally ambivalent and multilayered imagery that allows for symbolic readings.

At the same time the choice of (moving) images and their execution in staging, lighting, color design and animation sharpen the perception of certain emotions and overall atmosphere.

In this way the spectator can fully embrace the often contradictory back and forth of recovery from a big emotional loss yet still accompany the protagonist on his forward progressing journey. In my opinion the film demonstrates exemplary how a functioning hybrid between linear and nonlinear narrative can be created in service of expressing the essence of the source material.

But what to do, if the original poem offers even less of a concrete plot, not a really chronology of events, no story in the traditional sense at all?

What if instead of a "real" story we are given short glimpses of actions only, suggested atmosphere in the place of any progressive plotting; thoughts, moments instead of related events?

Where otherwise the "right" choice of images might be primarily suggested by their function for a narrative purpose new criteria need to be defined, if such is lacking. I argue that animation is particularly well-equipped as a medium to also convincingly adapt this type of more abstract storytelling that does not engage with plot primarily or at all.

Suggested Narratives: Between Concreteness and Abstraction

Entering the following discussion, it is important to clarify the subject of investigation first. We are now looking at an approach in poetry that still can be considered representational. Atmospheres, events, actions and places are described that related to concrete imagery. Only a conventional act-structure in the sense of a linear narrative is not given anymore. This is different from completely abstract poetry where the words would not carry concrete meaning and do away with any representation of "reality." Still these "suggested narrative(s)" negotiated here can arguably be seen as an interesting transitionary stage or connective tissue between more conventional narratives and complete abstraction.

Tan Wei Keong: *The Great Escape* (2015)

An excellent example for this approach is the poem *The Great Escape* (2012) by Alfian Sa'at (from the book *The Invisible Manuscript*) and its subsequent adaptation by independent Singaporean animation director Tan Wei Keong in 2015. The film was created as part of *UTTER 2015: Head Trips*, a series of five animated adaptations of written literature by contemporary Singaporean writers. The high quality of the film has been acknowledged by peer review, for example, its selection for official competition in the world's highest-ranking independent festival of animated film in Annecy (2016).

Figure 7.35: *The Great Escape* (2015) film still.

Alfian Sa'at's first unpublished collection of writings was composed when he was 22. It was first distributed unofficially to selected friends and colleagues. Bearing passionate testimony to private and public memories, this gathering of poems and prose fragments documenting the intimate challenges of Alfian longing to give voice to an invisible minority still struggling to be recognized today. *The Great Escape* is a tale about leaving the others behind.

The website of the Singaporean theatre company *Wild Rice* (n.d.) says about Sa'at: "Born in 1977, Alfian Bin Sa'at is currently a Resident Playwright with W!LD RICE (...)

Alfian has been nominated eight times for Best Script at the Life! Theatre Awards, eventually winning for *Landmark, Nadirah* and *Your Sister's Husband.* He has also won the Boh Cameronian for Best Original Script for *Parah* and Best Original Book or Lyrics for *The Secret Life of Nora*. He has also been nominated for the Kirayama Asia-Pacific Book Prize and the Singapore Literature Prize for *A History of Amnesia*.

In 2001, Alfian won the Golden Point Award for Poetry as well as the National Arts Council Young Artist Award for Literature. His plays have been translated into German, Swedish and Danish and have been read and performed in Singapore, Kuala Lumpur, London, Zürich, Hamburg, Munich, Berlin,

Figure 7.36: Tan Wei Keong, director of the film.

Copenhagen, Stockholm, Melbourne, Sydney and Brisbane."

The independent film director Tan Wei Keong holds a Bachelor of Fine Arts in Digital Animation from Nanyang Technological University, Singapore, from which he graduated in 2009. His animated short films *White* and *Hush Baby* received the Special Achievement and Special Mention awards, respectively, at the Singapore International Film Festival in 2007 and 2009, respectively. After graduation, he remained active and prolific as an independent animation director. He created *Pisfuskin* in 2013 that went on to be selected for official competition at the International Festival of Animation in Annecy 2014.

The Great Escape

By Alfian Sa'at

We will wake at dawn. You will fumble
for the car keys under your pillow.

The engine quivering: another kind of
  dawn.
I wind down the windows and a breeze

steals in to unfasten our smiles.
Each traffic light stands ceremonial.

Each blush of green approves of us
stealing away like this, with suitcases,

and enough memories to stay awake in
  motels
while I watch you sleeping on your side

and vice-versa. The radio plays our songs.
We only know the words to the choruses

but that is enough for now. My elbow
leans out from the window-edge

and picks up fresh gossip from the wind.
A secret dialogue, punctuated with caresses.

In the rear-view mirror our eyes search
  each other.
Who will we blame on the day we awake

to discover we had left something behind?
Who will we blame for what sneaked in

behind us in the car, that never aged,
to remind us of the time when we were
  young

and believed that love was a hermit whose
  cottage
we would find at the absolute end of the road,

at the end of the world where that
  question will sting
our severed lips: I am here now. Where are
  you?

Figure 7.37: Film still from Tan Wei Keong's adaptation of the poem "The Great Escape" (2015).

The approach to storytelling in the poem might be described as impressionistic. Describing a series of moments, connecting them to the idea of a voyage and then finally resulting in a question that chose a bigger framework of meaning.

The poem clearly talks about a sense of place, an idea of traveling and a relationship as well. Yet it stays open enough in the description to imply a variety of meanings or readings. Words and meanings are also connected in unexpected ways, for example, picturing love as a "hermit whose cottage we would find at the absolute end of the road."

How can an audiovisual adaptation do justice to this language of fleeting glances and enigmatic suggestions? There is obviously a need to find an equivalent to suggest an equally impressionistic narrative strategy through images and sounds.

I interviewed the director of *The Great Escape* to find answers to this and understand his specific adaptation strategy. We started our conversation, though, with a deeper look into the evolution of the project as a whole.

Interview with Tan Kei Keong

The Great Escape

Hannes Rall (interviewer)
Tan Wei Keong (interviewed)

Your animated short film *The Great Escape* is part of the bigger initiative "UTTER"—a creative endeavor by Singapore Writers Festival—in 2015, commissioning five animated adaptations of literary works. Can you start by telling us how you ended up being considered for this initiative?

David Lee and Eternality Tan (E.T.), producers of *The Great Escape,* had a list of directors they would like to approach when they were shaping up the proposal in 2014. I was invited to attend the screening of UTTER 2014, which exhibited the adaptations to live-action films. After that, we discussed potential ideas and a timeline, which remained open until the proposal was approved and supported by the National Arts Council, which came later in the year.

Was there any suggestion how your specific adaptation would have to fit into the bigger framework, or was the focus primarily on the selected artists—giving them "carte blanche" what to adapt? One could imagine that a balance between more concrete, plot-driven narratives and more experimental approaches might have been considered.

I was able to translate most of my personal ideas onto the film; David and E.T. gave full creative control to the artists. The only request they had was to include a cat character in the film, a motif that ties the film works together under the theme *Head Trips* and, of course, a reference to the mind-boggling conversations the Cheshire Cat had with Alice from *Alice's Adventures in Wonderland*. When edits of the five films started coming in, both producers mentioned that it is rather entertaining how the distinct style and direction of each artist complement each other, which made the program a balanced one.

Figure 7.38: The anthology poster and two other examples of films commissioned for the *Head Trips* series of animated adaptations: *The Fat Cat Ate Dadadaptat* (2015), directed by Darran Kuah, and *5 Shades of Solitude* (2015), directed by Ang Qing Sheng.

The Great Escape is inspired by the poem of the same title by Alfian Sa'at. I believe you use the term "inspired by" deliberately instead of "adapted from." I am very interested in this approach as opposed to a straightforward adaptation in the more traditional sense. Can you elaborate on that and also tell us what attracted you to the poem as a source of inspiration in the first place.

Alfian is a well-respected and prolific author and playwright in Singapore, and his works travel internationally. His works cover minority concerns, like Malays in the Chinese-majority Singapore and homosexuals. I began reading works by gay writers in Singapore after the initial meeting with the producers. My primary idea was to shape a story on two characters in a daily routine, something that everyone does in a normal relationship, straight or gay. The first thing I noticed in Alfian's poem is his sensitivity in his words and how his words created a world for the characters I have in mind. It also reminds me very much of Shimoda, a place in Japan where my husband and I spend our time together. *The Great Escape* is eventually shot in Shimoda, with its landscapes serving as a backdrop for the film.

Figure 7.39: Film still from *The Great Escape* showing the importance of the landscape for the film.

Did you actually communicate with the writer of the original poem about your approach to adaptation? Did he comment on the final outcome?

Alfian and I met only once before production, and I shared with him a vague outline of what I had in mind, something that was quite close to the finished film. That outline is obviously a huge jump from the original text of the poem, and Alfian was very open to how I interpreted his poem and my direction in this adaptation. What's interesting is that he mentioned that there is no point in a direct translation from the text to a film, because why would the audience want to experience the same thing twice? By being more free with the interpretation, the audience is able to have different experiences. After he heard my outline, he said that he viewed my adaptation as basically a continuation of his text—picking up where it ended. I thought that was a very perceptive observation.

What would you say is the more universal topic that the original poem and your film have in common?

The human relationship.

Am I right to assume that your film is more about creating an atmosphere than communicating a concrete plot? And would you agree that the choice of landscape and environment was essential for your film? I find the strange beauty on display quite mesmerizing and a big contributor to the artistic success.

How are the narrative content and the visual style connected in your film?

Yes, it is more of an atmosphere or mood that my film gives to the audience than what the characters are actually doing, which are mostly daily tasks like gardening and cooking. It was a conscious decision to include many shots of nature, like forests and the ocean, and to remove everything else, except the two characters in this paradise-like sanctuary, where they can get away from distractions and judgments. Even the characters are reduced to gender-neutral, plain grayscale characters, to balance the complexity of the relationship between man and nature.

Why did you end up choosing a multimedia approach, which mixes live-action plates with 2D animation and includes several other techniques, for example, time-lapse shooting?

I am always fascinated by a multimedia approach, because different techniques satisfy my various intentions and directions I have for my work. Photography is a direct way of capturing real life, and I feel my imagination stems from manipulating these ready images. By putting 2D animation with photographs onto a single image, I hope that I create a curious interest in the eyes of the audience, who recognize or acknowledge each of the individual elements but may have never seen them pieced together this way before. The passing of time between the two characters is an idea that is best conveyed through time lapse. And both frame-by-frame and time-lapse techniques share the same concept of creating drawings to depict an illusion of movement and choosing specific images to imply the passing of time. Sometimes, I think nature is beautiful enough in photographs, so I don't feel the need to create matte paintings for environments, and I choose to use time lapse instead.

In general, the integration of real-life photographs (live-action plates in time lapse—if you will) and the 2D characters is extremely well done. What were technical considerations to achieve such a seamless integration?

I think it wasn't too difficult to place the 2D characters onto the real-life photographs, as long as the photographs were taken with the characters in mind—as in the composition, the range of movement by the 2D characters, etc. After getting the time lapse of the photographs, I usually record references of myself within the frame, so that it's easier to animate later. A stable tripod is necessary for outdoor shooting too.

Figure 7.40: A still from the film that demonstrates the convincing and aesthetically appealing way of integrating 2D-drawn-characters into real life environments.

The visual style for some specific shots is even more unique and interesting, particularly in the scenes where you seem to be integrating real-life photographs of yourself with graphic textures. Can you give us a more detailed technical run-down of the process here—if you don't mind sharing some of your secrets?

There isn't much secret except, perhaps, patience. The process is tedious. In the shot of the minuscule man rolling the olive, I built a giant olive, almost 2 × 2 meters, using umbrellas, as a prop I could act with in front of the camera, which was placed frontally straight, very much like how the audience watches a theatrical stage. For the shot where the man was born from the olive, his movement is much more fluid and requires the limbs to be in mid-air at times. Therefore, the camera was angled from the ceiling, down at the floor. The poses were then recorded with me on the floor. These images were later digitally manipulated, printed out, colored, and scanned back in, to achieve the analogue style.

Often overlooked in discussions, but nonetheless extremely important is the role of sound. I dare say, it contributes majorly to the artistic success of your film. Who has created the soundscape for your film, and how did you go about it conceptually?

Darren Ng is such a delight to work with. He is a talented artist who is intuitive to music and sound. After completing the first edit of the film, I passed it on to Darren with the following notes.

> "His poem tells the relationship of two characters in an impossible relationship and the author questions his uncertain future. Alfian did say he wrote it before his first love relationship, and his text, ever so gentle, hints at a hopeless, distant future."

Figure 7.41: The highly sophisticated combination of various live action and animation filmmaking techniques becomes evident in this image from the finished film. Processed live action footage of the director himself is rescanned and painted over to achieve the final look. This approach was necessary to arrive at the surreal, dreamlike atmoshere the director wanted to suggest in his film.

> "I would like to think that there is a future for impossible relationships, for I have met one. The animation continues from where Alfian left off in his text: The two characters live in, or escaped to, a space of promising nature; where time suspends and moves organically; where judgements don't matter."

Here's what Darren said after he created the music and sound,

> "There is a sense of nothingness and helplessness to it that resonated within me when I watched it. There is also a certain quiet grandeur, suggesting something larger than life, bigger than us, that is not within our control, yet we always believe it is. We keep living in commas and semicolons, as we destine ourselves to be locked down in time, in a certain pocket of time, while the world, seemingly static, moves on in a time invisible to us….
>
> How do I design or suggest this emptiness/nothingness? There is also this world that is omnipresent (inside or outside) that embraces the self-fulfilling tragedy. And the sense of helplessness. My idea as of now is to create an immersive design of a world (as suggested by your scenics)... of a room, of a world that exist outside the room perpetually, and when they are outside, the world will 'embrace'

them, embrace us; as we become microscopic. Hyper-realistic perhaps. It's more real than perceived. The sounds of movement and activities will happen naturalistically—stark and clean—realistic when they are outdoors, intimate when they are indoors. The design will be binaural to aid perceptions. When it comes to the olive man, it will be more pronounced and in-your-head by using the contact mic method. This gives a sense of 'being' for the audience as they experience and become the olive man when those scenes happen, while they become observers when it is about the other two characters."

Let's now open up to a broader look on adaptations of poems for animated short films. What is your take on their specific suitability for animation or experimental animation?

Poems are very open-ended and allow varying interpretations and understandings by readers. They also use a sparse structure to convey vivid imagery and moods. Therefore, I find poems very suitable for experimental animation, especially animation that does not rely on significant dialogue.

Looking forward: Can you imagine returning to adaptation as a narrative strategy in the future? Where do you see the specific appeal in doing that, and what are the challenges you are being faced with as an artist?

Definitely. A good story begins as words most of the time, and a good director can't always be a good writer.

And finally, what do you believe can go wrong when adapting poetry for animation? Any obvious artistic pitfalls you can advise to stay clear of?

It is challenging for me to adapt a work that I do not exceptionally like or have trouble agreeing with, so I think it is important to start with a work, be it poetry or a short story, that excites or brings you new ideas and realizations. It's also not advisable to go into adaptations simply because an opportunity comes along. Sit with an idea and the original text for a while, let it simmer and grow, and see if it becomes a part of you. Otherwise, put it aside, move on, or come back to it later.

Tan introduces some interesting points here in terms of fidelity toward the literary source: He does not really see the point of any (too) literal adaptation as he asks provocatively "why would the audience want to experience the same thing twice." His decision-making in his adaptation also reiterates an argument that we have encountered previously: To honor the original author by actually being similarly inventive and original in the adaptation as Sa'at has been in his poem. The FBW review of Anna Kalus-Goessner's adaptation *Seemannstreue* had acknowledged a similar approach earlier in this chapter.

Being more free in the interpretation allows the audience to read different meanings into the animated adaptation, once again entirely in line with what the underlying source material achieves as a written piece.

In that sense, a less-plot-driven literary piece can also prove ultimately liberating for the adapter.

A concrete linear narrative, a narrowly defined plot, or even final twist creates certain expectations toward an animated adaptation. If these are not fulfilled entirely or at all, there is a high probability that the spectator (who knows the literary source) will be disappointed.

A more abstract poem will not create any of those expectations in the first place, because of its inherent ambiguity. There is much less of a "wrong" or "right" understanding of the story.

An adaptation of such material, therefore, can explore many different artistic pathways expanding on and improvising on the basis of the written foundation.

Consequently, the final step in this investigation is a closer look on the form of poetry (and its animated adaptation) that relinquishes any form of narrative entirely: Meaning is replaced by sound and rhythm.

Abstract and Experimental Poetry Adaptation

Abstract poetry is the term for a poetic movement, as coined by English poet Dame Edith Sitwell (1887–1964) in her book *Façade*. "The poems in *Façade* are abstract poems–that is, they are patterns of sound. They are...virtuoso exercises in technique of extreme difficulty, in the same sense as that in which certain studies by Liszt are studies in transcendental technique in music." (Sitwell, 1949)

McCaffery (1978) further observes that "in a period roughly stretching from 1875 to 1928, sound poetry's second phase had manifested itself in several diverse and revolutionary investigations into language's non-semantic, acoustic properties. In the work of the Russian Futurists Khlebnikov and Kruchenykh, the intermedia activities of Kandinsky the bruitist poems of the Dadaists (Ball, Schwitters, Arp, Hausmann, Tzara) and the 'paroles in liberta' of the Italian Futurist Marinetti, the phonernatic aspect of language became finally isolated and explored for its own sake. Prior to this there had been isolated pioneering attempts by several writers including Christian Morgenstern (ca. 1875), Lewis Carroll ('Jabberwocky'), August Stramm (ca. 1912), Petrus Borel (ca. 1820), Moliere, the Silesian mystic Quirinus Khulman (17th century), Rabelais and Aristophanes."

This non-narrative content of abstract and experimental poems can resonate perfectly with the abstract and nonlinear approach of experimental animation artists. Vice versa, the "unique aspects of the distinctive vocabulary of animation" (Wells 2002) are an ideal match to express abstract wordplay visually—to be more precise, the unlimited possibilities of animation to create exciting images and juxtapose them in a similar way as poetry combines words.

Poetry often prioritizes rhythmic composition and wordplay over a structure that answers to the demands of a concrete storyline.

Does that, therefore, mean that the adaptation of abstract or experimental poetry completely liberates the animation director from establishing any direct correspondence with the adapted poem, in essence, going one step forward from the previously described approach of vaguely inspired interpretation with Tan Wei Keong's *The Great Escape*?

In my opinion, the opposite is the case: *The Great Escape* is a very loose interrelation of the original poem by Alfian Sa'at. In musical terms, it could be likened to an improvisation over a known melody, with the melody itself still recognizable. This motif provides a loose structure and therefore is considered appealing by an audience.

In the case of *The Great Escape*, the reader would recognize the quotes from the poem, while the non-reader would respond positively to the thematic thread and connective tissue provided by it for the film. The spectator has something to relate.

Abstract poetry, in contrary, relies on the attraction of rhythmic patterns and the sound of the words entirely. There is no meaning per se or ever so vague storyline that allows the audience to empathize with. There is nothing to be recognized anymore if the adaptation gives up the connection with the source material! The adapted animation, therefore, needs to correspond with the appeal of the poem through rhythm and sound(s) in my opinion. In completely abstract animation, there is little else that can create an empathy with the audience, keep it "hooked."

In other words, if the animation is perfectly in sync with the rhythmic structure of a (recited) version of an experimental poem, the result will likely be recognized as appealing.
This can be further improved by creating visual equivalents for the phonetic language of the poem. In very simple terms, a word or sound in the poem could be recited loudly and then paired with a big shape. Certain words or phonetics in the poem could be paired with specific colors and so on.

As with experimental animation in general, it is important to provide structure, which can be entirely non-narrative but allows the audience a sense of orientation. This is evident in many pieces of the most outstanding experimental animation of artists like Oskar Fischinger (*Allegretto* 1936) and James Whitney (*Yantra* 1957) or their modern counterpart Michel Gagne in his Academy Award—shortlisted film *Sensology* (2010). These are not adaptations but examples for avant-garde animation that employ structure for their artistic success.

A concrete example will explain this further. First, I will talk about one of the classics to demonstrate significant characteristics of abstract poetry. I will then continue to devise strategies for adapting abstract poetry for animation.

Zang Tumb Tumb (usually referred to as *Zang Tumb Tuuum*) is a sound poem and concrete poem written by Filippo Tommaso Marinetti, an Italian futurist. It appeared in excerpts in journals between 1912 and 1914, when it was published as an artist's book in Milan. It is an account of the Battle of Adrianople, which he witnessed as a reporter for L'Intransigeant. The poem uses Parole in libertà (words in freedom)—creative typography— and other poetic impressions of the events of the battle, including the sounds of gunfire and explosions. The work is now seen as a seminal work of modernist art and an enormous influence on the emerging culture of European avant-garde print.

> "[The] masterpiece of Words-in-freedom and of Marinetti's literary career was the novel 'Zang Tumb Tuuum'... the story of the siege by the Bulgarians of Turkish Adrianople in the Balkan War, which Marinetti had witnessed as a war reporter. The dynamic rhythms and onomatopoetic possibilities that the new form offered were made even more effective through the revolutionary use of different typefaces, forms and graphic arrangements and sizes that became a distinctive part of Futurism. In 'Zang Tumb Tuuum;' they are used to express an extraordinary range of different moods and speeds, quite apart from the noise and chaos of battle.... Audiences in London, Berlin and Rome alike were bowled over by the tongue-twisting vitality with which Marinetti declaimed 'Zang Tumb Tuuum.' As an extended sound poem it stands as one of the monuments of experimental literature, its telegraphic barrage of nouns, colours, exclamations and directions pouring out in the screeching of trains, the rat-a-tat-tat of gunfire, and the clatter of telegraphic messages" (Tisdall, Bozzola 1977, 95–99).

Excerpt from the poem:

> 1 2 3 4 5 seconds siege guns split the silence
> in unison tam-tuuumb sudden echoes all
> the echoes seize it quick smash it scatter it
> to the infinite winds to the devil
>
> "In the middle these tam-tuuumb flattened
> 50 square kilometers leap 2-6-8 crashes clubs
> punches bashes quick-firing batteries. Violence
> ferocity regularity pendulum play fatality"
>
> ...these weights thicknesses sounds
> smells molecular whirlwinds chains nets
> and channels of analogies concurrences
> and synchronisms for my Futurist friends
> poets painters and musicians zang-tumb-
> tumb-zang-zang-tuuumb tatatatatatatata
> picpacpampacpacpicpampampac
> uuuuuuuuuuuuuuu
>
> ZANG-TUMB
> TUMB-TUMB
> TUUUUUM.

As there is no tangible storyline provided, there is not much to work with for the animator, or is there? While, indeed, a more conventional visual storyteller might get lost, this abstract proposal of rhythm and sound can provide a real treasure trove for the more experimentally oriented animator.

Strategies for Adapting Non-Narrative Poetry for Animation

Rhythm is also an element central to animation. Animation can excel at offering imaginative visualization(s) over a defined period of time.

Any adaptation of this type of poetry will largely have to succeed on two accounts: For one, the syncing of sounds (as implied by the language), and second, the aesthetic quality of the chosen means of visualization.

Within the time of delivery, a structured approach to timing is paramount to achieve good animation. This includes contrast in timing: slow versus fast, abrupt change versus uninterrupted flow of images, repetitive versus diverse, and monotonous versus varied. The poetic source material, that is, the lyrics, can already propose such a structure to the animator, who is able to transform the written concepts into time-based visuals.

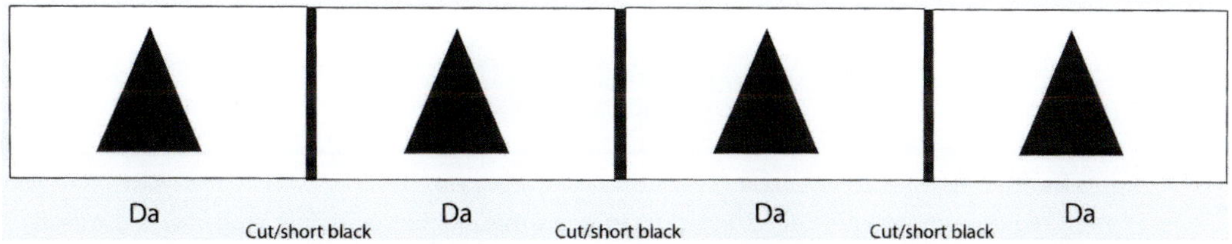

Figure 7.42: A very simple example: The written words (or phonetics) "da-da-da-da" might inspire the animator to match the repetitive structure of the words with exactly the same image repeated four times.

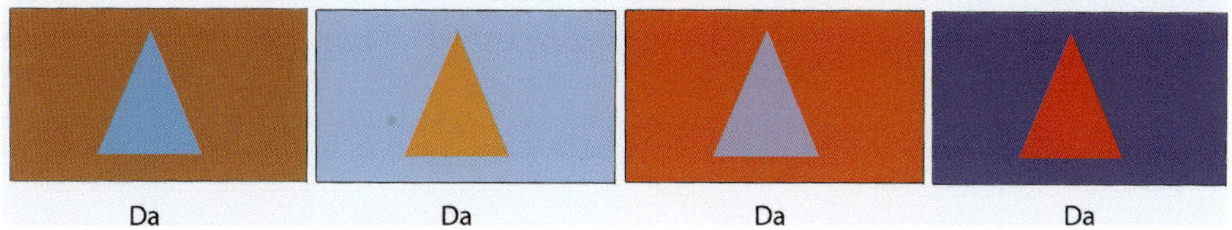

Figure 7.43: One could also add variations in color.

Figure 7.44: Or invert images, but essentially keep the same visual content.

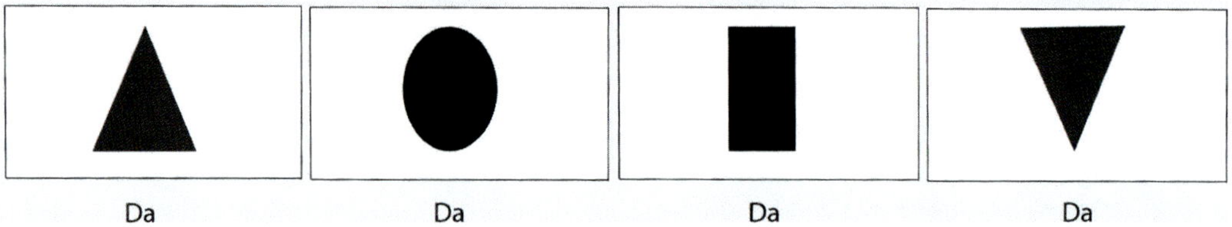

Figure 7.45: Alternatively, quite on the contrary, the animation artist could decide to combine the repetition of the same word with a new image for each new "da" accent.

In all cases, the "da-da-da-da" lyrics can offer a potential rhythmic structure for the timing, which can be answered to in various ways.

Figure 7.46: It is equally possible that a director decides to ignore that proposed structure altogether and instead prefers to hold one single image unchanged over the whole course of "da-da-da-da."

Whatever decision is made, it needs to be literally seen in the "bigger picture," that is, how it plays out in the framework of the movie as a whole.

Contrast is the keyword here. Unless a director deliberately intends to keep the audience in a monotonous lull, variety in timing is of the essence.

To continue from our previous example, we will assume that our imaginary poem will follow the initial "da-da-da-da" with a long "daaaaaaaaaaaaaaaaaa." This being the case, a strong proposal for a potential rhythmic structure is at hand for an animated adaptation.

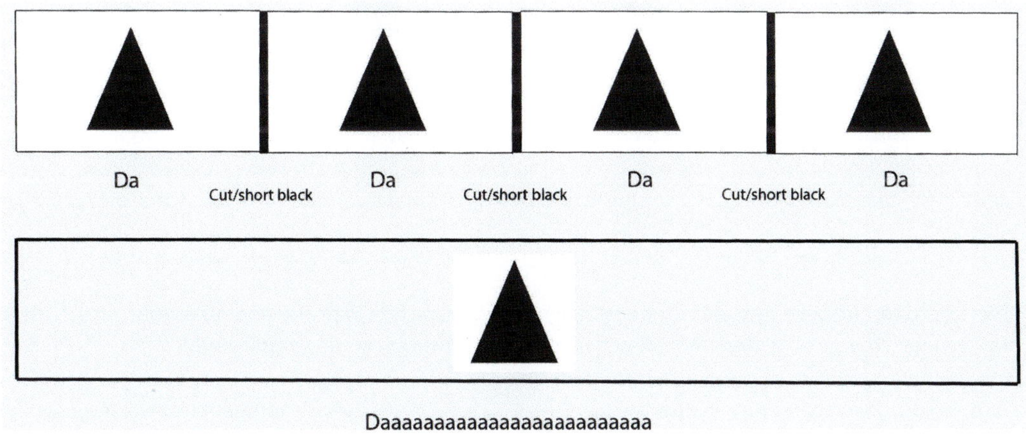

Figure 7.47: Let's now combine this with our first visual examples.

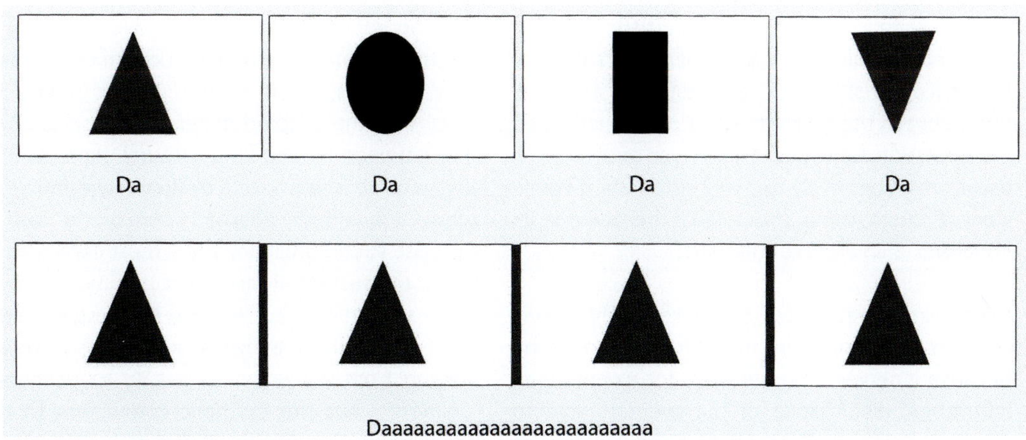

Figure 7.48: Or on the reverse.

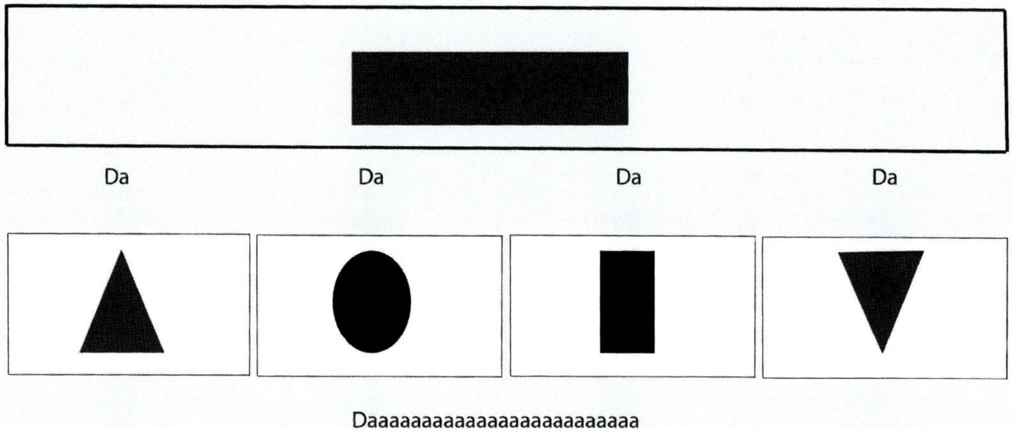

Figure 7.49: When seen in the context of the move as a bigger whole, even the example from Fig. 7.45 might work, assuming that, in further course, visual (and rhythmic) contrast will be provided by answering the words on offer in a similarly contradictory way. (by combining the long "daaaaaaaaaaaaaaaaaa" now with a varied sequence of images).

This approach, however, would not necessarily be an obvious choice, as it does not directly reflect the rhythmic structure of the poem through a corresponding timing structure in the animation—it would instead contradict it.

If not used by an extremely well-versed and experienced filmmaker with a strong artistic vision, it might easily look like a typical beginner's mistake (which it often is). It would fail to establish a connection between the source material and its animated interpretation. Generally speaking, an audience will usually react positively to a well-established equivalent of the rhythmic structure of the poem in its visualized (animated) counterpart.

Given an experienced filmmaker deliberately chooses to ignore this approach, it would be because it serves a bigger idea, for example, an intentional disturbance of the spectatorship to create a mood of discomfort. If the creation of such a mood would be in line with the original artistic intent of the poem's author, an artistic justification can be established.

It becomes quickly apparent from all the previously shown examples that there is a wide variety of approaches possible to answer to the written structure of an abstract poem through sequential visualization. All of these examples have one thing in common, though, and that is crucial to understand: They all correspond in synchronicity (if in different ways) with the adapted material. A close relationship between writing (and its aural expression) is always established! Such a deliberately established connection with the adapted poem on the basis of a precise sound breakdown will most likely lead to artistically successful results—if the imagery in itself is aesthetically convincing. The aesthetic concepts used in this framework can be highly diverse, ranging from conventional beauty to deliberate "ugliness"—but the rhythmic connection to the poem remains essential.

This form of animated adaptation of poetry is closely related to the concept of visual music (Moritz 1986) that encompasses the visualization of music and sound through the moving (and mostly animated) images. In some cases, there are clear overlaps between this field and the adaptation of experimental or more abstract poetry—a dividing line is hard to define at times. After examining the wide artistic variety poetry can offer to animation, the next chapter will take us further into modernity: It talks about the adaptation of contemporary literature.

Bibliography

Anderson, David Alan. 2008. *Tongue of the Hidden*. Animated short film. UK/Iran.

Algar, James, dir. 1940. *The Sorcerer's Apprentice*. Animated short film segment in *Fantasia*, animated feature film (anthology). Burbank, CA: Walt Disney Productions.

Autour de Minuit, prod. 2014. *En sortant de l'école-PREVERT*. Animated short film series, 2012.
Film list: *Les Oiseaux du souci* – Marie Larrivé, Camille Authouart (ENSAD), *En sortant de l'école* – Lila Peuscet (EMCA), *Tant de forêts* – Burcu Sankur, Geoffrey Godet (Supinfocom Valenciennes), *Les Belles familles* – Armelle Renac (Supinfocom Valenciennes), *Âne dormant* – Caroline Lefevre (EMCA), *Je suis comme je suis* – Marion Auvin (EMCA), *Page d'écriture* – Marion Lacourt (ENSAD), *Le Cancre* – Chenghua Yang (EMCA), *Le Gardien du phare aime trop les oiseaux* – Clément de Ruyter (GOBELINS), *Le Dromadaire mécontent* – Morgane Le Péchon (La Poudrière), L'Ecole des beaux arts – Anne Huynh (Ste Geneviève), *Quartier libre* – Marine Blin (La Poudrière), *Presque* – Mélia Gilson (LISAA).

Axén, Annelie. 2005. *Langz*. Bergen, Norway: Gasspedal.

Barbera, Joseph, and William Hanna, dir. 1941. *The Night Before Christmas*. Animated short film. Los Angeles, CA: Metro-Goldwyn-Mayer.

Baudelaire, Charles. 1857. *Les Fleurs du Mal*. Paris, France: Auguste Poulet-Malassis.

Blake, William. 1794. *The Tyger*. In *Songs of Experience*. London, UK: William Blake. Accessed July 22, 2016. http://www.blakearchive.org/exist/blake/archive/copyinfo.xq?copyid=songsie.c.

Bódy, Gábor, dir. 1985. *Novalis: Walzer*. Experimental video clip.

Bormann, Alexander von. 1996. *Erlkönig*. In: *Goethe Handbuch. Bd. 1: Gedichte*, edited by Regine Otto and Bernd Witte, 212–217. Stuttgart, Weimar, Germany: J.B. Metzler.

Bowring, Edgar Alfred. 1853. The Erl-King (translated from original poem by Johann Wolfgang von Goethe). In: *The Poems of Goethe*. London, UK: Clarke and Co.

Buñuel, Luis. 1960. *A Statement*. In *Film Culture*, No. 21, 41–42. New York: Film Culture.

Chiesa, Elena. n.d. *Elena Chiesa*. Accessed July 22, 2016. http://www.elenachiesa.it.

Chiesa, Elena, dir. 2008. *Polifemi*. Animated short film.

Chin, Staceyann. 2010a. *Crossfire*. New York: Alyson Books.

Chin, Staceyann. 2010b. *Jazz*. Polari Journal, 1. Accessed July 22, 2016. www.polarijournal.com/resources/Chin-Elsewhere_Trini_Jazz.pdf.

Curtiz, Michael, aka Kertesz, Mihály, dir. 1919. *Jön Az Öcsem (My Brother Is Coming)*. Silent short film (live action).

Darwish, Mahmoud. 2008. *La Eb Al-Nard*. London, UK: Al-Quds Al-Arabi.

Dekeukelaire, Charles, dir. 1927. *Combat de boxe*. Experimental short film.

Dencker, Klaus Peter, dir. 1971. *astronaut (Deutscher Film mit Untertiteln)*. Experimental short film. Baden-Baden, Germany: SWF (TV) production.

Dencker, Klaus Peter, dir. 1971. *Rausch (Buchstabiertafel mit anschließender Diskussion)*. Experimental short film. Baden-Baden, Germany: SWF (TV, production).

Dencker, Klaus Peter, dir. 1971. *Starfighter (Geschichte eines Fronteinsatzes)*. Experimental short film. Baden-Baden, Germany: SWF (TV, production).

Demuynck, Arnaud, and Rémi Durin, dirs. 2014. *Le Parfum De La Carotte*. Animated short film.

Deren, Maya, dir. 1943. *Meshes of the Afternoon*. Experimental short film.

Desmos, Robert. 1928. *La Place de l'Etoile*.

Dickinson, Emily. 1929. *If I can stop one heart from breaking*. In *Further Poems of Emily Dickinson*., edited by by Martha Dickinson Bianchi and Alfred Leete Hampson. Boston, MA: Little, Brown and Company Boston.

Disney, Walt, prod. 1929–1939. *Silly Symphonies*. Animated short film series. Burbank, CA: Walt Disney Productions.

Droste-Hülshoff, Annette von. 1844. *Loup Garou*. In *Letzte Gaben*. Vaduz, Liechtenstein: Liechtensteinverlag.

Dulac, Germaine, dir. 1927. *L'Invitation au Voyage*. Silent drama film.

Eesti Joonisfilm Studio, prod. 2007. *Must Lagi (Black Ceiling)*. Animated short film series.

Film-und Medienbewertung Wiesbaden. 2003. Jury commentary (translated from German) on rewarding *Der Erlkönig* the "Seal of Approval: Highly Recommended." Accessed September 11, 2015. http://www.fbw-filmbewertung.com/film/der_erlkoenig.

Film-und Medienbewertung Wiesbaden. 2008. Jury commentary (translated from German) on rewarding *Seemannstreue* the "Seal of Approval: Highly Recommended." Accessed July 11, 2016. http://www.fbw-filmbewertung.com/film/seemannstreue.

Fischinger, Oskar. 1936. *Allegretto*. Animated short film.

Gagné, Michel. 2010. *Sensology*. Animated short film.

Goethe, Johann Wolfgang von. 1797. *The Sorcerer's Apprentice*. In *Musen-Almanach für das Jahr 1798*, edited by Friedrich Schiller, 32–37. Tübingen, Germany: J.G. Cottaische Buchhandlung.

Griffith, D.W, dir. 1910. *The Unchanging Sea*. Silent short film (live action).

Hafez. 2006. *The Peacock and the Fish*. In *Ten Poems by Hafez*, edited by Jila Peacock. London, UK: Sylph Editions.

Hagerup, Simon. 2009. *De Døde Står Opp For Å Fortære De Levende*.

Halliwell, Stephen, and Aristotle. 1998. *Aristotle's Poetics*. Chicago, IL: University of Chicago Press.

Henze, Martin, and Robert Pohle, dirs. 2008. *Der Conny Ihr Pony*. Animated short film.

Hemmingway, David, and Nirid Pelet, dirs. 2007. *Poetry in Motion: Jazz. Crossfire. Frenzied Days*. Trilogy of animated short films.

Hess, Gary R. n.d. *History of Poetry*. Poem of Quotes. Website. Accessed September 27, 2015. http://www.poemofquotes.com/articles/history-of-poetry.php.

Hofmann, Joachim. 2010. *Augustins* Miniaturen. DVD. Bremen, Germany: Hochschule für Künste Bremen (production). Bremen, Germany: Edition Temmen (distribution).

Jackson, Wilfred, dir. 1933. *The Night Before Christmas*. Animated short film. Part of animated short film series *Silly Symphonies*. Burbank, CA: Walt Disney Productions.

Jandl, Ernst. 1966. *Bestiarium*. In *Laut und Luise*, 154–159. Olten und Freiburg im Breisgau: Walter-Druck.

Kalus-Goessner, Anna, dir. 2008. *Seemansstreue*. Animated short film.

Kencana, Rain, Miguel Angelo Pate, and Jalaludin Trautman, dirs. 2014. *The Thing With Feathers*. Dance short film (live action).

Klemm, Rudi, and Julius Pinschewer, dirs. 1930. *Chad Gadjo*. Animated short film.

Kuhligk, Björn. 2005. *Die Liebe in Zeiten der EU*. In: *Großes Kino*. Berlin, Germany: Berlin Verlag.

Kuhn, Jochen, dir. 2005–2012. *Sonntag*. Animated short film series.

Kuhn, Jochen, dir. 2005. *Sonntag 1*. Animated short film series.

Kuhn, Jochen, dir. 2010. *Sonntag 2*. Animated short film series.

Kuhn, Jochen, dir. 2012. *Sonntag 3*. Animated short film series.

Leuchtenberg, Stefan, and Martin Wallner, dirs. 2010. *The Lost and Found Box of Human Sensation*. Animated short film.

Lyons, Alice, dir. 2009. *The Polish Language*. Animated short film.

Mali, Taylor. 2005. The Impotence of Proofreading. In *Taylor Mali–A gifted poet*. Accessed July 22, 2016. https://englishwithlinda.wordpress.com/english-is-funny/taylor-mali-a-gifted-poet-the-the-impotence-of-proofreading/.

Mali, Taylor. 2007. *Pizza*. Track 16 on *Icarus Airlines*. CD. New York: Words Worth Ink.

Man Ray, dir. 1928. *L'Etoile de Mer*. Experimental short film.

Marcondes, Guilherme, dir. 2006. *Tyger*. Animated short film.

Marie de france. n.d. (12th century France). *Le Lai de Bisclavret*.

McCaffery, Steve. 1978. *Sound Poetry–A Survey*. In: *Sound Poetry: A Catalogue*, edited by Steve McCaffery and Barrie Phillip Nichol, 6–18. Toronto, Ontario: Underwich Editions.

Mercier, Emilie, dir. 2011. *Bisclavret*. Animated short film.

Mickiewicz, Adam. 1822. *Świteź*. In: *Ballady y Romanse*. Vilnius, Lithuania: Josef Zawadzki.

Miller, Frank. 1991–2000. *Sin City*. Comic series. Milwaukie, OR: Dark Horse Comics.

Moore, Clement Clark. 1822. *A Visit From St. Nicholas*.

Moritz, William. 1986. *Towards an Aesthetics of Visual Music*. ASIFA Canada Bulletin. Accessed July 16, 2016. http://www.centerforvisualmusic.org/TAVM.htm.

Moore, Clement Clarke. 1840. *Twas the Night Before Christmas*. In: *Selections from The American Poets*, edited by William Cullen Bryant, 285–286. New York: Harper & Brothers.

Motionpoems. n.d. *Motionpoems*. Accessed July 22, 2016. http://motionpoems.org.

Nathan, Merav, and Yaval, dirs. 2014. *Robin*. Animated short film, 2014.

Neys, Mark, dir. n.d. *Swoon*. Accessed July 22, 2016. http://www.swoon-videopoetry.com.

Oxford Dictionaries. 2015. *Poetry*, Oxford University Press. Accessed September 27, 2015. http://www.oxforddictionaries.com/definition/english/poetry?q=poetry.

Pedersen, Kristian, dir. 2011. *Kliniken*. Animated short film from the series *Gasspedal Animert*. Bergen, Norway: Gasspedal (production and distribution).

Pedersen, Kristian, dir. 2013. *Bølgeslag*. Animated short film from the series *Gasspedal Animert*. Bergen, Norway: Gasspedal (production and distribution).

Pedersen, Kristian, dir. 2014. *Pipene/The Pipes*. Animated short film from the series *Gasspedal Animert*. Bergen, Norway: Gasspedal (production and distribution).

Pedersen, Kristian, dir. 2012. *Skogen*. Animated short film from the series *Gasspedal Animert*. Bergen, Norway: Gasspedal (production and distribution).

Pedersen, Kristian, dir. 2011. *Viva Zombatista*. Animated short film from the series *Gasspedal Animert*. Bergen, Norway: Gasspedal (production and distribution).

Pedersen, Kristian, dir. 2011. Kliniken. Animated short film from the series *Gasspedal Animert*. Bergen, Norway: Gasspedal (production and distribution).

Pieper, Andreas, dir. 2005. *Die Begegnung*. Live action short film.

Pieterson, Taatske, dir. 2005. *One Person-Lucy*. Experimental short film.

Pignatari, Décio, dir. 1957. *Bebe Coca Cola*. Animated short film.

Poe, Edgar Allan. 2004. *"The Raven."* In: *The Selected Writings of Edgar Allan*. Poe, edited by G. R. Thompson, 57–59. Norton Critical Edition. New York: Norton.

Polak, Kamil, dir. 2010. *The Lost Town Of Świteź*. Animated short film.

Porter, Edwin S., dir. 1905. *The Night Before Christmas*. Thomas Alva Edison (studio).

Pound, Stuart. n.d. *Poetry with* Video. Accessed July 22, 2016. http://www.stuartpound.info/stills.html.

Priestley, Joanna, dir. 2012. *Dear Pluto*. Animated short film. Portland, OR: Priestley Motion Pictures (studio).

Priestley, Joanna, dir. 2009. *Missed Aches*. Animated short film. Portland, OR: Priestley Motion Pictures (studio).

Rall, Hannes, dir. 2013. *Das kalte Herz (The Cold Heart)*. Animated short film.

Rall, Hannes, dir. 2003. *Der Erlkönig* (*The Erl-King*). Animated short film.

Rall, Hannes, dir. 2000. *Der Rabe (The Raven)*. Animated short film.

Reading, Peter. 1983. *Diplopic*. London, UK: Secker & Warburg.

Rexroth, Kenneth. n.d. *Literature*. Accessed March 20, 2019. https://www.britannica.com/art/literature.

Richter, Hans. 1971. *Hans Richter*. London, UK: Thames & Hudson.

Rijken, Arnoud, and Michiel Snijders, prod. 2004b. *Dicht/Vorm Klassiekers*. Animated short film series. Il Luster Productions (production).

Rijken, Arnoud, and Michiel Snijders, prod. 2004b. *Dicht/Vorm Modern*. Animated short film series. Il Luster Productions (production).

Rimbereid, Øyvind. 2013. *Pipene*. In: *Orgelsjøen*. Oslo, Norway: Gyldendal Norsk Forlag.

Ringelnatz, Joachim. 1924. *Seemannstreue*. In: *Kuttel-Daddeldu*, 12–15. München, Germany: Kurt Wolff Verlag.

Roshdy, Nissmah, dir. 2013. *The Dice Player*. Animated short film.

Rozanov, Mysh. 2013. *Imaginary Encounters*. Motion comics/video-clip-series. Accessed July 22, 2016. https://www.indiegogo.com/projects/imaginary-encounters-a-visual-haiku-series#/.

Rühm, Gerhard, dir. 1969. *3 Kinematografische Texte*. Experimental short film sequences.

Sa'at, Alfian. 2012. *The Great Escape*. In: *The Invisible Manuscript*. Singapore: Math Paper Press.

Sandars, Nancy Katharine. 1972. *The Epic of Gilgamesh*. Harmondsworth, UK: Penguin.

Sandig, Ulrike Almut. 2007. *poem [meine heimat]*. In: *BELLA Triste: Zeitschrift für junge Literatur*, edited by Arpana Aischa Berndt, Moritz Heuwinkel, Hannah del Mestre, Mariusz Hoffmann, Luca Lienemann, Romana von Mengershausen und Jana Zimmermann. Issue 17. Hildesheim, Germany: BELLA triste e. V.: 77.

Schmerberg, Ralf, dir. 2003. *Poem*. Live action feature film (anthology). Berlin, Germany: Radical Media, Trigger Happy Productions (production).

Schwarm, Betsy. 2014. *Erlkönig-Song by Schubert*. In: *Encyclopaedia Britannica*. Accessed September 11, 2015. http://global.britannica.com/topic/Erlkonig.

Schwizgebel, Georges. 2015. *Erlkönig*. Animated short film. 6 minutes.

Selick, Henry, dir. 1993. *The Nightmare Before Christmas*. Animated feature film. Los Angeles, CA: Skellington Productions; Burbank, CA: Touchstone Pictures (production).

Sheeler, Charles, and Robert Strand, dirs. 1921. *Manhatta*. Experimental short film.

Sielecki, Hubert, dir. 2007a. *Sehen*. Animated short film.

Sielecki, Hubert, dir. 2007b. *Witz*. Animated short film.

Sitwell, Edith. 1949. *Facade*.

S.O.I.L. (Sight of an Ignored Landscape), prod. 2006. *Dicht/Vorm Vlaanderen*. Animated short film series.

Tan, Wei Keong. 2015. *The Great Escape*. Animated short film. 6 minutes. Singapore.

Tatarkiewicz, Wladyslaw, and Christopher Kasparek. 1975. *The Concept of Poetry*. In: *Dialectics and Humanism* Volume 2, Issue 2, Spring, p. 13.

Tenningen, Sigurd. 2010. *Bokstavene*.

Tisdall, Caroline and Bozzola, Angela. 1977. *Futurism*. London: Thames & Hudson.

Tolås, Elvind, and Ole Mads Velve, dirs. 2003. *Love Is The Law*. Experimental short film. Bergen, Norway: Flimmer Film (production).

Ulven, Tor. 1981. *Where the settlement ends*. In: *Forsvinningspunkt (Vanishing Point)*. Oslo, Norway: Gyldendal Norsk Forlag.

Ulven, Tor. 1981a. *It Requires*. In: *Forsvinningspunkt (Vanishing Point)*. Oslo, Norway: Gyldendal Norsk Forlag.

Ulven, Tor. 1981b. *When Disappearance Shine Brightly Enough*. In: *Forsvinningspunkt* (*Vanishing Point*). Oslo, Norway: Gyldendal Norsk Forlag.

Valie, Export, dir. 1986. *See-Text: Fingerpoem*. Experimental short video.

Viel, Anne, dir. 2014. *La Confiture De Carottes*. Animated short film.

Villanger, Aina. 2012. *langsang – et flytans habitat*. Oslo, Norway: Forlaget Oktober.

Volk, Gordon, dir. 2007. *Loup Garou*. Live action short film.

Wand, Eku, dir. 1989. *Bestiarium*. Animated short film.

Webb, Tim, dir. 1995. *15th February*. Animated short film.

Weibel, Peter, dir. 1975. *Video Texts*. Experimental short video.

Wells, Paul. 2002. *Animation: Genre and Authorship*. New York: Wallflower Press, 32.

White, Eddy, dir. 2006. *Carnivore Reflux*. Animated short film.

White, Eddy, dir. 2009. *The Cat Pian*. Animated short film.

Whitney, James, dir. 1957. *Yantra*. Animated short film.

Wiegner, Susanne, dir. 2010. *Just Midnight*. Animated short film.

Wild Rice. n.d. *Alfian Sa'at Resident Playwright*. Accessed July 16, 2016. http://www.wildrice.com.sg/about/artistic-team/83-resident-playwright.

Wilkinson, Mark, dir. 2011. *Human Condition*. Spoken-word music video.

Zemeckis, Robert, dir. 2007. *Beowulf*. Animated feature film. Los Angeles, CA: Shangri-La Entertainment; Los Angeles, CA: Image Mover (production). Los Angeles, CA: Paramount Pictures (domestic distribution). Burbank, CA: Warner Bros. Pictures (international distribution).

Uncharted Territories

Adapting Contemporary Literature for Animation

The preceding chapters have focused on different genres and angles for adaptation. But they largely had one thing in common: The adapted original texts are mostly in the public domain. That means that no permission to adapt needs to be attained and therefore no financial compensation paid to the author of the respective source material. This offers an easy explanation why the number of public-domain adaptations for animation outnumbers transpositions of contemporary authors by far, particularly in the area of animated shorts, because they are often student films—a segment of authors with extremely limited financial resources. Besides the mere financial constraints, the other factor holding back is the need for an initial contact and ongoing dialogue with a living writer. This adds more steps to the production process that can appear taxing to the adaptation director—student or not.

What is often forgotten in this equation is that there are rich possibilities such collaborations can yield. It might be extremely difficult, if not impossible, to obtain the rights for adaptation from a major best-selling author (although there is no harm in trying).

But there are many excellent contemporary authors of literature that remain comparatively underappreciated or are simply not writing "literary blockbusters." They might be very open to collaboration and welcoming to the idea of having their work adapted for the screen.

Even better, their active input or approval can add authenticity to the adaptation and benefit script development and filmic transformation.

Figure 8.1: Singaporean animators Harry and Henry Zhuang. (Courtesy of website Mothership Singapore, https://mothership.sg.)

Singaporean twin brothers Henry and Harry Zhuang are independent animation directors who have achieved a high level of artistic success in their comparatively young career. This was largely built on their interpretations of pieces by modern writers:

Their animated short film, *The Tiger of 142B* (2015), is an adaptation of contemporary Singaporean author Dave Chua's short story. It plays with the notion of a tiger appearing in modern Singapore, in the middle of a housing estate. One of its major appeals lies within a playful ambiguity that never clarifies if the "tiger" is real or only a figment of the protagonist's imagination. The directors masterfully apply the vocabulary of animation to achieve a dreamlike quality and add a uniquely local touch to the proceedings.

Figure 8.2: A collage of still frames from *The Tiger of 142B*. © Zhuang Bros 2015.

The film traveled to numerous international film festivals such as the Bucheon International Fantastic Film Festival (BiFan) and the prestigious Animafest Zagreb. The same film won "Best Film" in SEAShorts Film and the "Rising Talent" award in Beijing's China Independent Animation Film Forum.

Their latest project *Giant* (2018) is a stop-motion animation piece that is also inspired by the work of a living author: Tan Swie Hian's poem titled "巨人."

Building from these successes, they continue to produce animations that explore creative storytelling in their company Weaving Clouds. Most recently, they are both working as executive producers and creators for *Sticker Together*, a 20 × 5 minutes animation series that will be aired on Okto, a TV channel of Mediacorp Singapore.

It is fair to say that their determination to adapt modern Singaporean authors in highly artistic fashion has ultimately led to a significant success with commissioned work.

Their work on these adaptations can serve as a case study on how such adaptations can be carried out successfully. It will hopefully also inspire many aspiring filmmakers of any generation to further add to this comparatively underused field of animated adaptation.

Interview with Harry and Henry Zhuang

"Be Brave to Make It Your Own and Make It Personal"

Interview conducted at Nanyang Technological University Singapore on June 11, 2018

Hannes Rall (interviewer)
Henry Zhuang (interviewed)
Harry Zhuang (interviewed)

I'm here with Harry and Henry Zhuang to talk a little bit about *The Tiger of 142B*, their 2015 adaptation of the short story by contemporary Singaporean author Dave Chua. Can you start by telling me what sparked this collaboration in the first place?

There is this festival in Singapore called Utter—a fringe festival that is dedicated to adapt Singaporean literature into another form or medium. So, in the past, there was theater, then there was live-action film, and finally, in 2015, it was animation's turn. The festival curators picked a few animation artists to do an adaptation based on Singaporean literature. They gave a list of Singaporean writings, and we had to pick from that list.

Initially, we chose a poem that was written by Haresh Sharma, and we submitted it to the festival, but the curators replied that it was too outdated. They wanted us to choose some piece that was more current. That is when fellow Singaporean independent animator Tan Wei Keong told us about this story about a tiger roaming in the HDB premises *(editor's remark: HDB means Housing Development Board, a form of housing very common in and specific to Singapore. Typically, HDB flats are apartments in high-rise buildings that are subsidized by the government to provide affordable housing for the larger population).*

That concept really attracted us, and we went to a library and started reading, and that's when we decided that this is the story that we wanted to adapt.

Figure 8.3: Typical HDB flats in Jurong West, a neighborhood in Singapore. (Courtesy of I luv erky.)

The film's production was initially completed at the beginning of 2015, but we went on to further change and polish it. The final product was screened in Zagreb in 2015.

That means that you did not know or approach the writer of the story before?

We actually knew Dave Chua already through Animation Nation—a local animation festival, which he organized. We had a few contacts with him. After we graduated, I bumped into him during a book signing session. He asked me how I was doing?. I answered that I was intending to be a teacher, and Harry was planning to become a police officer. Then, Dave actually told us to keep animating and not to give up.

And that was the last time I spoke to him. That was in 2012. The interesting thing is that *The Tiger of 142B* came back to us, and the story was actually about this guy who was struggling between his ideals and what the society expected of him. If you read the story, you find that it is about this guy who is struggling to choose whether to work or to follow his heart. And so, it all came full circle in a way.

Which year was the original story *The Tiger of 142B* written? Dave Chua is a contemporary Singaporean writer, correct?

The story was written in the 1980s. If you read through the story, there were no mobile phones. People were still using pagers and similar devices. I think Dave Chua wrote the story quite some time ago and published it much later.

How did you obtain the rights? Was it already on a proposal list for the Utter initiative, or did you just learn about it from Tan Wei Keong? Did Wei Keong encourage you to ask Dave Chua directly for the rights for adaptation, or how did that work?

Everything was basically done through The Filmic Eye. The Filmic Eye is a company that is in contact with the National Arts Council (NAC) that was funding the initiative. They paid for the extra fee to get the rights.

So, you didn't have to deal with it directly.

No.

For the adaptation process, did you communicate in any kind of way with Dave Chua about your adaptation?

To get the permission to adapt, we only had 1 minute completed. And at that point of time, we had of course read the story, and we were very curious about what the tiger really meant in this story.

From this point on, after this first minute was laid out, Dave Chua gave us the freedom to adapt in any way we wanted. And I think that put us under some pressure, because we were not quite sure if we could deliver to his standard. When we were writing the screenplay, we kept sending him updated versions. He did not voice any concern except for one: He did point out that there was one line from the original text that he thought should be removed for the adaptation, because it would have felt out of place there.

Figure 8.4: Storyboarding and storyboards. © Zhuang Bros 2015.

So, basically, the author himself supported a change toward the original text?

Yes.

Okay, that's interesting. The aspect of fidelity toward the source material forms a big part of the academic discussion on adaptation. Did Dave Chua, in any kind of way, interfere or ask for approval of your visualization—of the characters or the locations in his story?

No. He gave us a lot of freedom. In fact, we changed quite a fair bit of the story. We changed the pivot of the story, I think. And we also removed a lot of the parts that we think were not needed, and then, we also changed the ending of the story.

So, how was the original ending of the story versus your film version?

I remember that the ending was that the police came. They were all finding the tiger.

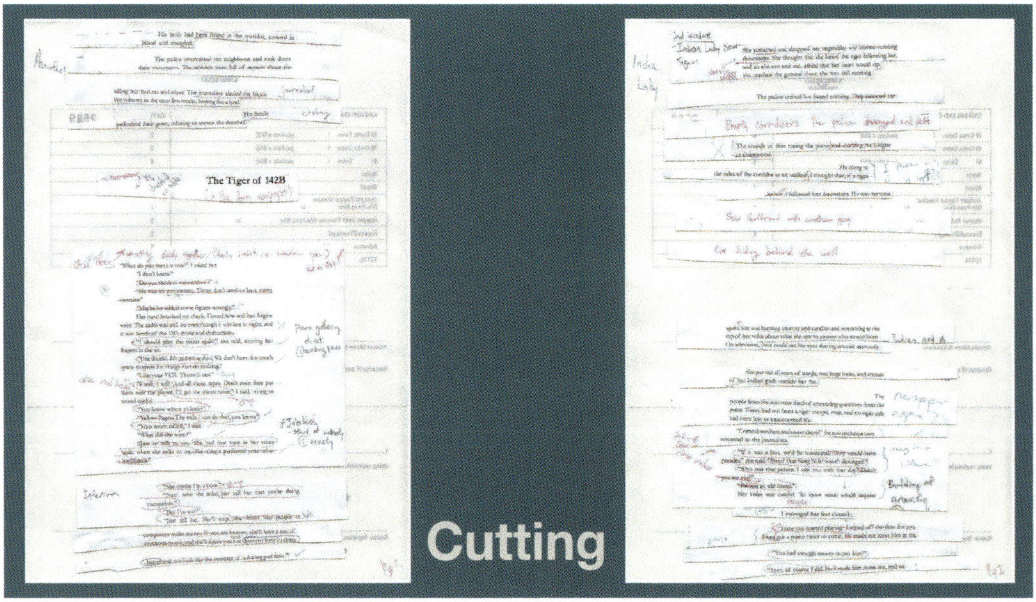

Figure 8.5: Editing the story. © Zhuang Bros 2015.

Actually, the ending of the original story was that there was a group of people roaming around, combing the HDB flats for the tiger, and the protagonist himself joined in with the crowd. And he was holding a knife. They were just following the crowd, and they just wandered around the HDB flat until the police appeared to stop them. And then, the crowd dispersed, and the protagonist ran back to his empty home and started playing the piano. That was already in the morning, after the events of the night.

But in my understanding, when I watch your film, it's never really clarified, (which is probably one of the major strengths of the film) if this tiger is just a figment of the imagination or if the tiger is actually real. Was that the same in the original story?

Yes, because nobody really saw the tiger.

So, where is this ambiguity there? There is one pivotal moment in the film where you start to feel that the tiger could be real, but then, it's not so clear anymore. I find that's very interesting to keep it in that balance. Is that faithful to the original story?

In the original story, the tiger did appear briefly, and the protagonist was just describing his feeling toward the tiger, but it is more of a monologue. And then, he just joined the crowd.

There wasn't a clear moment where they really met the tiger and he actually walked around a human being, like in our film. All of that was added by us, if I recall it correctly.

In this book, I talk a lot about the connections between the original story and the narrative approach you take to adapt it for animation. And I continue to talk about the implications for visualization. So, how did you come up with your concept for the graphic design? How would you define the connection between the narrative content and the way it turned out looking on the screen?

The original story was about 20 pages long. For adaptation, we had to edit it, we had to abridge. At the very beginning, we were wondering a lot what to leave out and what to keep. And then, we finally brought it down to a story of nine pages. We decided to go with these nine pages, because we had in mind to focus on the relationship between the boy and the girl. And these nine pages reflect just the relationship between the two of them.

After we turned it into a screenplay, we had to rewrite certain parts. In the story, this new protagonist seems like a smart person, but at the same time, he remains kind of aloof. He doesn't want to interact with society. We wanted to reflect that in our art direction.

So, we started exploring this character visually, holding an "audition" for the guy. And throughout this exploration, we eventually started adding colors and eventually liked this flat-color approach, but we were not satisfied yet. So, we edited; we kept exploring different versions.

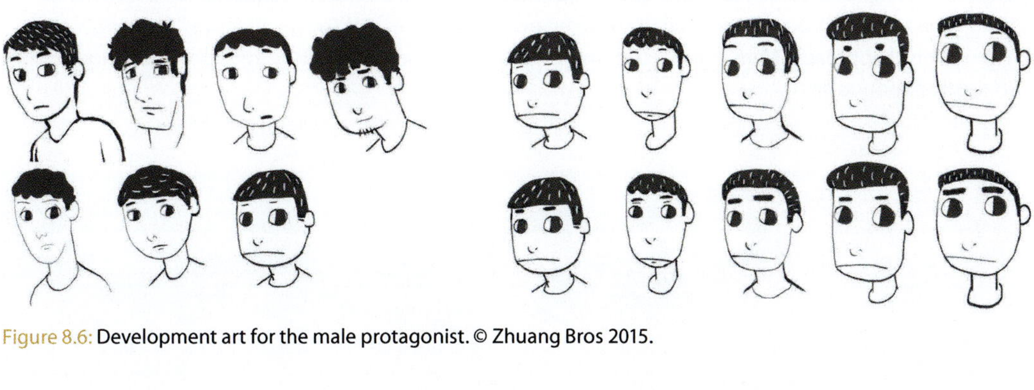

Figure 8.6: Development art for the male protagonist. © Zhuang Bros 2015.

Some of our thoughts were that this looks like an alien; this looks too Chinese for our approach. The other thing that we were struggling with was the background art. Initially, we were thinking that we could use a background with realistic perspective and use watercolor.

We started exploring this. At the same time, we were thinking why not try something else? This guy is living in his own world. The environment should reflect his state of mind, like in the art of Vincent Van Gogh—a kind of fragmented environment.

Figure 8.7: Development art for the background images. © Zhuang Bros 2015.

We were also putting a lot of thought into the look of the line work. We tried a look of wobbly lines combined with a limited color palette. And we continued to explore. We liked the idea of using a perspective that disperses with the conventional Western vanishing point approach. The perspective is deliberately slightly "wrong." We were influenced by the film *A Cat in Paris* (dirs. Felicioli, Gagnol 2010), a French animation. In our backgrounds, we similarly gave up on the idea of a "realistic perspective," favoring a more expressionist approach. Then, there is the limited color palette as well, and we added all these dotted lines in the background art.

Figure 8.8: Alternative versions of the background design. © Zhuang Bros 2015.

The character of a tiger is also reflected in the background concept. It adds to the visual storytelling. What I can see from the amount of work you created is that it was a long stage of visual development, which means that you were really trying very hard to match the story and the visual?

The original story isn't as fragmented as our adaptation. It's not like the "hero" is living in his own universe. But if we did it in a too conventional style, it would have felt like it didn't really reflect his state of mind. And so, we decided to go with a more restrained and stylized approach. Some attempts turned out to be too colorful. Imagine everything is moving. It would have looked too much like Vincent Van Gogh.

Figure 8.9: More variations. On the right, the background design inspired by Van Gogh paintings is shown. © Zhuang Bros 2015.

What I like about your film is its very unique approach—both visually and narratively. I believe this is a film that could not really have been made anywhere else. It is capturing the special atmosphere of HDB flats and so forth. So, how do you think the visuals and the storytelling achieve that? Maybe you can elaborate a bit more about how concrete you are in the storytelling and the resulting implications for the visual approach. Why do you think your film is perceived as very unique in style, despite the fact that it also wears a lot of European influences proudly on its sleeve?

I think the reason is that it is some kind of eclectic mix of several influences. It combines inspirations from Japanese animation with European influences. Look at the eyes: They resonate the "big-eye style" in manga and anime. At the same time, the background displays major influences from European animation.

When we were developing the backgrounds, we actually did a lot of research. The two of us went down to HDB flats, and we started taking pictures. The strong local flavor emerges partially because we grew up in Singapore. When we take pictures, we take pictures that reflect our impression of the HDB flat. So, we'll take pictures of the newspapers, boxes, and all these props in the flat. When we look at the reference that we draw, we can identify the elements that represent the Singaporean experience. That is the reason it works.

Figure 8.10: Still frames from the film. © Zhuang Bros 2015.

When we are illustrating, we have to cut out certain elements and add others to achieve a balance that creates an authentic impression.

In HDB flats, there are often many growing plants, and then, the residents tend to use these small corners where they used to put a lot of extra things for convenience and put newspapers outside.

So, what is also interesting for the readers of this book is that you started by researching the "real thing" first. Only then your personal point of view came on top of it, and you added the artistic interpretation.

Correct.

As pointed out before, after this initial meeting with the author Dave Chua, you were more or less allowed to go on your own. Was that until you completed the final film?

Dave Chua never saw the film until the second screening.

Did we send the animatics to him?

I think we did send them, but he said that he didn't want to watch them.

Figure 8.11: Model sheets for the film's protagonists. © Zhuang Bros 2015.

So, he wanted to be surprised. I think that's a very good situation for the adapter. It requires a lot of generosity on the end of the original author. It also reflects good judgment by understanding that animation is a different medium. I understand that this was overall a very positive experience for you.

The first time when Dave Chua watched, he said that we managed to capture the spirit of the story.

What I also like about the film is that it succeeds in getting the dialogue right. It reflects a very specific situation that a lot of people can empathize with: a slowly deteriorating relationship of a couple. Did you alter a lot of dialogue from the original text, or was it mainly really based on the dialogue from the original text?

Figure 8.12: The awkward situation of the couple: still frame. © Zhuang Bros 2015.

I think we did alter the dialogue a bit here and there to make it sound more adequate for our means. We first copied and pasted the dialogue into the screenplay, and then, we were not sure how well it flowed.

We did some table reads, with me and Harry dividing the roles among ourselves. Harry read the girl. We realized that the dialogue sounded a bit weird at times. That was when we started to make some minor adjustments here and there.

I think that's also good tip for the readers of this book that a table read can help in such instances. It is always a good stage to test, if dialogue really works when spoken or feels rather awkward.

Yes, I think the reading helps a lot.

I remember, in the original story, there was no texting.

Yes. So, we had to add the text, for example: "Why you never reply?"

We realized that the tiger stands for anxiety, and the interesting thing is that, in today's society, we have all these digital devices, which actually increase our speed in communication, but at the same time, they increase our anxiety as well.

When someone doesn't reply to your e-message, you start to wonder… did I write something wrong? Did I offend this person? That adds on to the anxiety. Back in the 1980s, people had to return calls using pay phones or similar devices; that form of anxiety didn't really exist. We took the liberty to change the story for the better, I guess.

Considering that there was a change of time period compared with the original text, it feels completely appropriate. I actually think it is very fitting as a chosen time period. This also supports the theory that changes, be it in terms of pure story or in terms of visualization, certainly can be for the better in adaptations, to keep things current or contemporary. And I think it worked really well with *The Tiger of 142B*.

Regarding the period, we struggled with that change for quite some time, because of the reason why Dave Chua wrote it in the 1980s: During the 1980s, it sounds possible that a tiger might be around in Singapore, but if you set it in today's context, it's much different: If you say that a tiger is roaming around in an HDB flat, no one will believe you. We had to struggle.

We had to decide on this.

It had to be…

Contemporary.

Today.

Have there ever been real tigers in Singapore, or was it always just an urban legend?

I think Dave Chua started to write this story because of a news article.

A news article that talked about a tiger in Singapore. I think also that is very nice, because it makes the whole motive of a tiger work on two levels. One is this kind of fantastic element. It could be a supernatural story in a way, but then again, it's very much related to real life. Are you planning to return to any adaptations of modern literature in the future?

I think we did one, right now: *The Giant*, which is an adaptation of Tan Swie Hian's poem as a stop-motion animation with newspaper. It's not an adaptation of a traditional linear narrative. It is a poem turned into a narrative animation.

巨人 (1968)

Figure 8.13: The Zhuang brothers with author Tan Swie Hian and the title of his poem *The Giant*.

Is there an English translation of this poem? Or is it only in Chinese?

It's only in Chinese, yes.

The synopsis of your filmic adaptation certainly describes a story: "*Giant* will be an experimental and surrealistic short film that shows how a mysterious island saves a fish, prides for the trees and when the volcano erupts, revealing that he is a giant bigger than the universe. The short film will present the island as an invisible hero, a protagonist who is always willing to sacrifice oneself to provide for the living." Was this narrative already suggested by the original text?

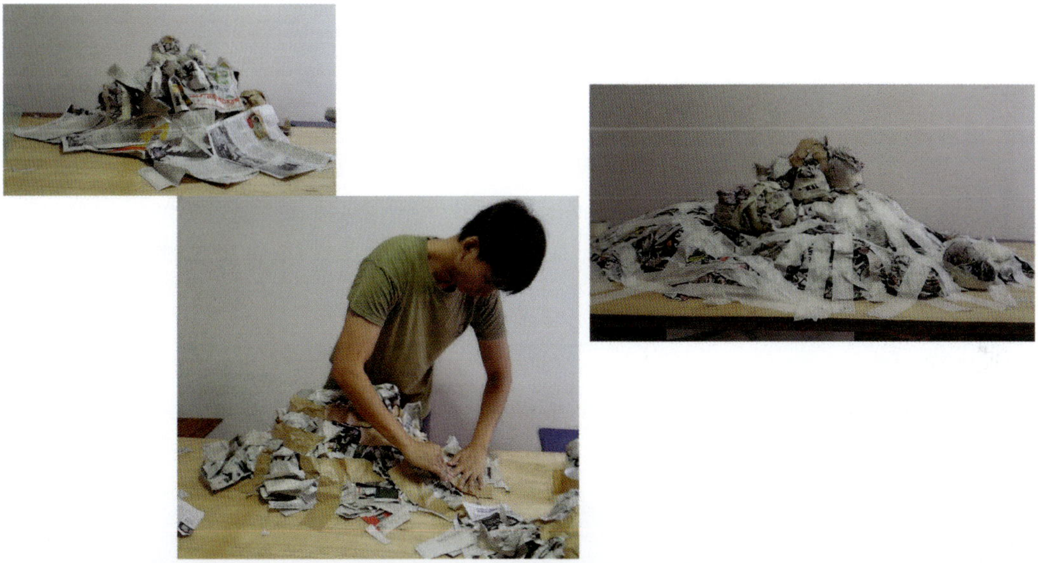

Figure 8.14: Building the island set for the film, all made from newspapers. © Zhuang Bros 2015.

The poem is written in a very open way; not sure, if fish are even mentioned in it.

It is a three-part poem. When we first read the poem, we had to decide for the part we wanted to adapt. We went to meet Tan Swie Hian, and we told him our interpretation of the poem.

We were guessing that his first poem is about his father. Then, we realized that the first poem is also about pioneers coming to Singapore, which he said was right. He was actually writing about his father, who is also a pioneer who came to Singapore.

We thought the second poem was about God.

We thought it was about God, but he said it was referring to spirituality in general.

I understand Tan Swie Hian is also a contemporary writer?

He wrote the poem in the 1980s. He's still alive. He is 75 years old now.

He's famous for being the richest artist in Asia.

Oh, I see.

He sold artwork for two million dollars. (*Editors remark:* In 2012, Tan's oil and acrylic painting *When the Moon Is Orbed* sold for S$3.7 million, a record at the time in Southeast Asia, see Asia News Network 2012).

He didn't make so much money with his poems, or did he?

Not that I know of. He is famous for his Chinese calligraphy.

He gave you permission to adapt the poem without charging anything for it?

We had to just give a very small fee.

So, it was more a goodwill contribution toward using the poem. I understand the film is not quite finished yet.

It was screened, but we were not very happy with it. We wanted to continue working on it. Back then, we were working from home. The studio was very small, but the topic is about a giant. So, you need very huge props.

They really look very impressive still.

Figure 8.15: The studio setup for *The Giant*; pictured here is the island.

For some shots, they are okay, but for the giant, we were not too happy with the results.

Once more returning to the subject of *The Tiger of 142B*. Can you give any recommendations for the adaptation of contemporary literature for animation?

When I attended the animation festival KROK in Moscow, I saw this animation piece that was also an adaptation. And I remember the judges were saying that they liked this adaptation—the animator was not chasing after the words of the original text, which, I think, was a useful piece of advice for us.

And when we were doing *The Tiger of 142B*, we were very clear that we didn't want to chase after what Dave Chua wrote. That gave us a lot of freedom, and at the same time, we could empathize with this

character. That allowed us to include personal elements. If you personalize the content, it becomes more real. I think that's what audience wants to see.

Although we are adapting someone else's story, there's a reason why you appear to be personally involved. You empathize with the character, and when you adapt it, you should make it your own: Be brave to make it your own and make it personal. Use the story as a skeleton, and you'll be the meat, the master, the shape. And, ultimately, that film would become yours.

That was very poetic. That was a very good statement. This approach comes through in the final result. I think it works because you found a way to empathize with the story and find your own access. Vice versa, the audience finds its way into the story too. You really empathize with the main character. We all know this fear of underachieving and not fitting; it is a universal topic. Yet, you very convincingly add a Singaporean twist to it that defies expectations.

It all really depends on the perspective. I don't think there will be one answer that can fit all. We have friends who went on with what the society wants, and they are still perfectly happy. I think, ultimately, it's up to the individual.

There's no easy "right or wrong."

It can also be that somebody really wants to create "super-commercial" art and be very happy with it, because it's authentic; it is what he/she really aims for. In any case, it is about staying true to yourself, being authentic, even if it's more difficult at times.

References

Asia News Network. 2012. Singapore artist's work sells for US$3m. Posted December 3. http://www.asianews-net.net/news-39718.html.

Chua, Dave. 2011. *The Tiger of 142 b*. In: *The Beating and Other Stories*. Singapore: Ethos Books.

Felicioli, Jaen Loup, and Alain Gagnol, dirs. 2010. *A Cat in Paris*. Animated feature film. Paris, France: Digit Anima/Flimage/France 3 Cinéma/Emage Animation Studios (production). Lyon, France: Gébéka Films (distribution).

Tan, Swie Hian. 1968. *The Giant*.

Image sources

HDB flats in Jurong West. Photography by I luv erky. 2007. Accessed August 22, 2018. https://commons.wikimedia.org/wiki/File:JurongwestHDB.JPG.

Visual Development and Artistic Research

How Story Defines Style for Animated Adaptations

The previous sections of this book have looked at animated adaptation from a variety of angles, always also touching on the interdependency between content development and design choices. This final chapter delves deeper into the mechanics of the process by analyzing the visual development of a variety of projects through case studies.

This also will serve to refute false notions that concept art does somehow miraculously and spontaneously "emerge" from the creator's mind, without any deeper engagement on an intellectual level. In fact, visual development carries a lot of similarities to a scholarly research approach. This is particularly true for adaptation, where the source material requires a complex thought process to arrive at the right choices. The preceding interviews and conversations with scholars and creators have already highlighted this aspect. But it will become even more evident from the examples shown and explained later in this chapter.

The initial steps of visual development, the artistic research through the assembling of **mood boards**, resemble the stage of literature review or contextual review in scholarly research in many ways.

Figure 9.1: Mood board assembled by Hannes Rall from original art by various romantic nineteenth-century landscape painters. Collage for the project *Hölderlin's Echo.*

A mood board collects samples of existing artwork to narrow down the choice of the desired artistic style. These examples can then serve to more closely determine the artistic direction and be an important communication tool for the artists working on a project. It gives them an idea of the direction they should work toward. Of course, the provided samples serve as a starting point only, to which the individual style of the concept artists is added and transferred to the images that are needed for the adaptation project they are working on. This way, something new can emerge by combining influences from the existing pieces with artistic innovation. Luckily, each artist's "handwriting" is entirely unique; even then, recreating in a traditional style will lead to an individual piece that avoids plagiarism and simple copying.

Figure 9.1 shows a collection of paintings by nineteenth-century romantic landscape painters from Europe and North America. The mood board suggests the stylistic direction for an animated sequence in the documentary feature *Hölderlin's Echo*. This is a project under development that celebrates the life of the famed German poet in a live-action documentary with interspersed animated segments. The piece is part of a dossier that is used to apply for a grant from German film-funding institutions to find additional financing partners. Partnering for this production are the Eberhard Karls University of Tübingen as well as several German film-production companies. The final production is intended for the celebration of Hölderlin's 250th anniversary in 2020.

The mood board suggests the intended style for the first of these sequences: A multiplane camera moves through wildly romantic landscapes, with limited animation of a few elements.

It becomes apparent from the mood board that a very cohesive design is suggested to keep the various elements stylistically unified. The goal is to create assets that can all believably be part of the same universe. The imagery is supposed to visually represent the early stage of Hölderlin's artistic and personal life—a period of youthful enthusiasm and exuberance and wildly romantic aspirations.

Adaptation content, that is, the choices for story and visual development are inseparably linked in animation, even more so in animated adaptation. This starts with the need to research a specific historical or cultural setting and continues with defining visual equivalents for the expression of a mood, atmosphere, or dramatic structures inherent in the source material. The visual and the narrative tone must match each other; otherwise, the artistic outcome will feel disparate and lack cohesion.

They complement each other, but together, they also form a completely independent narrative dimension, which is far more than just the simple addition of narration and image. That's why, it's so important to find the right pictures for the story.

This is only seemingly simple, because first one is confronted with limitless visual possibilities today more than ever before.

Important questions need to be considered, which help to narrow down the selection of a certain visual style:

What do I want to tell: What is the desired atmosphere of my animation?
What are the specific requirements and challenges when considering story as adaptation from a source text?

How does the visual style correspond with my narrative intent of adaptation: Will it be extremely faithful, historically accurate, and/or transferred to a different cultural setting or genre?

How can I match this by selecting my graphic means and artistic tools?

Can I transform the chosen design style into an animation production technique that works in various ways: Are the visual design, technical approach, and production schedule for the project compatible well? (Realistic estimation of the production effort).

At this stage, the previously introduced mood board would be the instrument of choice for trying out different stylistic approaches and artistic directions. It is absolutely necessary to look at concrete visual examples to enable team discussion or even the individual decision-making process. In the beginning, these could still be rather diverse, with many possibilities open—moving further along the multitude of options will be narrowed to the most suitable approach.

Figure 9.2: A typical example of an early mood board that "casts the net as wide as possible" to gather a wide diversity of possible artistic inspirations. Clockwise works by: Howard Pyle, unknown medieval artists, Franz Gaul (nineteenth century), Franz Marc (early twentieth century), Alb. Vogel, Ernst Ludwig Kirchner (twice, early twentieth century), and Hartmann Schedel. For the animated feature film project *Die Nibelungen* (WiP), written and directed by Hannes Rall.

Figure 9.3: Examples of character and environment designs for *Die Nibelungen* that integrate the above inspirations to create an entirely new and cohesively designed universe for the adaptation. Designs by Hannes Rall (left) and Hans Bacher (right).

The visual style must correspond with the content and be able to achieve the intended narrative effect for the viewer. For adaptations from literary texts, it takes on an even heightened importance: The decision to adhere to historic accuracy proposed by the source material has clear implications for the artistic research and visual development.

Breaches of style should usually be avoided, as the viewer will be irritated—the virtual animated universe is suddenly no longer "true." A realistic figure combined with a strongly caricatured figure defines such a break in style, unless it has a clear narrative basis. The same applies to hyper-realistically drawn figures combined with strongly stylized backgrounds. A tragic/realistic story told with funny characters creates an alienating effect. That is unless the very concept of adapting a source text motivates and justifies such a design decision: Maybe the alienating effect is the specific approach that the adapter has in mind for his animated version of the source text.

Such stylistic breaks can be used deliberately for narrative purposes, but they must not undermine them unintentionally. Otherwise, the narrative approach fails—the viewer remains perplexed (and disappointed).

For beginners, the choice of style is, of course, also often inseparably linked with their very own artistic styles and limitations. Young artists have to define these for themselves first—if they do the whole film alone or in very small teams. This certainly is true for most "author-based" projects such as independent animation films or student films. In such cases, it is crucial for the visual development artist(s) to consider if a member of the production team can pull off the proposed design style in production.

An experienced production designer must be able to move beyond a "personal" style and be able to offer a wide diversity of styles according to what story concept or budget demands. If a visual development artist or production designer can consider a complete studio or staff for final production, it obviously immediately widens the options for visual styles: The designer must not rely on himself/herself only to pull off his/her proposed styles in production. In any case, the visual development must always consider the capabilities of the artists and the economic constraints of the budget to make his/her vision succeed in production. This will be demonstrated by several case studies in this chapter. They cover a wide range in terms of adaptation strategies and final outcomes: Concepts aimed at different target audiences and delivered in diverse formats. The chapter closes with a visual development study that has actually been developed in 2017/2018, with several professional partners on board. But we begin with a widely known classic.

Case Study 1: *Moby-Dick*

Why *Moby-Dick*?

The famous book by Herman Melville tells the story of Captain Ahab, who is completely possessed by the idea to take revenge on the white whale Moby Dick. This is a universally relatable story of obsession, revenge, and ultimately redemption (of some sort). The book has been widely adapted for various media, including comics and film: A search in IMDB currently reveals 142 adaptations (August 2018). Among the comic adapters are prominent names such as Will Eisner and Bill Sienkiewicz, along with several adaptations in the *Classics Illustrated* series. In his 2015 essay, Christian Muschweck provides an excellent overview and compares the different design approaches—an excellent starting point for every Melville adaptation.

And there are good reasons for *Moby Dick*'s popularity among adapters Although Melville's source material almost works like a biblical allegory, the basic constellation can easily be transferred to other belief systems and cultural contexts. Ahab can take on a whole variety of incarnations, as long as his almost demonic appearance and dark charisma remain intact.

Similarly, it is not really essential that Moby Dick remains a whale—the basic theme would work with any animal or monstrous creature as well. The 1977 film *The White Buffalo* (dir. Thompson) is a *Moby-Dick* remake, all but in name, as the director himself was happy to confirm: "It's a *Moby Dick* of the west..." (as quoted by Gallo 1976).

Although Melville's original novel (in its unabridged form) engages deeply with the details of whaling in the nineteenth century, this author would argue that its timeless appeal lies in the strong conflict and characters. Therefore, this first case study will present a wide variety of options for animated adaptations. It will begin by exploring how various degrees of realism can correspond with the type of narrative chosen by the adapter.

General considerations on visual styles for *Moby-Dick*

Some stylistic main categories can be defined, which can be distinguished by their claim to realism and degree of abstraction on the one hand and target audience/genre on the other. The following illustration demonstrates how the famous character of Captain Ahab can be designed in different styles, serving different types of narratives.

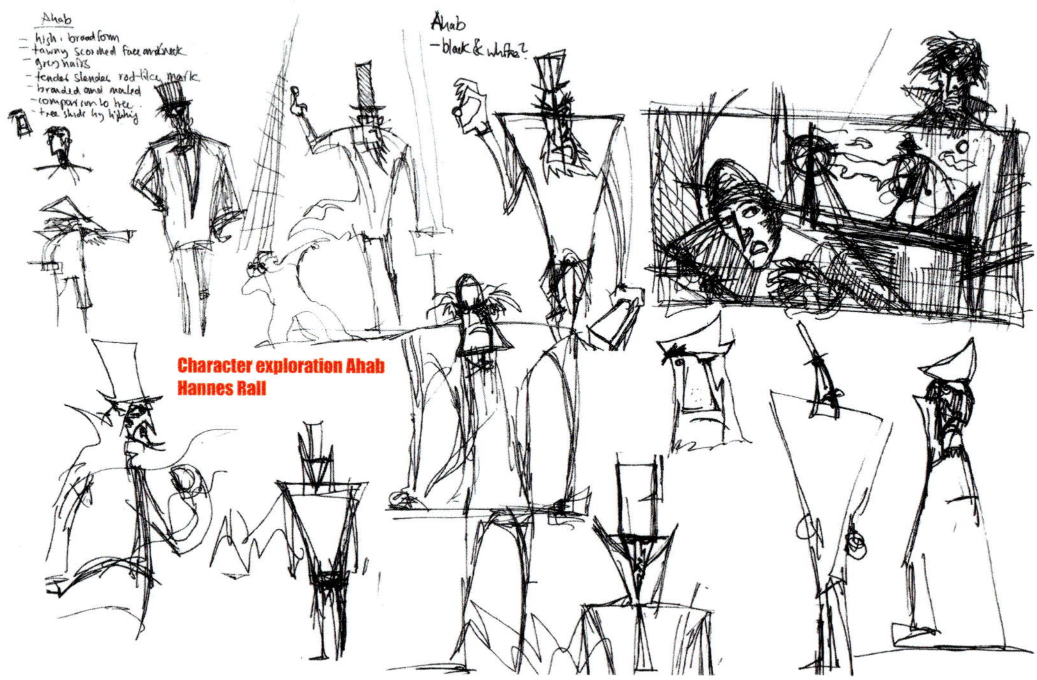

Figure 9.4: First loose sketches for Ahab by Hannes Rall.

To allow for comparison, Melville's own description of Ahab is quoted from the original text:

> "Reality outran apprehension; Captain Ahab stood upon his quarter-deck.
>
> There seemed no sign of common bodily illness about him, nor of the recovery from any. (…) His whole high, broad form, seemed made of solid bronze, and shaped in an unalterable mould, like Cellini's cast Perseus. Threading its way out from among his grey hairs, and continuing right down one side of his tawny scorched face and neck, till it disappeared in his clothing, you saw a slender rod-like mark, lividly whitish. It resembled that perpendicular seam sometimes made in the straight, lofty trunk of a great tree, when the upper lightning tearingly darts down it, and without wrenching a single twig, peels and grooves out the bark from top to bottom, ere running off into the soil, leaving the tree still greenly alive, but branded. Whether that mark was born with him, or whether it was the scar left by some desperate wound, no one could certainly say. (…) So powerfully did the whole grim aspect of Ahab affect me, and the livid brand which streaked it, that for the first few moments I hardly noted that not a little of this overbearing grimness was owing to the barbaric white leg upon which he partly stood. It had previously come to me that this ivory leg had at sea been fashioned from the polished bone of the sperm whale's jaw." (Melville 2011, 164)

Figure 9.5: "Captain Ahab" in various styles. Character designs by Hannes Rall (2016).

1) Cartoony/highly stylized

Strongly stylized and abstracted. Hardly any details: In essence, the icon of the figure. Examples of artists who work with a similar style: Walter Moers, Brösel (partly), Jean-Marc Reiser, Claire Bretecher.

Adaptation approach: Due to the level of abstraction, not suitable for (smaller) children but rather targeted at a mature, sophisticated audience.
Fits: Parody, satire, black humor, and independent animated films for adults.
Animation technique: Suggests traditional drawn animation; otherwise, the style is difficult to implement to its full potential.

2) Funny for children's programs

Strongly stylized, simplified, few details, and a high "cuteness factor."

Adaptation approach: Clearly aimed at children ca. ages 5–12 years. The friendly design style implies a somewhat-toned-down version of the original novel that avoids showing explicit cruelty, violence, and blood, which, in the case of *Moby-Dick*, creates a severe problem for keeping the "spirit" of the source material intact. Yet, it is not an uncommon requirement when it comes to demands of TV editors, which might go as far as to ask: "Shouldn't Ahab and the whale become friends in the end?"
Suitable for: A simplified version of the story for children, with omission of the darker elements. It could also function as a relatively neutral style for an educational series, which, for example, prepares information about whaling for children, generally animated series for children.
Animation technique: To be cost-efficient here, the suggested approach would be two-dimensional (2D) cutout animation, created in the computer. TV budgets are tight; therefore, the idea of reusable assets fits the bill, literally!

3) Funny

Another word for comic styles that are categorized as "funny" style. Basically, the two preceding examples are also included. But this example fits the definition of a "classical" funny more. Very caricatured: Large knob nose, exaggerated, "unrealistic" proportions, more details, and more complex coloring. See Greg's *Achille Talon* (42 albums, 1966–1996), Albert Uderzo's *Asterix* (23 albums, 1961–1978), and Morris'/Goscinny's *Lucky Luke*.

Adaptation approach: Matches the style of a faithfully adventurous retelling of the tale; can be paired with humorous elements. The style would fit a narrative that balances between straight adaptation and parody/spoof.
Fits: Parody, funny version of the story, and satire. It's hard to imagine the full tragedy of *Moby-Dick* taking place in this style. Or, it could create an interesting effect. Different layers of storytelling could address a youthful and a mature audience likewise.
Animation technique: The concept art leaves many options open: Traditional 2D, 2D computer, and three-dimensional (3D) computer. Budget considerations might imply—which way to go, as well as the artistic intent in terms of realism for the environment. The more naturalistic/detailed the design,

the more 3D computer animation becomes the best choice, artistically speaking.

3a) Anthropomorphic style (no visual example)

A special form of this style is the anthropomorphic funny style (humanized animals) in all its variations. This style approach takes up the narrative tradition of fables. Examples: Walt Disney characters Donald Duck, Mickey Mouse, and Peg Leg Pete and Walt Kelly's *Pogo* (1948–1975).

Adaptation approach: A younger audience is implied here. However, one could also achieve an interesting effect by pairing this style with a truly dark retelling of the source material. In this, it would rather match an older audience.

Fits: TV series for children, ages 6 years and up, or an older audience, depending on narrative tone.

Animation technique: Open to various techniques ranging from traditional 2D animation to 3D computer animation or even stop motion (if budgets can be afforded).

4) Semi-funny

The term "semi-funny" is interestingly enough a German invention. Thus, a distinction between "pure" funnies and funnies, with a higher proportion of realistic elements, is made. Sometimes, it is not so easy to differentiate between them; that is, where does the style "funny" end and where does "semi-funny" begin? A possible distinguishing feature is the extent of realism and detail in the backgrounds, like in Hergé's *Tintin*, a textbook example for the definition of a "semi-funny." The example here shows a clear difference to Figure 9.3: This captain Ahab is drawn in the classic "Ligne Claire" style, as invented by Hergé. It shows more realistic proportions in comparison.

Adaptation approach: The higher level of abstraction and increased level of "realistic" detail will allow for a completely faithful retelling of the source novel, without seeming at odds with the design style.

Fits: One could imagine this style for a "true-to-life" adaptation of *Moby-Dick*. It should match a slightly older audience (ages 8 years and up) for a TV series or feature film.

Animation technique: In terms of artistic and economic considerations, a hybridized style that smartly combines drawn animation with 2D computer techniques (digital cutout) could be the best choice.

5) Semi-realistic

When realistic elements are combined with caricatured stylization, one could define such an approach as "semi-realistic." Once again, the distinction from a "semi-funny" style remains somewhat a matter of perspective. But a "semi-realistic" style would clearly have the degree of realism dominate over the amount of caricature it uses for characters and environment.

Here, cartoon elements mix with more realistic proportions. This style could also be described as strongly stylized realism. Hatching is completely absent, and flat colors are used with minimal shading. In terms of environment, the viewer will expect a graphically reduced but historically accurate illustration.

Adaptation approach: This type of character design suggests an adaptation that keeps the serious tone, darker elements, and authenticity of *Moby-Dick*.

Fits: This style can easily reproduce the whole tragedy of Melville's masterpiece. The emotions of the actors can be represented very effectively with appropriate graphical enhancement.

Animation technique: A mix between drawn animation and digital cutout, or entirely relying on the latter.

6) Realistic

Realistic proportions, dramatically exaggerated, but not extremely caricatured. High detail density and elaborate hatching to show material properties. Modeling of the figure through light and shadow.

Adaptation approach: Dark, serious, and a rather natural match for the source material.
Probably more for a feature film than a TV series, also in terms of the production costs.

Fits: Of course, this style is ideal for the dramatic/dark side of *Moby-Dick*. But it is also a good choice to illustrate the documentary details about whaling, with detailed and well-researched backgrounds.

Animation technique: Owing to the strongly suggested textured details and degree of realism, 3D computer animation combined with non-photorealistic rendering (NPR) would be the best choice. In terms of purely artistic considerations, traditional hand-drawn animation could also work nicely yet simply be too expensive to produce. In any case, this is probably the most expensive version to produce, compared with stylistic choices 1–5.

The next sections will explore how this approach can be expanded from a single character to the design of a whole cast. The main characters in the source text are, besides Ahab and the "hero" and narrator Ishmael, the mates, as paired with their respective harpooneers:

Chief mate Starbuck with harpooneer Queequeg, second mate Stubb with harpooneer Tashtego, and third mate Flask with harpooneer Daggoo. Finally, Fedallah—Ahab's own harpooner. Melville describes them all in great detail:

The mates

"The chief mate of the Pequod was **Starbuck**, a native of Nantucket, and a Quaker by descent. He was a long, earnest man, and though born on an icy coast, seemed well adapted to endure hot latitudes, his flesh being hard as twice-baked biscuit. (…) Only some thirty arid summers had he seen; those summers had dried up all his physical superfluousness. But this, his thinness, so to speak, seemed no more the token of wasting anxieties and cares, than it seemed the indication of any bodily blight. It was merely the condensation of the man." (Melville 2011, 154)

"**Stubb** was the second mate. He was a native of Cape Cod; and hence, according to local usage, was called a Cape-Cod-man. A happy-go-lucky; neither craven nor valiant; taking perils as they came with an indifferent air; and while engaged in the most imminent crisis of the chase, toiling away, calm and collected as a journeyman joiner engaged for the year. Good-humored, easy, and careless, he presided over his whale-boat as if the most deadly encounter were but a dinner, and his crew all invited guests (…) He kept a whole row of pipes there ready loaded, stuck in a rack, within easy reach of his hand; and, whenever he turned in, he smoked them all out in succession, lighting one from the other to the end of the chapter; then loading them again to be in readiness anew. For, when Stubb dressed, instead of first putting his legs into his trowsers, he put his pipe into his mouth." (Melville 2011, 158)

"The third mate was **Flask**, a native of Tisbury, in Martha's Vineyard. A short, stout, ruddy young fellow, very pugnacious concerning whales, who somehow seemed to think that the great leviathans had personally and hereditarily affronted him; and therefore it was a sort of point of honour with him, to destroy them whenever encountered." (Melville 2011, 159)

Figure 9.6: Character sketches for the mates by Hannes Rall.

The harpooneers

Queequeg: "Such a face! It was of a dark, purplish, yellow colour, here and there stuck over with large blackish looking squares. (...) But at that moment he chanced to turn his face so towards the light, that I plainly saw they could not be sticking-plasters at all, those black squares on his cheeks. There was no hair on his head—none to speak of at least—nothing but a small scalp-knot twisted up on his forehead. His bald purplish head now looked for all the world like a mildewed skull. Had not the stranger stood between me and the door, I would have bolted out of it quicker than ever I bolted a dinner."(Melville 2011, 52)

"Next was **Tashtego**, an unmixed Indian from Gay Head, (...) Tashtego's long, lean, sable hair, his high cheek bones, and black rounding eyes—for an Indian, Oriental in their largeness, but Antarctic in their glittering expression—all this sufficiently proclaimed him an inheritor of the unvitiated blood of those proud warrior hunters, who, in quest of the great New England moose, had scoured, bow in hand, the aboriginal forests of the main. (...) To look at the tawny brawn of his lithe snaky limbs, you would almost have credited the superstitions of some of the earlier Puritans, and half-believed this wild Indian to be a son of the Prince of the Powers of the Air. Tashtego was Stubb the second mate's squire." (Melville 2011, 160)

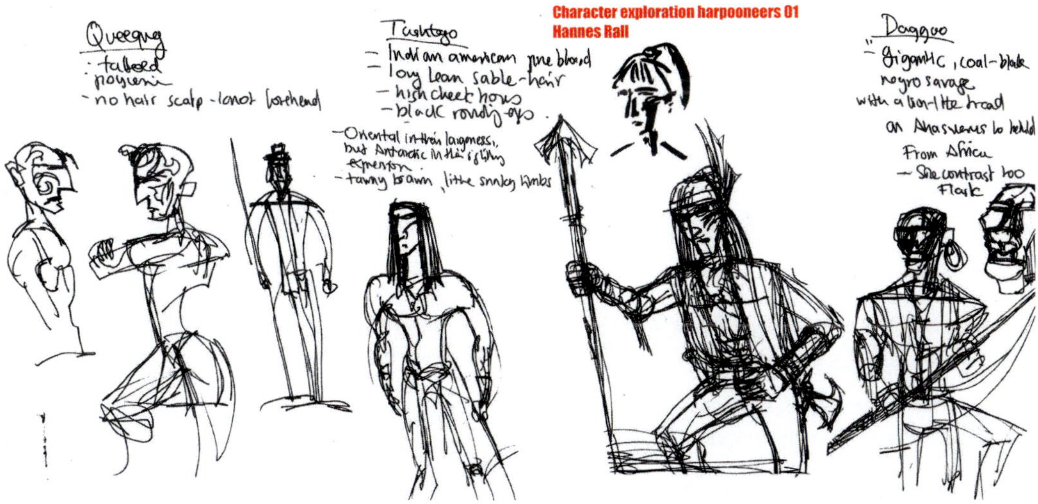

Figure 9.7: Loose sketches by Hannes Rall, exploring designs for the harpooneers. Quick and simple sketches are the necessary next step after the mood board exploration of the concept. This guarantees a vitality that seldom can be achieved when starting with overly detailed and polished design right away. Always work from the simple and rough towards the refined!

"Third among the harpooneers was **Daggoo**, a gigantic, coal-black negro-savage, with a lion-like tread—an Ahasuerus to behold. Suspended from his ears were two golden hoops, so large that the sailors called them ring-bolts, and would talk of securing the top-sail halyards to them. (...) Daggoo retained all his barbaric virtues, and erect as a giraffe, moved about the decks in all the pomp of six feet five in his socks. There was a corporeal humility in looking up at him; and a white man standing before him seemed a white flag come to beg truce of a fortress. Curious to tell, this imperial negro, Ahasuerus Daggoo, was the Squire of little Flask, who looked like a chess-man beside him."(Melville 2011, 161)

Fedallah (original description paraphrased by Shmoop Editorial Team 2018):

"Fedallah is the harpooneer whom Ahab secretly smuggles aboard the Pequod in order to staff his whaling boat. Fedallah's origins are mysterious, and we know little more than that he is a Parsee, or Persian fire-worshipper, that he wears a black Chinese-style jacket, and that he has his long white hair wound like a turban around his head."

Figure 9.8: Further sketches by Hannes Rall, exploring designs for the harpooneers. Contrast between characters is essential to create a functioning "cast."

The following examples show how to create a stylistically cohesive character ensemble for different adaptation approaches. The concept art will demonstrate the potential of *Moby-Dick* for transcultural and cross-genre adaptations, besides a more faithful/traditional version, which, in return, once again, attest to the universality of themes negotiated in the original written text. The character designs were created by Singaporean concept artist Jasper Liu Yingxian.

A "semi-realistic" approach

Accurate

The proportions maintain a high level of naturalism with elements of exaggeration and graphic stylization that make each character easily distinguishable. Even when reduced to silhouettes, each character remains different. This is achieved by using strongly diverse basic shapes to build the characters. Instead of relying on speculation, the costumes are accurately based on historical references. Artist Jasper Liu followed the descriptions of the characters in the novel, giving them suitable looks based on their ethnicities.

Figure 9.9: Character line-up "semi-realistic" by Jasper Liu Yingxian.

Figure 9.10: Size comparison sheet ("Moby Dick" versus the human characters) for the "semi-realistic" version by Jasper Liu Yingxian.

Designer's thought process

- **-Ahab** is designed with a rigidity in his motivation to hunt Moby Dick, through his shape and posture. By giving him crooked lines, especially in his face, hair, and harpoon, Ahab is made more intimidating.
- **-Queequeg** looks like a "dangerous cannibal" but is dressed very well. The artist contrasted Queequeg's bulky and roughened physique with neat and well-fitting clothes. This also adds an interesting contrast through the design that contradicts the cliché one would typically expect. It also resonates with the character properly that Queequeg is actually a very gentle and noble person once you get past his seemingly threatening physique.
- **-Stubb** is a happy-go-lucky kind of guy, who kills whales for the (strange) fun of it. Thus, he was designed to be asymmetrical to reflect his personality—his cap pulled to one side and one side of his shirt pulled out.

This results in a set of designs that keeps a high fidelity to the source text. The costumes were also researched to meet the high standards of authenticity proposed by the original novel. As will be demonstrated later, this is by far not the only option for adapting *Moby-Dick*. Yet, if one decides to go through with such an approach, it is of essence to maintain that standard throughout all production design. This includes characters, costumes, props, backgrounds, environments, and color design.

A "cross-cultural" approach

Japan has a long history of whaling, making this setting very appropriate for an adaptation of *Moby-Dick*. The visual development is inspired by the Japanese Ukiyo-e (Japanese for "pictures of the floating world") art style. According to the *Encyclopaedia Britannica* (1998), Ukiyo-e is described as "one of the most important genres of art of the Tokugawa period (1603–1867) in Japan." It further notes that "the ukiyo-e style also has about it something of both native and foreign realism (…) Common subjects included famous courtesans and prostitutes, kabuki actors and well-known scenes from kabuki plays, and erotica. More important than screen painting, however, were wood-block prints, ukiyo-e artists being the first to exploit that medium. (…) The essence of the ukiyo-e style was embodied in the works of Utamaro, Hokusai, and Hiroshige."

Designer's thought process

Hokusai's wood-block prints and those of his less famous contemporaries were the main source of reference for developing a related style for this visual *Moby-Dick* adaptation.

Figure 9.11: A collection of works in the Ukiyo-e art style, from left to right:

1. *An actor in the role of Kurando Yukinaga : Two actors in the roles of Saitogo Kunitake and a female Buddhist devotee : An actor in the role of Osadanotaro Nagam* by Utagawa, Kuniyoshi, (1798–1861)
2. *Beauty wearing a kimono with a pattern of waterwheels in waves* by Kaigetsudō, Dohan, (active 1710–1720)
3. *Whale hunting at the island of Goto in Hizen* by Utagawa, Hiroshige, (1826–1869).
4. *Sawamura Sojuro as Soga Juro and Ichimura Takenojo as Soga Goro* by Nishimura, Shigenaga, (1697–1756).
5. *Mukōjima miyamoto musashi* by Utagawa, Kuniyoshi, (1798–1861)
6. *Shoki and a courtesan beneath an umbrella* by Nishimura, Shigenobu, (active 1730s–early 1740s)
7. The actor Ichikawa Monnosuke. by Katsukawa, Shunkō, (1743–1812).

As expressed in its name, Ukiyo-e art exudes an atmosphere of otherworldliness and weightlessness that the concept artist tried to capture in his designs. The characters are based on Japanese whalers and fishermen, wielding fishing knives and harpoons. Fedallah was described in the source text as a devil in man's disguise. Hence, he is drawn with a face looking like the Japanese "oni" (demon). Flask's body is designed based on a sumo wrestler.

Figure 9.12: Character line-up for the "Japanese" version by Jasper Liu Yingxian.

Figure 9.13: Size comparison sheet ("Moby Dick" versus the human characters) for the "Japanese" version by Jasper Liu Yingxian.

A "cross-genre" approach

Had the aforementioned live-action film *The White Buffalo* transferred *Moby-Dick* to the Western genre, this variation shows the potential for recontextualizing the source material in outer space and future worlds.

Designer's thought process

The characters were reimagined as aliens in this set. In the first attempt, Jasper Liu designed the characters to look very different from one another. However, the relationship of the mates and harpooners became too unclear. In the second round of designs, the designer grouped the mates together through a reptilian theme and their spacesuit designs. In contrast, the harpooners came from different planets and looked completely different from each other. Also, their spacesuits were designed to be improvised and incomplete, built from whatever material they had.

Figure 9.14: Early version of character line-up.

Figure 9.15: Final character line-up for the "science fiction" version by Jasper Liu Yingxian.

Visually, **Ahab** was designed with long curling shapes, almost like a predatory snake. Ahab's posture was designed to resemble a strict army officer.

Instead of giving **Queequeg** tattoos, the designer gave him curling shapes coming from his head and his extra arms. His fierce eyes and sharp teeth are meant to suggest his predatory instincts, like a beast barely kept in control.

Figure 9.16: Size comparison sheet ("Moby Dick" versus the alien characters) for the "science fiction" version by Jasper Liu Yingxian.

Figure 9.16 demonstrates that the animal species of Moby Dick can be changed, as long as the evolving character keeps the defining trait of monstrosity and menace—more of a supernatural character, a god-like figure, than an actual animal. Further concept art would explore the design's potential for displaying different moods and emotional states. This would help to do the complexity of the titular character in the source material justice.

Melville has offered a lot of detailed visual description in his original text. This challenges the adapter to either consequently reference it or move entirely away from any direct visual reference. This is entirely different from the next author, an old acquaintance from this book.

Case Study 2: *Back to the Bard*: Visual Variations on Shakespeare

Roberta E. Pearson (2004, 91–92) notes:

> "The humanist Shakespeare, set free from the stifling historicism of a particular English heritage is a transcendent genius who wrote of universal themes and emotions and created emblematic characters recognized by all (...) A humanist Shakespeare is a cosmopolitan who speaks to all the world in contemporary terms."

Shakespeare is by far the most popular author for filmic adaptations. In 2011, Forrest Wickman conducted an analysis of IMDB data to identify the most adapted authors of written literature. Shakespeare leads clearly with 831 listings; second is Anton Chekhov, with merely 320 "writer" listings, followed by Dumas (243) and Poe (240). This already provides ample reason to return to his works in the visual development section.

But there is an additional aspect that make his texts particularly suitable for visual exploration: The reason for the high appeal of Shakespeare's work for filmic adaptation might also be that he offers little to no description of the visuals in his plays. The actual look of the characters, clothing, and locations are almost entirely left to the imagination of the audience or reader. This enables a very free visual interpretation of the source material. This certainly contributes to the universal and timeless appeal of his plays that overcomes time and spatial limitations, as well as cultural barriers.

The following section explores this diverse potential through examples that visually adapt the texts in different time periods, geographical surroundings, and cultural contexts. They also demonstrate how Shakespeare can be transferred to entirely fictional or imaginary worlds. The art is created by Singaporean visual development artist Jasper Liu Yingxian, in close collaboration with Hannes Rall as the visual supervisor. These are all concepts exclusively created for this book to serve as an inspiration for visually diverse interpretations of Shakespeare.

Macbeth

Macbeth cannot only be considered among Shakespeare's best-known plays, but it has also been wildly popular for film adaptation: IMDB.com lists no less than 200 examples. In comparison, the similarly famous *A Midsummer Night's Dream* has 142 adaptations listed (as of August 2, 2018). In addition there are films that are adaptations all but in name, like Akira Kurosawa's masterpiece *Throne of Blood* (1957). By successfully transferring the story to a Japanese samurai setting, it also demonstrates the universality of Shakespeare's themes and its potential to transcend cultural boundaries. *Macbeth* offers a colorful cast of characters along with some of the Bard's most iconic scenes—like the first meeting with the three witches.

The medieval version

> This first visual development version references the time period that Shakespeare based the play on: "Shakespeare's plot is only partly based on fact. Macbeth was a real eleventh century Scottish king, but the historical Macbeth, who had a valid right to the throne, reigned capably in Scotland from 1040 till 1057. (...) Shakespeare found his version of the story of Macbeth in the Chronicles of Holinshed, a historian of his own time." (BBC n.d.).

Because this historical setting remains unchanged, the design approach here can be considered the most "faithful" in that respect. But the stylistic approach would work best for a narrative that adds humorous undertones to a straight retelling of the story. Plot details can remain the same, but even without any alteration, the design would rather suggest a dark comedy than a "deadly serious" adaptation.

Figure 9.17: Thumbnail sketches for the "medieval" version by Jasper Liu Yingxian.

Figure 9.18: Character line-up for the "medieval" version by Jasper Liu Yingxian.

Design thinking: Medieval

Jasper Liu explored how shapes can make characters look humorous, in particular looking at artist Nicolas Marlet, with his wild and iconic character designs. **King Duncan**'s beard and round belly reflected his jolly nature, and he is a king who did not deserve to die by Macbeth's hands. **Malcolm** ran away after his father's assassination; therefore, he was portrayed as a lanky and awkward character. The designer was further inspired by the witch characters in Studio Ghibli films such as *Spirited Away* (dir. Miyazaki 2001) and *Howl's Moving Castle* (dir. Miyazaki 2004), which had the witches transform into birds. Therefore, he based the concept for the **three witches** on crow and owl. While this idea is transposed to a European setting, the design remains entirely original.

The Japanese version

The mention of *Throne of Blood* already demonstrated the potential to adapt *Macbeth* for a Japanese setting. The following examples apply this idea to visual concepts for an animated feature film. Please compare with the Japanese version of *Moby-Dick*, which clearly references a specific historic art style. Here, inspiration is drawn from various manga, for example, writer Kazuo Koike's and artist Goseki Kojima's *Lone Wolf and Cub* (1970–1978).

Merged with Jasper Liu's very own vivid brushwork, an appealing fusion of Asian line styles emerges. The transposition to a different cultural context also resonates well with fresh takes on clichéd visualizations of major characters—like the three witches.

Figure 9.19: Thumbnail sketches for the "Japanese" version by Jasper Liu Yingxian.

Figure 9.20: Character line-up for the "Japanese" version by Jasper Liu Yingxian.

Design thinking: Japanese

Here, the designer took great inspiration from the dry-brush aesthetic of certain Japanese manga, particularly from Takehiko Inoue's *Vagabond* series. To distinguish itself from Kurosawa's famous *Throne of Blood*, the artist chose to set this version of *Macbeth* in a later era (e.g., Meiji era) when the samurais did not wear heavy armor anymore.

Macbeth and **Macduff** were given similar shapes, representing them as skilled samurai destined to fight each other. Macduff, however, has a straw hat and cape, giving him a more rugged look, as an exiled samurai ("ronin"): an outsider coming back for revenge.

Banquo was designed with broad shoulders and a square shape to represent his righteousness and his refusal to be tempted by the witches' prophecy.

The **witches** were visualized as beautiful young geishas instead of ugly old witches. This idea also implies their magical powers that keep them eternally young.

The Western version

This genre requires the artist to consider the many well-established stereotypes and multiple subgenres such as the classical Western, the Spaghetti Western, the post-modern Western, and so on. This is important, because quoting from these will definitely have an effect on the perception of the audience: The use of certain clichés or visual stereotypes will immediately create an expectation about this character's behavior. In this case, the designer chose to use the iconic "stranger with the poncho" for Macbeth. This is a quote from Sergio Leone's Spaghetti Westerns, like *A Fistful of Dollars* (dir. Leone 1964), in which this iconic character was played by Clint Eastwood, only that, here, the role cliché is smartly subverted: Instead of being the rightful avenger, the "stranger with the poncho" becomes the bad guy. This defies established audience expectation and creates a surprise. For other characters, precise equivalents of the original roles in the source text were chosen: Duncan turns from a king into the local sheriff. This works because both of these roles constitute the highest degree of authority in their respective communities. The playful integration of stereotypes would support a comedic approach to storytelling.

Figure 9.21: Thumbnail sketches for the Western version by Jasper Liu Yingxian.

Figure 9.22: Character line-up for the Western version by Jasper Liu Yingxian.

Design thinking: Western

The characters become more stylized and graphical in shapes. The construction of the designs is based on appealing contrasts between vertical, horizontal, and diagonal axes. **Macbeth** is designed to be a character who is a skilled cowboy but is afraid of his wife. He is pressured into killing Duncan, who is the sheriff of the town. **Macduff** is designed with rigid angles, to show that he is an unforgiving and experienced gunfighter. The artist deviated from the previous sets in the way that he designed the **three witches** as a cohesive group. Each of the witches is an individual entity, each a formidable gunfighter that is not to be messed with. This suggests that they came from different backgrounds and formed a notorious guild.

The Roaring Twenties version

One could argue that *Macbeth*'s central theme is the fight for power, "when ambition goes unchecked by moral constraint" (Sparknotes n.d.). Therefore, it appears like a natural match to transfer the text to a setting in the Roaring Twenties, with rivaling gangs fighting for dominance.

Figure 9.23: Thumbnail sketches for the Roaring Twenties version by Jasper Liu Yingxian.

Figure 9.24: Character line-up for the Roaring Twenties version by Jasper Liu Yingxian.

Design thinking: Roaring Twenties

For the gangster genre, real mafia figures such as Lucky Luciano and Al Capone were researched for design inspiration. As mafia members typically wear similar clothing, great care was taken to vary the body silhouettes and postures between the characters. This achieves a cast of characters that are easily distinguishable from each other. Drawing inspiration from Al Capone, the designer gave **Macbeth** an overall V shape and sharp features, to foreshadow his betrayal of **King Duncan** (also a mob boss here) and taking over the throne. The sharp features are repeated in **Lady Macbeth** and the **three witches** as well, representing their malevolence. **Duncan** has a large rectangular shape to represent his imposing position as the don of the mafia; yet, as the leader, he is always fair to his "soldiers"—in this version, the members of the "family."

The science fiction version

This makes for an interesting comparison with the previous science fiction setting for *Moby-Dick*. In many ways, this environment frees the adapter to come up with outlandish characters, letting the imagination roam freely. Yet, in its own way, the adaptation must adhere to the concept to define visual equivalents for the main character properties. This can be easily demonstrated by the example of **King Duncan**: His authority as a ruler is visualized through his imposing figure and dominating pose.

Figure 9.25: Thumbnail sketches for the "science fiction" version by Jasper Liu Yingxian.

Figure 9.26: Character line-up for the "science fiction" version by Jasper Liu Yingxian.

Design thinking: Science fiction

French comic artist's Moebius (pseudonym of Jean Giraud 1938–2012) design language was referenced for this set of characters and combined with the wild shapes of modern avant-garde fashion. The end result is also vaguely inspired by Luc Besson's film *The Fifth Element* (1997), which Moebius had worked on. To represent the power-hungry (soon-to-be) queen, **Lady Macbeth** was given an enveloping coat and an over-the-top crown. As every character is already wearing impractical clothing, the **three witches** are further based on the Sun, the Moon, and the Cosmos, in order to differentiate them from ordinary mortals.

Reinventing iconic scenes

Three iconic scenes from *Macbeth* are reinvented here for the new adaptation settings. By picking major turning points and dramatic peaks from the story, a good impression of the design approach in a narrative context can be achieved. Such **key visuals** are an important first test to check if the overall approach to production design will work. A character design can be approved only if the figure has been explored in various poses and moods and combined with various backgrounds needed for the film. The key visuals can also serve to communicate the final production look toward the production team or to convince financial investors and funding institutions.

Macbeth and Banquo encounter three witches

World War One setting

Classical setting with regular witches

Feudal period Japan setting

Hindu mythological setting

Figure 9.27: Macbeth's encounter with the three witches. Art by Jasper Liu.

Lady Macbeth convinces Macbeth to kill King Duncan

Science fiction setting

Chinese wuxia (martial hero) setting

Western setting

Figure 9.28: Lady Macbeth persuades Macbeth to kill Duncan. Art by Jasper Liu.

Macduff fights Macbeth

Historical setting

Tribal setting

Gangster setting

Figure 9.29: Macduff fights Macbeth. (Courtesy of Jasper Liu.)

Exploring story options and stylistic variations for Shakespeare adaptations

A Midsummer Night's Dream and *Antony and Cleopatra* are developed here for a variation of major **story beats** (major story points that alter the direction of the narrative). The different genres and cultures referenced unpack the vast potential for Shakespeare adaptation. The possibilities are practically limitless.

These examples can also serve as an inspiration for the reader to develop any of these concepts into a full-fledged pre-production "package" or design "bible" that will include character cast, environment, and prop design plus the color design. All concept art by Jasper Liu Yingxian.

Story beats: *A Midsummer Night's Dream*

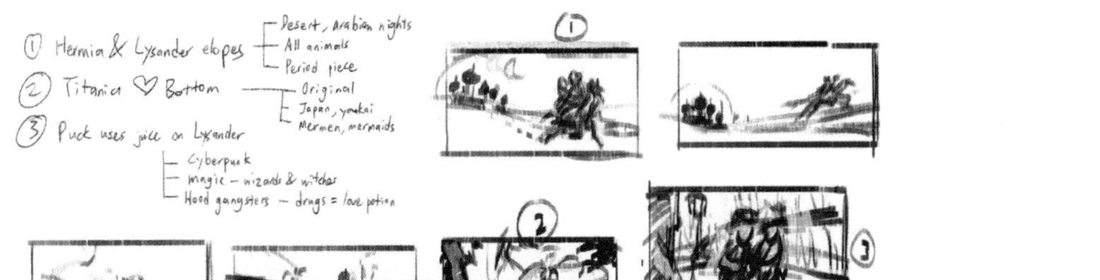

Figure 9.30: Identifying major story beats for *A Midsummer Night's Dream* through quick thumbnail sketches.

Story and style variations: *A Midsummer Night's Dream*

Hermia and Lysander elope

Figure 9.31: Arabian.

- Appeal of a previously unseen setting: The couple attempts to escape into the desert under the moonlight, atop a camel.
- A subtle touch of Van Gogh (1853–1890) in the lighting (referencing his *Starry Night* 1889).

Figure 9.32: Animals.

- The forests in the original inspired the designer to use anthropomorphic characters.

Animals, being agile, can move around in the forest, as if it is a playground.

Figure 9.33: Period piece.

- The couple blends in with the crowd to get away via a train.
- Hermia and Lysander are cautiously looking around their surroundings to make sure they are not being followed.

Figure 9.34: Faithful to the original setting.

Titania falls in love with Bottom

This certainly is one of the most popular moments from the original play. It is therefore particularly challenging and interesting for the visual adapter to move away from the iconic image of the donkey-head for Bottom.

- A more line-centric image, designed to look like it could be a page from a children's storybook.

Figure 9.35: Japan, youkai style.

- Japanese Shinto mythology is rich with kami (gods/deities) and youkai (demons).
- The fairies could impersonate a type of youkai, and Bottom's head turns into a monstrous-looking one.
- This drawing references Japanese art drawn with sumi ink (ink made from an inkstick, commonly used in Japanese and Chinese brush painting).

Figure 9.36: Mermaids and mermen.

- Soft, curvy forms to illustrate the underwater world of mermen.
- Bottom gets his head turned into an angler-fish, which creates a contrast with Titania, who is a mermaid.

Puck uses potion on Lysander

Figure 9.37: Cyberpunk.

- In a cyberpunk setting, Puck becomes a cyborg armed with a syringe instead of flower juice.
- Sketchy lines and texture to give a run-down, dystopian look.

Figure 9.38: Magic, witches, and wizards.

- Lysander and Hermia sleep in the library, while Puck fires a spell at Lysander.
- Wonky shapes to give more character to the environment.

Figure 9.39: Hood gangster.

- More realistic proportions, but lines, describing the flesh and clothes, are exaggerated.
- The love potion is now a hallucinogenic drug.

Story beats: *Antony and Cleopatra*

This play is among Shakespeare's lesser-known plays; a 2016 survey ranks it at number 14 and in the niche category (Dahlgreen). This seems to automatically liberate the designer to neglect any established visual tradition. Yet, this proves wrong, because the protagonists Antony and Cleopatra are universally known—the image of Elizabeth Taylor in the role (*Cleopatra*, dir. Mankiewicz 1963) lingers on in cultural memory, and it has become an icon of pop culture in the twentieth century.

Their story is also situated in a concrete time period:

> "In 41 BC, Mark Antony, at that time in dispute with Caesar's adopted son Octavian over the succession to the Roman leadership, began both a political and romantic alliance with Cleopatra" (BBC 2014).

This suggests that the production designer should thoroughly research the period detail if he decides for a "faithful" adaptation.

Figure 9.40: Exploring story options for the adaptations through quick thumbnail sketches.

This can be somewhat mitigated by moving away from any realism in the style; yet, whenever suggesting a specific historical setting, the author believes in the value of accuracy. Unless any information is lacking, this leaves no alternative to invention or an informed guess.

The other option is, of course, to entirely move away from an "authentic" historical timeline and completely reinvent the story for a different time and place. Not seeing the main characters in Egyptian and Roman costumes, respectively, will immediately create a sense of displacement or alienation. But, precisely this effect can be put to good use when matching it with a suitable story.

Story and style variations: *Antony and Cleopatra*

Antony with Cleopatra before he returned to Rome

Figure 9.41: "Faithful" adaptation, true to historical setting (Egypt and Roman empire).

- A flat, graphical style—cartoony and strongly stylized form.
- Focusing on shapes to allow further contrast between characters: Antony, a Roman general, and Cleopatra, a smart ruler capable of seducing men.

Figure 9.42: Aviation.

- Watercolor look.
- Took inspiration from Charlie Brown's simple characters.
- Instead of battles at sea, here, battles will be in the sky.

Figure 9.43: Fantasy.

- Elves and humans instead of Egypt and Rome.
- Lines blend into the shapes at some areas.
- Giving the image more of a dreamy and otherworldly look.

Triumvirate and Pompey celebrate peace

Figure 9.44: Chinese, Romance of the Three Kingdoms.

- Elaborate armor commonly seen in Chinese graphic novels.
- Four Chinese generals sharing wine as a symbol of brotherhood.
- A Chinese saying "Easily a thousand brothers will share your wine and meat, but when misfortune calls, hardly one of them will be left" (Lau, Ma 1986, 4).

Figure 9.45: African.

- Interesting patterns in African clothing and masks that provide localized context.
- Thin figures, taking inspiration from puppet designs in indigenous African art.

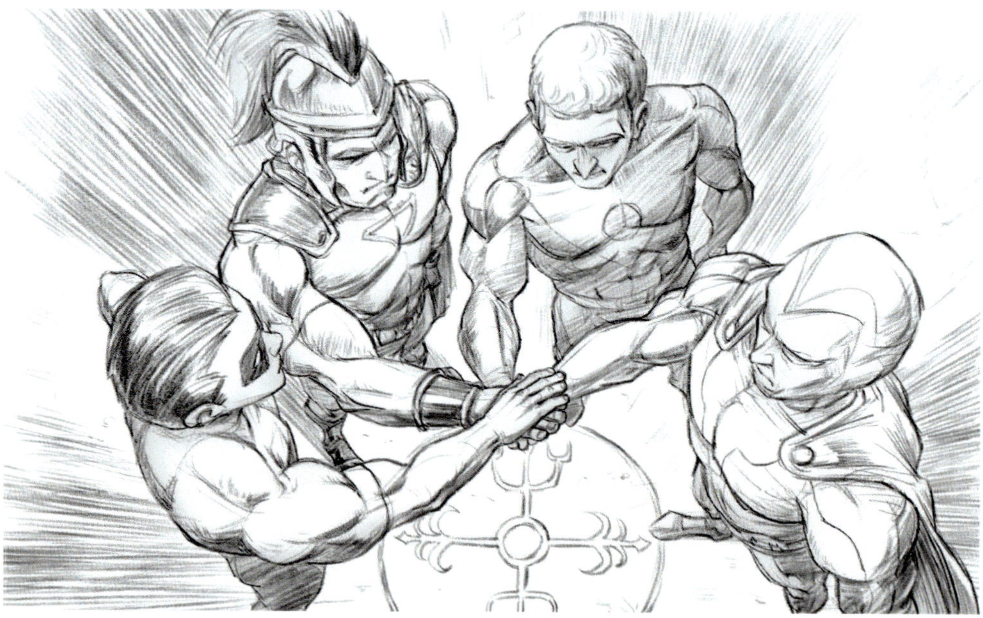

Figure 9.46: Superheroes.

- This story beat matches superhero comics, when several superheroes put aside their differences and unite together.
- The second guy from the left is wearing a Roman costume, while the third guy from the left is modeled after Octavius' bust.

Death of Antony

Figure 9.47: Science fiction: robot mecha genre.

- The characters are pilots of giant robots.
- *Antony and Cleopatra* is a political story, just like the *Gundam* franchise (a fictional universe created by a Japanese toy manufacturer—pilots in giant robots fighting political battles).

Figure 9.48: Steampunk/post-apocalyptic.

- Inspired by *Mad Max: Fury Road* (dir. Miller 2015).
- Gritty look with smoke and dust reflects the hopelessness of the situation—a tragic story in which the tyrant wins.

Figure 9.49: Police crime drama.

- A story where the police fail and the criminals take over the city. Perhaps, Antony was part of the criminal gang and defected to the police's side.
- Referenced the animated film *Tekkon Kinkreet* (dir. Arias 2006) for its quirky character design.

Case Study 3: *Westboy*

Figure 9.50: *Westboy* is a concept that tells the story of a German immigrant boy in the Wild West of 1850, loosely based on the popular novels by German author Karl May (1842–1912).

This case study distinguishes itself from the previous examples by its close proximity to concrete production reality: *Westboy* was developed in 2017/2018 as a TV-series concept by the author, together with Jörg von den Steinen. Jörg is a veteran editor of children and youth programs with Germany's biggest broadcaster Zweites Deutsches Fernsehen (ZDF). In his career, he has helped to develop and supervised many animated children's TV series and feature films, including *Enyo der Erbe des Schamanen (Legend of Enyo), Dog Star, Die Wilden Kerle, Ritter Trenk (Trenk, the little knight), Lauras Stern (Laura's Star), Tupu – Das wilde Mädchen aus dem Central Park (Tupu)*, and, most recently, *Inui*. He also works as a free author and brought his longstanding experience into the collaboration with Hannes Rall. This ensured that the developed concept was realistically conceived to meet with expectations of broadcasters for a youthful audience.

The first draft was developed as an illustrated treatment (a "series bible") between late November 2017 and early January 2018. It contained the concept for a 13-episode first season and included completed character designs, production design key visuals, and a detailed treatment for the first episode. The general narrative arc of the series was also demonstrated by including synopses of several other episodes later in the season.

The team then submitted the concept to the competition "Germany's Next Animation Talent," held by the Stuttgart International Festival of Animated Film, with support by Studio 100.

Studio 100 is a major international production company that has succeeded in Germany with box office successes like *Die Biene Maja (Maya the Bee*, dir.

Stadermann 2014) and its sequel *Die Biene Maja–2-Die Honigspiele Maya the Bee: The Honey Games* (dir. Cleary, Delfino, Stadermann 2018). Representatives from the studio were also part of the jury for the competition, which added a realistic producer's point of view to the proceedings—potential for commercial exploitation firmly in check.

Westboy succeeded at the competition by being among the five final nominees selected from around 40 submissions. This was not only rewarded with prize money but also resulted in a contract for continued development with Studio 100—still ongoing at the time of writing. This proved the commercial potential of the concept, qualifying the study as a good example for developing a feasible adaptation concept for a young audience (ca. ages 8 years and up).

Moreover, it is also interesting in terms of adaptation theory, because it very loosely adapts the original source material of one of Germany's most famous authors of youth literature.

Who was Karl May?

Karl May has been one of the most popular German writers for more than 100 years. His heroes Winnetou, Old Shatterhand, Apanatschi, and Kara Ben Nemsi have become German icons. He wrote about 100 books, which have been printed about 200 million times and translated into more than 40 languages. He invented the blood brothers Winnetou (a Mescalero Apache chief) and Old Shatterhand (a famous "man of the West" of German origin, supposedly May himself). He was most certainly inspired by James Fenimore Cooper's heroes Hawkeye and Chingachgook from the *Leatherstocking Tales* (1826–1841).

Figure 9.51: The author's own take on Karl May's famous heroes. Left to right: Old Shatterhand, Winnetou, Kara Ben Nemsi, and Hadschi Halef Omar. Hannes Rall, digital, 2016/18.

Amusingly, May even quoted Cooper's work in his own writing and complained about the former writer's lack of personal experience in traveling the territories he described: "Cooper has been a very good novelist, and I too enjoyed his Leatherstocking Tales; but he wasn't in the West. He understood perfectly how to connect poetry with reality; but in the West one only has to deal with the latter." (in *The Scout*, 1888/1889).

Figure 9.52: Left: Old Shatterhand and Winnetou. Illustration by Oskar Herrfurth for the book edition of the story *The Oil Prince* by Karl May published in 1897. Right: *Chingachgook and Hawkeye*. Illustration by Michał Elwiro Andriolli; engraving by M. Jules Huyot. In: James Fenimore Cooper. *Le dernier des Mohicans (The Last of the Mohicans)*. Paris: Firmin-Didot, 1884.

This carries a certain irony, as May had made his readers only believe that he had experienced all "his" adventures himself—in his disguises as superheroes Old Shatterhand and Kara Ben Nemsi, respectively. Wildly imaginative, he completely invented a romantic Wild West panorama and a picturesque Orient that had never truly existed. It was not until 1899/1900 (at the age of 57 years) that he first traveled the Orient and in 1908 America, but his major works had long since been written.

He did, however, meticulously research the regions traveled by his heroes through all available literature and research sources. Therefore, his completely fictional "Reiseerzählungen" (travel tales) appeared rather believable at the time. May frequently took photos of him dressed up as his heroes and even had their iconic rifles fabricated for him: the "Bärentöter" (bear slayer), the "Henry-Stutzen" (Henry-rifle), and Winnetou's "Silberbüchse" (silver rifle). But all stories were an expression of his great longing for the world and adventure.

Figure 9.53: Left: Karl May dressed up as his hero and alter ego Old Shatterhand. Shot, according to *"Karl May und seine Zeit"* by Max Welte, "probably in the first days of April 1896." Right: *Old Shatterhand*, illustration (1899) by Oskar Herrfurth for the book edition of *Der schwarze Mustang* (later *Half-Blood*).

Lütkehaus (2012) notes:

> "Karl May's fame was based on a truly enormous work, written with unparalleled diligence, in which global exoticism, fantastic adventures and literary high tension came together. But three legends made it really irresistible. The first claims that he was Old Shatterhand and the first-person narrator Kara Ben Nemsi in one person. The second says that he saw the countries that he himself had experienced stories about. And the third claims that throughout his life he had been a bourgeois person and writer, who in his late work had become the proclaimer of a global Christian-humanistic message of peace."

Figure 9.54: Left: Karl May dressed up as his "Oriental" hero Kara Ben Nemsi. (Courtesy of Alois Schiesser, 1896). Right: Karl May Postcard No. 3 *"Hamdulillah!" whispered Halef. "We have them."* From: *Karl May's travel stories vol. IV In the Gorges of the Balkans*. Freiburg: Friedrich Ernst Fehsenfeld. 1898. Page 600. Illustration by unknown artist.

Karl May's film adaptations

Karl May's popularity in Germany soared to new heights in the course of Karl May's film adaptations of the 1960s, the most successful German cinema series (Stark 2005, 207). Contrary to earlier adaptation attempts, this time, the films largely focused on May's Wild West tales, beginning in 1962 with the hugely successful *Der Schatz im Silbersee* (*The Treasure of Silver Lake*). Most of them were produced by Horst Wendlandt or Artur Brauner. Recurring leading actors were Lex Barker (Old Shatterhand, Kara Ben Nemsi, and Karl Sternau), Pierre Brice (Winnetou), Stewart Granger (Old Surehand), Milan Srdoč (Old Wabble), and Ralf Wolter (Sam Hawkens, Hadschi Halef Omar, and André Hasenpfeffer).

Figure 9.55: Left: Pierre Brice as Winnetou, Karl-May-Festspiele Elspe. (Courtesy of Elke Wetzig/CC-BY-SA.) Right: "Old Shatterhand" Lex Barker with actress Karen Kondazian May 1973. (Courtesy of Karen Kondazian.)

The romantic symphonic scores by Martin Böttcher contributed hugely to the success of the series and remain iconic until today in Germany. The impressive landscapes of (mostly) Croatia, such as the famous Plitvice lakes, also were a major factor, as they work surprisingly well as a substitute for the real "Wild West." After the boom of the 1960s film series had come to an end by 1968, later years also saw several new adaptations of Karl May's works for the big screen or television. Interestingly, these were carried out with varied levels of fidelity to the source material: The popular TV series *Kara Ben Nemsi Effendi* for the German broadcaster ZDF (dir. Gräwert 1973/75) was a highly faithful adaptation of Karl May's Oriental cycle of novels. The stop-motion feature film *Die Spur führt zum Silbersee* (dir. Rätz 1990) was also way more faithful than the 1962 live-action adaptation (dir. Reinl). A production of the formerly East German DEFA studios, it unfortunately failed to succeed at the box office. *Winnetou – Der Mythos lebt* (dir. Stölzl 2016), the most recent TV live-action adaptation, seeks to achieve a balance between a faithful adaptation of elements from the source material, paying homage to the iconic 1960s movies and complete reinvention with a more realistic approach. The series contains wonderful moments, and the enthusiasm of cast and crew shows in the result. Yet, the author would argue that particularly the idea to demythologize the heroes to a certain extent, does not fully work. The fairy-tale element is crucial for the appeal of all Karl May–based adaptations, and it is difficult to retain the unique charm without it.

This short overview demonstrates the (continued) relevance of Karl May's adaptations, before looking more closely into the development of the author's own adaptation. The following conversation between *Westboy* co-authors Hannes Rall and Jörg von den Steinen is not so much a formal interview but an insight into the thought process of creation. It demonstrates the interdependency of narrative and visual development through many examples. The interview took place in Stuttgart on December 1, 2017.

Interview on *Westboy* with Jörg von den Steinen

Concept and Story

Hannes Rall (interviewer)
Jörg von den Steinen (interviewed)

Let's talk a bit about our joint development project, the animation series *Westboy*, which is very freely based on Karl May's original Wild West stories, primarily centered around the heroes and blood brothers Winnetou, who is an Apache chief, and Old Shatterhand, a German Westerner. They experienced a continuing immense popularity in Germany, which still comes to bear today, mainly through the film versions of the 1960s, with Lex Barker and Pierre Brice in the leading roles, which were seen by a huge audience of millions.

Figure 9.56: The young version of the blood brothers, as developed for *Westboy*. This concept piece pays homage to the classic 1960s live-action adaptations. Art by Jasper Liu and Jochen Rall. Creative direction by Hannes Rall.

At the same time, however, the increasing digitization has caused the consumption of the original novels to decline sharply. So, it is no longer as widespread as it was in our youth. And I think there is also the fact to consider that the popularity of the main characters is still there. I think there are also some surveys, also in the context of the recent remake of German broadcaster RTL (dir. Stölzl 2016), that this awareness of the heroes Winnetou and Old Shatterhand is still very much there. But this means you may also have to think of new ways of dealing with it again, and perhaps you can or even have to take more freedom to make it interesting in keeping with the times. You have also supervised this great live-action film for children, *Winnetou's Son* (dir. Erkau 2015), where the point is that a boy of our time—small, fat, with glasses, which actually reminded me immediately of myself, who is a big Winnetou fan—wants to take over this role in such an open-air play, based on Bad Segeberg or the like. And the movie manages to bring this balancing act across in a very credible way and it works extremely well. Based on this, perhaps we can tell a little bit about how we also try to think further to define an adaptation that could be interesting for today's audience.

Yes. I'm just telling you what the writers told me, how they arrived at the concept for *Winnetou's Son*. Karl May is difficult to grasp today, depending on the age of the targeted audience, which will certainly also have some influence on our common project. Near to author Anja Kömmerling's home, there was a horse farm that offered birthday parties for families. And there was a birthday party taking place. I don't know, if her own child was involved. But it was definitely there, which means there were horses. There was one person who was guiding that. And there were very different children. And there was a big tent and so on. So, this idea, we are Indians today, is played out at such a children's birthday party. The next point is, of course, everywhere in Germany, not only in Bad Segeberg but also in Elspe and elsewhere "Karl May Festivals" take place—mostly, big family events. You go there with the children. What particularly fascinates the children there is apparently an open-air stage combined with real horses, clearly mixed with evil cowboys and good Indians or the other way around, based on some vaguely familiar stories.

So, what I wanted to emphasize is that it is interesting to actually see that although the books themselves are nor selling as much as they used to, the number of open-air theatres playing Karl May has increased almost inflationary. Traditionally, there were Elspe and Bad Segeberg, the oldest, I think, at which Pierre Brice then actually performed in certain years. And that has expanded by leaps and bounds. And this culture seems to be very enticing, and they are still very popular.

Figure 9.57: These examples show how the visual concept was developed to display the epic dimensions of the landscape, taking full advantage of the CinemaScope format. Art by Jasper Liu (left) and Hannes Rall (right), creative direction by Hannes Rall.

They're popular because they also offer a great show value. I mean, it's like going to an amusement park somewhere. It's all mixed up. And, of course, everyone, mostly the boys, discover Indian or cowboy gameplay when they're little. These are still the most popular carnival costumes, however. This world remains extremely attractive. There's clearly separated good and evil. You can hide. You can sneak. You can shoot with wooden arrows and what else. So, all those stories you love to do. Karl May offers a lot of adventure. And that's something that connects us all. That the former Karl May readers are now partly the parents or grandparents who go to these open-air games with their own good memories and have a great time there. And that's well marketed. And there, the stories are well prepared, that there is somehow something for everyone. And then, this is a great experience. That in our time today, the experiences and events have always become bigger than they used to be, that's how it is. In this respect, one can do something good with this term Karl May, especially

with the term Winnetou. He's already an icon. And then, someone like Bully Herbig (popular German stand-up comedian) comes along and makes a really funny and family-compatible parody of it, so to speak, *Der Schuh des Manitu / The Shoe of Manitou*, (dir. Herbig 2001), and takes all these figures and really creates a huge box-office success, albeit as a great spoof of the "original" 1960s movies.

Winnetou and Old Shatterhand are, of course, satirized here. But, of course, they are absolutely adorable people. You can reach younger people with this approach, or a middle-aged audience. Because that's Bully Herbig. Therefore the older ones can share and enjoy the experience of the festivals together with the younger generation. The memory of the books is kept. Reading the original novels today can actually be quite strenuous. I wouldn't give them to very young children either. They are more suitable for ages 10 years and up. What is problematic today is Karl May's strong focus on the fact that all the great Western heroes are Germans. The Indians are "very wild." And there are also some very clichéd villains among them. Winnetou is a noble Indian, a great friend. But on every third page, someone gets shot or even scalped. And that almost happens in passing.

Winnetou, that is already the prototype of the so-called "noble savage"—in the tradition of, for example, James Fenimore Cooper's *Leatherstocking Tales* (originally published between 1823 and 1841, in non-chronological order). And I think there is a seemingly paradoxical aspect of May's work that can be played on in different ways. Karl May's work also features this strong respect for other cultures, besides certain nowadays surely problematic tendencies of German nationalism. The pacifist tendencies in Karl May's writings became stronger and stronger in his later work, which then led to the fact that the Nazis were often strongly editing original material by Karl May, and certain passages were also shortened because they at that time were not in conformity with the Nazi ideology. The Nazi ideology wanted to propagandize the German superiority versus other cultures.

But this is not inherent in Karl May's work, most certainly not in his later work.

There is more complexity to be found, and his work resists such simplification.

Yes, this aspect is also in there. It is also becoming a bit more "missionary" in parts, also as far as religion is concerned. So, this also concerns poor Winnetou. In the end, he becomes a Christian and wants people to sing "Hail Mary" when he dies.

Which, of course, also partly leads to borderline parodistic tendencies in the original films from the 1960s. When you think about the topic in a contemporary way, you would have to reconsider such elements. And probably, you don't want to have these elements in a modern film version.

Well, let's put it this way: The success of the old films (which you can still watch today, albeit with a smirk on your face) can also be attributed to them being the first big German adventure films. They had a good look. Although everything was done in former Yugoslavia, it was claimed that was the "Wild West." And from the look of it, you certainly believed it. Back then, the trip to northern Italy was the "world trip" you could make. Not like today, when everyone can go to Australia at age 18. Different times. It was all in these movies. There was an element of longing. There were adventures. There were happy endings, mostly. Even when there were angry citizens who threatened Karl May (and later the filmmakers) because they let Winnetou die. So, he was "revived" for more films, chronologically taking place during the time before his fictional death.

Figure 9.58: Concept art: Buffalo hunt. Used primarily to communicate the desired mood and composition, this collage artwork by Hannes Rall integrates an existing classic Western painting. This is, of course, not for use in a later production but to quickly explore and demonstrate the visual potential. Again, the emphasis lies on the major role of the environment combined with silhouetted characters.

But somehow, such a tragic death also carries dramatic weight, a narrative device that remains very much in practice. Think of the death of Han Solo in *Star Wars: The Force Awakens*: This approach is a courageous decision, which deliberately cuts a narrative thread and gives a different significance to everything that has happened before. So, the magic of these 1960s movies still exists, although one is certainly influenced by nostalgia there. In a certain sense, this is "German Western" that somehow defined its very own brand and was not so easily interchangeable with Hollywood productions. And the interesting thing is, the more the film series tried to turn toward an internationalization, or a very generic Western story toward the end of their success, the less successful they became. The first Harald Reinl-directed filmic Karl May adaptations (1962–1965) could almost be qualified as "German Western fairy tales." And this is where their specific charm lies—this "uber-romanticized" vision of the "West."

Well, they also take specific motives from the Karl May novels that add nature and adventure and reflect certain values, friendship in particular. What I find appealing about our approach to Karl May is that there's a modern trend to "show" the youth of popular adult heroes: I know Sherlock Holmes as a grown man. Well, he did grow up sometime. So, there can be a book series about "young Sherlock Holmes." I can tell "young" Peter Pan. A "young James Bond." And there are plenty of books around where writers have adapted this as an idea.

You are adapting somebody else's ideas, but you are creating an underlying foundation that expands the universe beyond what is known from the original novels. And that's a bit like that here: with our idea of *Westboy*, the story of a "young" Shatterhand. In the original novels, we are experiencing a literally "Old" Shatterhand, who comes along as a grown man.

And meets Winnetou for the first time as an adult. We take a little poetic license here, referring somewhat back to May's own tradition as a highly imaginative storyteller. Karl May, who proclaimed for a long time: Yes, I have done all of this myself.

We let a German emigrant get there at a young age, and he meets the young Indian Winnetou, which gives rise to completely different things. But we can then somewhat contextualize this "prequel" idea either within the narrative continuity of May's work or be similarly inventive and imaginative as May himself.

A kind of adaptation in "spirit," if you will.

Precisely. How did they become who they are? This is always interesting for us, particularly for the children and youth program. Now, I think our exciting topic is that we said we have the invented universe of Karl May, which is historically situated in the years from 1865. We're going back a bit. We're going somewhere around 1850. And during these times, indeed, we had a large stream of emigrants, who then came over from Europe and especially also from Germany. And in this wave comes a single boy and that's just our Karl May. Just for the sake of argument. What would happen to him? What emotional baggage does he carry with him? And how does he get into a new landscape that opens up before him, that is spectacular, huge, big and still populated by people like these Indians, who at that time were not yet under the thumb of the whites?

Figure 9.59: Visual development for *Westboy*: In Mescalero-Apache territory. Art by Jasper Liu, creative direction by Hannes Rall.

This balance was tilting over at that time. There is the appeal of the completely different culture, with its own, completely different customs than those that I know. And now, let us emphasize Karl May's central point and look at the white emigrant not as a conqueror but as a friendly explorer. It's someone who says I'm curious and I want to meet someone. And I'm ready to build a bridge. That is very important for me now, for example, that if that is the core of the whole, this can be our defining value. The value is friendship. In many films and series I appreciate, the value of friendship is told in different variations. And that is a good value, which also represents well in programs for public broadcasters.

Figure 9.60: Again, historical reference forms the basis for these explorations of the main character Westboy and his friends: German immigrants arriving in St. Louis. Art by Jasper Liu, creative direction by Hannes Rall.

And that is certainly present as an element in Karl May's work. So, in this respect, one would be true to the work in this sense. Well, you can't walk away from it. And I think it's always important to me when it comes to adaptation; basically, that one tries to capture this somewhat-elusive "spirit of the original," instead of really being literal in the sense that one has to translate everything one to one. This approach often contradicts the idea of adaptation in the first place. As mentioned before, Karl May as a writer himself is, of course, also a genius spinner of tales. He had never been to America before writing his Western novels. In some sense, we might continue this tradition "in the spirit of Karl May" by creating an alternative universe about the youth of his heroes. What would have happened if he had come to America earlier? Maybe this even reflects Karl May's own narrative approach to a certain extent. And could be seen as a loving homage as well?

Yes, I think that's absolutely right. It somehow also represents the idea of the storyteller taking his own spin of the tale; I mean, here, too, you encounter the great American-Indian culture, where telling stories around the campfire was their own experience of writing history. So, this is a classic principle: We tell each other stories. You got one for me, I got one for you, and so on. And in many of these older cultures, we don't have the history books; they use oral traditions instead. They know the stories. And they tell them three times, with slight variations. And then, the younger generation contributes to them too. There are still cultures where nothing is written down. It is only possible through oral communication.

Let's just assume that we embrace this idea of fantasizing, of "spinning a yarn." We are metaphorically "sitting around the campfire." At some point, someone could start to tell something that is actually rooted in authentic American-Indian culture, possibly a story that you somehow pull out of Karl May's work, which, of course, you would have to be very familiar with—so you are quoting correctly. But possibly also something that is historically documented or where one can agree, yes, it could have been that way. This approach to storytelling would make this show so appealing. We could "make it up."

But we must remember, we must also include the element of adventure here. That's got to be great and exciting. And the adventure of a series targeted at children and youth cannot be based on murder and death. We have to restrain ourselves and make sure that this does not happen. We have to engage in a smaller idea of drama that does not necessarily need the big "exit by death" to create suspense and excitement. We should allow ourselves to go off on tangents that represent an authentic facet of the culture of the Indians.

Figure 9.61: Exciting adventure and the discovery of authentic American-Indian culture. Concept art by Jasper Liu and Jochen Rall. Creative direction by Hannes Rall.

We could also weave in memories of our hero's time in Germany, where things were quite different during the March Revolution of 1848. That should not go too far, because these are all complex historical backgrounds, which we have now simply adapted for our character(s). But, of course, he can tell us what that was like. And he can tell his friend Winnetou about that too. In this way, they exchange their life experiences, so to speak.

It was part of our consideration that Karl May's work features this element of German nationalism, by claiming that most great Western heroes were of German origin. We thought, however, that this could be counteracted by adding values, which are "typically German" but which could be seen as very positive in a contemporary context. So, when you think of the value of democracy and the importance of the revolution of 1848 and so on. And also with the topic of 'immigration,' our young Karl would be an immigrant to America. So there presents itself an opportunity to positively occupy the idea of 'German values' by redefining them as positive instead of negative: Tolerance, openness towards other cultures, democratic values."

Well, I'd say, yes. I would say the German-slanting European. I mean, that's what happened. So, most of the people who went over there, or quite a few, just came from Europe from certain situations.

Yes, also, for example, fleeing the notorious Irish "Potato Famine."

There are many stories. Of course, too many stories: Tales of colonialism and seafaring, many diverse historic events. You can't integrate all that in one concept now. But it's definitely in the game. And, of course, today, a modern perspective on America is extremely important. I was just looking at biographies of emigrant families again. There were also many Jews who emigrated. Other members of other religions. So that one can also tell about the exodus for certain reasons, of people with this diversity of views, also of religions, which are now gathering in America. Now, of course, this is not supposed to be a historical journey. But the appeal would emerge, if you took the characters' development seriously, if you embraced the complexities proposed by May's source material. I could, for example, look at Sam Hawkens as a "funny" character. He always thinks that the next guy is less able than himself. And finds himself surprised what "the other" (mostly the "greenhorn" Old Shatterhand) is actually capable of. Otherwise, he is a rather brave guy himself, an experienced trapper, and a good friend. He looks extremely bizarre and also talks funny. And has a couple of male friends on top, who are similarly bizarre in appearance and behavior.

Classic Sam Hawkens illustrations (with pals Will Parker and Dick Stone as the "clover leaf" (Kleeblatt). by Oskar Herrfurth from early publications of May's works (late 19th century).

Figure 9.62: Sam Hawkens and his pals, as seen by German illustrator Oskar Herrfurth in the late-nineteenth century.

But this alone might not be sufficient for the narrative structure yet. The character needs to have some dramatic function for me. He has to be a little bit more than just a funny figure; he also needs to have a past and thus also a certain depth. And that's what I mean, that's when we're at this crucial moment, that's when we start digging. We haven't completely defined this whole system yet, but both of us have the impression that, if we turn toward the historical circumstances, especially to the Indians at their rites and customs, we get a lot of topics that are unusual and that can supply us with interesting stories.

Absolutely, and this also bridges to the original Karl May material. Despite the fact that he never traveled in the described countries himself, he had done some surprisingly accurate research: Germanist and May expert Helmut Schmiedt in his *Karl May. Studien zu Leben, Werk und Wirkung eines Erfolgsschriftstellers* (as quoted in Thielke 2017) was amazed: "Some readers have travelled through the described areas following his descriptions and, if one may believe them, have always arrived at their destination." Other scholars, though, point out the immense "poetic license" May took with the facts and his invention of an entirely imaginary "Western" language (Wolff 2003). So, we are looking at a mix of comparatively accurate description and complete fabrication. We had also talked about the Winnetou comics of Helmut Nickel (1963), who actually holds a doctorate in ethnology and art history and was a curator at the Metropolitan Museum of Art for many years and who has applied this scientific knowledge in his adaptations, where he added pages of "infographics" with accurately researched ethnological information. So, there's a rich field to mine in that respect.

What I find very appealing for animation is the great potential with these somewhat-bizarre characters in the source material. These were always taken back or played down in the live-action adaptations, because then, they were not seen or felt as contemporary. Interestingly, in the very first live-action adaptations (*Der Schatz im Silbersee, Winnetou 1–2*), there are actually still some of these characters. But most of them end up with Sam Hawkens as the only character left in that direction—like in the latest film adaptation by RTL in 2016. However, there certainly is narrative potential. And, of course, it would be important to integrate this in a meaningful way into the dramatic structure, that is, to give the figures depth.

Figure 9.63: Sam Hawkens character design for *Westboy*. Art by Hannes Rall and Jasper Liu, creative direction by Hannes Rall.

So, let's put it this way: It's always a big topic for children and youth, for example, how the so-called "comic characters" are also used in live-action film adaptations. Well, there are some (mostly adults) who hate our actor Armin Rohde as sheriff in *Winnetou's Son*. They don't like it. Because they just say the character has been deteriorated to a "campy" figure. My experience is when the humor is adequately balanced, children like such characters very much. Children love clowns. This has nothing to do with adult perception. If an adult acts "funny" or "weirdly" in a children's movie, that can create an enjoyable moment for the young audience. The child can feel stronger. And there is also a transformation of the "funny" adult character: I mean, in the end, the "General" (Uwe Ochsenknecht) accepts our child hero Max as "Winnetou's son." And that is a huge achievement for him. There is a character arc. So, I wouldn't condemn him so much. He's been acting very stupid or funny or something a few times before, but in the end, there is a serious character transformation.

Well, interestingly, you find that "incredibly credible." I think *Winnetou's Son* takes this children's perspective very seriously—as far as I can judge for myself, at my advanced age. Well, it felt very reminiscent of my own childhood. And that came across as very credible. And also, how that is played with the other characters—this works very well. And I think it will always be difficult and not so easy to get the balance right with "real" actors, as opposed to cartoon characters.

And that, I think, is always the art of being aware of what and for whom I am telling a story with funny and bizarre figures. In the case of children and young people, one simply has to consider the fact that we have this great theme that always stays current for a child audience: "Cowboys, Indians, Wild West." That is the big issue, with big discussions, of course. May I bring my pistol to the kindergarten for carnival? And so on. The child actually wants to act out such stories. I think a child doesn't have this subtext of what can actually happen with guns. I don't know. But still, they're only allowed to throw cotton balls. And that might be (overly) politically correct. In essence, however, the attraction, the appeal lies somewhere else—I mean, we have a chance there: The closeness to nature. So according to the motto, ask children today, if they ever climbed a tree. And many will say they never did. I think every kid should have done this. And every child should have broken his knees and tore his pants. And that's exactly the spirit that our series, if it were successful, could capture. You can do that. And it's a beautiful experience. And that's certainly a value inherent in Karl May's original work. It was so widespread in its readership. For some, it was exotic. Of course, all the other aspects were also included: the missionary and the "particularly good German." And, of course, Karl May himself has played a role

in this, because he has become more and more involved in this role. And that's what he wanted for his life. And ended up lying about it, too. He even commissioned to have "Winnetou's" silver rifle built for him. Then, somehow, an attentive reader notices that the silver rifle was actually placed in the tomb with Winnetou. Why do you have it still? Yeah, he says, "it's a different story. I still have to write that down."

So, we're back to fantasizing, to "spinning a yarn."

Now, I want to move on to a specific character detail that demonstrates our story concept quite well: the figure of Klekih Petra. He is the white advisor of the Apache chief Intschu tschuna and the teacher of Winnetou and his sister Nscho-tschi. He is a German immigrant, who has almost completely assimilated himself within the Apache culture. We both agreed that it would be nice to tell his backstory in more detail, which is only hinted at in Karl May's original material. In *Winnetou the Red Gentleman* (aka *Winnetou 1*), the character talks about his involvement as a scholar in the German revolution of 1848:

"I was a teacher at a higher school (...) My greatest pride was to be a free spirit, to have deposed God, to the point of being able to prove that believing in God is nonsense. (...) Then came the time of the revolution. [...] I appeared publicly as the leader of the dissatisfied (…)" (p. 40).

He also calls himself a "German, a student, a renowned scholar, and now a real Apache; that seems wonderful" (ibid).

Figure 9.64: **Visual development of Klekih Petra. Art by Hannes Rall and Jasper Liu, creative direction by Hannes Rall.**

His tragic backstory connected to the 1848 revolution is detailed there as well.

He ultimately had to flee his homeland, haunted by remorse and guilt.

Yet, there are a lot of gaps left in his biography for us to fill in, particularly after his arrival in America. Maybe you'd like to tell us something about that?

That is certainly part of the appeal of this concept. When you discover these particularly interesting figures. A character like Klekih Petra, for example, is more or less portrayed as someone who has, so to speak, made a development toward the Indian culture and has since then been highly regarded and respected by the Indians for a long time. On the one hand, one would assume, he has "simply" become a wise Indian himself, but apparently, he has also brought something with him, which is somehow particularly interesting for the chief and Winnetou now. The attraction of bringing this forward to Karl May's "younger years," so to speak, is that Klekih Petra is then younger as well. Accordingly, we could now bring such figures together in our concept. We could say there is a much earlier encounter, when Klekih Petra is not yet with these Apache and he has not yet arrived with them. He brings some European knowledge and influence, which is attractive. It is also important here that he should not arrive as a patronizing scholar at the time, and the indigenous and local people say: "Yoo-hoo, we'll follow your instructions." But somehow, he arrives with a broader knowledge. That's the way to put it. But he also comes to this country as an immigrant and lets himself be fascinated by what he finds. If he is on a different level than Karl, already being an adult, maybe the paths will separate too. You will have to see, you can tell everything. But, of course, it is a charming figure. This is also true for all the other characters that somehow appear in Karl May's work. You could say Sam Hawkens has some kind of history and we'll tell it. Or we take others… Aunt Droll has some kind of history, which is not told by Karl May—either not at all or in parts as contradictory. And we say we take something from the original and transfer it into our model. Our model is simple, we set a time, we have a historical environment, so to speak, where we also get to know a little bit what really happened at that time. And transfer the fictional characters and give them background and depth. And that's what we work with: That is a delightful mixture of authentic reference, quoting from the original source and reinventing, re-fabricating. I think that's what both of us like about this concept.

Visual development

Based on the discussion so far, we can now examine how content development and visual design can be connected. There was an initial piece of concept art on the city of St. Louis, which, in its first incarnation, did not quite do justice to the actual historical situation. And then, we both agreed that it would actually be nice, to present the city of St. Louis as it really looked at the time, based on authentic reference: With a very large main road, where covered wagons are lined up, which is documented on the basis of a historical photo. And, continuing from this, to actually create the design of the corresponding background and to apply any stylization only afterward.

Rough sketches by Jasper Liu that develop the Mississippi environment in St. Louis, the landscape going into the West and the diverse steamboat variants.

Figure 9.65: Visual development for the city of St. Louis (early sketches). Art by Jasper Liu, creative direction by Hannes Rall.

Absolutely correct. Based on materials and images that can be found. Of course, you have to research. On the other hand, I think it's always nice to approach the design from the story. We have a young man here who doesn't know America, who knows more closely-knit cities from Europe—in this special case, somebody from Germany. And he is now coming to a country that has tried, so to speak, to create a logistics system at great speed. The railway does not exist yet. So, what did they do? You had to build quickly, you had to build with wood. You had to build roads, but they could not be perfectly tarred, but planned on the basis of what transport needed at that time, they were made up rather quickly. And the whole thing is a dynamic striving for a certain size on the one hand but also, by many people who are already there, a striving to move on at once. There was a big wave of immigrants that came there. It is historically accurate that these were predominantly German and Irish migrants arriving (ushistory.org n.d.). So, there is the need for a big road right now to provide space for them. We don't need all the details of St. Louis. But we should focus on illustrating this major factor of the layout of the city. The design concept should illustrate who's settled down a little bit now. Or, we show some of them, just shopping to move on. And that is also our intention in general; we know that our hero should not cling to this place, but he should move on. Let us lead him into the prairie. And then, you might find a clue that some metal-processing industries in St. Louis, for example, have just had an upswing. Then, you know that there are indeed courageous traveling traders who loaded all kinds of household objects into their covered wagons: We're going west now, because you can make a profit from it. So, it is not only the settlers, who say: "We want to build up our place somewhere." There are also traders with the intention to make a good deal, to make profits.

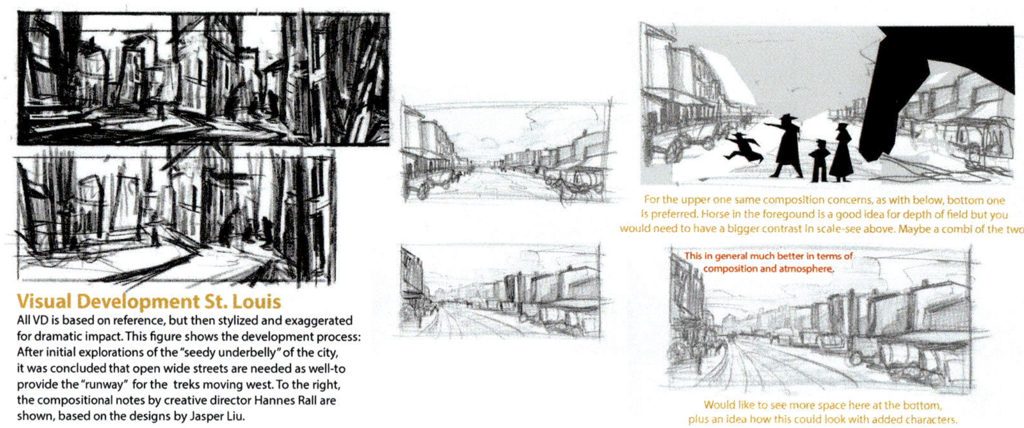

Figure 9.66: Visual development for the city of St. Louis (later development stages). Art by Jasper Liu, creative direction by Hannes Rall.

How does our young hero fit into this situation? We could just as well say now: Okay, there is a wagon train of 40 big covered wagons, and they all want to move to the West, or they are still to be pulled on the trip to be gold hunters. We have to consider that. Also, of course, from the point of view of the production effort that this would require. Such a 40-wagon trek, that's then somehow at least 100 people and more. We can't show so many—too expensive. Of course, we must put our hero in there somehow. Therefore, it is perhaps nicer to find a smaller unit, and this must somehow have a historically credible background. We can find an inventive solution. And then, we combine it with characters like Sam Hawkens, who will accompany the trek as scouts: "I'll take care of you a little bit. You have no idea, you greenhorns." Something along these lines. And we will have integrated the fictional character into a historically credible environment, and we will be moving our protagonist toward the moment of encounter with Winnetou. That's the point. And then, we can think, in the context of such a series, in how many intermediate stages we will tell this. When do we create the situation of the first encounter? We would, at the same time, think about exciting, disruptive situations. Adversaries, opponents who want to prevent this first encounter from happening. You can tell it all over and over, or you can tell it very briefly. Of course, we are looking for small subtle hints and possibilities and finally also for the tonality and rhythm—how we want to tell it.

It is also very nice how our opening scene re-engages with this all-important visual aspect, meaning the initial journey on the steamboat. All happening on the impressively big river, the Mississippi. And then, Aunt Droll and Sam Hawkins on the canoe come along for the rescue of our young hero. I find this to be a very nice combination of narrative idea and an opulent visual scenario.

Figure 9.67: Visual development for the river-rescue scene. Art by Jasper Liu, creative direction by Hannes Rall.

And in the very same scene, we are already being introduced to "young Klekih Petra"—I think you renamed him Tom Kleemann to "keep the secret."

Maybe you can say a little more about that?

You want a scene that's driven by some action, that offers some narrative and visual excitement. You especially want to see our hero, who is alone at this point, isolated from the crowd. He distinguishes himself from the others, emigrants, who have already forcefully claimed their territory on the boat, in that he makes small sketches. He observes the other people, and because of that, he becomes the target of some bullies there. You can play with it: One is German, the others are Irish. That's playful for now, it's not absolutely fixed at this stage. It's about showing the situation after such a long journey. Everybody's kind of tired. So that a conflict can easily emerge. And my thought was that you could visualize the hero's origins somewhere. That's why I thought if his father was a blacksmith, he gave him a horseshoe for luck. As it happens. That means a lot to him. That means that's an important object to him, very meaningful. This is a nice bridge, because we can tell later that Indians have totems. If you like, he's got his totem, it's a horseshoe. How can these two be connected? Horseshoes are made of metal. It's an ingredient the Indians don't know. That means you already introduce the meeting of two fundamentally different worlds. Karl can later probably get a whistle from the Indians. Something carved out of wood. I can start playing with that at some point, in the sense of connections and in the sense of exchange. So, you give me yours, I give you mine. Or, I'll show you mine, and I'll show you the opposite. And by that, I have established a conflict. Karl shows that he's good at throwing horseshoes. He's such a hero. The others get upset. Then comes Klekih Petra, he's a mediator. This means that he creates a moderating situation that does not lead to them immediately pummeling their fists on the nose. People consent, and then, the situation calms down for a moment. I'll show you what it's "always like" in the Wild West. People like to bet. They are choosing favorites, a competition ensues. I'm getting a little liveliness.

By introducing this throwing competition (that follows) on the boat?

Then comes a throwing competition. For now, I have simply assumed that this has a tradition from Europe. That there was that famous horseshoe throwing. Our hero then can show again that he is also clever and that he is also strong. Because he worked for his father, the blacksmith, even at a very young age. He wins this. But then, he has to escape to flee the situation of emerging conflict. That means by a trick: He simply throws his suitcase into the water. And then comes something you wouldn't really expect: This suitcase seems to float. Doesn't go down. So, our hero jumps off the steamboat. Then, the Mississippi shows that it has power, that it is a big, mighty river. So, this leap into the cold water was also a bit too optimistic. Our hero gets into trouble, but two imaginary characters, invented by Karl May, come and help him. And on the raft, it briefly shows what they're like. That they're like an old couple, bitching with each other, bickering about, and so on: Meet Sam Hawkens and Aunt Droll for the first time! That means I solve what I was just trying to tell in an exciting way. I introduce the characters with a few saucy sayings. Show, don't tell means demonstrating personalities through action.

That is very nice in the sense of introduction, because these are motives directly inserted from Karl May: These two bizarre Westerners, completely integrated to serve the dramatic structure. Moreover, the motif of a scene on a paddle steamer is actually quoting from the novel *Der Schatz im Silbersee (The Treasure of Silver Lake)*. It is the initial scene there—but becomes newly contextualized here and thus "breathes" the spirit of May.

Exactly. It quotes from there, but it also mitigates it very much, because the actual scene in *"Der Schatz im Silbersee"* ends in murder and manslaughter and in a brutality that I naturally need to avoid using in a children's and youth series in this form.

A thought that I would take up, because it demonstrates again the interlocking of narrative thoughts and visual implementation. What remains important in this aspect is authenticity, by saying: If we show Apache, we also reference the background that the Mescalero Apache don't live only in tipis but also might have used different housings as well (so called "wicki ups"). That the Apache look like Apache (and specifically Mescalero in the case of Winnetou's tribe) and not like any American Indians of the Great Plains (like the Sioux or Cheyenne). That's thinking along the same lines of authenticity.

Figure 9.68: **Visual development for the look of Winnetou's clothing, attire, and overall appearance. It was important to consider authentic reference on Apache costumes, particularly Mescalero, as shown in the historic photography by Frank Randall (ca. 1883–1887) and the illustration by Arthur Schott (1857) on the right. Art by Jasper Liu and Hannes Rall, creative direction by Hannes Rall.**

And we also brought in this other thought, of a fictitious journal, that Sam Hawkens might have written about his life previous to his "Karl May-biography." This could also bring in a connection with historical events, the Lewis and Clark Expedition of 1804–1806, for example. This did happen a bit too early to match our fictional timeline (1853), but we could reminisce by creating a similar endeavor that echoes that spirit of early discovery. And a young(ish) Sam Hawkens at the forefront to discover this frontier.

Figure 9.69: Capturing the spirit of early expeditions into uncharted Western territories. Visual Art by Hannes Rall (top) and Jasper Liu/Hannes Rall (bottom), creative direction by Hannes Rall.

Yes, of course. So, we define a certain age for him and then give it a range between 15 and 20 years, during which he could have experienced other things at a certain age. Which he can talk about at some point. And sometimes, this also comes in handy, if you need just such a building block for the story. On these early expeditions, the conditions were quite different. The territory was still completely unexplored. Not everything went well, either. That means that's a wealth of experience he has. The charming thing is that I get a more differentiated figure. At first glance, he just seems to be a bit of a clown. Because he looks the way he does. Because he talks the way he talks. He's always getting into the crosshairs with Aunt Droll. Initially, you'd think I wouldn't trust too much in the abilities of this person. But such a character constellation is a common trait of Karl May: Sam Hawkens can shoot well, he knows his way around, and so on. That means there is a different side to him. He's actually a quite complex character. That has got to come from somewhere.

This backstory adds depth to the character and should be reflected in his visual design as well.

And that makes the character more interesting. And it gets stronger when you introduce his surprising abilities in combat. This creates the biggest appeal if you don't immediately reveal this, if you don't tell the audience right away. Instead, you give the character a background and a certain depth, from which you can extract this ability, make it believable, and then use it in surprising ways.

I think what came out very nicely in the development discussion is the general idea of basing our fiction in fact. In the sense that we take some liberties in terms of visual stylization, but what is shown is still referencing authentic historical facts. So, when we then show a Western city, we base it in reference we can find. This is a concept similar to the approach of the comic series *Lucky Luke* (Goscinny, Morris 1955–1977). That is not a realistic style. That's a "funny" style. Strongly caricatured characters. But Morris as the artist, and Goscinny as the writer back then did an awful lot of research and then built this very exaggerated style based on historical facts, based on their research.

What would make such a children's and youth series exciting today?

I have to create excitement, and that can work from just an underlying tension—one that does not need manslaughter and scalping to excite. Just to give you an example: The freestanding house. If there is prairie only around there, I have no cover, nothing. That means, now, if our heroes want to approach that house unseen, they must have a good idea. You have to think of something to get there unnoticed. And their performance and the suspense are built on whether this idea works out. When I have grassland around such a house, I create the classic situation: I can sneak up through the grass. Unfortunately, by chance, a dangerous animal could be hiding in this grass as well. That means, on the one hand, I have the advantage that the grass is covering me, but I possibly have the danger that I can become the victim of a predator myself or that someone is after me. And the great thing is, in this case, I don't need murder and manslaughter at all, I can build the suspense from these elements only.

And this results from backdrops, from places, and, of course, from abilities of my comrades-in-arms, and I can "paint" these accordingly. For example, you could say that Aunt Droll looks not exactly like a in drag but she wears such strange clothes that you underestimate her. Or totally makes you think he ran away from the nuthouse. But, of course, and that would be something to think about: Why is it so? And how come someone can survive like that in an extremely wild or rough landscape. So, he may have certain abilities. He can be a fantastic knife thrower. You just underestimate him. He can throw this one knife that can be in a moment exactly the gadget you need to survive—just to give you an example. It has to be someone who hits the fly on the wall right there, so that we can still get out of any dangerous situation. Of course, I can also establish it. I've got it up my sleeve with him. At the same time, I have bizarreness. He's a positively weird character. Use that throughout the whole narrative. So that the audience constantly underestimates him, for example.

This is a very nice narrative device. As a spectator, you are always relishing such an "aha-experience," an element of surprise—I think even more so for a youthful audience. We were talking about identification, about empathy with the characters. This creates empathy, because a children's audience identifies with a character who is underestimated or feels small, and then, there is this moment when he can exceed these expectations to become a hero—defying expectations.

We can use this as a general principle. We tell about Karl, who encounters these Western characters with open eyes and much curiosity—people he might not have met in Europe in this form. That's what makes it attractive. And then comes the next level, of course, the encounter with Indian culture and especially with someone like Winnetou, who represents his counterpart from an entirely different culture.

We had already talked about this earlier that Karl May was probably inspired by James Fenimore Cooper's *Leatherstocking Tales*, where we already find a blood brotherhood that is just not named as such. So, with Chingachgook and "Hawkeye" Nathaniel Bumpoo, there is already this element of cross-cultural bonding, this respect for Indian culture. Karl May took that up and made it even stronger in his own writings.

Yes, that's strong there. And the element of curiosity, of discovering the new frontier, the other culture(s).

Another slightly bizarre May character comes to mind: Lord Castlepool—your archetypical British gentleman—or a spoof of it, actually: a wealthy gentleman who has money, who moves to the West, who seeks adventure that he wants to document with the newly invented device of a "photographic camera apparatus." A completely new and young art form back then. This would be nice to play with narratively as well.

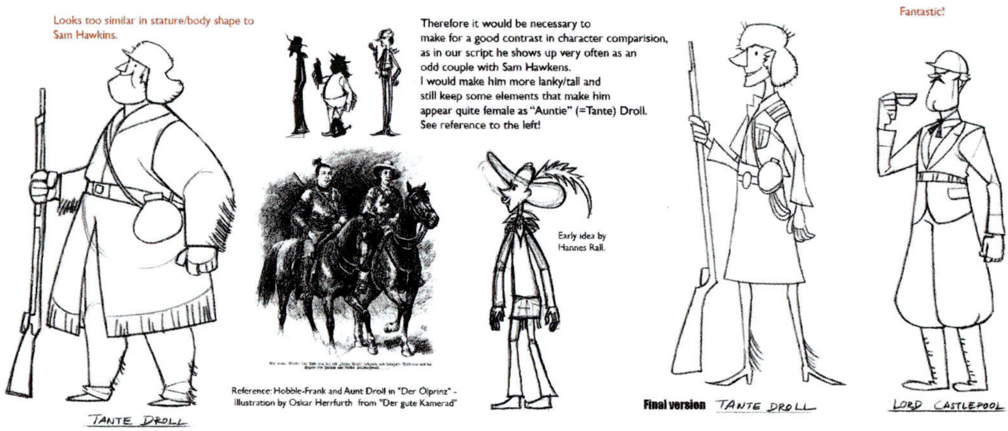

Figure 9.70: Character design development for Aunt Droll and Lord Castlepool. Art by Hannes Rall and Jasper Liu, creative direction by Hannes Rall.

There is another important aspect to consider for a modern adaptation: Finding a balance between male and female characters. That means you have to go back to the source and do a little research. Because Karl May predominantly tells his tales through male characters. There are some women but rarely in heroic or leading roles. Not always fit for military service. There are exceptions, though. There is the daughter of Old Surehand, Ellen, who is obviously an "amazon," who can do everything. How to install such a character could enrich the narrative, make it exciting—not the easiest thing to do but certainly an interesting and ultimately rewarding challenge.

You can do that, and interestingly enough, you are opening up the narrative that way. For example, the 2016 live-action film version took the poetic license of not letting the female character of Nscho-tschi die, which, of course, was a big thing for the Karl May purist. Now, if you consider a prequel, then this topic is definitely not an issue at all. And a character like Nscho-tschi, Winnetou's sister, could also be thought of and played on in a much more modern way than may have been the case in the past. Well, there are already openings, which you can use, maybe.

Exactly. That's a huge advantage. You immediately have this relationship: Winnetou must protect someone smaller: his sister. There is the potential for a whole story arc by itself. This emerges from the natural desire to shield your own family. And there is May's character of Ribanna (from *Winnetou 2*), another female American-Indian, and Karl adores her. Then, it's the other way around. Then, he wants to protect her too, and then, he might want to meet her.

Figure 9.71: In this comparison sheet for *Westboy*, the major American-Indian characters shown, including the female characters of Winnetou's mother, his sister Nscho-tschi, and the mentioned potential "love interest" for the heroes, Ribanna—an Assiniboin girl. Character designer: Jasper Liu. Creative Director: Hannes Rall.

If you now think about the possibilities of the Karl May adaptation we are planning to do, what would you see as the specific properties of animation (versus live action) that would benefit our narrative approach? We thought about the idea of magic before, maybe to use such a supernatural approach for Klekhi Petra?

For one, you couldn't finance what we are having in mind as live action. Second, there are the content-related considerations: We want to enter into possibly the culture, into certain rituals. So historical fact is, I believe, that the Indians knew some herbs, which allowed them to access some state of trance: a "dreamtime" condition if you will. Someone might have dreamt something and then told the medicine man what he had dreamed. The medicine man then might have concluded that the buffalo will arrive tomorrow at noon. That's something you can express incredibly well through the medium of animation.

Figure 9.72: Developing the supernatural aspect of *Westboy*: A shaman working his magic. Development art by Jochen Rall, creative direction by Hannes Rall.

We can create scenes with flickering fires that throw dancing shadows, which morph into magical figures. You have this hilly landscape, you have this Pueblo architecture, you can have a full moon, you have two friends sitting up there on the mud hut and one has a vision and has an idea, and you visualize that. These are narrative elements and situations that need strong visuals to support them. And animation is the perfect medium to do that.

And that actually allows to implement these elements at a reasonable cost. The difference is that if you were to combine live action and visual effects now, it would actually be impossible in a television budget.

Absolutely yes. One would have to go more deeply into research about the diverse beliefs and religious traditions of the Indian tribes to get this all right. There are many interesting concepts to explore there, for example, "what comes from nature, returns to nature." One would have to be careful what to adapt and how it would prove adequate for a youthful audience.

Of course, one could also first get the facts right and create corresponding scenes. Ideally, these should integrate forms of indigenous art in a respectful way, moving carefully to avoid any notion of appropriation there. That would add an authenticity that could be quite interesting.

Let's discuss the example of the totem. American Indians obviously thought that each person is only part of a bigger whole and accompanied by a spiritual counterpart impersonated by a certain animal. They tried to read from certain natural phenomena and attributed specific meaning to those. Things that, at least partially, appear entirely strange to the European mindset. Partially, though, also similar to a connectedness to nature, which even here in Europe, traditional farmers could relate to, because they live out of nature and keep reading signs: when the clouds form in a specific way or when the swans move to the south, which signifies a certain meaning for the quality of the soil (or interpretations). One simply reads in the nature, or we look into the weather report or in the Internet. And at that time, it was possible to retrieve such information directly from nature, and that is not even the worst approach today either. Like the things you learn in a simple survival course, where you have to do without modern technology: We move through a landscape here, where the west wind brings us rain. So, if you want to head into a certain direction, look where the moss is on the trees. We could make that part of our story—why not?

The close relationship of the American Indians to nature can become one of our central narrative devices. The supernatural elements would be firmly anchored in that idea. All these magic things could happen. And from this wealth of meticulously researched knowledge, I can try to invent beautiful fictional stories.

That was a great conclusion. Thank you for this interview.

Further to the interview, the following section adds insight into the aspects of the visual development that haven't been covered yet. It also contributes a more comprehensive overview of character development and environment design in various stages.

Character development

Here, the different iterations of the characters and final character line-ups are shown, particularly the development of the hero, Charlie. It is part of the artistic concept that a color version and a silhouetted version of the figures exist side by side. The silhouetted versions of the characters are to be used in the adaptation for different dramatic purposes (dreamlike states, magic, and drama) and lighting situations (sunsets and fire). This creates a unique idea for the character design that helps to make the concept stand out, as it defies convention.

Besides all artistic considerations and matching the adaptation idea, an important aspect was the fact that all characters' designs needed to work for the technique of digital cutout animation (with occasional use of traditional 2D animation). This technique was chosen for both artistic and budget purposes: Animating as cutouts allows for animating with richly ornamented figures while keeping the budget under control. The reason is simply that the character assets are only built once and then can be "moved around." They don't need to be redrawn for every second frame. To build these character models, the body and limbs must be "breakable" into segments connected through joints. This is demonstrated well in the design sheets for horses and bisons.

Figure 9.73: Character design development for Charlie. Final version on the right. Art by Jasper Liu, creative direction by Hannes Rall.

Charlie went through many different designs, before the final character design was arrived at. As the "good" protagonist, the "hero," it was particularly challenging to balance the notion of a little boy with the idea of the hero he would grow into later: the legendary "Old Shatterhand." There needed to be a balance between a certain daring quality and a childlike curiosity and innocence in the character. Age was also an important consideration—with our hero supposedly being around the age of 8–10 years.

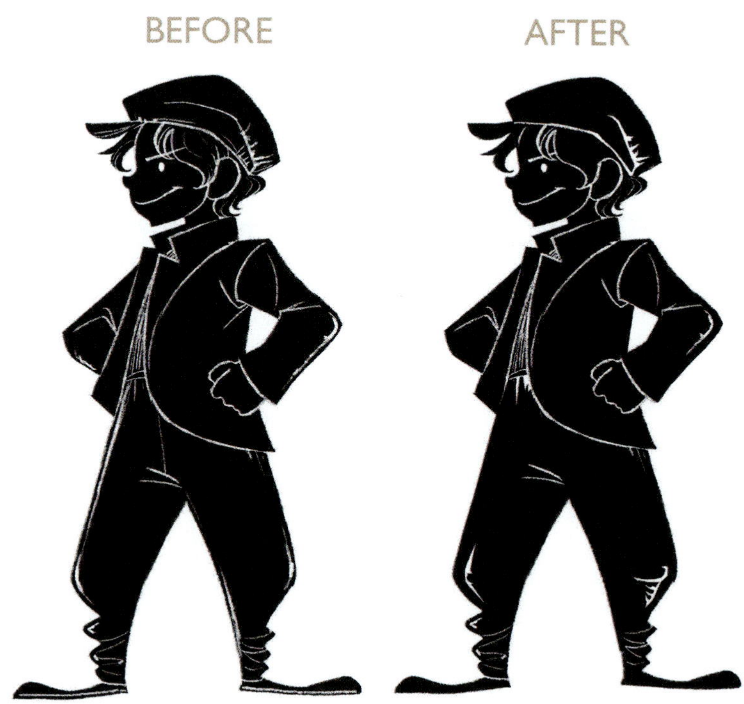

Figure 9.74: Character development of silhouette versions of the character "Charlie" by Jasper Liu Yingxian and Hannes Rall.

The illustration in Figure 9.74 shows an early draft of the silhouetted version of "Charlie" by Jasper Liu (visual development artist) on the left and the later improved/revised draft by Hannes Rall (creative director) on the right. The second draft is far less busy, more graphic, and going for sharply defined lines instead of "broken/brushy" ones. Details in white line are significantly reduced but sharp and graphic. Wherever the black silhouette already perfectly defines the shape, it is rather counter-productive and not necessary to place additional white lines close to the edge.

Figure 9.75: Development sketches (pencil) for German immigrant characters. Art by Jasper Liu, creative direction by Hannes Rall.

Figure 9.76: Final German immigrant characters in color and silhouette versions. Art by Jasper Liu, creative direction by Hannes Rall.

Figure 9.77: Final American-Indian characters in color and silhouette versions. Art by Jasper Liu, creative direction by Hannes Rall.

Figure 9.78: Final character line up for horse and bisons. Art by Jasper Liu, creative direction by Hannes Rall.

Early development stages

The following two figures show early concept art for characters and environments. These were ultimately discarded and replaced by the stronger designs, which were shown in the previous figures. Although all are pleasant enough, the characters did not really match the adaptation ideas closely enough—they did not sufficiently represent equals of the older versions of the characters Karl May had described in his books. The environments for the Indian territories and St. Louis were also deemed a tad too generic and therefore revised on the basis of more authentic reference.

Figure 9.79: Early development art: Apache land. Art by Jasper Liu, creative direction by Hannes Rall.

Figure 9.80: Early development art: St. Louis. Art by Jasper Liu, creative direction by Hannes Rall.

Additional backgrounds and environments: Stylistic variations

Figure 9.81: *Westboy* visual development study *St. Louis* by Hannes Rall (2017).

Figure 9.81 shows a visual development study for *Westboy* that combines a historic etching of St. Louis with the character of "Charlie" in full color. Of importance here is to create a strong contrast between the character and the background, to make the character literally "stand out." All graphic elements work in tandem to achieve a strong composition: tone (dark against light), scale (big foreground objects), and framing (the background provides an "empty stage," where the character is placed). The connection between the narrative intent of the adaptation (authenticity of historic buildings and landscapes) becomes immediately evident: Using historic graphics or photographs answers to these demands, even when considering the potential inaccuracies of the respective artists.

Figure 9.82: *Westboy* visual development study integrating historic photographic reference on the Badlands territory in South Dakota. Hannes Rall (2017).

The author did one more finished piece that combines a revised/expanded historic photograph (public domain) with silhouetted characters. What it has in common with the previous St. Louis piece is to demonstrate some epic scale in CinemaScope (the landscape becomes important) and how to balance characters and backgrounds in terms of scale/tone/composition. Plus: Restraint in color for maximum contrast—that is a general rule: never lose contrast start with strong basic contrast, and then build from it. Layers with various levels of opacity between character layer and background layers also help, for example, a 34% blue or similar, to achieve a clear separation between characters and background.

It is an absolutely normal process in visual development that designs undergo many revisions until a final approved version is arrived at. This has absolutely nothing to do with the talent or capabilities of the involved artist(s) but is more resembling a long communication process to match directorial vision and design. In fact, one of the most important aspects of the visual development process is to try out different stylistic iterations through a "trial and error" method, until an artistic concept emerges that fits all narrative, artistic, and technical requirements.

References

Abrams, Jeffrey Jacob, dir. 2015. *Star Wars: The Force Awakens*. Live action feature film. San Francisco/Santa Monica, CA: Lucasfilm/Bad Robot Productions (production). Burbank, CA: Walt Disney Studios Motion Pictures (distribution).

Arias, Michael. 2006. *Tekkon Kinkreet*. Animated feature film. Tokyo, Japan: Aniplex (production). Culver City, CA: Destination Films (distribution).

Besson, Luc. 1997. *The Fifth Element*. Live action feature film. Neuilly-sur-Seine, France: Gaumont (production). Neuilly-sur-Seine, France: Gaumont Buena Vista International (distribution: France); Los Angeles, CA: Columbia Pictures (distribution: United States).

BBC. *Macbeth Background*. n.d. Accessed August 2, 2018. http://www.bbc.co.uk/bitesize/higher/english/macbeth/background/revision/2/.

BBC. 2014. *Cleopatra*. Accessed August 2, 2018. http://www.bbc.co.uk/history/historic_figures/cleopatra.shtml.

Cleary, Noel, Sergio Delfino, and Alexs Stadermann, dirs. 2018. *Die Biene Maja 2 – Die Honigspiele* (*Maya the Bee: The Honey Games*). Animated feature film. Paris, France: Studio 100 (production). Paria, London: Studio Canal (distribution).

Cooper, James Fenimore, and Susan Fenimore Cooper. 1898a. *The Deerslayer: Or, The First War-path, The Leather Stocking Tales by James Fenimore Cooper*. New York: Sully and Kleinteich.

Cooper, James Fenimore, and Susan Fenimore Cooper. 1898b. *The Last of the Mohicans: Or, A Narrative of 1757, The Leather Stocking Tales by James Fenimore Cooper*. New York: Sully and Kleinteich.

Cooper, James Fenimore, and Susan Fenimore Cooper. 1898c. *The Pathfinder: Or, The Inland Sea, The Leather Stocking Tales* by James Fenimore Cooper. New York: Sully and Kleinteich.

Cooper, James Fenimore, and Susan Fenimore Cooper. 1898d. *The Pioneers: Or, The Sources of the Susquehanna, The Leather Stocking Tales* by James Fenimore Cooper. New York: Sully and Kleinteich.

Cooper, James Fenimore, and Susan Fenimore Cooper. 1898e. *The Prairie, The Leather Stocking Tales by James Fenimore Cooper*. New York: Sully and Kleinteich.

Dahlgreen, Will. 2016. *Shakespeare 400 years on: every play ranked by popularity*. Accessed August 3, 2018. https://yougov.co.uk/news/2016/04/22/shakespeare-400/.

Erkau, André, dir. 2015. *Winnetous Sohn (Winnetou's Son)*. Live action TV movie. Erfurt, Germany: Kinderfilm GmbH (production). Mainz, Germany: ZDF (broadcast/distribution).

Gallo, William. 1976. *An Intrepid Gunfighter Meets Fear. Los Angeles Times*, c.1.

Goscinny, René, and Morris (pseudonym for De Bevere, Maurice). 1955–1977. *Lucky Luke*. Comic-album series. Marcinelle, Belgium: Dupuis (1955–1967). Paris, France: Dargaud (1968–1977).

Goscinny, René, and Albert Uderzo. 1961–1976. *Asterix*. Comic-album series, 23 volumes. Paris, France: Dargaud.

Goseki, Kojima, and Koike Kazuo. 1970–1976. *Lone Wolf and Cub*. Manga. Tokyo, Japan: Futabasha.

Gräwert, Günter, dir. 1973–1975. *Kara Ben Nemsi Effendi*. TV series, 2 seasons, 26 episodes. Mainz, Germany: ZDF (production/broadcast/distribution).

Greg (pseudonym for Regnier, Michel Louis Albert). 1966–1996. *Achille Talon*. Comic-album series, 42 volumes. Paris, France: Dargaud.

Herbig, Michael, dir. 2001. *Der Schuh des Manitu (The Shoe of Manitou)*. Live action feature film. Munich, Germany: HerbX Medienproduktion GmbH (production). Constantin Film (distribution).

Hergé (pseudonym for Remi, Georges). 1939–1986. *Tintin*. Comic-album series, 24 volumes. Tournai, Belgium: Casterman.

IMDB.com. n.d. "Moby Dick." Website keyword search. Accessed August 2, 2018. https://www.imdb.com/find?q=moby%20dick&s=tt&ref_=fn_al_tt_mr.

IMDB.com. n.d. "Macbeth." Website keyword search. Accessed August 2, 2018. https://www.imdb.com/find?ref_=nv_sr_fn&q=macbeth&s=tt

IMDB.com. n.d. "A Midsummer Night's Dream." Website keyword search. Accessed August 2, 2018. https://www.imdb.com/find?ref_=nv_sr_fn&q=+a+midsummer+night%27s+dream&s=tt.

Irish and German Immigration. n.d. ushistory.org. Accessed July 22, 2018. http://www.ushistory.org/us/25f.asp.

Kazuo, Koike, and Kojima Goseki. 1970–1978. *Lone Wolf and Cub*. Manga series. Tokyo, Japan: Futabasha.

Kelly, Walt. 1948–1975. *Pogo*. Comic-strip series. New York: Post Hall Syndicate.

Lau, Joseph S.M., and Y.W. Ma, eds. 1986. *Traditional Chinese Stories: Themes and Variations*. Boston, MA: Cheng & Tsui.

Leone, Sergio. 1964. *A Fistful of Dollars*. Live action feature film. Munich, Germany: Constantin Film (production). Beverly Hills, CA: United Artists (distribution).

Lütkehaus, Ludger. 2012. *Genie und Hochstapler*. Accessed May 30, 2017. https://www.zeit.de/2012/14/L-S-Karl-May.

Mankiewicz, Joseph L., dir. 1963. *Cleopatra*. Live action feature film. Century City, CA: Twentieth Century Fox (production and distribution).

May, Karl. December 1888–August 1889. *Der Scout. Reiseerlebniß in Mexico von Karl May*. In: *Deutscher Hausschatz*. Regensburg, Germany: Verlag Friedrich Pustet.

May, Karl. 1894. *Der Schatz im Silbersee*. Stuttgart, Germany: Union Deutsche Verlagsgesellschaft.

May, Karl. 1893. *Winnetou-der Rote Gentleman*. Freiburg, Germany: Fehsenfeld, p. 40. As documented by the facsimile of the original edition under https://www.karl-may-gesellschaft.de/kmg/primlit/reise/gr07/gr07-txt.pdf.

Melville, Herman. 2011 *Moby-Dick*. Ignatius Critical Editions. Edited by Mary R. Reichardt and Joseph Pearce. San Francisco, CA: Ignatius Press.

Miller, George, dir. 2015. *Mad Max: Fury Road*. Live action feature film. Sydney, Australia: Kennedy Miller Mitchell; Los Angeles, CA: Village Roadshow Pictures; Los Angeles, CA: RatPac-Dune Entertainment (production). Burbank, CA: Warner Bros (distribution).

Miyazaki, Hayao. 2004. *Howl's Moving Castle*. Animated feature film. Tokyo, Japan: Studio Ghibli (production). Tokyo, Japan: Toho Co. Ltd. (distribution).

Miyazaki, Hayao. 2001. *Spirited Away*. Animated feature film. Tokyo, Japan: Studio Ghibli (production). Tokyo, Japan: Toho Co. Ltd. (distribution).

Muschweck, Christian. 2015. *Moby Dick im Comic – Ein Vergleich ausgewählter Beispiele von 1942 bis heute*. Accessed August 2, 2018. http://comicgate.de/hintergrund/moby-dick-im-comic-ein-vergleich-ausgewaehlter-beispiele-von-1942-bis-heute/.

Nickel, Helmut. 1963. *Winnetou*. Comic-book series. Vol. 1–8, 10. Hannover, Germany: Walter Lehning Verlag.

Pearson, Roberta. 2004. *Heritage, Humanism, Populism: The Representation of Shakespeare in Contemporary British Television*. In: *Janespotting and Beyond: British Heritage Retrovisions Since the Mid-1990s*, edited by E. Voigts-Virchow, 87–97. Tübingen, Germany: G. Narr Verlag.

Rätz, Günter, dir. 1990. *Die Spur führt zum Silbersee* (*The Trace Leads to the Silver Lake*). Animated feature film. Dresden, Germany: DEFA-Studio für Trickfilme (production).

Reinl, Harald. 1962. *Der Schatz im Silbersee* (*The Treasure of Silver Lake*). Live action feature film. Hamburg, Germany: Rialto Film Preben Philipsen/Jadran Film (production). Munich, Germany: Constantin Film (distribution).

Reinl, Harald. 1963. *Winnetou 1. Teil* (*Winnetou part 1*). Live action feature film. Hamburg, Germany: Rialto Film Preben Philipsen/Jadran Film (production). Munich, Germany: Constantin Film (distribution).

Reinl, Harald. 1964. *Winnetou 2. Teil* (*Winnetou part 2*). Live action feature film. Hamburg, Germany: Rialto Film Preben Philipsen/Jadran Film (production). Munich, Germany: Constantin Film (distribution).

Reinl, Harald. 1965. *Winnetou 3. Teil* (*Winnetou part 3*). Live action feature film. Hamburg, Germany: Rialto Film Preben Philipsen/Jadran Film (production). Munich, Germany: Constantin Film (distribution).

Shmoop Editorial Team. 2008 Fedallah in Moby-Dick. Shmoop University, Inc. Last modified November 11, 2008. Accessed July 30, 2018. https://www.shmoop.com/moby-dick/fedallah.html.

Sparknotes. n.d. *The Corrupting Power of Unchecked Ambition*. Accessed August 3, 2018. http://www.sparknotes.com/shakespeare/macbeth/themes/.

Stadermann, Alexs, dir. 2014. *Die Biene Maja (Maya the Bee*). Animated feature film. Paris: Studio 100 (production). Babelsberg, Germany: Universum Film (distribution).

Stark, Isolde. 2005. *Elisabeth Charlotte Welskopf und die Alte Geschichte in der DDR: Beiträge der Konferenz vom 21. bis 23. November 2002 in Halle/Saale*. Stuttgart, Germany: Franz Steiner Verlag, 207.

Stölzl, Philipp, dir. 2016. *Winnetou-Der Mythos lebt.* Three-part TV movie: 1.) *Winnetou – Eine neue Welt (Winnetou-A New World)*, loosely based on Karl May's original novel *Winnetou 1.* 2.) *Winnetou – Das Geheimnis vom Silbersee (Winnetou-The Secret of Silver Lake)* loosely based on Karl May's original novel *Der Schatz im Silbersee (The Treasure of Silver Lake).* 3.) *Winnetou – Der letzte Kampf (Winnetou-The Last Battle)* loosely based on Karl May's original novel *Winnetou 3.* Munich, Berlin, Germany: Rat Pack Filmproductions (production). Köln, Germany: RTL (broadcast/distribution).

Takehiko, Inoue. 1999–ongoing. *Vagabond.* 37 volumes. Tokyo, Japan: Kodansha.

The Editors of Encyclopaedia Britannica. 1998. *Ukiyo-e.* Accessed December 29, 2017. https://www.britannica.com/art/ukiyo-e.

Thielke, Thilo. 2017. *Karl May Der tollkühne Deutsche im Land des Herdenwürgers. (Karl May The daring German in the Land of the Herd Slayer).* Accessed July 22, 2018. http://www.spiegel.de/einestages/karl-may-die-sudan-abenteuer-um-kara-ben-nemsi-a-1140775.html.

Thompson, J. Lee. 1977. *The White Buffalo.* Live action feature film. Universal City, CA: Dino De Laurentiis Company (production). Beverly Hills, CA: United Artists (distribution).

Van Gogh, Vincent. 1889. *Starry Night.* Oil on canvas. New York: Museum of Modern Art.

Wer war Karl May? 2017. Accessed May 30, 2017. https://www.mdr.de/figarino/webchannel/karl-may-100.html.

Wickman, Forrest. 2011. *The Most Adapted Authors: Revised and Expanded Edition (INFOGRAPHIC).* Accessed July 13, 2017. http://www.slate.com/blogs/browbeat/2011/03/23/the_most_adapted_authors_revised_and_expanded_edition_infographic.html.

Wolff, Felix. 2003. *How to build worlds with words Karl Mays virtueller "Wilder Westen." (Karl May's virtual "Wild West").* In: *Namen und Wörter. Freundschaftsgabe für Josef Felixberger zum 65. Geburtstag*, edited by Gerald Bernhard, Dieter Kattenbusch, and Peter Stein, 223–242. Regensburg, Germany: Verlag Christine Lindner.

Image Sources

Royalty-free Ukiyo-e Images.

http://www.loc.gov/pictures/collection/jpd/http://www.loc.gov/pictures/collection/jpd/.

http://www.loc.gov/pictures/collection/jpd/item/2002700001/.

http://www.loc.gov/pictures/collection/jpd/item/2002700000/.

http://www.loc.gov/pictures/collection/jpd/item/2002700002/.

http://www.loc.gov/pictures/collection/jpd/item/2002700008/.

http://www.loc.gov/pictures/collection/jpd/item/2002700015/.

http://www.loc.gov/pictures/collection/jpd/item/2002700018/.

http://www.loc.gov/pictures/collection/jpd/item/2002700017/.

http://www.loc.gov/pictures/collection/jpd/item/2002700035/.

http://www.loc.gov/pictures/collection/jpd/item/2008660495/.

http://www.loc.gov/pictures/collection/jpd/item/2008660155.

Gaul, Franz. 1871. Nibelungen/ Hagen. Watercolor. Costume For Hebbel's *Die Nibelungen.*

Herrfurth, Oskar. n.d. *Das Kleeblatt.* Accessed July 23, 2018. http://rooschristoph.blogspot.com/2013/09/sam-hawkenswenn-ich-mich-nicht.html.

Herrfurth, Oskar. n.d. *Butler und das Kleeblatt.* Ilustration by Oskar Herrfurth for *Der Ölprinz, in Der gute Kamerad.*

Herrfurth, Oskar. 1893–1894. *Sam Hawkens auf seinem Maultier Mary und Kantor Matthäus Aurelius Hampel (Sam Hawkens on his mule Mary and Cantor Matthäus Aurelius Hampel).* Illustration.

Kirchner. Ernst Ludwig. n.d. *Portrait of Van de Velde.*

Kirchner. Ernst Ludwig. 1928. *Street in the Rain.* Woodcut – 22,8 × 17,4 cm. Kirchner Museum Davos.

Kurosawa, Akira, dir. 1957. *Throne of Blood.* Live action feature film. Tokyo, Japan: Toho Studios (production/distribution).

Marc, Franz. 1912. *Tiger.* Painting, oil on canvas.

Pyle, Howard. 1899. *The Story of Siegfried: Homecoming*. In: *The Story of Siegfried*, by James Baldwin. New York: Scribner & Sons.

Rackham, Arthur. *Siegfried hands the drinking-horn back to Gutrune, and gazes at her with sudden passion*. Arthur Rackham's illustrations to: *Richard Wagner's The Ring of the Nibelung*.

Randall, Frank. [between 1883 and 1888]. *Seated studio portrait of a Native American Mescalero Apache boy*. Public domain. Accessed July 23, 2018. https://commons.wikimedia.org/wiki/File:Mescalero,_Painted_boy.jpg.

Schott, Arthur. 1857. *A Lipan Apache warrior*. Public domain. Accessed July 23, 2018. https://commons.wikimedia.org/wiki/File:Lipan_apache_1857.jpg.

Schedel, Hartmann. 1493. *Schedelsche Weltchronik or Nuremberg Chronicle*.

Unknown artist. 1353. *Battle of Legnica (Legnitz) 1241*. From Legend of Saint Hedwig. Source/Photographer: Medieval illuminated manuscript, collection of the J. Paul Getty Museum.

Unknown artist. 1480–1488. *Armoured Hungarian infantry in a castle*. National Széchényi Library, Budapest. Probably made in Buda. Parchment.

Unknown seamsters. Circa 1051–1099. *Bayeux tapestry, scene 8: Guido of Ponthieu guides the prisoners to his castle*.

Vogel, Alb. 1840–1841. *Die Nibelungen – Der nächtliche Überfall (The Nibe/ungs-Attack at Night)*. In: Rethel, Alfred. 1909. *Die Nibelungen*. Berlin: Fritz Heyder.

1a.) Illustration by Oskar Herrfurth for the book edition of Karl May's novel *The Oil Prince* published in 1897.
https://commons.wikimedia.org/wiki/File:Karl_May_Der_Oelprinz_Herrfurth_001.jpg

1b) *Chingachgook and Hawkeye*. Illustration by Michał Elwiro Andriolli; engraving by M. Jules Huyot. In: James Fenimore Cooper. *Le dernier des Mohicans (The Last of the Mohicans)*. Paris: Firmin-Didot, 1884.
https://commons.wikimedia.org/wiki/File:Le_dernier_des_Mohicans_-_Cooper_James_-_Andriolli_-_Huyot_-_p29.jpg

2a.) Karl May dressed up as his hero and alter ego Old Shatterhand. Recorded according to "Karl May und seine Zeit" by Max Welte, "probably in the first days of April 1896."

2b.) *Old Shatterhand*, illustration (1899) by Oskar Herrfurth for the book edition of *Der schwarze Mustang* (later *Half-Blood*).
https://commons.wikimedia.org/wiki/File:Karl_May_Der_schwarze_Mustang_Herrfurth_001.jpg

3a.) *Karl May as Kara Ben Nemsi*. Photograph (1896) by Alois Schiesser.
https://commons.wikimedia.org/wiki/File:Karl_May_as_Kara_Ben_Nemsi.jpg

3b.) *Karl May Postcard No. 3 "Hamdulillah!" whispered Halef. "We have them."* From: *Karl May's travel stories vol. IV (In the Gorges of the Balkans)*. Freiburg: Friedrich Ernst Fehsenfeld. 1898. Page 600.
https://commons.wikimedia.org/wiki/File:Karl_May_Postkarte_Fehsenfeld_003.jpg

4a.) Piere Brice as Winnetou, Karl-May-Festspiele Elspe. „Foto: Elke Wetzig/CC-BY-SA.
https://commons.wikimedia.org/wiki/File:Piere_Brice_als_Winnetou,_Karl-May-Festspiele_Elspe_2.jpg

4b.) Lex Barker Karen Kondazian May 1973. Karen Kondazian. May 1, 1973. http://www.thewhipnovel.com/blog/?attachment_id=2223
https://commons.wikimedia.org/wiki/File:Lex_Barker_Karen_Kondazian_May_1973.jpg

Afterword

This is the journey's end. And arriving here, the reader might hopefully have learned some things on the way. There is more than one way to create a "good" adaptation. A bad film can't be a good adaptation. The adaptation must be able to succeed on its own—and within the qualitative parameters of the art form it is created for. Absolute fidelity to the source material doesn't guarantee that. Sometimes, the opposite is the case. Being too literal can get in the way of a successful adaptation for another medium because it neglects the most important requirement for such transposition: Change it must.

Yet, the contributors agree that it remains essential to create with the "spirit of the author" in mind, considering the source text for adaptation. What precisely is meant by this ever-elusive term? This remains a different question to give a general answer to. It rather should be explored in context with the specific work and how the adaptation narrative and design answer to it. Examinations in this book have offered concrete answers in multifaceted ways. It could, for example, mean to mirror the narratively-random structure of a Shakespeare play through similarly playful story and design concepts in the corresponding animated adaptation. This means employing more abstract ideas instead of slavishly copying period details for visualization.

For the reader who wasn't familiar with the creative practice of animation before, the author also hopes to have achieved another important insight:

Any notion of a "genius creator" suddenly struck by "creative lightning" is (mostly) wrong. Animation is an art form that requires a very structured and controlled process, maybe more so than any other (audio-) visual art form. This rings even more true for animated *adaptations*. Visual development and artistic research are key here, as the design cannot be created in isolation but must resonate with the requirements of the literary source material. This can manifest itself in meticulously researched historical detail, if the intent of the adapter is to recreate a visually authentic setting for an adaptation (see adaptation *Westboy* in Chapter 9). Or, it can require a laborious process of experimentation to define visual equivalents of more abstract narrative concepts in a source text (see *The Tiger of 142b* by the Zhuang Bros., Chapter 8).

The author hopes that this book offers a solid foundation to examine animated adaptations through an integrated research approach that considers theoretical context and artistic practice on equal terms. And he hopes to have provided a treasure trove of inspiration for future animated adaptations. The brilliance of many artists presented here would surely suggest that.

Therefore, this end is also a beginning: Good luck on your continued journeys of discovery.

Figure A.1: Production still from *As You Like It*, directed by Hannes Rall (WiP). Design by Hannes Rall, Lim Wei Ren Darren and Khoo Siew May.

Acknowledgments

The author wishes to thank Nanyang Technological University Singapore (NTU), for providing an ideal environment for research and creation that made this book possible in the first place.

Special thanks to Prof. Alan Chan, Vice President (Alumni and Advancement); Prof. Luke Kang Kwong Kapathy, Chair of the School of Humanities and Associate Dean (Research) for the College of Humanities, Arts and Social Sciences (HASS); Prof. Vibeke Sorensen, Chair of the School Art, Design and Media (ADM); Assoc. Prof. Andrea Nanetti, Associate Chair (Research), ADM; and Prof. Michael Walsh for their constant encouragement and support.

The research for this book was supported by the Ministry of Education (MOE) Singapore Tier 1 Grant "Adaptation for Animation—Transforming Literature Frame by Frame."

I would also like to thank my research partners at NTU: Prof. Seah Hock Soon, School of Computer Sciences (SCE); Assoc. Prof. Daniel Keith Jernigan (School of Humanities) and Tissina George, co-authors and co-producers of *The Beach Boy*, *Si Lunchai*, and *All the World's a Stage*; and my research team at ADM who contributed to many of the projects mentioned in this book: Sulaiman Abdul Bin Rahman, Khoo Siew May, Xue Enge, Alvin Tay, Chen Juntao, Lim Wei Ren Darren, Andre Quek.

A special shout-out to former team member Jasper Liu for his amazing work created exclusively for this book.

Last but not least, I thank all the students at the Digital Animation and Media Art programs at ADM—you all continue to inspire and amaze me.

People I have constantly admired (and continue to do so) and who were so kind to contribute generously to this book are Hans Bacher, Giannalberto Bendazzi, John Canemaker, Ishu Patel, and Georges Schwizgebel. I would have never dreamed to be able to work with you—but the dream came true!

A very special thanks also goes to Prof. Michael Dobson, Director of the Shakespeare Institute Stratford-upon-Avon for many years of perfect and enthusiastic research collaboration.

I would also want to show gratitude to friends and family: my brother Jochen Rall for design advice and fantastic contributions, and my partner Dr. Angela Takano for constant support and advice.

Thanks also go to all the collaborators, interview partners, and providers of artwork for this book. All of them can't be named here, but their names can be found throughout the book—thank you so much!

Index

Note: Page numbers in italic refer to figures respectively.